AGILE BUSINESS TRANSFORMATIONS

Priorities, Lessons, and Practices

AGILE BUSINESS TRANSFORMATIONS

Priorities, Lessons, and Practices

Edited by

Satyajit Chakrabarti, PhD

Subrata Chattopadhyay, PhD

Udit Chawla, PhD

Sundeep Singh Sondhi, PhD

Arunava Dalal, PhD

AAP | APPLE ACADEMIC PRESS

First edition published 2025

Apple Academic Press Inc.
1265 Goldenrod Circle, NE,
Palm Bay, FL 32905 USA

760 Laurentian Drive, Unit 19,
Burlington, ON L7N 0A4, Canada

CRC Press
2385 NW Executive Center Drive,
Suite 320, Boca Raton FL 33431

4 Park Square, Milton Park,
Abingdon, Oxon, OX14 4RN UK

Library and Archives Canada Cataloguing in Publication

Title: Agile business transformations : priorities, lessons, and practices / edited by Satyajit Chakrabarti, PhD, Subrata Chattopadhyay, PhD, Udit Chawla, PhD, Sundeep Singh Sondhi, PhD, Arunava Dalal, PhD.
Names: Chakrabarti, Satyajit, editor | Chattopadhyay, Subrata (Teacher of Electrical Engineering), editor. | Chawla, Udit, editor. | Sondhi, Sundeep Singh, editor. | Dalal, Arunava, editor.
Description: First edition. | Includes bibliographical references and index.
Identifiers: Canadiana (print) 20240536150 | Canadiana (ebook) 20240536169 | ISBN 9781774918586 (hardcover) | ISBN 9781774918579 (softcover) | ISBN 9781003559344 (ebook)
Subjects: LCSH: Organizational change. | LCSH: Business enterprises—Technological innovations.
Classification: LCC HD58.8 .A35 2025 | DDC 658.4/06—dc23

Library of Congress Cataloging-in-Publication Data

CIP data on file with US Library of Congress

ISBN: 978-1-77491-858-6 (hbk)
ISBN: 978-1-77491-857-9 (pbk)
ISBN: 978-1-00355-934-4 (ebk)

About the Editors

Satyajit Chakrabarti, PhD

Satyajit Chakrabarti, PhD, is a professor, technologist, serial entrepreneur, and venture capitalist. He is an avid philanthropist and social entrepreneur. He has published extensively in the fields of artificial intelligence, IoT, and data science and has over 20 patents filed in various fields of technology. Dr. Chakrabarti is the Pro Vice Chancellor at the University of Engineering and Management, Newtown, Kolkata, West Bengal, India. He has special expertise in management consulting, strategic management, technology applications, and problem solving using innovation and innovative technologies. He earned his PhD in Nanotechnology at the National Institute of Technology, India, and his master's in Computer Science from the University of British Columbia, Canada.

Subrata Chattopadhyay, PhD

Subrata Chattopadhyay, PhD, is presently working as a Professor in the Business Administration Department at the Institute of Engineering & Management, School of University of Engineering and Management, Kolkata, India. He is well-versed in cutting-edge teaching techniques and has extensive industry connections. He has published more than 23 articles in seminars and conferences and contributed to more than 30 international journals. In addition, he is the author of three books, *Values and Ethics for Engineers and Managers, Transport Management,* and *Computations in Estate Management.* As a life member of ISTD, CMA, PRSI, NIPM, NHRD, NFED, and ISABS, he also provides mentorship and consulting services to a number of other organizations. He holds MSc, MBA, and PhD degrees from IIT-ISM Dhanbad, India.

Udit Chawla, PhD

Udit Chawla, PhD, is presently working as an Associate Professor in Business Administration Department at the Institute of Engineering & Management, School of University of Engineering and Management, Kolkata, India. He is an accomplished academician with a track record of employment in the higher education sector and is a strong education professional focused on business analytics, data science, machine learning, and artificial intelligence. He has expertise in R, SPSS, SAS, PYTHON, etc. He has published more than 20 articles in reputed international journals, which are indexed in ABDC, Scopus, SCI, etc., and he has contributed more than 30 articles presented at international conferences such as IIMs, etc. He holds BTech, MBA, and PhD degrees in Management.

Sundeep Singh Sondhi, PhD

Sundeep Singh Sondhi, PhD, is currently serving as the Dean of the Department of Business Administration (BBA and MBA programs) at the Institute of Engineering & Management, School of University of Engineering and Management, Kolkata, India. He has been associated with academics and the department for the last five years. Prior to this, in his corporate life, he was involved in business development through direct and indirect sales, partner recruitment, and training across multiple industries. He has more than 25 years of rich experience in the industry. His area of interest is developing solutions and relationships with both internal and external customers that result in win-win situations. He completed his PhD from the Indian Institute of Management, Indore, India, in the area of Strategic Management.

Arunava Dalal, PhD

Arunava Dalal, is presently working as an Assistant Professor in Business Administration Department at the Institute of Engineering & Management, School of University of Engineering and Management, Kolkata, India. He has published more than five articles in reputed international journals, which are indexed in ABDC, Scopus, etc. He also has a rich experience working in the industry for more than 17 years. He is also currently pursuing PhD at the University of Engineering & Management, Kolkata, India.

Contents

Contributors

Muskan Aggarwal
Xavier Institute of Social Service, Ranchi, India

Dominic Appiah
Royal Holloway, University of London, United Kingdom

Sudin Bag
Department of Business Administration, Vidyasagar University, Midnapore, India

Sanjib Bhattacharjee
School of Management, Presidency University, Bengaluru, India

Satyadip Biswas
Institute of Engineering & Management, School of University of Engineering and Management, Kolkata, India

Suchandra Bose
Institute of Engineering & Management, School of University of Engineering and Management, Kolkata, India; PhD Scholar, Adamas University

Satyajit Chakrabarti
Institute of Engineering & Management, School of University of Engineering and Management, Kolkata, India

Subrata Chattopadhyay
Institute of Engineering & Management, School of University of Engineering and Management, Kolkata, India

Udit Chawla
Institute of Engineering & Management, School of University of Engineering and Management, Kolkata, India

Vishal Choudhary
The Heritage Academy, Kolkata, West Bengal, India

Sushmita Choudhury
Pinnacle Infotech, Durgapur, West Bengal, India

Manali Chowdhury
Department of Business Administration, University of Engineering & Management, Kolkata, India

Mrinal Kanti Das
Department of Commerce, Kanchrapara College, Kanchrapara, North 24 Parganas, West Bengal, India

Anirban Datta
MESCIA Engineers; West Bengal State Centre, The Institution of Engineers (India); MIE, Kolkata, West Bengal, India

Joysri Datta
Institute of Engineering & Management, School of University of Engineering and Management, Kolkata, India

Aryan Deb
Institute of Engineering & Management, School of University of Engineering and Management, Kolkata, India

Priyanka Dey
Institute of Engineering & Management, School of University of Engineering and Management, Kolkata, India

Subhanan Dey
Faculty of Management Studies, ICFAI University, Ranchi, Jharkhand, India

Sakshi Dhiman
School of Business and Management, Christ (Deemed to be University), Delhi, India

Saptaparni Dhol
Institute of Engineering & Management, School of University of Engineering and Management, Kolkata, India

Sumanta Dutta
Postgraduate and Research Department of Commerce, St. Xavier's College (Autonomous), Kolkata, India

Soumik Gangopadhyay
Institute of Engineering & Management, School of University of Engineering and Management, Kolkata, India

Ruchi Gautam
Jharkhand Raksha Shakti University, Ranchi, India

Rikta Ghorui
Institute of Engineering & Management, School of University of Engineering and Management, Kolkata, India

Saptaparna Ghosh
Institute of Engineering and Management, Kolkata, India
University of Engineering & Management, Kolkata, India

Abhijit Kumar Gupta
D Empressa Pvt. Ltd, Kolkata, India

Cynthia Simon El Hajj
Holy Spirit University of Kaslik (USEK), Lebanon

Hena Iqbal
Ajman University, Ajman, UAE

Sadia Islam
Department of Environmental and Resource Economics, Dhaka School of Economics, Dhaka, Bangladesh

M. A. Jabbar
Department of CSE (AI & ML), Hyderabad, Telangana, India

Md Kaif Reyaz Jaliawal
Bengal Institute of Technology, Kolkata, West Bengal, India

Zidan Kachhi
School of Commerce, Finance & Accountancy, CHRIST (Deemed to be University) Pune, Lavasa Campus, India

Manohar Kapse
Symbiosis Center for Management and Human Resource Development (SCMHRD), Symbiosis International (Deemed University), Pune, India

Abhishek Kumar
Department of Management Studies and Industrial Engineering, IIT Dhanbad, Dhanbad, India

Akanksha Kumari
Xavier Institute of Social Service, Ranchi, India

Rajkumar M.
Faculty of Management Studies, ICFAI University, Ranchi, Jharkhand, India

Kousik Mandal
Department of Business Administration, Vidyasagar University, Midnapore, India

Varsha Mishra
Royal Holloway, University of London, United Kingdom

Debolina Mitra
University of Engineering and Management, Kolkata, West Bengal, India

Rajesh Mohnot
Department of Finance, Ajman University, Ajman, United Arab Emirates

Sourav Mondal
Department of Management Studies and Industrial Engineering, IIT(ISM) Dhanbad, Dhanbad, India

Indraneel Mukhopadhyay
Institute of Engineering and Management, Kolkata, India
University of Engineering & Management, Kolkata, India

Soumya Mukherjee
Department of Management Studies, Techno India (Hooghly Campus), Chinsurah, West Bengal, India

Devika Mulchandani
The Calcutta Anglo Gujarati College, Kolkata, West Bengal, India

Raunak Pandey
The Calcutta Anglo Gujarati College, Kolkata, West Bengal, India

Pinku Paul
Management Development Institute, Murshidabad, West Bengal, India

Soumyajeet Paul
Institute of Engineering & Management, School of University of Engineering and Management, Kolkata, India

Shreya Periwal
Techno India, Kolkata, India

Jeanne Poulose
School of Business and Management, CHRIST (Deemed to be University), Delhi, India

Ashutosh Rai
PhD Scholar, University of Engineering and Management, Kolkata, India

Swecha Ram
Future Institute of Technology, Kolkata, India

Anugu Harshavardhan Reddy
School of Business & Management, CHRIST (Deemed to be University) Pune, Lavasa Campus, India

Moin Reza
D Empressa Pvt. Ltd, Kolkata, India

Arijit Roy
Chikitsa Medicare Pvt. Ltd, Kolkata, India

Suchana Roy
Institute of Engineering & Management, School of University of Engineering and Management, Kolkata, India

Cynthia Saha
Postgraduate and Research Department of Commerce, St. Xavier's College (Autonomous), Kolkata, India

Mitali Sengupta
Institute of Engineering & Management, School of University of Engineering and Management, Kolkata, India

Kirti P. Sharma
Techno India University, Kolkata, India

Manjari Sharma
School of Commerce, Finance & Accountancy, CHRIST (Deemed to be University) Pune, Lavasa Campus, India

Shivam Prem Sharma
Techno India University, Kolkata, West Bengal, India

Vinod Sharma
Symbiosis Center for Management and Human Resource Development (SCMHRD), Symbiosis International (Deemed University), Pune, India

Sahil Shaw
Techno India University, Kolkata, India

Shubham Kumar Shaw
Techno India University, Kolkata, West Bengal, India

Rikitha Shetty
School of Business and Management, CHRIST (Deemed to be University), Delhi, India

Ganga Show
The Calcutta Anglo Gujarati College, Kolkata, India

Amaan Singh
Techno India University, Kolkata, West Bengal, India

Ankita Singh
Jagdish Sheth School of Management (JAGSoM), Bangalore, India

Ayush Kumar Singh
Future Institute of Technology, Kolkata, India

Aditya Vikram Singh
Jagdish Sheth School of Management (JAGSoM), Bangalore, India

Harsh Vikram Singh
Techno India University, Kolkata, West Bengal, India

Saumya Singh
Department of Management Studies and Industrial Engineering, IIT Dhanbad, Dhanbad, India

Foreword

Revolution is the single thing that never stays the same in the dynamic world of modern business. Agility must be embraced as a key philosophy by organizations if they have to succeed in this constantly changing environment. This important and essential manual *Agile Business Transformations: Priorities, Learnings, and Practice* helps readers navigate the treacherous landscape of agile transition in business.

You will discover a gold mine of tips, tricks, and best practices suggested by professionals who have transformational experiences in these sections. This book serves as a guide for leaders and practitioners alike, from comprehending the priorities that support successful agile transitions to learning from real-world experiences.

The authors guide you through the complexities of adopting agility while highlighting the obstacles and successes encountered along the route. This book contains priceless insights that may be implemented in a variety of organizational scenarios, regardless of whether you are an experienced CEO, a project manager, or an agile enthusiast.

Greater than just a book, *Agile Business Transformations* provides a road map for thriving in a time of rapid change. Let this book serve as your trustworthy guide as you set out on your own agile journey. It will illuminate the way ahead and assist you in transforming your company with assurance and purpose.

—Phillip Kotler

American marketing author and consultant, and professor emeritus; the S. C. Johnson & Son Distinguished Professor of International Marketing, Kellogg School of Management at Northwestern University, Illinois

Preface

The requirement for adaptation and agility is more important than ever in the quickly changing corporate environment of today. Organizations always struggle to navigate complex markets, new technologies, and shifting client demands as they work to remain competitive. Businesses all across the world have embraced agile approaches as a way to promote transformation, innovation, and sustainable growth in response to these dynamic pressures.

This book is a thorough compilation of the opinions, encounters, and best practices of academics, professionals, and thought leaders who have started the agile transformation path. It acts as a road map for businesses looking to successfully launch, carry out, and optimize agile programs. The book goes deeply into the core of agile ideas, methods, and frameworks, showing how they can be modified and put into reality to suit various business domains and operational scales. Readers will learn insightful perspectives on agile approaches and their significant influence on numerous facets of contemporary businesses, such as project management, product development, human resources, customer engagement, and strategic planning, with each new chapter.

This volume illustrates the real-world struggles through entrepreneurship and accomplishments experienced by organizations from a variety of industries in their agile transformations through the contributions of various authors of different countries.

CHAPTER 1

Sustainable Food Delivery Apps: A Study on Consumer Satisfaction Toward the Usage of These Applications in the United Arab Emirates

UDIT CHAWLA[1], HENA IQBAL[2], M. A. JABBAR[3], and VARSHA MISHRA[4]

[1]*Institute of Engineering & Management, School of University of Engineering and Management, Kolkata, India*

[2]*Ajman University, UAE*

[3]*Department of CSE (AI&ML), Hyderabad, Telangana, India*

[4]*Royal Holloway, University of London, UK*

ABSTRACT

In recent times, the expansion of the field of food delivery through online apps has put the hospitality industry on digital distribution channels. Several scholars have recently tried to comprehend how consumers use these apps. However, many facets of the use of apps have not been investigated yet. Food delivery is a rapidly growing industry. Food is a very important aspect of life, and this industry makes it possible for clients to get delicious restaurant-made treats at home at affordable prices. Due to its promising present and future, this industry has a large number of brands and businesses. We found five aspects in this study: service (SR), technology (TN), convenience (CV), security (SC), and rewards and discounts (RD). SR and TN have the biggest effects on customer satisfaction.

Agile Business Transformations: Priorities, Lessons, and Practices. Satyajit Chakrabarti, Subrata Chattopadhyay, Udit Chawla, Sundeep Singh Sondhi, & Arunava Dalal (Eds.)

1.1 INTRODUCTION

Mobile phones, particularly smart ones, have become an indispensable need in the present culture (Lee et al., 2019). It was reported that in 2019, more than 5 billion people across the globe owned a mobile phone, the majority of which were smart, internet-enabled mobile phones (Silver, 2019). The accelerated rate of advancement in Information Communication Technology (ICT), has made smart mobile phones, advanced technology, and application software an essential part and a necessity in our regular day-to-day activities (Lal and Dwivedi, 2009; Shareef et al., 2012; Dwivedi et al., 2016; Baabdullah et al., 2019; Lu et al., 2019; Malaquias and Hwang, 2019; Ismagilova et al., 2019). Application software was invented and created to be used on mobile phones, iPods, and tablets. They can be accessed from application stores, reportedly at the beginning of 2017, there were more than 2.2 million applications on the IOS application store, and about 2.8 million on the Android application store (Statista, 2018a). Among these million applications, it was reported that food delivery applications had the second-highest number of downloads from the Apple store (Ariel, 2015). Therefore, more than 60% of eateries and food caters had enrolled themselves on at least one such food delivery application (BCG, 2017).

Delivery of food items in the UAE started very early (Baindur and Macário, 2013). The popularity of food delivery applications around the world began in the 2000s (Pigatto et al., 2017). UAE is one of the most popular countries in the world, and without a doubt, a large market for such business. The majority of the UAE population is younger than 25, which is the target audience for these applications. The demand for food, to satisfy this specific age group is the decisive part of the F & B industry of the country (AIMS Report, 0000).

The food delivery applications can be for a specific eatery and its various branches. Domino's and Pizza Hut (Sjahroeddin, 2018; Yeo et al., 2017), and some other food delivery applications are for various eateries, and not specific ones (Sjahroeddin, 2018). Some food delivery applications also let users get information about different eateries, access their menu, then place their orders, and pay through the app itself. This helps users to get their food delivered to their doorstep without any specific communication with the eatery and its staff (Okumus and Bilgihan, 2014; Wang et al., 2019).

Such food delivery applications usually turn profitable only after gaining much popularity and obtaining users' trust and loyalty. The revenue earned is usually from the payment for membership from eateries and prime memberships from users, promotions, and ads. The amount received from a delivery payment almost entirely goes to the eatery itself (Tarun, 2019). However, there is a growing engagement of users with food delivery applications, allowing them to access information about different hotels and eateries, weighing them based on reviews, price, etc., and then ordering from the one they prefer the most reviews (Carlson et al., 2019; Thakur, 2016; Yang et al., 2016; Yang et al., 2017).

1.2 REVIEW OF LITERATURE

Studies pertaining to food delivery apps are still in their beginning stages. Research is now attempted to understand the factors affecting consumer satisfaction relating to this application (Okumus and Bilgihan, 2014; Wang et al., 2019). Detailed analysis has found that most of the studies undertaken are from the customer's perspective and to understand their acceptance of food delivery apps. In a study based in the country of Brazil, consumers were seen to care more about the usefulness, and service quality of Online Food Applications, (Pigatto et al., 2017). In a similar study by (Okumus and Bilgihan, 2014) using the Technology Acceptance MODEL (TAM), a few factors were found to be major forecasters for customer satisfaction relating to food delivery apps, like perceived convenience, usefulness, societal pressure, and ease of use (Convenience) is one of the major factors that lead to customer satisfaction, especially in the e-industry (Silva et al., 2016). In the food delivery industry too, convenience leads to satisfaction, which further leads to loyalty. It was reported in the same study that restaurant owners genuinely look for customers of the younger generation, because they are found to be ordering more frequently, and in the near future the revenue earned out of them only would be more than 3.39 trillion dollars since they have more technological understanding and prefers comfort (Lee et al., 2017). In a study by Lee et al. (2017), it was found that individuals less than the age of 30 years of age are seen to order more frequently and are now the target customers for these applications. This age group consists mostly of students and they were found to be more inclined toward technology and, therefore, could easily order, and have food delivered to their houses. According to Chorneukar (2014), consumers have the option of deciding their food on the basis of their preference, without having to converse with anybody. It is one of the advantages of online delivery that if the required order is placed correctly by the consumer, the right order will be delivered to them (Weng and Chao, 2013). Therefore, it is the responsibility of the consumer to place their required order correctly. Some consumers may have problems placing orders in their first few times, but they would come along later, owing to the easy user interface. As stated by Silva et al. (2016), customers do not only place their orders from a certain restaurant, because of the taste of their food, they also care about the ambiance, SR, and décor of the restaurant. In a study by Rezaei (2016), it was similarly found that customers get more attracted to patterns present in their vision naturally, and it was recommended that additional items should be presented in the same way to motivate customers to purchase an extra item. Food delivery apps have an option for customers to put their reviews and feedback about the food taste, packaging, and also delivery reviews (Bert et al., 2014). Such reviews are available to everybody including other customers, thus they can work as advertisements (Filieri, 2015; Mudambi and Schuff, 2010; Wei and Lu, 2013). These reviews are useful for customers to refer to before placing their orders. This can make consumers make an informed choice (Filieri, 2015; Huang et al., 2015). It was found in research by Elwalda et al. (2016) that consumers usually are more attracted to the characteristics mentioned in reviews and end up purchasing the same items. Therefore, consumer preference highly depends on online ratings and reviews (Cheung et al., 2008).

The potential that a new software holds, to help consumers achieve their requirements and demands in a better advantageous and beneficial manner is called the Performance expectancy (Venkatesh et al., 2003). Applications and software that seem to be faster, smoother, and more beneficial tend to have a pragmatic effect on consumers (Khalilzadeh et al., 2017; Dwivedi et al., 2017; Sharma and Sharma, 2019; Tamilmani et al., 2019; Venkatesh et al., 2003). It was found that the insight and intent a customer has on a certain product, especially a new one holds a great influence on customer satisfaction and their tangible acceptance of the product (Alalwan et al., 2017; Rana et al., 2016; Shareef et al., 2018; Venkatesh et al., 2003). Social Influence is considered to be the most significant factor on which a consumer's acceptance toward a certain brand depends, especially an online brand. In the words of Venkatesh et al. (2003), Social Influence is the acceptance of a certain scheme by the consumer's friends or family, whose discretion is important to them. Consumers are often found to consult individuals in their societal group for advice, and opinions about a product or scheme (Alalwan et al., 2017; Okumus et al., 2018). Sometimes they talk about it to gather more data, and personal experiences of others relating to the particular item or service, or rather just to achieve communal support for using the same (Verkijika, 2018). Social influence holds a great impact on customer satisfaction relating to virtual applications and services; Verkijika (2018) found that it had a progressive impact on the usage of online payments.

Price is the most important parameter that affects a consumer's buying intention and satisfaction, especially relating to virtual software, apps, and services (Venkatesh et al., 2012). Consumers generally equate the benefits received with the amount they paid for the same, they also associate the cost they would be paying if getting the food, the orthodox way with the cost they pay through food delivery apps (Alalwan et al., 2017; Venkatesh et al., 2012). Researchers like Shaw and Sergueeva (2019) have also found that users who intend to use virtual shopping and other services highly depend on the price they will pay for it.

1.3 OBJECTIVE

To study a conceptual model for distinguishing the variables impacting customer satisfaction of consumers utilizing food delivery applications.

1.4 RESEARCH METHODOLOGY

For this study, the United Arab Emirates was chosen as the study location. This is a developed country, as they have the highest app usage for food delivery compared to other countries. Two hundred and fifty samples were collected from various locations in the United Arab Emirates using a structured questionnaire emailed to respondents. First, we identified approximately 50 quality parameters to determine customer perceptions and preferences for the food delivery application. A five-point Likert scale were used ranging from 1: completely disagree to 5: completely agree was introduced to measure each parameter. In addition to these parameters, respondents' demographic and psychological variables were also recorded. To achieve our research objectives, the data were used for multiple multivariate analyses, after appropriate cleansing and validation.

1.5 FINDINGS AND ANALYSIS

1.5.1 MEASUREMENT MODEL

Usually, we use confirmatory factor analysis in public research. Both exploratory, as well as CFA, are involved in comprehending the variance of all variables. The overall model was assessed by chi-square (χ^2), the goodness of fit index

(GFI), adjusted goodness of fit index (AGFI), comparative fit index (CFI), and root mean square error of approximation (RMSEA). GFI values should be over 0.9. and AGFI values over 0.8 indicate good data fitting. A RMSEA value between 0.05 and 0.10 was considered an indication of fair fit, and values above 0.10 indicated poor fit. Composite reliability (CR) is defined as a measure of the consistency of contented construct pointers. A higher CR indicates that possible variables are reliable; the values should be greater than 0.5.

TABLE 1.1 Goodness of Fit Indices (CFA).

CMIN/DF	P	GFI	AGFI	NFI	TLI	CFI	PCLOSE	RMSEA
3.116	0.000	0.841	0.778	0.837	0.91	0.93	0.06	0.057

From Table 1.1, we can see that we are getting satisfactory results for the confirmatory factor analysis.

TABLE 1.2 Discriminant Validity.

	SR	CV	TN	SC	RD
SR	**0.84**				
CV	0.366	**0.81**			
TN	0.311	0.645	**0.75**		
SC	0.482	0.563	0.629	**0.91**	
RD	0.700	0.702	0.733	0.66	**0.93**

Thus, from Table 1.2, we can conclude that congruence validity is accepted for this model, except for the construct NR which has very low value. From Table 1.3, we can see that AVE and CR are very less for the construct NR. From Figure 1.1, we can also conclude that convergent validity is also accepted as the variables associated with the factors are greater than 0.7.

TABLE 1.3 Results of the Measurement Model.

Measurement items	AVE	CR
SR	0.84	0.89
CV	0.81	0.8
TN	0.90	0.88
SC	0.91	0.85
RD	0.93	0.75

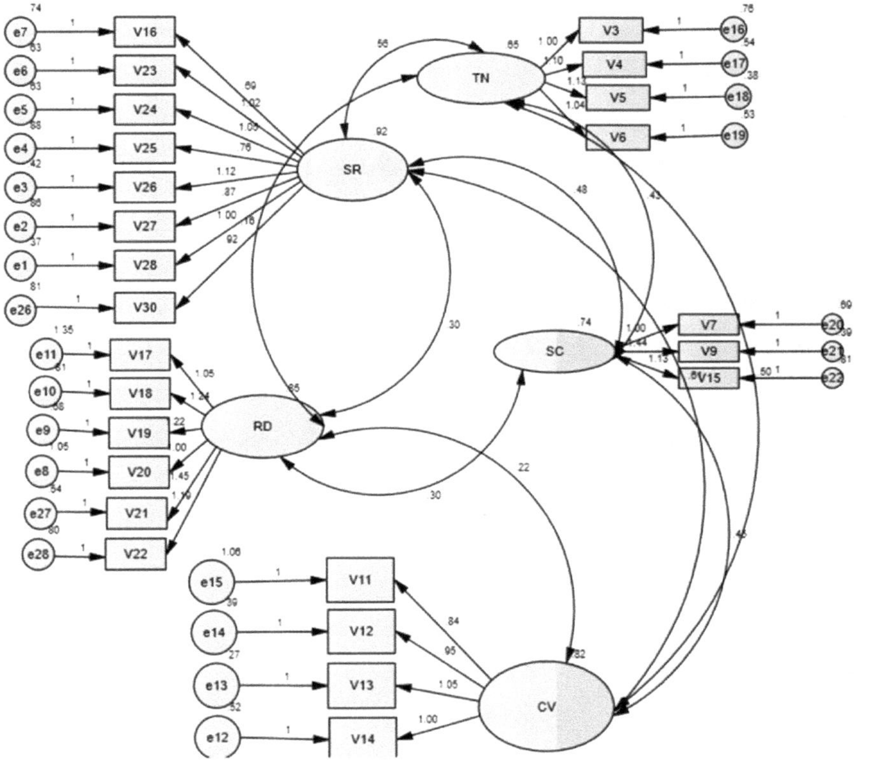

FIGURE 1.1 Confirmatory factor analysis.

TABLE 1.4 Goodness of Fitness (SEM).

CMIN/DF	P	GFI	AGFI	NFI	TLI	CFI	PCLOSE	RMSEA
3.671	0.000	0.82	0.80	0.833	0.84	0.91	0.000	0.091

From Table 1.4, we can see that we are getting satisfactory results for the Structured Equation Modelling. The structural model of the FOOD DELIVERY APP (Figure 1.2) suggests that TN and SR impose a larger impact on customer satisfaction (SATF) as it signifies the most important construct as the regression weight is 0.93 and 0.50. The study also signifies that there is a positive relationship between SATF—"Overall Customer Satisfaction" and the construct CV, construct SC and also construct RD as the regression weights are 0.27, 0.19, and 0.13. Thus, it may be hypothesized that patients in general consider that TN and SR play a very important role in determining customer satisfaction.

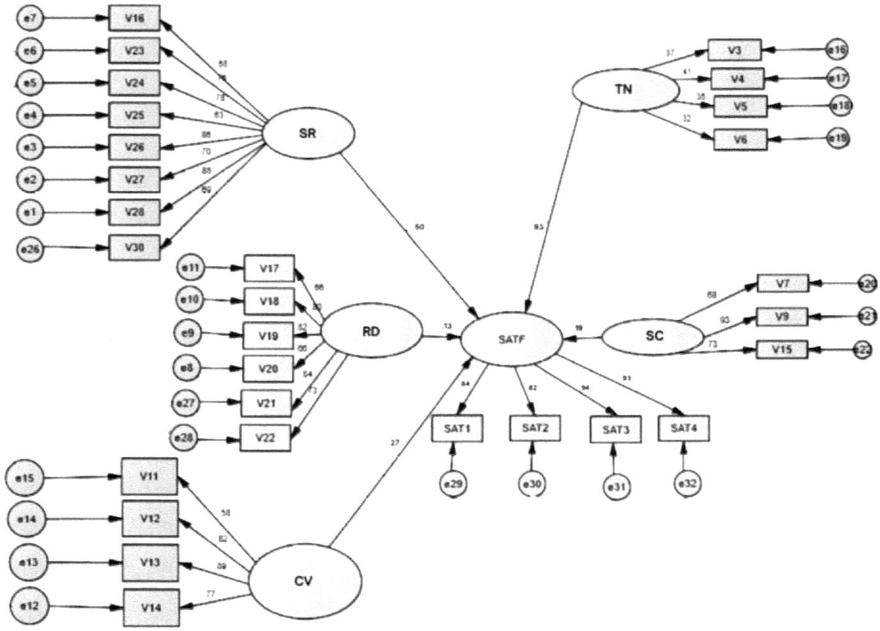

FIGURE 1.2 Structural equation modeling.

1.6 CONCLUSION

New developments in technologies have given birth to many application-based service industries, and the companies under all such industries are scoring fairly. Food delivery apps are one such industry that has boomed only in a few years of existence. Customers can enjoy food from their favorite restaurants in the comfort of their houses. Using food delivery apps, they can order food and indulge in their food without the hassle of being stuck in traffic and waiting in lines for hours in restaurants. This study was done to analyze the satisfaction of customers using food delivery apps, with the help of identified factors. It was found that all the factors have significance in customer satisfaction relating to food delivery apps. Technology acceptance is considered for the growth of a food delivery business because it has a good impact on overall customer retention and provides information at the touch of a single button, making online shopping more favorable thanks to a large selection of goods and simple evaluation; which results in increase in demand for FDA services. This study was conducted to learn more about how consumers felt about the different meal delivery services and the industry as a whole considering both transitional objectives and far-sighted corporate growth plans and foresight techniques. To prepare for the upcoming technological revolution, they must develop an omnichannel marketing plan and upskill their personnel which is done by using an analytical approach to consumer profiling, keeping track of orders, and behavioral way of giving orders in terms of income generation, consumer configuration, and consumer holding with which the businesses could implement suitable drives to boost customer approval and lower the customer drop-outs.

KEYWORDS

- **SR**
- **TN**
- **SC**
- **customer satisfaction**

REFERENCES

AIMS Report 0000 [Online]. https://theaims.ac.in/resources/online-food-service-in-indiaan-analysis.html.

Alalwan, A. A.; Dwivedi, Y. K.; Rana, N. P. Factors Influencing Adoption of Mobile Banking by Jordanian Bank Customers: Extending UTAUT2 With Trust. *Int. J. Inf. Manage.* **2017,** *37* (3), 99–110.

Ariel. App Stores Growth Accelerates in 2014 [Online]; 2015. https://blog.appfigures.com/app-stores-growth-accelerates-in-2014/ (accessed Jan 2, 2019).

Baabdullah, A. M.; Alalwan, A. A.; Rana, N. P.; Kizgin, H.; Patil, P. Consumer Use of Mobile Banking (M-Banking) in Saudi Arabia: Towards an Integrated Model. *Int. J. Inf. Manage.* **2019,** *44,* 38–52.

Baindur, D.; Macário, R.M. Mumbai Lunch Box Delivery System: A Transferable Benchmark in Urban Logistics? *Res. Transport. Econ.* **2013,** *38* (1), 110–121. https://doi.org/10.1016/j.retrec.2012.05.002

BCG The new digital reality for restaurants [Online]; 2017. https://www.bcg.com/publications/2017/technology-value-creation-strategy-new-digital-realityrestaurants.aspx (accessed Jan 3, 2019).

Bert, F.; Giacometti, M.; Gualano, M. R.; Siliquini, R. Smartphones and Health Promotion: A Review of the Evidence. *J. Med. Syst.* **2014,** *38* (1), 1–11. *Bus. Res.* *68* (6), 1261–1270.

Carlson, J.; Rahman, M. M.; Taylor, A.; Voola, R. Feel the VIBE: Examining Value-in-the-Brand-Page-Experience and Its Impact on Satisfaction and Customer Engagement Behaviors in Mobile Social Media. *J. Retail. Consum. Serv.* **2019,** *46,* 149–162.

Cheung, C. M.; Lee, M. K.; Rabjohn, N. The impact of Electronic Word-of-Mouth. 2008.
Chorneukar. *To Study the Customer Perceptions of Electronic Food Ordering*, St. Joseph's Evening College—Pondicherry University: Bangalore; 2014.
Dwivedi, Y. K.; Rana, N. P.; Janssen, M.; Lal, B.; Williams, M. D.; Clement, M. An Empirical Validation of a Unified Model of Electronic Government Adoption (UMEGA). *Gov. Inf. Q.* **2017,** *34* (2), 211–230.
Dwivedi, Y. K.; Shareef, M. A.; Simintiras, A. C.; Lal, B.; Weerakkody, V. A Generalised Adoption Model for Services: A Cross-Country Comparison of Mobile Health (m-health). *Gov. Inf. Q.* **2016,** *33* (1), 174–187.
Elwalda, A.; Lu, K.; Ali, M. Perceived Derived Attributes of Online Customer Reviews. *Comput. Hum. Behav.* **2016,** *56,* 306–319.
Filieri, R. What Makes Online Reviews Helpful? A Diagnosticity-Adoption Framework to Explain Informational and Normative Influences in e-WOM. *J. Food J.* **2015,** *119* (3), 639–657.
Huang, J.; Baptista, J.; Newell, S. Communicational Ambidexterity as a New Capability to Manage Social Media Communication within Organizations. *J. Strateg. Inf. Syst.* **2015,** *24* (2), 49–64.
Ismagilova, E.; Hughes, L.; Dwivedi, Y. K.; Raman, K. R. Smart Cities: Advances in Research—An Information Systems Perspective. *Int. J. Informa. Manag.* **2019,** *47,* 88–100.
Khalilzadeh J.; Ozturk, A. B.; Bilgihan, A. Security-Related Factors in Extended UTAUT Model for NFC based Mobile Payment in the Restaurant Industry. *Comp. Hum. Behav.* **2017,** *70,* 460–474.
Lal, B.; Dwivedi, Y. K. Homeworkers' Usage of Mobile Phones: Social Isolation in the Home-Workplace., **2009,** *22* (3), 257–274.
Lee, E.; Lee, S.; Jeon, Y. Factors Influencing the Behavioral Intention to Use Food Delivery apps. *Soc. Behav. Pers. Int. J.* **2017,** *45,* 1461–1474.
Lee, S. W.; Sung, H. J.; Jeon, H. M. Determinants of Continuous Intention on Food Delivery Apps: Extending UTAUT2 with Information Quality. *Sustainability* **2019,** *11* (11), 3141. https://doi.org/10.3390/su11113141
Lu, C. C.; Wu, L.; Hsiao, W. H. Developing Customer Product Loyalty through Mobile Advertising: Affective and Cognitive Perspectives. *Int. J. Inform. Manage.* **2019,** *47,* 101–111.
Malaquias, R. F.; Hwang, Y.Mobile Banking Use: A Comparative Study with Brazilian and US Participants. *Int. J. Inf. Manage.* **2019,** *44,* 132–140.
Mudambi, S. M.; Schuff, D. Research Note: What Makes a Helpful Online Review? 2010.
Okumus, B.; Bilgihan, A. Proposing a Model to Test Smartphone Users' Intention to Use Smart Applications when Ordering Food in Restaurants, *J. Hospitality Tour. Technol.* **2014,** *5* (1), 31–49.
Okumus, B.; Ali, F.; Bilgihan, A.; Ozturk, A. B. Psychological Factors Influencing Customers' Acceptance of Smartphone Diet apps when Ordering Food at Restaurants. *Int. J. Hosp. Manag.* **2018,** *72,* 67–77.
Pigatto, G.; Machado, J. G. D. C. F.; Negreti, A. D. S.; Machado, L. M. Have you Chosen Your Request? Analysis of Online Food Delivery Companies in Brazil. *British* 2017.
Rana, N. P.; Dwivedi, Y. K.; Williams, M. D.; Weerakkody, V. Adoption of Online Public Grievance Redressal System in India: Toward Developing a Unified View. *Comput. Hum. Behav.* **2016,** *59,* 265–282.

Rezaei, S. S. Determinants of App Stores Continuance Behavior: A PLS path Modelling Approach. *J. Internet Commercial.* **2016,** 408–440.
Shareef, M. A.; Archer, N.; Dwivedi, Y. K. Examining Adoption Behavior of Mobile Government. *J. Comp. Inform. Syst.* **2012,** *53* (2), 39–49.
Shareef, M. A.; Baabdullah, A.; Dutta, S.; Kumar, V.; Dwivedi, Y. K. Consumer Adoption of Mobile Banking Services: An Empirical Examination of Factors According to Adoption Stages. *J. Retail. Consum. Serv.* **2018,** *43,* 54–67.
Sharma, S. K.; Sharma, M. Examining the Role of Trust and Quality Dimensions in the Actual Usage of Mobile Banking Services: An Empirical Investigation. *Int. J. Inform. Manag.* **2019,** *44,* 65–75.
Shaw, N.; Sergueeva, K. The Non-monetary Benefits of Mobile Commerce: Extending UTAUT2 with Perceived Value. *Int. J. Inform. Manag.* **2019,** *45,* 44–55.
Silva, F. Q.; Freire, O.; Lima-Filho, D. O.; Brandão, M. M.; Isabella, G.; Moreira, L. B. Intentions to Purchase Food Through the Internet: Developing and Testing a Model. *Br. Food J.* **2016,** *3* (118), 572–587.
Silver, L. Smartphone Ownership is Growing Rapidly Around the World, but Not Always Equally. *Pew Research Center's Global Attitudes Project*; February 5, 2019. [Online]. https://www.pewresearch.org/global/2019/02/05/smartphone-ownership-is-growing-rapidly-around-the-world-but-not-alwaysequally/
Sjahroeddin, F.; In *The Role of E-S-Qual and Food Quality on Customer Satisfaction inOnline Food Delivery Service*, 9th International Research Workshop and National Seminer; 2018. Available at: https://jurnal.polban.ac.id/index.php/proceeding/article/viewFile/1097/898.
Statista *Mobile app Usage – Statistics & Facts*; 2018a [Online]. Available from: https://www.statista.com/topics/1002/mobile-app-usage/ (accessed Dec 15, 2018).
Tamilmani, K.; Rana, N. P.; Prakasam, N.; Dwivedi, Y. K. The Battle of Brain vs. Heart: A Literature Review and Meta-analysis of "Hedonic Motivation" use in UTAUT2. *Int. J. Inf. Manage.;* **2019,** *46,* 222–235.
Tarun. How do Food Delivery Apps Earn their Revenue? *Medium*; Dec 31, 2019 [Online]. https://medium.com/@nagartarun/how-dofood-delivery-apps-earn-their-revenue-ee945633d634.
Thakur, R. Understanding Customer Engagement and Loyalty: A Case of Mobile Devices for Shopping. *J. Retail. Consum. Serv.* **2016,** *32,* 151–163.
Venkatesh, V.; Morris, M.; Davis, G.; Davis, F. User Acceptance of Information Technology: Toward a Unified View. *MIS Q.* **2003,** *27* (3), 425–478.
Venkatesh, V.; Thong, J. Y. L.; Xu, X. Consumer Acceptance and Use of Information Technology: Extending the Unified Theory of Acceptance and Use of Technology. *MIS Q.* **2012,** *36* (1), 157–178.
Verkijika, S. F. Factors Influencing the Adoption of Mobile Commerce Applications in Cameroon. *Telemat. Inform.* **2018,** *35* (6), 1665–1674.
Wang, W. T.; Ou, W. M.; Chen, W. Y. The Impact of Inertia and User Satisfaction on the Continuance Intentions to use Mobile Communication Applications: A Mobile Service Quality Perspective. *Int. J. Inf. Manage.* **2019,** *44,* 178–193.
Wang, Y. S.; Tseng, T. H.; Wang, W. T.; Shih, Y. W.; Chan, P. Y. Developing and Validating a Mobile Catering app Success Model. *Int. J. Hospitality Manag.* **2019,** *7,* 19–30.
Wei, P. S.; Lu, H. P. An Examination of the Celebrity Endorsements and Online Customer Reviews Influence Female Consumers' Shopping Behavior. *Comput. Hum. Behav.* **2013,** *29* (1), 193–201.

Weng, T. S.; Chao, I. C. Evaluating Factors Influencing the Intention to Use Online Ordering System—A Case Study of Lunch Box Purchasing. *J. Contemp. Manag.* **2013.**

Yang, S.; Lin, S.; Carlson, J. R.; Ross, W. T.; Jr. Brand Engagement on Social Media: Will Firms' Social Media Efforts Influence Search Engine Advertising Effectiveness. *J. Mark. Manag.* **2016,** *32* (5–6), 526–557.

Yang, Y.; Asaad, Y.; Dwivedi, Y. Examining the Impact of Gamification on Intention of Engagement and Brand Attitude in the Marketing Context. *Comput. Hum. Behav.* **2017,** *73,* 459–469.

Yeo, V.C.S.; Goh, S.-K.; Rezaei, S. Consumer Experiences, Attitude and Behavioral Intention toward Online Food Delivery (OFD) Service. *J. Retail. Consum. Serv.* **2017,** 150–162.

CHAPTER 2

A Study on How Green Marketing Strategies Affect Consumer Purchasing Behavior Across the Automobile Sector

JOYSRI DATTA[1], SUCHANDRA BOSE[1,2], SOUMYAJEET PAUL[1], and RIKTA GHORUI[1]

[1]*Institute of Engineering & Management, School of University of Engineering and Management, Kolkata, India*

[2]*Adamas University, Kolkata, India*

ABSTRACT

Businesses have started changing their business practices to cater to society's promoting environmental concerns via "Green Marketing" strategies as customers are concerned about the environment. Through a thorough study of the literature, it seeks to comprehend the Green Marketing concept, its pertinent elements, and in particular, the practices and consequences of these techniques on purchasers' buying habits in the Indian automobile sector. Sustainable marketing is the practice of promoting ecological goods as well as services that are ethical and environmentally friendly. Businesses that engage in environmentally friendly advertising take advantage of devoted clients as well as a positive brand reputation while also preserving the environment and promoting a more sustainable future. To produce vehicles with less impact on people and the environment, Automobile manufacturing companies throughout the world utilize techniques and technologies that are sustainable, environmentally friendly, and optimized. It is crucial to understand how "Green" consumers are in terms of their knowledge,

Agile Business Transformations: Priorities, Lessons, and Practices. Satyajit Chakrabarti, Subrata Chattopadhyay, Udit Chawla, Sundeep Singh Sondhi, & Arunava Dalal (Eds.)

attitudes, and behavior since our article examines how approaches for Ecological Marketing impact consumers' buying habits. We have studied various impacts of demographic factors like sexuality, Age Group, Revenue, Academic Qualifications, and Profession on Consumer Purchase Behavior. Research and in-depth study are carried out to understand several other factors regulating Consumer Purchase Behavior for buying Electric Vehicles in detail.

2.1 INTRODUCTION

The practice of "Green Marketing" has been elevating significantly in terms of demand in the modern marketplace. During the latter half of the 1980s first half of the 1990s, the expression "Green Marketing" initially surfaced. In the same year, 1975, the American Marketing Association organized its inaugural session on "Ecological Marketing." The notes from the workshop were published in "Ecological Marketing," the initial text about "Green Marketing." As a consequence, "Green Marketing" covers a diverse array of actions, like adjustments to the manufacturing process, changes to products and packaging, and adjustments to advertising. Green purchasing behavior is the practice of consumers buying products that are regarded as "green" or environmentally advantageous (Sondhi et al., 2023). It deals with advertising goods and services in light of how great they are for the environment. Nowadays, it is increasingly usual to promote ecologically friendly goods and services. It involves creating, generating, spreading, using, and discarding. Customers are also more concerned about sustainability. Nowadays, people are more likely to seek high-quality goods that are also affordable and ecologically sustainable. Recent advancements in automotive technology are a result of growing transportation problems such as traffic congestion, noise, and carbon emissions (Chawla et al., 2023). According to the "IBEF" study from 2023, the two-wheeler market has grown at a 10% annual pace during the previous five years. India is ranked fifth in the market for commercial vehicles and thirteenth in the market for passenger cars. Along with all these successes, the Indian automotive sector employs over 10 million people. Last year, the domestic passenger car market in India saw its biggest yearly sales ever. Despite the fact that owning a car has become more of a necessity, the environment is now the biggest threat to our civilization (IBEF, 2023). India was listed as the seventh most polluted nation in the world in 2022, according to "The Times of India" citing The Swiss IQAir's "World Quality Report" published in 2023. Among the top 50 filthy towns worldwide, there are 50 towns included, 39 within India. Other sources of pollution include industrial facilities, coal-fired power stations, and biomass burning, while the transportation sector is responsible for 20–35% of the PM2.5 pollution (IANS, 2023). As a result of greenhouse gas emissions from vehicles, the ozone layer is harmed, air temperatures rise, and this results in global warming. Global warming has an effect on all living things, including animals. Humans are experiencing significant respiratory issues as a result of rising carbon monoxide and other toxic gas emissions. Modern times have seen a sharp rise in air pollution. The introduction of the E Vehicle, which produces zero emissions, is crucial given the rise in demand for passenger cars since it would lessen the damage done to all forms of biodiversity. Electric Vehicles (EVs) have seen a significant rise in popularity recently as a more efficient, environmentally friendly alternative to traditional vehicles powered by gasoline. EVs have become a reasonable selection for numerous drivers throughout the world as a cause of developments in battery design, a developing infrastructure system for growing demand among customers, and charging. Since these cars are powered by energy stored in batteries rather than petrol to turn the wheels, they are altering the way we think about driving. According to an article in "The Invest India Outlook" from 2023, India has become the world's third-most populous marketplace for motor vehicles as a share sales volume, trailing only Germany and Japan. Governments and businesses are advised to cooperate in order to shift consumer preferences toward greener goods. The automobile industry is a major employer in India and contributes 7.1% of its GDP to the nation's GDP. Between 2022 and 2030, India's domestic market for electric cars will grow at a pace of 49%, with 10 million vehicles sold annually by that time (Singh, 2023). Nirmala Sitharaman, the minister of finance suggested a monetary distribution of INR 35,000 crore for sizable financial expenditures intended for accomplishing zero emissions goals and the power shift until 2070 in the Union Budget 2023–2024. For a battery-operated energy preservation mechanism along with 4000 MWH capability, she added, the Government will provide funds to close the viability gap. For manufacturers of EVs, the Government has in the past introduced programs including the Production Linked Incentive Scheme (PLI) and the Faster Adoption of Manufacturing of Electric Vehicles Scheme II (FAME-II). The FAME-II initiative, which aims to support and promote the usage of renewable energy automobiles, has received INR 51.72 billion (about $631 million) from the budget. This budget allocation has grown by 80% from the previous years and reduced customs fees on lithium-ion batteries used in electric cars as well as excise duty discounts on natural gas and biogas may encourage more international

EVs to be imported into India (Bureau, 2023). Tata Motors and Mahindra & Mahindra, two significant Indian manufacturers, have started creating EVs, and other overseas businesses have entered the industry. India emerges as a possible rival in the race to install a new electrical car manufacturing facility outside of China for the Swedish luxury automaker Volvo Cars. The Tata Nexon eclipsed other well-known models from Maruti Suzuki and Hyundai to become popular sellers of SUV in India in December 2021, according to news from "The Zed News" published on January 4, 2022. With just two models—the Nexon EV and Tigor EV—and 86% of the market in terms of yearly sales, Tata controlled the EV sector (Garg, 2022). From the explanation above, it is reasonable to infer that over the next several years, the market for electric cars in India will grow dramatically. The nation is in a good position to switch to an increasingly viable and ecologically pleasant kind of mobility because of favorable Government policies, rising consumer awareness, and technological improvements. There is a huge chance for national as well as global firms to support and contribute to growth the development of the nation's EV environment as the need for EV grows. Specifically, how the Green Marketing methods used by various companies influence customer choices throughout the automotive sector, this paper explores some of the significant aspects that have the ability to affect consumers' preferences to purchase eco-friendly automobiles.

2.1.1 PRIOR STUDIES

2.2 OBJECTIVE OF THE STUDY

To understand whether the variables of demographics are significantly associated with Customer Purchasing Behavior.

2.3 RESEARCH METHODOLOGY

Our research is based on a primary survey. The goal is to identify the variables that affect customer choice throughout the automotive industry. A structured questionnaire is created incorporating a non-probability convenience sampling technique and distributed across social media platforms, online forums, and various online communities resulting in a sample size of 226 respondents with no partial response recorded. Responses from both the Male and Female category audience were taken into consideration.

TABLE 2.1 Literature Review.

Authors	Research design	Dependent variable	Independent variable	Finding
Bhatia and Jain 2013	Questionnaire	Environmental concerns, green products	Communication Campaigns, Awareness of environmental degradation	Consumers have actually given the seriousness a higher rate because of several distinct reasons which are falling under the purview of environmental concerns. Consumers' agreement when it comes to environmental degradation was high and, in this case, green products may be preferred over conventional products that cannot impact the environment positively. Here, the important point to consider is that protecting the environment is very necessary. Marketers may discover new green products and let the consumers know about the benefits of it. Respondents have marked the seriousness of different environmental concerns high.
Sharang Karurkar, Seema Unnikrishnan, Swapna Sonali Panda	Questionnaire	Environmental impacts, safety impacts	Green Product design, green technology implementation	First, to know the present environmental aspects in different companies. Second, to get an idea of the impact of the present manufacturing processes on the environment. Thirdly, to get to know about the focus points of the companies in regard to competitive environmental policies, that will help to stay in the competition. In the case of the automobile industry in India, logistics is the primary angle that received the first rank. Followed by green logistics, the second most factor of importance is green energy or in other words, power.
Nigam and Sharma 2022	Descriptive Research	Customer buying electric two-wheelers	Rise in petrol price, charging time, mileage, service provided by the company	Statistically speaking, there exists a significant relation between customers buying electric two-wheelers and the increase in petrol prices, again, there exists a significant relationship between charging time with customers buying electric two-wheelers, but there is an absence of any significant relationship between customers buying electric two-wheelers and its mileage. A significant relationship

TABLE 2.1 *(Continued)*

Authors	Research design	Dependent variable	Independent variable	Finding
				prevails in between customers buying electric two-wheelers and after-sales service provided.
Udit Chawla, Rajesh Mohnot, Varsha Mishra, Harsh Vikram Singh, Ayush Kumar Singh	Questionnaire	Customer Recommenda-tions	Charging Time, Innovation, Perceived Quality, Perceived, Affordability, Awareness, Comfort	In order to gain a better understanding of consumer buying decisions, researchers have looked at EVs. The analysis reveals that the biggest non-financial barrier to adoption is the battery's range. In more than 70% of transportation assessments, it has been discovered that each of the three responders considers the range for driving to be either a "major drawback" or a "roughly of a drawback."
Pandey et al., 2021	Survey	Electric Cars Purchase Intentions	Perceived Monetary Benefits, Perceived Costs, Perceived	The study concluded that factors like perceived monetary benefits plus aspects like personnel innovativeness impact to a great level of the purchase intention of EVs. While other factors such as perceived cost as well as perceived risk alongside
			Environmental Benefits, Perceived Risks	perceived environmental benefit do not create influence on electric car buying intention to a great level. The influence of demographic factor (including gender) on EV purchase intention has also been investigated and developed; and it can be concluded that gender bears no significant impact in this case.
Vatsa et al., 2016	Questionnaire	Demand for green vehicles	Eco-friendly features	Considering the degradation that is happening in the condition of air, Nowadays, Preference for sustainable automobiles is increasing as more individuals seek to drive automobiles with sustainable characteristics. Simultaneously, by incentivizing green cars the Government is opening up the chances for players in the automotive industry..

TABLE 2.1 *(Continued)*

Authors	Research design	Dependent variable	Independent variable	Finding
Vatsa et al., 2021	Descriptive	Inclusion of theme in advertisements	Performance, Luxury, Economy good value	The analysis puts forth the distribution of primary themes of advertisements. Efficiency was very important when often used as the main idea portrayed in the advertising with 44% of usage, and next is Luxury/prestige themes (21%), Innovative technology, security, novel sales enticements, environmental issues, and a way out, among various other subjects were utilized.
Dsouza Prima Frederick, Ganesh Bhat S., Sujaya H. 3 & Meghana Salins	Survey	Adoption of Green Marketing	Inventory, Operation, Research & Development, Resources, Eco-Innovation, Consumption, Innovation, Consumerism, Expenditure	The factors that influence Green Marketing for Sustainable Development is exhibited as ABCD analysis framework and it shows the results in terms of mean scores, one—the "Advantageous" construct has ranked first, signifying satisfaction. Second—"Benefits" signifying a neutral impact on Green Marketing for Sustainable Development and Third for "constraints and disadvantages," respectively, resulting as a not satisfactory factor for Green Marketing for Sustainable Development (Frederick et al., 2022).
Nozari et al., 2021	Survey	Aiding business sector organizations and Green Marketing	IoE Technologies	Business sector organizations, like social marketing for citizens, strategic branding of organizations, structures, marketplaces, and governments, are some of the most important players in this area. The notion of environmentally sustainable practices should get serious consideration by businesses because it is Perhaps among the most crucial aspects of significance. Sustainable marketing deals with an area that businesses should focus a high level of attention, and is a highly effective instrument for gaining knowledge regarding the requirements that are related to the customers, of businesses and meeting the preference of ecologically conscious goods.

TABLE 2.1 *(Continued)*

Authors	Research design	Dependent variable	Independent variable	Finding
Viet 2022	Survey	Customer-based brand equity	Green Marketing Mix Tools	The findings showed that sustainable advertising blended instruments actually have a favorable implication for the creation of consumer-based equity in green brands. Additionally, the findings demonstrate the connection of green brand equity components in the context of Vietnam.
Vaitone et al., 2022	The multi-step process to create GMaS	Eco Labeling	Safety, Recyclability, Reusability, Innovativeness of green products, and Marketing Communication	Measurement of a crucial variable in a sustainable era is provided by the newly developed GMaS. GMaS is nothing more than a 14-item measure with four parts: planning, goods and corporate advertising, and interaction in advertising. These parts are the ones that have shown sufficient factorial validity and reliability. The scale includes planning, which covers principles, culture, and policies as the cornerstones of Green Marketing, internal marketing, which considers the notion of Green Marketing arousal from workers, and other categories of views.

There were distinct sets of responses, segregated into five categories based upon chronological age: 18–25 years, 26–30 years, 31–35 years, 36–40 years, and >40 years. The questionnaire also consisted of questions related to various parameters such as Income Range, Occupation, and Educational Qualifications of the respondents and how the customer buying decisions for EVs are impacted by Green Marketing methods used by different automakers. The following characteristics were assessed on a five-point Likert scale to determine their significance when buying a vehicle: EVs are environment friendly since they have zero emissions hence reducing air pollution, Better Technology is associated with EVs, thereby a reason for high demand, and EVs may substantially decrease the cost of zero fuel costs, lower maintenance costs, and various tax advantages and subsidies from the Government.

2.4 FINDINGS AND DISCUSSIONS

2.4.1 CONSUMER PURCHASE BEHAVIOR VARIABLES

V7-EVs are environment friendly since they have zero emissions hence reducing air pollution.

V9-Better Technology is associated with EVs, thereby a reason for high demand.

V11-EVs save a significant sum of funds on zero fuel costs, lower maintenance costs, and various tax advantages and subsidies from the Government.

2.5 GENDER

H_0—There is no significant association between Gender and Consumer Purchase Behavior

H_1—There is a significant association between Gender and Consumer Purchase Behavior

The chi-square value for V7 is 15.512[a], and the asymp sign is 0.004—less than 0.05—as can be seen in the data table (Table 2.2). Similar to V9, where the significance level is 10.809[a] and the asymp sign is 0.029 (about 0.03), below 0.05 is indicated, and V11, where the chi-square value is 17.048[a] and the asymp sign is 0.002, less than 0.05 is indicated. These suggestions arrived here are alternative hypotheses that have been accepted and the null

TABLE 2.2 Chi-Square Test and Symmetrical Measures.

		Value	df	Asymp. sig. (2-sided)			Value	Approx. sig.
V7	Pearson Chi-Square	15.512[a]	4	.004	Nominal by Nominal	Contingency Coefficient	.253	.004
	Likelihood Ratio	16.008	4	.003			226	
	N of Valid Cases	226			N of Valid Cases		226	
V9	Pearson Chi-Square	10.809[a]	4	.029	Nominal by Nominal	Contingency Coefficient	.214	.029
	Likelihood Ratio	10.858	4	.028			226	
	N of Valid Cases	226			N of Valid Cases		226	
V11	Pearson Chi-Square	17.048[a]	4	.002	Nominal by Nominal	Contingency Coefficient	.265	.002
	Likelihood Ratio	17.775	4	.001			226	
	N of Valid Cases	226			N of Valid Cases		226	

hypothesis remains rejected. Thus, Gender has an alliance with Consumer Purchase Behavior concerning variables V7, V9, and V11. Likewise, it is evident that the variable's contingency coefficient for V7 is 0.253 (approx. 0.3), indicating the connection of sexuality and Consumer Purchase Behavior is Average in comparison to the variable. The Contingency Coefficient of variable V9 is 0.214, which indicates that the connection of Gender and Consumer Purchase Behavior is weak compared to the variable. Lastly, the Contingency Coefficient of Variable V11 is 0.265 (approx. 0.3), indicating the connection of Gender and Consumer Purchase Behavior is Average with the variable.

In Graph 2.1, we have shown two genders: Male and Female, and their responses have been recorded.

2.6 GRAPHICAL INTERPRETATION

It has been observed that for variable 7, the higher proportion of males agrees that EVs are environment friendly since they have zero emissions hence reducing air pollution. According to the survey response, female respondents, who mostly are housewives hardly use vehicles or EVs, they are less cautious about the harmful emissions of toxic gases emitted from vehicles. On the other hand, males use vehicles or E vehicles more on a daily basis, they are aware of the environmental damage caused due to vehicular emission, and thereby they agree to the fact that EVs are safer for the environment. For variable 9, it has been observed that a higher proportion of females agree that Better Technology is associated with EVs, thereby a reason for high demand. While on the other hand, according to the survey conducted, males believe that due to environmental awareness, greater vehicle choice has an implicit effect on consumer buying patterns, henceforth the widespread usage of EVs is predominantly rising in the modern era across the Automobile Sector. For variable 11, it has been observed that higher proportions of females agree that EVs are saving a significant sum of funds on zero fuel costs, lower maintenance costs, and various tax advantages and subsidies from the Government. While on the other hand, male considers that though it is environmentally friendly to use EVs, these batteries are made with lithium-ion technology, which is more expensive to produce since it requires rare earth elements. Even more money is spent on this for bigger cars. Therefore, the battery is the primary cause of electric automobiles' high price.

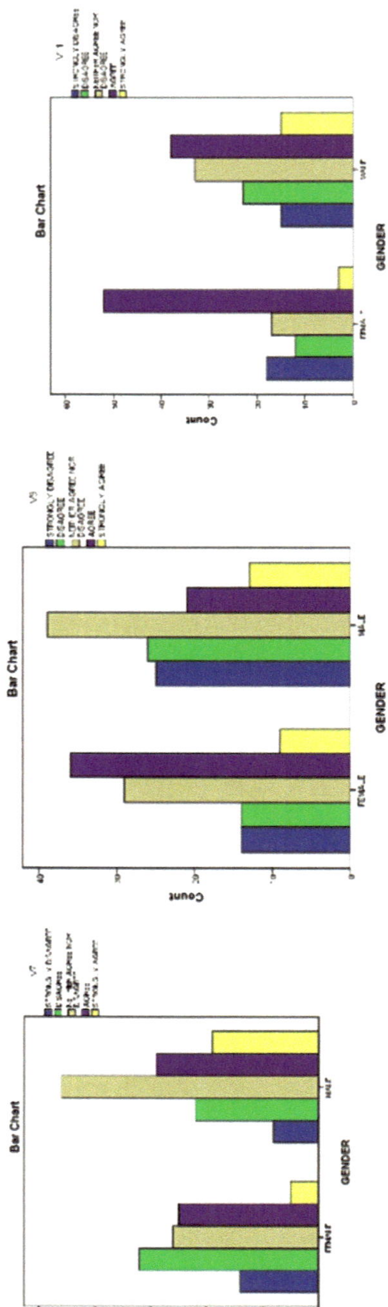

GRAPH 2.1 Responses as per gender.

2.6.1 CONSUMER PURCHASE BEHAVIOR VARIABLES

V7—EVs are environment friendly since they have zero emissions hence reducing air pollution.

V9—Better Technology is associated with EVs, thereby a reason for high demand.

V11—EVs save a significant sum of funds on zero fuel costs, lower maintenance costs, and various tax advantages and subsidies from the Government.

2.7 AGE

H_0—There is no significant association between Age and Consumer Purchase Behavior

H_1—There is a significant association between Age and Consumer Purchase Behavior

The chi-square value for V7 is 49.733[a], and the asymp sign is 0.000, a value below 0.05, according to the data table (Table 2.3). Similar results were found for V9, where the chi-square value was 84.468[a] and the asymp sign was 0.000, below 0.05, and for V11, where the chi-square value was 77.773[a] and the asymp sign was 0.000, below 0.05. This suggests that the alternative hypothesis is accepted, and the null hypothesis is rejected. Age and Customer Purchase Activity are related to variables V7, V9, and V11, respectively. Similarly, we observe that the Contingency Coefficient of the variable for V7 is 0.425 (approx. 0.4), indicating the connection of Age and Consumer Purchase Behavior is average with the variable. The Contingency Coefficient of variable V9 is 0.522, which indicates that the connection of Age and Consumer Purchase Behavior is average with the variable. Lastly, the Contingency Coefficient of Variable V11 is 0.506 (approx. 0.5), indicating that the connection of Age and Consumer Purchase Behavior is average with the variable.

In Graph 2.2, we have shown five Age Groups: The Age Groups representing those surveyed collected are ranging from 18 to 25 years, 26 to 30 years, 31 to 35 years, 36 to 40 years, and > 40 years. The response to their satisfaction level is recorded and studied.

2.8 GRAPHICAL INTERPRETATION

It has been observed that for variable V7, higher proportions of the 26–30 years age group strongly agree that EVs are environment friendly since

TABLE 2.3 Chi-Square Test and Symmetrical Measures.

		Value	df	Asymp. sig. (2-sided)			Value	Approx. sig.
V7	Pearson Chi-Square	49.733[a]	16	.000	Nominal by Nominal	Contingency Coefficient	.425	.000
	Likelihood Ratio	62.803	16	.000			226	
	N of Valid Cases	226			N of Valid Cases		226	
V9	Pearson Chi-Square	84.468[a]	16	.000	Nominal by Nominal	Contingency Coefficient	.522	.000
	Likelihood Ratio	85.282	16	.000			226	
	N of Valid Cases	226			N of Valid Cases		226	
V11	Pearson Chi-Square	77.773[a]	16	.000	Nominal by Nominal	Contingency Coefficient	.506	.000
	Likelihood Ratio	83.700	16	.000			226	
	N of Valid Cases	226			N of Valid Cases		226	

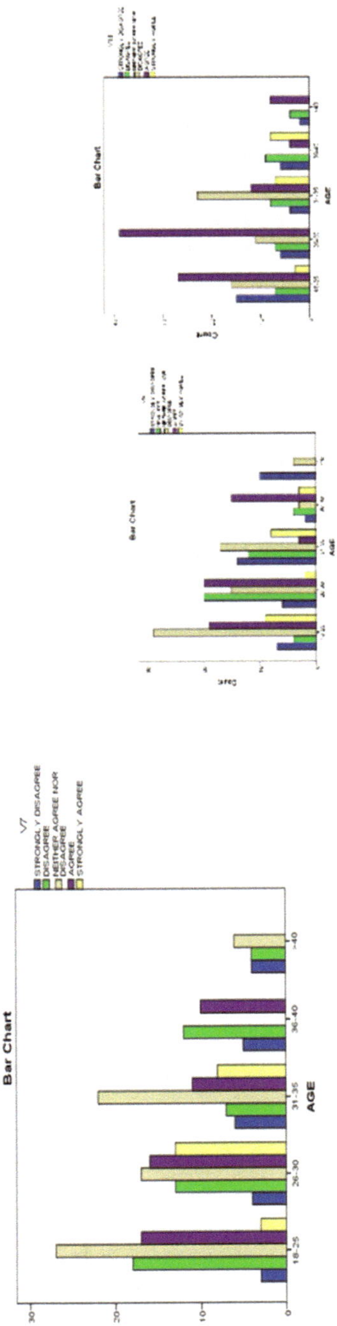

GRAPH 2.2 Responses as per age groups.

they have zero emissions hence reducing air pollution. Being active users of vehicles or EVs, they are aware of the advantages of using and why it is safe to use for the environment and biodiversity in general. While on the other hand, the age group of 31–35 years disagrees with the statement as they use vehicles or EVs in lesser proportions, not very much aware of the technological evolution across the automobile sector. For variable V9, it is observed that the age group of 18–25 years strongly agrees that Better Technology is associated with EVs, thereby a reason for high demand. Being the most progressive age group, they are technologically more updated about the current trends across the automobile sector. They keep on exploring new vehicles for new technology, designs, and models. While on the other hand, the age group 31–35 disagrees with the statement, they think that due to societal influence, social awareness contributed to the adoption of EVs, contributing toward their high usefulness in the modern era.

For variable, V11, it is observed that the varied ages ranging from 36 to 40 years agree that EVs might save a substantial sum of cash on zero fuel costs, lower maintenance costs, and various tax advantages and subsidies from the Government. As per the survey, there are comparatively fewer users of EVs, not aware of the higher electronics cost, higher initial maintenance cost, higher initial purchase cost, and so on. While on the other hand, the age group 18–25 years disagrees with the statement. They proactively use and know that there are several problems like replacing batteries is expensive, finding charging stations, which are few in number, longer hours of charging of batteries, and so on.

2.8.1 CONSUMER PURCHASE BEHAVIOR VARIABLES

V7—EVs are environment friendly since they have zero emissions hence reducing air pollution.

V9—Better Technology is associated with EVs, thereby a reason for high demand.

V11—EVs save a significant sum of cash on zero fuel costs, lower maintenance costs, and various tax advantages and subsidies from the Government.

2.9 INCOME

H_0—There is no significant association between Income and Consumer Purchase Behavior

H_1—There is a significant association between Income and Consumer Purchase Behavior

TABLE 2.4 Chi-Square Test and Symmetrical Measures.

		Value	Df	Asymp. sig. (2-sided)			Value	Approx. sig.
V7	Pearson Chi-Square	35.845[a]	16	.003	Nominal by Nominal	Contingency Coefficient	.370	.003
	Likelihood Ratio	40.816	16	.001			226	
	N of Valid Cases	226			N of Valid Cases		226	
V9	Pearson Chi-Square	56.100[a]	16	.000	Nominal by Nominal	Contingency Coefficient	.446	.000
	Likelihood Ratio	57.961	16	.000			226	
	N of Valid Cases	226			N of Valid Cases		226	
V11	Pearson Chi-Square	47.746[a]	16	.000	Nominal by Nominal	Contingency Coefficient	.418	.000
	Likelihood Ratio	52.515	16	.000			226	
	N of Valid Cases	226			N of Valid Cases		226	

One can observe through the data table (Table 2.4) that the chi-square value for V7 is 35.845[a] as well and the asymp sign is 0.003 which is less than 0.05. Likewise, for V9 the value is 56.100[a], and the asymp sign is 0.000 which is below 0.05, and for V11 the chi-square value is 47.746[a], and the asymp sign is 0.000 which is below 0.05. This implies that the null hypothesis is rejected and the alternate hypothesis is accepted. Thus, Income has a relationship with Consumer Purchase Behavior concerning variables V7, V9, and V11. Likewise, it is apparent that the Contingency Coefficient of the variable for V7 is 0.370 (approx. 0.4), indicating the connection of Age and Consumer Purchase Behavior is average with the variable. The Contingency Coefficient of variable V9 is 0.446, which indicates that the connection of Age and Consumer Purchase Behavior is average with the variable. Lastly, the Contingency Coefficient of Variable V11 is 0.418 (approx. 0.4), indicating that the connection of Age and Consumer Purchase Behavior is average with the variable.

Graph 2.3 shows Income Groups ranging from less than 25k, 25k–50k, 50k–75k, 75k-1L, >1L. The response of the following income range has been recorded and studied.

2.10 GRAPHICAL INTERPRETATION

For the variable V7, it has been observed that people having income ranging from above 1 lakh strongly agree with the statement that EVs are environment friendly since they have zero emissions hence reducing air pollution. They are active users of EVs, a conscious buyer, and know the benefits of driving a car powered by electricity. While on the other hand, income groups ranging from 50–75 K are fewer users of EVs, as well as the affordability ratio of purchasing Electric Vehicles is less as compared to the other income groups. They are not aware of its advantage. Hence, they strongly disagree with the statement. For the variable V9, it has been observed that people having income ranging from less than 25 K strongly agree with the statement that Better Technology is associated with EVs, thereby a reason for high demand. Due to the innovative features of conventional cars, societal influence makes them high in demand. While on the other hand, the income group ranging from 50–75 K strongly disagrees with the statement, they use EVs more not because of the technology, but for social awareness, and greater vehicle choice. The primary benefit of battery-powered cars is the potential enhancement of the air quality of cities that they could offer. For the variable V11, it has been observed that people having income ranging from less than 25 K strongly agree with the

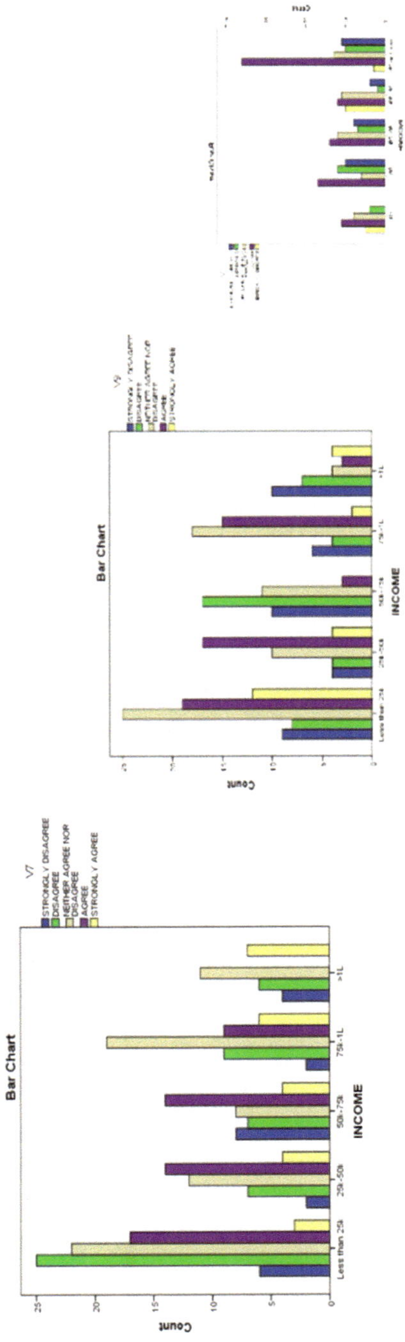

GRAPH 2.3 Responses as per income groups.

statement that EVs may significantly decrease the cost of zero fuel costs, lower maintenance costs, and various tax advantages and subsidies from the Government. They cannot afford to buy expensive EVs, are less aware of the high purchase cost, and so on. While the income group ranging from 75 k to 1 Lakh strongly disagrees with the statement. Being an active user of EVs the high purchase cost, higher battery cost and other designs associated with the EVs, lack of charge stations, which are few, and so on.

2.10.1 CONSUMER PURCHASE BEHAVIOR VARIABLES

V7—EVs are environment friendly since they have zero emissions hence reducing air pollution.

V9—Better Technology is associated with EVs, thereby a reason for high demand.

V1—EVs save a significant sum of funds on zero fuel costs, lower maintenance costs, and various tax advantages and subsidies from the Government.

2.11 OCCUPATION

H_0—There is no significant association between Occupation and Consumer Purchase Behavior

H_1—There is a significant association between Occupation and Consumer Purchase Behavior

It can be observed from the data table (Table 2.5) that the chi-square value for V7 is 59.217[a] and the asymp sign is 0.000 which is below 0.05. Likewise, for V9 the value is 17.738[a,] and the asymp sign is 0.023 which is less than 0.05, and for V11 the chi-square value is 24.584[a,] and the asymp sign is 0.002 which is below 0.05. This implies that the null hypothesis is rejected, and the alternate hypothesis is accepted. Hence, Occupation has a link with Consumer Purchase Behavior concerning variables V7, V9, and V11. Likewise, we can observe that the Contingency Coefficient of the variable for V7 is 0.456, which indicates the connection of Occupation and Consumer Purchase Behavior is average with the variable. The Contingency Coefficient of variable V9 is 0.270, which indicates that the connection of Occupation and Consumer Purchase Behavior is average with the variable. Lastly, the Contingency Coefficient of Variable V11 is 0.313, which indicates that the connection of Occupation with Consumer Purchase Behavior is Average with the variable.

TABLE 2.5 Chi-Square Test and Symmetrical Measures.

		Value	df	Asymp. sig. (2-sided)			Value	Approx. sig.
V7	Pearson Chi-Square	59.217[a]	8	.000	Nominal by Nominal	Contingency Coefficient	.456	.000
	Likelihood Ratio	68.585	8	.000			226	
	N of Valid Cases	226			N of Valid Cases		226	
V9	Pearson Chi-Square	17.738[a]	8	.023	Nominal by Nominal	Contingency Coefficient	.270	.023
	Likelihood Ratio	23.612	8	.003			226	
	N of Valid Cases	226			N of Valid Cases		226	
V11	Pearson Chi-Square	24.584[a]	8	.002	Nominal by Nominal	Contingency Coefficient	.313	.002
	Likelihood Ratio	26.644	8	.001			226	
	N of Valid Cases	226			N of Valid Cases		226	

Graph 2.4 shows the occupations of people ranging from Services, Business, and others. The response of the following income range has been recorded and studied.

2.12 GRAPHICAL INTERPRETATION

For variable V7, it has been observed that people from other professions apart from business or service agree with the statement that EVs are environment friendly since they have zero emissions hence reducing air pollution. Being the active buyer of EVs, they are a conscious buyer. The expenditure of recharging an electric automobile is less expensive than buying petrol or gasoline for our driving demands because of their higher effectiveness and fewer expenses of energy. While people doing business disagree with the statement as they are aware of the harm caused by vehicular emissions to the environment and biodiversity in general.

For the variable V9, it has been observed that some of the people doing business and few from other professions agree with the statement that Better Technology is associated with EVs, thereby a reason for high demand. They think that EVs have innovative features like batteries, and greater mileage than conventional vehicles making them more popular among the masses. While on the other hand, a few sections of people doing business disagree with the statement, as they think social awareness and societal influence resulted in predominantly high demand for EVs across the automobile sector.

For the variable V11, it has been observed that people doing business agree that EVs might save a substantial sum of funds on zero fuel costs, lower maintenance costs, and various tax advantages and subsidies from the Government. While on the other hand, people from other professions disagree with the statement. Being the potential buyer of EVs, they are aware of high purchasing costs, the cost of exchanging any parts, batteries of cars, the lack of charging stations, and so on.

2.12.1 CONSUMER PURCHASE BEHAVIOR VARIABLES

V7—EVs are environment friendly since they have zero emissions hence reducing air pollution.

V9—Better Technology is associated with EVs, thereby a reason for high demand.

V11—EVs save a significant sum of funds on zero fuel costs, lower maintenance costs, and various tax advantages and subsidies from the Government.

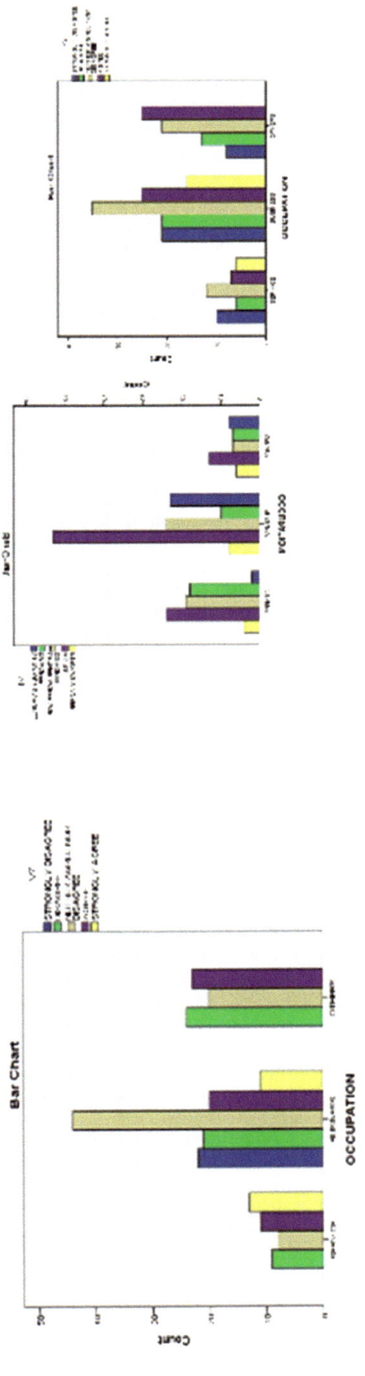

GRAPH 2.4 Responses as per income range.

2.13 EDUCATIONAL QUALIFICATIONS

H_0—There is no significant association between Educational Qualifications and Consumer Purchase Behavior

H_1—There is a significant association between Educational Qualifications and Consumer Purchase Behavior

It can be observed from the data table (Table 2.6) that the chi-square value for V7 is 17.506[a] and the asymp sign is 0.132 which is more than 0.05. Similarly, for V9 the value is 40.934[a], and the asymp sign is 0.000 which is below 0.05, and for V11 the chi-square value is 33.247[a], and the asymp sign is 0.001 which is below 0.05. This implies that the null hypothesis is rejected, and the alternate hypothesis is accepted in the case of V9 and V11. For variable V7, the null hypothesis is accepted, there is no significant association between Education Qualifications and Consumer Purchase Behavior. Thus, Occupation has an association with Consumer Purchase Behavior concerning variables V9 and V11 only. Likewise, we can observe that the Contingency Coefficient of the variable for V9 is 0.392, which indicates the connection of Education Qualification and Consumer Purchase Behavior is average with the variable. The Contingency Coefficient of variable V11 is 0.358, which indicates that the connection of Education Qualification and Consumer Purchase Behavior is average with the variable. Graph 2.5 shows the Education Qualification of people ranging from Madhyamik. HS, Graduate, Post Graduate. The response of the following income range has been recorded and studied.

2.14 GRAPHICAL INTERPRETATION

For variable V9, it has been observed that people having an Education Qualification: Graduate Degree agree that Better Technology is associated with EVs, thereby a reason for high demand. They keep themselves updated regarding the models and designs of vehicles, due to some innovative features, electrical charging, batteries, and so on, making it more appealing to the masses. While on the other hand, people having postgraduate degree disagree with the statement. They believe that customers are becoming more alarmed, they are socially aware of the degrading conditions of the environment. Hence, they are gradually shifting toward the concept of sustainability, hence social awareness, better use, lower maintenance cost, and effective operations are the cause of its high demand in the market. For the variable V11, it has been observed that some people having graduate degree agree

TABLE 2.6 Chi-Square Test and Symmetrical Measures.

		Value	df	Asymp. sig. (2-sided)			Value	Approx. sig.
V7	Pearson Chi-Square	17.506[a]	12	.132	Nominal by Nominal	Contingency Coefficient	.268	.132
	Likelihood Ratio	21.009	12	.050			226	
	N of Valid Cases	226			N of Valid Cases		226	
V9	Pearson Chi-Square	40.934[a]	12	.000	Nominal by Nominal	Contingency Coefficient	.392	.000
	Likelihood Ratio	42.180	12	.000			226	
	N of Valid Cases	226			N of Valid Cases		226	
V11	Pearson Chi-Square	33.247[a]	12	.001	Nominal by Nominal	Contingency Coefficient	.358	.001
	Likelihood Ratio	38.584	12	.000			226	
	N of Valid Cases	226			N of Valid Cases		226	

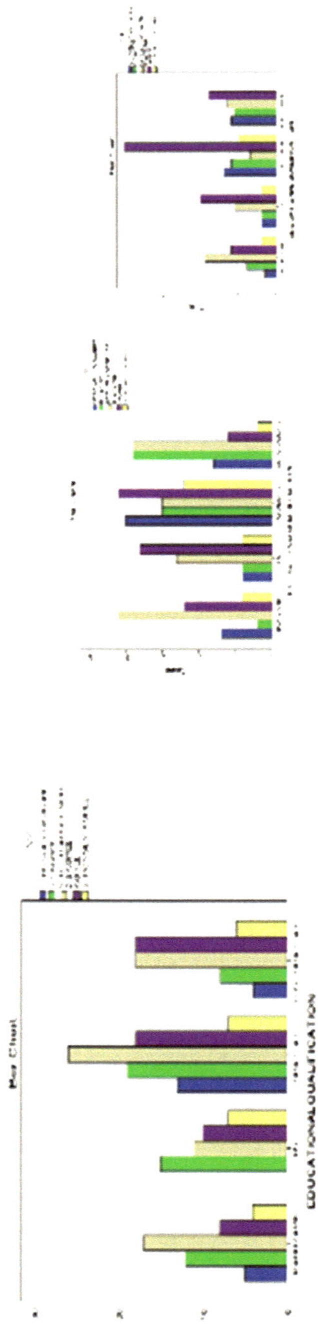

GRAPH 2.5 Responses of the specific income range.

with the statement that EVs are saving a significant sum of funds on zero fuel costs, lower maintenance costs, and various tax advantages and subsidies from the Government. These few sections of graduate people are not the users of EVs in higher proportions. They are unaware of the cost structure of EVs, their maintenance cost, and other investments associated with it. While on the other hand, certain sections of graduate people disagree with the statement, as they are aware of the other investments associated with EVs. In addition to the expensive initial purchase price, additional costs include the inconsistent electrical supply in many areas of the nation and the increased capacity and voltage required to refuel more powerful batteries. Due to the distances throughout India and its famously awful traffic, the fundamental EV Transmission issues and the danger of lacking electricity remain a concern. Additionally, electric cars can take a very long time to recharge. Another challenge with all-EVs is their fueling. The greater starting price of an electric car becomes a major barrier to purchase. The fact that one may purchase a larger petrol automobile for the same price as a smaller one makes this a determining factor for many, even if the reduced fuel, operating, and maintenance expenses, as well as tax credits, can counteract this.

2.15 CONCLUSION

We investigated the effects of several demographic parameters like Gender, Age, Income, Education Qualifications, and Occupation on Consumer Purchase Behavior. We have also studied various factors regulating Consumer Purchase Behavior for buying EVs. For developing countries like India, environmental education is crucial since it promotes and develops pro-environmental attitudes (Chawla et al., 2022). "Environmental Attitude" or "Green Attitude" refers to a person's perspective on protecting and enhancing the environment. Consumer Behavior Researchers have long thought that a person's beliefs might foretell their actions or behaviors. Our paper addresses the results of research and in-depth analysis done to determine consumer awareness, attitude, and behavior about the environment, particularly as it relates to the automobile industry. Consumers (auto owners) have amply demonstrated their awareness of the fact that emissions from moving vehicles are the primary cause of pollution. Despite the fact that most automobile owners are aware of the term "Global Warming," relatively few are familiar with the term "Green Marketing." It is clear that while people are talking about global warming in many venues, Green Marketing, a relatively unfamiliar idea, is not well known.

EVs should ideally replace internal combustion engine (ICE) cars in the aftermath of the ecological calamity (Chawla et al., 2023). Additionally, the majority of car buyers believe that the four-wheelers on the market in our nation are not environmentally friendly. Only a small percentage of buyers think that automakers adhere to green practices. The general level of awareness of all aspects of Green Marketing is quite high. On several assertions, there are considerable differences in the degree of awareness between Age Groups, Gender Groups, Income Groups, Occupation Groups, people with different education degrees, and so on. When it comes to taking action, it is frequently seen that even when consumers have the proper knowledge and attitude, their conduct shifts. Governments and marketers should distribute necessary information about environmental issues in order to push young consumers toward adopting green and environmentally friendly products (Chawla et al., 2022). India's consumers prefer electric vehicle pricing to be lower than those in other nations. If the policymakers of the Automobile industry modify the price, bridge the gap of demand and supply chain, improve the storage capacity of batteries, and build charge stations for effective charging, then would contribute to the surge in the nation's purchases of battery-powered cars. Hence more the purchase, environmental threats will be minimized.

2.16 MANAGERIAL IMPLICATIONS

This research paper is a potential guide to how several demographic factors like Age, Gender, Educational Qualifications, and Income impact Consumer Purchase Behavior. Besides there are other factors that also regulate the phenomenon. Proper Social Awareness, Affordable Pricing Strategies, Technological Innovations, Effective Demand and Supply chain, Distribution strategy, and so on are also studied in the paper in detail. Despite awareness, people do not act accordingly. The "Green Marketing" concept should be talked about more across public platforms. Policymakers should work on the Pricing Strategy of EVs, hence should be more affordable to the masses than any specific income and occupation group. Every Age group should be informed of depleting fossil fuels and should be encouraged to take action. This will make them participate in the evolution of sustainability. Automobile Makers should design the models of EVs feasibly so that various parts are less costly, batteries do not require frequent charging, more capacities of battery, and so on. Along with technological innovations, it should be cost-effective to serve the best. The distribution channel of EVs should be the main focus, many companies are yet to launch EVs, also there is a lack of power stations across metropolitan cities of India and improper charging facilities. The demand and supply chain of EVs should be modified. Thereby Automobile Makers will get ideas on how to improvise designs and other strategies to attract new customers across all Age Groups, Income Groups, and so on. Green Marketing is indeed the future of the Automobile Industry. In contrast to traditional motor vehicles, electric automobiles do not require fuel or petrol to operate. EVs, therefore, do not contribute to air pollution. Additionally, electric cars are quite affordable and help drivers use less gas. Using EVs not only protects the environment but also preserves our supply of renewable energy sources for the future. Hence more awareness should be built for the purchase of EVs, implementation of Green Marketing, and advantages of using E-Vehicles, thereby promoting sustainability across Automobile Sector.

KEYWORDS

- **green marketing**
- **Indian automobile sector**
- **sustainable development**
- **green practices**
- **sustainability**

REFERENCES

Auto, E. T. Kia India to Open Bookings for EV6 on April 15 - et auto, ETAuto.com; 2023 [Online]. https://auto.economictimes.indiatimes.com/news/passenger-vehicle/kia-india-to-open-bookings-for-ev6-on-april-15/99258793 (accessed Apr 17, 2023).

Bhatia, M.; Jain, A. Green Marketing: A Study of Consumer Perception and Preferences in India [Online]. *Semanticscholar*; 2013. https://www.semanticscholar.org/paper/

Bureau, T. H. India;s Electric Vehicle Market Grew 223% in 2022, The Hindu [Online] 2023. https://www.thehindu.com/sci-tech/technology/indias-electric-vehicle-market-grew-223-in-2022/article66516424.ece (accessed April 17, 2023).

Chawla, U.; Choudhary, S.; Mishra, V. 4 Young Consumers' Green Purchasing Behavior with Reference to Green Marketing. *Sustain. Mark. Custom. Value* **2022,** *59.*

Chawla, U.; Mohnot, R.; Mishra, V.; Singh, H. V.; Singh, A. K. Factors Influencing Customer Preference and Adoption of Electric Vehicles in India: A Journey towards More Sustainable Transportation. *Sustainability* **2023,** *15* (8), 7020.

IBEF. Automobile Industry, Indian Automobile Companies—IBEF. India Brand Equity Foundation [Online]; 20, November. https://www.ibef.org/industry/india-automobiles (accessed Apr 17, 2023).

Frederick, D. P.; S, G. B.; H, S.; Salins, M. *Quantitative ABCD Analysis of Green Marketing for Sustainable Development*. Srinivas Publication, 2022. https://doi.org/10.47992/IJCSBE.2581.6942.0240

Garg, A. Tata Records Highest Ever EV sales, Nexon Becomes Best-selling SUV in India, Zee News. 2022 [Online]. https://zeenews.india.com/automobile/tata-records-highest-ever-ev-sales-in-india-nexon-become-best-selling-suv-2425221.html (accessed Apr 17, 2023)

Nozari, H.; Szmelter-Jarosz, A.; Ghahremani-Nahr, J. The Ideas of Sustainable and Green Marketing Based on the Internet of Everything—The Case of the Dairy Industry. mdpi.com. Retrieved from Future Internet | Free Full-Text | The Ideas of Sustainable and Green Marketing Based on the Internet of Everything—The Case of the Dairy Industry (mdpi.com). 2021.

IANS *Most Polluted Cities in India: 39 Indian Cities Among World's 50 Most Polluted Says Report: India News-Times of India, The Times of India*. TOI, 2023 [Online]. https://timesofindia.indiatimes.com/india/39-indian-cities-among-worlds-50-most-polluted-report/articleshow/98636612.cms (accessed April 17, 2023).

Karukar, S.; Unnikrishan, S.; Panda, S. S. Study of Environmental Sustainability and Green Manufacturing Practices in the Indian Automobile Industry. 2018. www.oidaijsd.com [Online].http://www.ssrn.com/link/OIDA-Intl-Journal-Sustainable-Dev.html

Nigam, P.; Sharma, V. Study of Green Advertisements of Electric 2 W Vehicle for Environmental Sustainability in Bhopal Madhya Pradesh. 2022. Retrieved from https://www.researchgate.net/publication/369202317

Pandey, M.; Mohan, M.; Subha, K. A Study on Customer Perception Towards Purchase Intention of Electric Cars in India. 2021 [Online]. www.jetir.org

Sharma, N. K. Industry Initiatives for Green Marketing in India. *Bus. Econ. J.* **2015,** *07* (01). doi: https://doi.org/10.4172/2151-6219.1000192.

Singh, A. P. O. *India's EV Economy: The Future of Automotive Transportation*. Investment Promotion and Facilitation Agency, 2023 [Online]. https://www.investindia.gov.in/team-india-blogs/indias-ev-economy-future-automotive-transportation (accessed 17, April 2023).

Sondhi, S.; Chawla, U.; Iqbal, H. Relationship Between Social Cause, Environment Conservation and Environmental Attitude, Towards Promoting Green Purchasing Behavior. *Serbian J. Manag.* **2023,** *18* (1), 27–43.

Vaitone, N. V.; Kiene, I. S.; Meneses, G. D.Measuring Green Marketing: Scale Development and Validation. 2022. mdpi.com [Online]. Retrieved from (PDF) Measuring Green Marketing: Scale Development and Validation (researchgate.net)

Vatsa, M. et al., GMS is Powerful Force in Passenger Car Segment of Indian Automobile Industry to Enhance Innovation and Widen Profits. *Int. J. Eng. Res.* **2015,** *4* (09). doi: https://doi.org/10.17577/ijertv4is090377.

Vatsa, M.; Chakrabarti, M.; Kumar, R. *Analysis of Green Marketing Trend In Passenger Car Segment of Indian Automobile Industry*. IAEME Publication, 2016 [Online]. http://www.iaeme.com/ijm/issues.asp?JType=IJM&VType=7&IType=6

Vatsa, M.; Singh, S.; Chaudhary, S. Study of Green Advertisements in Indian Automobile Sector for Environmental Sustainability. 2021 [Online]. https://doi.org 10.1088/1757-899X/1091/1/012015

Viet, B. N. The Impact of Green Marketing Mix Elements on Green Customer Based & nbsp;brand Equity in an Emerging Market. Emerald Insight. Retrieved from The impact of Green Marketing Mix Elements on Green Customer Based Brand Equity in an Emerging Market | Emerald Insight. 2022.

CHAPTER 3

Driving Toward Sustainability: The Role of Eco-friendly Transportation in Reducing Carbon Emissions in the United Arab Emirates

HENA IQBAL[1], AYUSH KUMAR SINGH[2], SWECHA RAM[2], SHREYA PERIWAL[3], and GANGA SHOW[4]

[1]*Ajman University, Ajman, UAE*

[2]*Future Institute of Technology, Kolkata, India*

[3]*Techno India, Kolkata, India*

[4]*The Calcutta Anglo Gujarati College, Kolkata, India*

ABSTRACT

Purpose: The objective of this paper investigate the impact of electric vehicles (EV) on environment. Reduced carbon emissions and climate change have increased interest in eco-friendly transportation solutions. EV have emerged as a viable method for lowering carbon emissions from transportation. Transportation through electric vehicles plays a vital role in decreasing carbon emissions in the environment as the world seeks for a more sustainable future. EV have emerged as a viable and practical approach for reducing the transportation sector's carbon footprint. It is necessary to get dependent on electronic vehicles rather than carbon-emitting vehicles to protect the atmosphere.

EVs have greater starting prices than typical gas-powered vehicles; they offer lower lifetime expenses due to decreased maintenance and fuel

Agile Business Transformations: Priorities, Lessons, and Practices. Satyajit Chakrabarti, Subrata Chattopadhyay, Udit Chawla, Sundeep Singh Sondhi, & Arunava Dalal (Eds.)

expenditures. Furthermore, advances in the battery technology have enhanced EV range and performance, making them more feasible and reasonable for daily usage. However, an absence of charging substructure continues to be a key barricade that hampers mainstream EV adoption. Governments and private businesses must collaborate to provide a comprehensive charging network to facilitate EV adoption. Without a better and available charging network electronic vehicle has no benefit.

It is crucial to encourage the use of EVs due to the benefits of fewer carbon discharges, improved air quality, and decreased dependence on fossil oils. As the public is still dependent on carbon-emitting vehicle, availability of incentives like tax credits and rebates might influence customers to choose environmentally friendly products. The adaptation of electronic vehicle helps in the growth of people and environment.

Design/methodology: Data for this study was acquired in Howrah and Kolkata, where 250 replies were received from people of various genders, ages, occupations, and economic levels. The parameter studies for the investigation were derived using a 5-point scale (from 1—strongly disagree, to 5—strongly agree).

Findings: The following factors emerged from the investigation, which has been termed "Performance," "Infrastructure," and "Reliability." It has also been discovered that the factors "Performance" and "Infrastructure" have a major impact on consumer preference.

3.1 INTRODUCTION

In recent times, the United Arab Emirates (UAE) has witnessed tremendous urbanization and profitable expansion. With this expansion has come a rise in the amount of buses on the highway, performing in enlarged carbon emigrations and mischievous environmental goods. The transportation assiduity contributes significantly to global carbon emigrations, counting for roughly 23 of total energy-related CO_2 emigrations. Road transport accounts for more than 60 of total carbon emigrations in UAE metropolises, making it the major contributor to hothouse gas emigrations (Wang et al., 2016; Ali and Söffker, 2018). According to Zhang et al. (2020 and 2018 independently), promoting eco-friendly transportation choices similar as electric vehicles (EVs), cold-blooded buses, and public conveyance is one strategy to minimize these emigrations (Lee, 2020; Liu et al., 2021).

Electric vehicle (EV) request access in the transportation sector has dramatically increased in recent times. Energy cells, ultracapacitors, and battery technologies are the energy sources used by electric cars. As a result, less fossil energy is used, and no pollution is produced during operation (Khizir Mahmud et al., 2019). Several issues, including battery cost, effective charging ways, integration of the charging stations, and the impact of EV integration on the grid, need to be overcome for EVs to be competitive in the request (Yong et al., 2015). Such a problem is seen as one of the most important cerebral walls to EV relinquishment by the general population. Due to the diversity for EV trip decorations and variety nervousness, the electrical request of EVs is more nebulous than national energy requirements. Also, when the arraigning positions are associated with the network, the growing saturation and unpredictability for EVs may have numerous impacts on the power force. Former studies have investigated how EV charging and discharging affects the energy system (Tookanlou et al., 2020; Rodriguez et al., 2022). Electric vehicle (EV) charging and discharging might lead to enterprises with power quality and stability as well as force and demand mismatches (LeCun et al., 2015; Green et al., 2011).

Several countries are also aiming to phase out internal combustion machine (ICE) vehicles, and the focus is now on adding the use of electric vehicles (EVs) for the transference segment. Although EVs offer several advantages, similar as using lower reactionary energy and producing no pollution during operation, there are several challenges that need to be overcome for them to be competitive in the request. Because cybersecurity and sustainability are two distinct fields, difficulties crop. According to Wilkinson et al. (2001), Lubin and Esty (2010), sustainability refers to the ecological equilibrium between the terrain, profitable development, and social well-being. Cybersecurity, on the other hand, is the preparation of shielding systems, schemes, and agendas from online pitfalls. It is insolvable to dispute either sphere's significance. Experimenters in sustainability focus on structural and fiscal aspects, similar to EVs' shorter time to vend, lower prices, and the development of new environmental detectors. As a result, new technology is developed snappily, but its security measures may not be acceptable or defined at a rate that keeps up with the rate of product (Mihet-Popa and Saponara, 2018). This is due to the fact that sustainability professionals in the field of cybersecurity only occasionally do study in these areas (Salam, 2020). A sizable assiduity with a sizable cash inflow is EV manufacture. Still, there is little information accessible and little work being done to establish norms and recommendations that show how to negotiate sustainability without cybersecurity (Kumar et al., 2018).

3.2 LITERATURE REVIEW

The development of infrastructure has become a key factor in the acceptance of the electric vehicles (EVs). It is critical to comprehend how infrastructure influences consumer behaviors toward EVs as EVs gain in popularity. A study by Sierzchula et al. (2014) found that people's decisions to purchase EVs were significantly influenced by the accessibility of EV charging infrastructure. According to the study, the availability of indicting infrastructure increased people's perceptions of EV range and their propensity to purchase an EV. The study also found that drivers who frequently made long distance trips needed access to fast charging infrastructure. The impact of public charging infrastructure on the uptake of EVs in the United States was examined in another study by Liao et al. (2019). According to the study, the sales of EVs significantly increased as the number of public charging stations increased. The study also discovered that encouraging the acceptance for EVs depended significantly on the accessibility of Level 3 fast indicting organization. The effect of EV charging infrastructure on the electrical grid was investigated in a study by Pudjianto et al. (2019). Electric vehicles (EVs) are a key component of the transition to a low-carbon energy system because they can stabilize the erratic features of renewable liveliness foundations and increase capacity by modifying their own charging requirements (Chawla et al., 2023). The study discovered that while installing EV charging infrastructure may raise peak demand, with proper management, it may also open opportunities for grid balancing and greater use of renewable energy sources. The relationship between EV charging infrastructure and the growth of smart cities was examined by Wang et al. in 2019. It was discovered that the installation of EV charging infrastructure can be a crucial part of the growth of shrewd metropolises. It also emphasized the significance of combining renewable energy sources and EV charging infrastructure to support sustainable urban development. The influence of residential charging infrastructure on EV adoption was examined by Zhou et al. (2018). It was discovered that the likelihood of buying an EV increased significantly when home charging infrastructure was available. The ease and cost savings of home charging played a significant role in influencing consumer attitudes toward EVs. The decision to buy an EV is greatly influenced by the accessibility of EV charging infrastructure, especially fast charging infrastructure. Aside from that, the installation of EV charging infrastructure can facilitate grid balancing, rise the use of renewable liveliness sources, and support sustainable urban growth. More recent technology improvements in cars are an importance of the need to address growing transportation issues including noise pollution, carbon emissions, and congested roadways. The development of self-driving cars and electric propulsion has a big influence on environmentally friendly transportation systems (Chawla et al., 2023).

Due to their cost-effectiveness and environmental friendliness, electric vehicles (EVs) have become more and more popular in recent years. However, many potential buyers have expressed serious concerns about the performance of EVs. One of the most important performance elements that customers consider when buying a car is acceleration. Early electric vehicle models, however, accelerated more slowly than conventional gasoline-powered cars, which might have prevented their widespread use (Hidrue et al., 2011). A vast number of experiments have grown with the quickly increasing EV market. Even though the present amount of investigation on clients' driving patterns for electric vehicles, social aid programs, distribution methods, and technology developments is quite incisive, new analyses indicate that study often makes the same assumptions (Chawla et al., 2023).

Another essential performance aspect for EVs is range. It speaks of how far an electric vehicle (EV) can go on a single charge. Participants in a study by Axsen et al. (2016) rated range as one of the most crucial aspects to consider when buying an EV. Consumers were also discovered by the authors to be eager to get salary more for an automobile with a greater range. This suggests that the acceptance of EVs be contingent heavily on range. The range of EVs has increased as battery technology has advanced. A study by Santini et al. (2020) found that improvements in battery technology have enabled EVs to travel more than 400 miles on a single charge. This increased range might help to allay consumers' worries about the short driving range of EVs and broaden their appeal. The adoption of EVs depends heavily on their performance. Both acceleration and range are crucial performance elements that can affect consumer choices. Performance will probably become less of a concern for consumers as EV technology advances, which could hasten the adoption of these vehicles.

Customer satisfaction and perceptions of the vehicle's quality are influenced by reliability. A study by Bressan et al. (2019) looks at the dependability of EV lithium-ion batteries. The authors stress that a significant reliability issue is the deterioration of battery performance over time. They also point out that several variables, such as temperature, depth of discharge, and charging/discharging rate, affect how severely batteries degrade. The authors advise using predictive models to determine battery life expectations and enhancing battery management systems to increase reliability. The burning of limited properties (such as fossil fuels) in the transport and energy segments is regarded as the primary foundation of carbon emissions (Chawla et al., 2023).

The dependability of EV motors is examined in a study by Li et al. (2020). The performance and safety of the vehicle are both impacted by motor failure, according to the authors. The study emphasizes how temperature, vibration, and mechanical stress are just a few of the variables that affect how reliable a motor is. The authors suggest using fault diagnosis methods to find motor flaws and enhancing motor design to increase reliability.

According to the report, the major nonmonetary barrier to broad adoption is the range of electric vehicles. Over 70% of transportation reviews reflect the powerful variety to be a "major drawback" or "to some extent, a drawback" (Chawla et al., 2023). The researchers highlight that a faulty management system can lead to significant safety issues, such as loss of vehicle control. The study underscores that several elements, including software and hardware development, testing, and upkeep, impact the reliability of management systems. The authors recommend employing fault injection methods to assess the reliability of management systems and improve their dependability by implementing more robust system designs (Chen et al., 2019).

3.3 OBJECTIVE OF THE STUDY

The objective is to study the relationship between demographic factors and customer satisfaction on impact of usage of eco-friendly transportation among the residents of UAE.

3.4 RESEARCH METHODOLOGY

This research was conducted using well-organized questionnaires, and a total of 274 samples were gathered from individuals in the UAE who actively use eco-friendly transportation. The primary data for this study was collected from a diverse group of respondents, including men and women of various age groups, different income levels, and diverse occupational backgrounds such as business, service, and others. To assess the opinions of the participants, each parameter in the survey was measured on a five-point scale, ranging from "1" for "strongly agree" to "5" for "strongly disagree." In order to determine any significant relationships between demographic factors and customer satisfaction toward eco-friendly transportation, the researchers employed the chi-square test.

3.5 VARIABLE

V-5 Public Transport Development Significantly Reduces Carbon Emissions

V-8 Vehicles Face Challenges Due to High Costs, Limited Charging Infrastructure

V-13 Transportation mode plays a crucial role in determining carbon emissions.

3.6 FINDING AND ANALYSIS

3.6.1 GENDER

H_0—There is no significant association between gender and customer satisfaction related to eco-friendly transportation.

H_1—There is a significant association between gender and customer satisfaction related to eco-friendly transportation.

Based on the data presented in Table 3.1, we observe that the chi-square values for variables V5, V8, and V13 are 8.169a, 4.460a, and 3.118a, respectively. The corresponding asympsig values (p-values) for these variables are .086, .347, and .538, all of which are greater than the significance level of 0.05. This indicates that we fail to reject the null hypothesis and, in turn, reject the alternative hypothesis. In simpler terms, gender does not appear to have a significant association with customer satisfaction concerning variables V5, V8, and V13. Additionally, the contingency coefficients for V5, V8, and V13 are .170, .127, and .106, respectively. These coefficients signify a low level of relationship between gender and customer satisfaction concerning these variables. In summary, the statistical analysis suggests that gender does not play a significant role in influencing customer satisfaction for the aspects represented by V5, V8, and V13. The connection between gender and customer satisfaction appears to be relatively weak based on the calculated values of the contingency coefficients.

The combination of environmental awareness, scientific evidence, air quality improvements, traffic congestion reduction, cost-effectiveness, infrastructure development, convenience, and social benefits makes the

TABLE 3.1 Chi-Square Tests and Symmetric Measures.

		Value	**df**	**Asymp. Sig. (2- sided)**			**Value**	**Approx. Sig.**
V5	Pearson Chi-square	8.169[a]	4	0.086			0.17	0.086
	Likelihood ratio	8.295	4	0.081	Nominal by nominal	Contingency coefficient		
	No. of valid cases	274			No. of valid cases		274	
V8	Pearson Chi-square	4.460[a]	4	. 347	Nominal by nominal	Contingency coefficient	0.127	0.347
	Likelihood ratio	4.503	4	0.342				
	No. of valid cases	274			No. of valid cases		274	
	Pearson Chi-square	3.118[a]	4	0.538	Nominal by nominal	Contingency coefficient	0.106	0.347
V13	Likelihood ratio	3.137	4	. 535				
	No. of valid cases	274			No. of valid cases		274	

acceptance of public transport development a method to decrease carbon emissions more widespread among people. The acceptance of electric vehicles is steadily increasing as technology improves, costs decrease, and governments and private entities invest in expanding charging infrastructure. Individuals can make informed decisions about their transportation choices, opting for lower-emission modes when possible and contributing to overall efforts to reduce carbon emissions and combat climate change.

3.6.2 AGE

H_0—There is no significant association between age and customer satisfaction related to eco-friendly transportation.

H_1—There is a significant association between age and customer satisfaction related to eco-friendly transportation.

Based on the data provided in Table 3.2, we can observe that the chi-square values for variables V5, V8, and V13 are 11.274a, 9.433a, and 15.844a, respectively. The corresponding asympsig values (p-values) for these variables are .792, .894, and .464, all of which exceed the significance level of 0.05. As a result, we accept the null hypothesis and reject the alternative hypothesis. In simpler terms, age does not seem to have a significant association with customer satisfaction concerning variables V5, V8, and V13. Furthermore, the contingency coefficients for V5, V8, and V13 are .199, .182, and .234, respectively. These coefficients indicate a low level of relationship between age and customer satisfaction concerning these variables. In summary, the statistical analysis suggests that age does not play a significant role in influencing customer satisfaction for the aspects represented by V5, V8, and V13. The connection between age and customer satisfaction appears to be relatively weak based on the calculated values of the contingency coefficients.

The combination of environmental awareness, financial considerations, urban living, social factors, technological integration, shared mobility trends, environmental advocacy, and peer influence makes public transport development a compelling option for reducing carbon emissions within the 25 to 30 age group. As charging infrastructure expands, electric vehicles become more accessible and affordable. The transportation choices significantly impact their personal carbon emissions and contribute to broader labors to speech climate modification and decrease greenhouse gas releases in the transportation sector.

TABLE 3.2 Chi-Square Tests and Symmetric Measures.

		Value	**df**	**Asymp. Sig. (2-sided)**			**Value**	**Approx. Sig.**
V5	Pearson Chi-square	11.274[a]	16	. 792			0.199	0.792
	Likelihood ratio	11.728	16	0.762	Nominal by nominal	Contingency coefficient		
	No. of valid cases	274			No. of valid cases		274	
V8	Pearson Chi-square	9.433[a]	16	0.894	Nominal by nominal	Contingency coefficient	0.182	0.894
	Likelihood ratio	9.524	16	0.89				
	No. of valid cases	274			No. of valid cases		274	
	Pearson Chi-square	15.844[a]	16	. 464	Nominal by nominal	Contingency coefficient	0.234	0.464
V13	Likelihood ratio	18.115	16	0.317				
	No. of valid cases	274			No. of valid cases		274	

3.6.3 INCOME

H_0—There is no significant association between income and customer satisfaction related to eco-friendly transportation.

H_1—There is a significant association between income and customer satisfaction related to eco-friendly transportation.

Based on the data presented in Table 3.3, we can observe that the chi-square values for variables V5, V8, and V13 are 11.113a, 17.969a, and 34.616a, respectively. The corresponding asympsig values (p-values) for these variables are all reported as .000, which is less than the significance level of 0.05. This leads us to reject the null hypothesis and accept the alternative hypothesis. In simpler terms, income indeed shows a significant association with customer satisfaction regarding variables V5, V8, and V13. Furthermore, the contingency coefficients for V5, V8, and V13 are .197, .248, and .335, respectively. These coefficients indicate a low level of relationship between income and customer satisfaction concerning these variables. In summary, the statistical analysis reveals that income plays a significant role in influencing customer satisfaction for the aspects represented by V5, V8, and V13. However, it is important to note that the relationship between income and customer satisfaction is not particularly strong, as indicated by the calculated values of the contingency coefficients.

The benefits of public transport development in reducing carbon emissions are widely recognized, achieving broad public and political support for these initiatives may still require addressing concerns, investing in infrastructure, and creating effective communication strategies to emphasize the positive influences on the environment and overall excellence of life. The statement reflects widely recognized challenges faced by low-emission vehicles; it may not be universally accepted without exceptions or differing perspectives. The statement is widely accepted, there may still be isolated voices or groups with differing views, but the overwhelming scientific evidence supports the significant influence of transportation mode on carbon emissions.

3.6.4 OCCUPATION

H_0—There is no significant association between occupation and customer satisfaction related to eco-friendly transportation.

H_1—There is a significant association between occupation and customer satisfaction related to eco-friendly transportation.

TABLE 3.3 Chi-Square Tests and Symmetric Measures.

		Value	df	Asymp. Sig. (2-sided)			Value	Approx. Sig.
V5	Pearson Chi-square	11.113[a]	16	.000			0.197	.000
	Likelihood ratio	11.747	16	0.761	Nominal by nominal	Contingency coefficient		
	No. of valid cases	274			No. of valid cases		274	
V8	Pearson Chi-square	17.969[a]	16	.000	Nominal by nominal	Contingency coefficient	0.248	.000
	Likelihood ratio	18.238	16	0.31				
	No. of valid cases	274			No. of valid cases		274	
	Pearson Chi-square	34.616[a]	16	.000	Nominal by nominal	Contingency coefficient	0.335	.000
V13	Likelihood ratio	32.016	16	0.01				
	No. of valid cases	274			No. of valid cases		274	

TABLE 3.4 Chi-Square Tests and Symmetric Measures.

		Value	**df**	**Asymp. Sig. (2-sided)**			**Value**	**Approx. Sig.**
V5	Pearson Chi-square	6.743[a]	8	0.565			0.155	0.565
	Likelihood ratio	6.991	8	0.538	Nominal by nominal	Contingency coefficient		
	No. of valid cases	274			No. of valid cases		274	
V8	Pearson Chi-square	8.934[a]	8	0.348	Nominal by nominal	Contingency coefficient	0.178	0.348
	Likelihood ratio	9.012	8	0.341				
	No. of valid cases	274			No. of valid cases		274	
	Pearson Chi-square	10.433[a]	8	0.236	Nominal by nominal	Contingency coefficient	0.192	0.236
V13	Likelihood ratio	10.106	8	0.258				
	No. of valid cases	274			No. of valid cases		274	

Based on the information provided in Table 3.4, the chi-square values for variables V5, V8, and V13 are 6.743a, 8.934a, and 10.433a, respectively. The corresponding asympsig values (p-values) for these variables are .565, .348, and .236, all of which are greater than the significance level of 0.05. As a result, we accept the null hypothesis and reject the alternative hypothesis. In simpler terms, occupation does not show a significant association with customer satisfaction concerning variables V5, V8, and V13. Furthermore, the contingency coefficients for V5, V8, and V13 are .155, .178, and .192, respectively. These coefficients indicate a low level of relationship between occupation and customer satisfaction concerning these variables. In summary, the statistical analysis suggests that occupation does not play a significant role in influencing customer satisfaction for the aspects represented by V5, V8, and V13. The connection between occupation and customer satisfaction appears to be relatively weak based on the calculated values of the contingency coefficients.

Public transport development remains widely recognized as an operative strategy to decrease carbon emissions in inner-city areas. Many people acknowledge the challenges of high costs and limited charging infrastructure faced by electric vehicles; it is essential to continue raising awareness, investing in infrastructure, and addressing concerns to encourage broader acceptance and adoption of clean transportation options. The scientific community recognize the critical role of transportation in carbon emissions, achieving universal acceptance requiring continued education, public awareness campaigns, and evidence-based communication about the importance of sustainable transportation choices.

3.6.5 EDUCATIONAL QUALIFICATION

H_0—There is no significant association between educational qualification and customer satisfaction related to eco-friendly transportation.

H_1—there is a significant association between educational qualification and customer satisfaction related to eco-friendly transportation.

Based on the data presented in Table 3.5, we can observe that the chi-square values for variables V5, V8, and V13 are 33.351a, 25.178a, and 43.138a, respectively. The corresponding asympsig values (p-values) for these variables are .001, .014, and .000, all of which are less than the significance level of 0.05. As a result, we reject the null hypothesis and accept the alternative hypothesis. In simpler terms, educational qualification

TABLE 3.5 Chi-Square Tests and Symmetric Measures.

		Value	df	Asymp. Sig. (2-sided)			Value	Approx. Sig.
V5	Pearson Chi-square	33.351[a]	12	0.001			0.329	0.001
	Likelihood ratio	29.47	12	0.003	Nominal by nominal	Contingency coefficient		
	No. of valid cases	274			No. of valid cases		274	
V8	Pearson Chi-square	25.178[a]	12	0.014	Nominal by nominal	Contingency coefficient	0.29	0.014
	Likelihood ratio	21.983	12	0.038				
	No. of valid cases	274			No. of valid cases		274	
	Pearson Chi-square	43.138[a]	12	0	Nominal by nominal	Contingency coefficient	0.369	0
V13	Likelihood ratio	43.755	12	0				
	No. of valid cases	274			No. of valid cases		274	

indeed exhibits a significant association with customer satisfaction regarding variables V5, V8, and V13. Furthermore, the contingency coefficients for V5, V8, and V13 are .329, .290, and .369, respectively. These coefficients indicate a low level of relationship between educational qualification and customer satisfaction concerning these variables. In summary, the statistical analysis reveals that educational qualification plays a significant role in influencing customer satisfaction for the aspects represented by V5, V8, and V13. However, it is important to note that the relationship between educational qualification and customer satisfaction is not particularly strong, as indicated by the calculated values of the contingency coefficients.

The graduate people are more likely to accept the idea that public transport development significantly reduces carbon emissions due to their enhanced knowledge, critical thinking abilities, environmental awareness, and exposure to relevant information through their educational experiences. Aware of challenges related to electric vehicles and charging infrastructure associated with the universal populace, it is essential to recognize that individual perspectives can still vary significantly. The majority of graduates are likely to accept the importance of transportation mode in determining carbon emissions; it is essential to recognize that individual beliefs and perspectives can still vary.

3.7 CONCLUSION

It is impossible to overstate how important eco-friendly transport is to cutting carbon emissions in UAE cities. A more environmentally friendly future for the transportation industry has been made possible by the development and promotion of electric vehicles (EVs). This shift to sustainable mobility has been largely driven by three important factors: charging infrastructure, performance, and reliability.

The first factor supporting the adoption of EVs in UAE cities has been the development of a strong incriminating organization system. The accessibility and convenience of charging EVs have significantly increased thanks to an increase in public charging stations and incentives for private charging stations. More people are switching to environmentally friendly transportation as a result of this infrastructure expansion, which has reduced range anxiety and boosted EV users' confidence.

Second, concerns about the viability of EVs as an alternative to conventional vehicles have been addressed by a significant improvement in EV performance over time. The acceleration, range, and overall driving experience of modern EVs are impressive. The range anxiety that once troubled EV owners is dwindling as a result of ongoing advancements in battery technology. Due to their increased performance, EVs are now a popular choice among consumers, which contributes to the overall decline in carbon emissions.

Finally, as EV manufacturers place a priority on quality and durability, the dependability of eco-friendly transportation has become more and more apparent. Prospective buyers now feel more confident thanks to the expanded selection of EV models from reputable manufacturers as well as the extended warranties on batteries and other parts. Consumers are more likely to select EVs as their primary mode of transportation as they gain in reputation for dependability and trust, which results in a significant drop in carbon emissions.

In conclusion, improvements in the performance, dependability, and infrastructure for charging electric vehicles have helped the UAE focus on creating a sustainable transportation system. The transition to a greener and more sustainable transport system in UAE cities will undoubtedly quicken as these factors continue to get better, which will be advantageous to both the environment and the local populace. A vital first step in ensuring a sustainable future and lowering carbon emissions in the UAE and elsewhere is adopting eco-friendly transport.

KEYWORDS

- **eco-friendly transportation**
- **electric vehicles**
- **sustainability**
- **performance**
- **infrastructure**
- **reliability**

REFERENCES

Ali, A. M.; Söffker, D. Towards Optimal Power Management of Hybrid Electric Vehicles in Real-time: A Review on Methods, Challenges, and State-of-the-Art Solutions. *Energies* **2018,** *11* (3), 476. doi:10.3390/en11030476

Axsen, J.; Burke, A.; Kurani, K. S. Are Batteries Ready for Plug-in Hybrid Buyers? *Transp. Res. Part à Policy Pract.* **2016,** *94,* 414–425.

Bressan, J. D.; Li, J.; Sheng, Y.; Peng, H. Reliability of Lithium-ion Batteries for Electric Vehicles: A Review. *Energies* **2019,** *12* (7), 1213. doi:10.3390/en12071213

Chawla, U.; Mohnot, R.; Mishra, V.; Singh, H. V.; Singh, A. K. Factors Influencing Customer Preference and Adoption of Electric Vehicles in India: A Journey towards More Sustainable Transportation. *Sustainability* **2023,** *15* (8), 7020.

Chen, B. et al., *Reliability Assessment of Electric Vehicle Powertrain Systems.* 2019.

Green, R. C.; Wang, L.; Alam, M. The Impact of Plug-in hybrid Electric Vehicles on Distribution Networks: A Review and Outlook. *Renew. Sustain. Energy Rev.* **2011,** *15* (1), 544–553. doi:10.1016/j.rser.2010.08.015

Hidrue, M. K.; Parsons, G. R.; Kempton, W.; Gardner, M. P. Willingness to Pay for Electric Vehicles and Their Attributes. *Resour. Energy Econ.* **2011,** *33* (3), 686–705. doi:10.1016/j.reseneeco.2011.02.002

Khizir Mahmud, G. E.; Town, S. M.; Hossain, M. J. Integration of Electric Vehicles and Management on the Internet of Energy. *Sustain. Energy Syst. Group*, 2019. Retrieved from https://ideas.repec.org/a/eee/rensus/v49y2015icp365-385.html. NSW, Australia: School of Engineering. Australia.

Kumar, A. D.; Chebrolu, K. N. R.; Soman, K. P. A Brief Survey on Autonomous Vehicle Possible Attacks, Exploits and Vulnerabilities. arXiv. 2018, Retrieved from arXiv:1810.04144

LeCun, Y.; Bengio, Y.; Hinton, G. Deep learning. *Nature* **2015,** *521* (7553), 436–444. doi:10.1038/nature14539

Lee, M. An Analysis of the Effects of Artificial Intelligence on Electric Vehicle Technology Innovation using Patent Data. *World Pat. Inf.* **2020,** *63,* 102002. doi:10.1016/j.wpi.2020.102002

Li, X.; Huang, Y.; Lin, Y.; Sun, Y. Reliability Assessment and Improvement for Electric Vehicle Motor. *IEEE Access* **2020,** *8,* 153751–153760. doi:10.1109/access.2020.3017195

Liao, F.; Guan, X.; Chen, W. The Impact of Public Charging Infrastructure on the Adoption of Electric Vehicles: Evidence from the United States. *Appl. Energy* **2019,** *236,* 804–812.

Liu, D.; Wang, W.; Wang, L.; Jia, H.; Shi, M. Dynamic Pricing Strategy of Electric Vehicle Aggregators Based on DDPG Reinforcement Learning Algorithm. *IEEE Access* **2021,** *9,* 21556–21566. doi:10.1109/ACCESS.2021.3055517

Lubin, D. A.; Esty, D. C. The Sustainability Imperative. *Harvard Business Review* **2010,** *88,* 42–50.

Mihet-Popa, L.; Saponara, S. Toward Green Vehicles Digitalization for the Next Generation of Connected and Electrified Transport Systems. *Energies* **2018,** *11* (11), 3124. doi:10.3390/en11113124

Pudjianto, D.; Bialek, J. W.; Strbac, G. The Impact of Electric Vehicle Charging Infrastructure on the Electricity Grid. *Renew. Sustain. Energy Rev.* **2019,** *114,* 109327.

Rodriguez, A. A.; Perdomo, L.; Al-Sumaiti, A.; Santamaria, F.; Rivera, S. Management of Electric Vehicles Using Automatic Learning Algorithms: Application in office Buildings. *Smart Charg. Solut. Hybrid Electr. Veh.* **2022,** 143–157.

Salam, A. Internet of Things for Sustainable Community Development: Introduction and Overview. In *Internet of Things for Sustainable Community Development*, Springer: Berlin, Heidelberg, Germany, 2020; pp 1–31. doi:10.1007/978-3-030-35291-2_1

Santini, D. J.; Benato, A.; Dalla Riva, V. Future Prospects of EVs and HEVs Technologies: State-of-the-Art and Challenges. *Energies,* 2020.

Sierzchula, W.; Bakker, S.; Maat, K. The Influence of Financial Incentives and Other Socio-economic Factors on Electric Vehicle Adoption. *Transp. Res., Part A* **2014,** *69,* 1–18.

Tesla. Model S. 2021, Retrieved from https://www.tesla.com/models

Tookanlou, M. B.; Marzband, M.; Kyyra, J.; Al Sumaiti, A.; Hosani, K. A. In *Charging/Discharging Strategy for Electric Vehicles basedon bi-level Programming Problem: San Francisco Case Study, Proceedings of the 2020 IEEE 14th International Conference on Compatibility, Power Electronics and Power Engineering (CPE-POWERENG), Setubal,* Portugal, *1* (pp. 24–29), 2020.

Wang, S.; Fang, C.; He, Q.; Zhang, Y.; Chen, M. EV Charging Infrastructure Deployment in China: Opportunities and Challenges for Smart City Development. *J. Clean. Prod.* **2019,** *235,* 1329–1339.

Wang, X.; Yuen, C.; Hassan, N. U.; An, N.; Wu, W. Electric Vehicle Charging Station Placement for Urban Public Bus Systems. *IEEE Trans. Intell. Transp. Syst.* **2016,** *18* (1), 128–139. doi:10.1109/TITS.2016.2563166

Wilkinson, A.; Hill, M.; Gollan, P. The Sustainability Debate. *Int. J. Operat. Prod. Manag.* **2001,** *1,* 26.

Yong, J. Y.; Ramachandaramurthy, V. K.; Tan, K. M.; Mithulananthan, N. A Review on the State-of-the-Art Technologies of Electric Vehicles, Its Impacts, and Prospects. *Renew. Sustain. Energy Rev.* **2015,** *49,* 365–385. doi:10.1016/j.rser.2015.04.130

Zhang, C.; Liu, Y.; Wu, F.; Tang, B.; Fan, W. Effective Charging Planning Based on Deep Reinforcement Learning for Electric Vehicles. *IEEE Trans. Intell. Transp. Syst.* **2020,** *22* (1), 542–554. doi:10.1109/TITS.2020.3002271

Zhou, L.; Cui, H.; Zhou, B. Home Charging Infrastructure and Electric Vehicle Adoption: An Empirical Study in Shenzhen, China. *Appl. Energy* **2018,** *215,* 515–525.

CHAPTER 4

Exploring the Role of Sustainable Marketing in Shaping Consumer Attitudes toward Environmentally Friendly Products in the United Kingdom

DOMINIC APPIAH[1], UDIT CHAWLA[2], VARSHA MISHRA[3], DEVIKA MULCHANDANI[4], SHIVAM PREM SHARMA[5], and MD KAIF REYAZ JALIAWAL[6]

[1]*Marketing, Royal Holloway, University of London, London, United Kingdom*

[2]*Institute of Engineering & Management, School of University of Engineering and Management, Kolkata, India*

[3]*Royal Holloway, University of London, London, United Kingdom*

[4]*The Calcutta Anglo Gujarati College, Kolkata, West Bengal, India*

[5]*Techno India University, Kolkata, West Bengal, India*

[6]*Bengal Institute of Technology, Kolkata, West Bengal, India*

ABSTRACT

Purpose: Businesses are implementing sustainable marketing techniques to advertise their eco-friendly products as UK customers grow more ecologically aware. The study aims to determine sustainable marketing influences customer perceptions about these goods in the UK.

According to the report, UK consumers are quite aware of the practise known as "greenwashing," which involves deceiving customers about a product or service's environmental advantages. Customers stressed the need

Agile Business Transformations: Priorities, Lessons, and Practices. Satyajit Chakrabarti, Subrata Chattopadhyay, Udit Chawla, Sundeep Singh Sondhi, & Arunava Dalal (Eds.)

of clear and trustworthy sustainable marketing strategies that appropriately communicated a product's environmental effect.

Overall, this study demonstrates that customer attitudes toward environmentally friendly items in the UK may be significantly influenced by sustainable marketing. Sustainable marketing needs to be open, credible, and connected with the consumer values to be able to be fortunate. Consumer education on sustainable marketing strategies should be a top priority for businesses to help customers better understand how their purchases affect the environment.

Future studies should examine how well sustainable marketing works to influence customer choices in various situations and across various UK consumer categories. It could also look at how certifications and legal frameworks support honest and open sustainable marketing practices. In the end, this study may help create sustainable marketing plans for the UK that are advantageous to both companies and the environment.

Design/Methodology: Structured questionnaires were used to conduct this study. Men and women from diverse age groups, income ranges, and occupational backgrounds, including business, service, and others, provided the study's principal sources of data. Five points were used to calculate each parameter studied for the survey (ranging from 1—strongly disagree, to 5—strongly agree).

Findings: According to the study, environmental friendly product attitudes among UK customers are significantly improved by sustainable marketing. Customers have become prepared in order to compensate more for environmentally friendly items now that they are more conscious of sustainability challenges. To improve customer demand, there is a need for more effective education and communication on the advantages of sustainable products.

4.1 INTRODUCTION

Eco-friendly products, sometimes referred to as environmentally friendly products, are created without the use of toxins or other possibly hazardous ingredients and have no adverse effects on the user or the surroundings in which they are used (Ellison et al., 2016; Haghjou et al., 2013). The desire for environmentally friendly goods has increased globally as a consequence of increasing customer awareness and expertise. Thus, knowing customer behavior toward the environment is the basis of sustainable or environmentally friendly advertising (Wang et al., 2020; Xu et al., 2020). The difficulties are mostly important to environmentally carefree human actions (Hopkins, et al., 2020). Few research scholars agree that the complex difficulties may be addressed and remedied by pursuing the proper human activities in an ecologically friendly manner (Han, 2020; Steg and Vlek, 2009). Especially, the attitude toward individual consumption (approaching, purchasing, and consuming things in an environmentally friendly manner) is a primary requirement for ecological sustainability (Halder et al., 2020). Around four percent of the worldwide market is anticipated to be occupied by sustainable goods.

According to a few studies, customers account for more than sixty percent of overall consumption in the United Kingdom and are the inspiration behind environmentally responsible production. In recent studies, consumer awareness of environmental issues and their commitment to protecting the environment has expanded over time (e.g., Shazmin et al., 2016). Further to new research, consumer knowledge of environmental concerns and their dedication to environmental preservation has expanded over time (Rockström et al. 2009). The most curial step toward sustainable lifestyles is the manufacturing and consumption of more environmental-friendly products (Shi et al., 2013). Nevertheless, environmentally conscious or "green" items continue to be an obscure sector at the moment. Over the last ten years, GB Technologies have expanded dramatically. The development of various GB technologies is to increase the rate of practices of eco-friendly products toward sustainable lifestyles (Zhang et al., 2011a, 2011b). Resources-saving, environmentally responsible, and water- and energy-saving technology is now universally regarded as standard. New innovations like high-efficiency windows, green roofs, solar shading devices, solar water heaters, gray water treatment facilities, and high-efficiency HVAC systems have all acquired widespread adoption in the building industry (Koebel et al., 2015). Green brand recognition increases customer satisfaction and positive press for the company that manufactures ecologically friendly goods. Consumer loyalty is challenging to gain since it is determined not just by the superiority of environmentally friendly goods, but also by how the product has a positive impact on the environment (Mourad and Serag Eldin Ahmed, 2012).

The goal this study seeks is to learn further about how having a positive outlook concerning environmental issues, thinking for the natural world, and the urge to make a difference might influence individuals to purchase eco-friendly goods (Sondhi et al., 2023). This study has been done in the United Kingdom to acknowledge the consumer attitude toward environmental-friendly products. Additionally, there is very little actual data supporting the idea that pro-environmental attitudes and beliefs lead to environmentally aware actions like purchasing eco-friendly products. The present study was carried out to evaluate the pro-environmental issues, understanding of environment, and eco-product awareness among customers in the United Kingdom and the possible impact that these variables may have on green purchasing behaviors, as well as to understand the reasons behind the inconsistent attitude and behavior of these consumers.

4.2 LITERATURE REVIEW

The ethical perspective or the favorable or adverse evaluation of the ecosystem that consumers have of the environment influences their decision to buy green products (Sondhi et al.,2023). According to recent research, consumer awareness of environmental issues and their commitment to protecting the environment have grown over time; it has been proven that more customers have changed their purchasing habits over the previous several decades and are utilizing increasingly sustainable items in their daily lives (Holloway et al., 2007).

In respect to sustainable marketing, this study primarily looks at how innovation affects consumer perceptions toward sustainable goods. Customers are increasingly looking for sustainable choices as ecological issues continue to rise (Epstein and Buhovac, 2014). In order to favorably affect consumer views and promote the market acceptability of environmentally friendly products, this study aims to investigate how firms may effectively convey their environmental initiatives. This is accomplished through researching the connection between innovative strategies and sustainable marketing (Franceschini et al., 2016).

Typical external hurdles to sustainable consumption include product cost and availability or the practicality of handling and buying sustainable items (Janßen, and Langen, 2017). Selecting more environmentally friendly items might also be hampered by a lack of knowledge regarding product sustainability (Zsóka et al., 2013). Since constant access to information is anticipated in modern culture, it should come as no surprise that this information is quite significant and affects consumers on several psychological levels (Steg and Vlek; 2009). If offered through promotional tactics, knowledge may instantly change how customers view their level of behavioral control while they are at a business (Testa et al., 2015) and activate emotions with a strong impact (Kemp et al., 2012). Information can also influence consumers in various subsidiary ways and help them adopt pro-environmental views

(Cornelissen et al., 2008). The amount of consumer education and, consequently, characteristics like their care for environmental concerns, may be other significant impediments to adopting pro-environmental behavior. There are significant gaps in studies carried out in the United Kingdom on how conservational apprehension, additionally, the product sustainability evidence affects customer attitudes and purchase behavior, as well as how those factors interact (Kim and Seock, 2009).

The preference for ecologically sound and green goods over conventional products throughout the process of making choices is known as the consumer's environmentally conscious purchase behavior (Chawla et al. (2022). It ought to be emphasized that the majority of ecological studies ignore other types of promotion employed in marketing efforts and only consider green labels as delivering information about product sustainability (Rex and Baumann (2007). For firms to properly inform customers about their sustainability initiatives, marketing tactics are crucial. Companies are using a variety of marketing techniques, including branding, green labeling, and ecological marketing, to advertise their ecologically friendly products. Consumer views toward environmentally friendly items can be significantly influenced by sustainable marketing. Studies have demonstrated that marketing for sustainable products may have a favorable impact on customer sentiments (Bergkvist and Bech-Larsen, (2010). Adopting environmentally friendly practices, promoting them, engaging in ecofriendly utilization, supporting companies that make ecologically conscious goods, and increasing expenditure on them are all examples of green purchasing behavior (Sondhi et al., 2023). According to a study by Lee and Park (2017), consumers are more inclined to buy environmentally friendly items when they believe that such products would have a beneficial influence on the environment. Clients are more likely to trust and stick with firms that successfully communicate their sustainability initiatives (Bergkvist and Bech-Larsen, 2010). Furthermore, sustainable marketing may improve brand reputation and competitive advantage, resulting in higher income and sales (Polonsky and Rosenberger, 2001). Considering that they are considerate of their role in contributing to the environment's preservation, people who care about the natural world seem more inclined to be committed to preserve it (Sondhi et al., 2023).

Due to the high production costs, green items are typically more expensive than conventional products (Ling, 2013). Price has thus been recognized as a key barrier to green consumption (Gleim et al., 2013; Aslihan Nasir and Karakaya, 2014). Price is a major consideration when making purchases, especially for young customers residing in the United

Kingdom with low purchasing power. According to studies carried out in the UK, people who care about the environment are not very price sensitive, and the price has little impact on whether they choose to buy green items (Grankvist and Biel, 2001; Cronin et al., 2011). In a study by Choi and Parsa (2007), it was revealed that among state restaurant associations in the USA consumers are reluctant to pay a premium for environmentally friendly goods and services. Mixed results have been observed regarding consumers' being prepared to spend extra for green items in the cities in UK. The price sensitivity related to these customers has been revealed by a lot of research in the past. For instance, Manaktola and Jauhari (2007) found that customers with high EC appreciate hotels that use green practises but are hesitant to pay a higher price for it. In contrast, it was discovered by Yadav and Pathak (2017) and Prakash and Pathak (2017) that customers were prepared to pay more for environmentally friendly items. Examining the impact of the inclination to pay on green initiatives is essential in light of these contradicting findings.

Market demand, the supply chain, the channels of distribution, and governmental regulations can all have an effect on how readily available sustainable products are. Given the scarcity of resources and high production costs, businesses that provide sustainable products may encounter difficulties expanding their manufacturing, selling, and distribution operations. Major studies in UK have revealed that if sustainable items are easily accessible on the market, people are more inclined to buy them (Dangelico and Pujari, 2010). On the other hand, it may be difficult to develop sustainable consumption habits due to the restricted supply of sustainable items. The absence of sustainable items is a major impediment to sustainable purchasing habits, according to research by Luchs et al. (2010). Additionally, consumers may think that sustainable items are expensive or hard to locate, which may deter them from buying them. Consumer views toward environmentally friendly items are significantly influenced by the availability of sustainable products. Businesses that create sustainable products must make sure that consumers can easily find and acquire them on the market (Bodur et al., 2014). The development of sustainable purchasing habits may be hampered by the restricted supply of sustainable items. In order to develop a market that supports the accessibility of sustainable goods, governments, corporations, and consumers must collaborate (Griskevicius et al., 2010). However, while accessibility has been playing significant participation toward influencing customer attitudes about sustainable products, sustainability initiatives should not be sacrificed in the sake of accessibility.

4.3 STATEMENT OF THE PROBLEM

Businesses looking to successfully advertise eco-friendly items must comprehend how sustainable marketing strategies interact with cutting-edge strategies. This study aims to address the lack of comprehensive data on how sustainable marketing strategies affect consumer perceptions toward sustainable goods in the United Kingdom.

4.4 OBJECTIVE OF THE STUDY

The purpose of this study serves to determine consumer attitudes toward sustainable and environmentally friendly products in the United Kingdom with the help of different parameters like Innovation, Availability, Affordability, Information Awareness, and Reliability.

4.5 HYPOTHESES OF THE STUDY

- **H_1:** There is no significant difference between parameters like Innovation, Availability, Affordability, Information Awareness and Reliability and choice of their brands.

4.6 METHODOLOGY

The study has examined the Consumers Perception of sustainable products by using a structured questionnaire and causal interactions with customers, 242 models were collected from London. The data came from people of various ages, genders, jobs, and socioeconomic backgrounds. The parameter studies of the survey were each calculated on a five-point scale (from 1—strongly disagree, to 5—strongly agree).

4.7 RESULT AND ANALYSIS

Based on the analysis provided in Table 4.1, it is seen that the asymp. sig for Innovation, Availability, Affordability, and Information Awareness are lesser than 0.05, and hence null hypothesis was rejected in each case. Or to put it another way, there was a significant difference between Innovation,

TABLE 4.1 Results of ANOVA for Understanding Different Parameters of Sustainability for Different Brands.

	Sum of Squares		df	Mean Square	F	Sig
Innovation	Between groups	2444.279	4	611.07	2.768	0.028
	Within groups	53,874.877	244	220.799		
	Total	56,319.157	248			
Availability	Between groups	2456.731	4	614.183	2.791	0.027
	Within groups	53,689.469	244	220.039		
	Total	56,146.201	248			
Affordability	Between groups	2425.975	4	606.494	2.719	0.03
	Within groups	54,419.881	244	223.032		
	Total	56,845.855	248			
Information awareness	Between groups	2489.834	4	622.459	2.826	0.026
	Within groups	53,737.684	244	220.236		
	Total	56,227.518	248			
Reliability	Between groups	836.567	4	209.142	0.925	0.45
	Within groups	55,158.622	244	226.06		
	Total	55,995.189	248			

Availability, Affordability, and Information Awareness, with respect to brand preference. The alternative hypothesis H_1 was accepted.

Post Hoc Test (Table 4.2) was used for a more thorough study to determine the differences between the brands.

TABLE 4.2 Results of Post Hoc Analysis for "Innovation" Parameter of Sustainability.

Innovation	Brand A	Brand B	Brand C	Brand D	Brand E
Brand A		H1 Rejected	H1 Rejected	H1 Accepted	H1 Rejected
Brand B	H1 Rejected		H1 Rejected	H1 Rejected	H1 Rejected
Brand C	H1 Accepted	H1 Rejected		H1 Accepted	H1 Rejected
Brand D	H1 Rejected	H1 Rejected	H1 Accepted		H1 Accepted
Brand E	H1 Rejected	H1 Rejected	H1 Rejected	H1 Accepted	

As per Table 4.2, Brand B has been unique in providing better innovation in comparison with Brand A, Brand C, Brand D, and Brand E. Brand B, promotes the efficient use of resources and advancing the development of environmentally friendly technology. The Brand B addresses environmental challenges and builds a more durable and peaceful interaction among people and the environment.

TABLE 4.3 Results of Post Hoc Analysis for "Availability" Parameter of Sustainability.

Availability	Brand A	Brand B	Brand C	Brand D	Brand E
Brand A		H1 Rejected	H1 Rejected	H1 Accepted	H1 Rejected
Brand B	H1 Rejected		H1 Rejected	H1 Rejected	H1 Rejected
Brand C	H1 Accepted	H1 Rejected		H1 Accepted	H1 Rejected
Brand D	H1 Rejected	H1 Rejected	H1 Accepted		H1 Accepted
Brand E	H1 Rejected	H1 Rejected	H1 Rejected	H1 Accepted	

According to Table 4.3, Brand B product variety and accessibility in compared to product variety and accessibility in compared to Brand A, Brand C, Brand D, and Brand E are much improved. Customer attitudes toward environmental sustainability are substantially impacted by the availability of sustainable goods and services. BRAND B provides accessible options to the customers, making them more inclined toward making environmentally friendly decisions. This encourages a move toward sustainable practices.

TABLE 4.4 Results of Post Hoc Analysis for "Affordability" Parameter of Sustainability.

Affordability	Brand A	Brand B	Brand C	Brand D	Brand E
Brand A		H1 Rejected	H1 Rejected	H1 Accepted	H1 Rejected
Brand B	H1 Rejected		H1 Rejected	H1 Rejected	H1 Rejected
Brand C	H1 Accepted	H1 Rejected		H1 Accepted	H1 Rejected
Brand D	H1 Rejected	H1 Rejected	H1 Accepted		H1 Accepted
Brand E	H1 Rejected	H1 Rejected	H1 Rejected	H1 Accepted	

According to Table 4.4, Brand B provides more affordability of products, when compared to Brand A, Brand C, Brand D, and Brand E. In determining client attitudes toward sustainability, affordability acts as a crucial strand. The brand provides sustainable products at reasonable prices, making customers more likely to make eco-friendly decisions. This makes sustainability readily available to a wider market and promotes the adoption of environmentally beneficial behaviors.

According to Table 4.5, BRAND B provides more affordability of products, while contrasted with Brand A, Brand C, Brand D, and Brand E. In order to influence consumer attitudes regarding sustainability, information awareness is essential. The brand preference makes customers further probable in choosing ecologically favorable practises along with products once individuals become conscious of how their choices affect their surroundings, which raises the demand for sustainable solutions and encourages companies to use greener business practises.

TABLE 4.5 Results of Post Hoc Analysis for "Information Awareness" Parameter of Sustainability.

Information Awareness	Brand A	Brand B	Brand C	Brand D	Brand E
Brand A		H1 Rejected	H1 Rejected	H1 Accepted	H1 Rejected
Brand B	H1 Rejected		H1 Rejected	H1 Rejected	H1 Rejected
Brand C	H1 Accepted	H1 Rejected		H1 Accepted	H1 Rejected
Brand D	H1 Rejected	H1 Rejected	H1 Accepted		H1 Accepted
Brand E	H1 rejected	H1 rejected	H1 rejected	H1 accepted	

4.8 CONCLUSION

The impact of sustainable marketing in influencing customer attitudes toward green products in the UK has been examined in this study. Businesses need sustainable marketing strategies in order to influence consumer attitudes toward sustainable products effectively communicate their sustainability efforts to consumers, build brand trust and loyalty, and increase competitive advantage.

Additionally, accessible sustainable marketing techniques are essential in influencing customer attitudes in the UK toward green products. Businesses may appeal to a larger consumer base, boost sales and profitability, and promote sustainability by combining affordable techniques with sustainable marketing initiatives. Although the demand for ecologically friendly items is rising in the UK, there are still many places where they are hard to get. This means that companies must concentrate on enlarging their distribution networks and increasing customer access to sustainable products. Businesses can use a variety of tactics to raise consumer awareness, including informing customers about the sustainability of their products, developing sustainable marketing campaigns that emphasize the effects of their products regarding ecology along with community as a whole, and collaborating with nonprofit groups to advance sustainability. The current study adds toward expanding the knowledge about ecological marketing and offers guidance to companies wishing to use sustainable marketing tactics to attract eco-aware customers.

TABLE 4.6 Results of Post Hoc Analysis for Multiple Comparisons of Parameters with Sustainability.

Dep. Var.	(I) Brand	(J) Brand	Mean difference (I-J)	Std. Error	Sig.	95% Confidence Interval		Dep. Var.	(I) Brand	(J) Brand	Mean difference (I-J)	Std. Error	Sig.	95% Confidence Interval	
						LB	UB							LB	UB
Innovation	A	B	–2.367	3.589	0.51	–9.44	4.7	Reliability	A	B	2.642	3.631	0.468	–4.51	9.79
		C	1.276	3.332	0.702	–5.29	7.84			C	1.64	3.371	0.627	–5	8.28
		D	–6.883*	3.323	0.039	–13.43	–0.34			D	–2.433	3.362	0.47	–9.06	4.19
		E	0.15	3.323	0.964	–6.39	6.69			E	1.45	3.362	0.667	–5.17	8.07
	B	A	2.367	3.589	0.51	–4.7	9.44		B	A	–2.642	3.631	0.468	–9.79	4.51
		C	3.642	3.043	0.233	–2.35	9.64			C	–1.002	3.079	0.745	–7.07	5.06
		D	–4.517	3.033	0.138	–10.49	1.46			D	–5.075	3.069	0.099	–11.12	0.97
		E	2.517	3.033	0.408	–3.46	8.49			E	–1.192	3.069	0.698	–7.24	4.85
	C	A	–1.276	3.332	0.702	–7.84	5.29		C	A	–1.64	3.371	0.627	–8.28	5
		B	–3.642	3.043	0.233	–9.64	2.35			B	1.002	3.079	0.745	–5.06	7.07
		D	–8.159*	2.724	0.003	–13.53	–2.79			D	–4.073	2.757	0.141	–9.5	1.36
		E	–1.126	2.724	0.68	–6.49	4.24			E	–0.19	2.757	0.945	–5.62	5.24
	D	A	6.883*	3.323	0.039	0.34	13.43		D	A	2.433	3.362	0.47	–4.19	9.06
		B	4.517	3.033	0.138	–1.46	10.49			B	5.075	3.069	0.099	–0.97	11.12
		C	8.159*	2.724	0.003	2.79	13.53			C	4.073	2.757	0.141	–1.36	9.5
		E	7.033*	2.713	0.01	1.69	12.38			E	3.883	2.745	0.158	–1.52	9.29
	E	A	–0.15	3.323	0.964	–6.69	6.39		E	A	–1.45	3.362	0.667	–8.07	5.17
		B	–2.517	3.033	0.408	–8.49	3.46			B	1.192	3.069	0.698	–4.85	7.24

TABLE 4.6 *(Continued)*

Dep. Var.	(I) Brand	(J) Brand	Mean difference (I-J)	Std. Error	Sig.	95% Confidence Interval		Dep. Var.	(I) Brand	(J) Brand	Mean difference (I-J)	Std. Error	Sig.	95% Confidence Interval	
		C	1.126	2.724	0.68	–4.24	6.49			C	0.19	2.757	0.945	–5.24	5.62
		D	–7.033*	2.713	0.01	–12.38	–1.69			D	–3.883	2.745	0.158	–9.29	1.52
	A	B	–2.367	3.583	0.51	–9.42	4.69		A	B	–2.667	3.584	0.458	–9.73	4.39
		C	1.252	3.326	0.707	–5.3	7.8			C	0.923	3.328	0.782	–5.63	7.48
		D	–6.917*	3.317	0.038	–13.45	–0.38			D	–7.267*	3.318	0.029	–13.8	–0.73
		E	0.15	3.317	0.964	–6.38	6.68			E	–0.25	3.318	0.94	–6.79	6.29
	B	A	2.367	3.583	0.51	–4.69	9.42		B	A	2.667	3.584	0.458	–4.39	9.73
		C	3.619	3.038	0.235	–2.37	9.6			C	3.59	3.04	0.239	–2.4	9.58
		D	–4.55	3.028	0.134	–10.51	1.41			D	–4.6	3.029	0.13	–10.57	1.37
		E	2.517	3.028	0.407	–3.45	8.48			E	2.417	3.029	0.426	–3.55	8.38
Availability	C	A	–1.252	3.326	0.707	–7.8	5.3	Information awareness	C	A	–0.923	3.328	0.782	–7.48	5.63
		B	–3.619	3.038	0.235	–9.6	2.37			B	–3.59	3.04	0.239	–9.58	2.4
		D	–8.169*	2.72	0.003	–13.53	–2.81			D	–8.190*	2.721	0.003	–13.55	–2.83
		E	–1.102	2.72	0.686	–6.46	4.26			E	–1.173	2.721	0.667	–6.53	4.19
	D	A	6.917*	3.317	0.038	0.38	13.45		D	A	7.267*	3.318	0.029	0.73	13.8
		B	4.55	3.028	0.134	–1.41	10.51			B	4.6	3.029	0.13	–1.37	10.57
		C	8.169*	2.72	0.003	2.81	13.53			C	8.190*	2.721	0.003	2.83	13.55
		E	7.067*	2.708	0.01	1.73	12.4			E	7.017*	2.709	0.01	1.68	12.35

TABLE 4.6 *(Continued)*

Dep. Var.	(I) Brand	(J) Brand	Mean difference (I-J)	Std. Error	Sig.	95% Confidence Interval		Dep. Var.	(I) Brand	(J) Brand	Mean difference (I-J)	Std. Error	Sig.	95% Confidence Interval	
	E	A	−0.15	3.317	0.964	−6.68	6.38		E	A	0.25	3.318	0.94	−6.29	6.79
		B	−2.517	3.028	0.407	−8.48	3.45			B	−2.417	3.029	0.426	−8.38	3.55
		C	1.102	2.72	0.686	−4.26	6.46			C	1.173	2.721	0.667	−4.19	6.53
		D	−7.067*	2.708	0.01	−12.4	−1.73			D	−7.017*	2.709	0.01	−12.35	−1.68
Affordability	A	B	−2.367	3.607	0.512	−9.47	4.74	Affordability	D	A	6.850*	3.339	0.041	0.27	13.43
		C	1.282	3.349	0.702	−5.31	7.88			B	4.483	3.048	0.143	−1.52	10.49
		D	−6.850*	3.339	0.041	−13.43	−0.27			C	8.132*	2.738	0.003	2.74	13.53
		E	0.15	3.339	0.964	−6.43	6.73			E	7.000*	2.727	0.011	1.63	12.37
	B	A	2.367	3.607	0.512	−4.74	9.47		E	A	−0.15	3.339	0.964	−6.73	6.43
		C	3.649	3.059	0.234	−2.38	9.67			B	−2.517	3.048	0.41	−8.52	3.49
		D	−4.483	3.048	0.143	−10.49	1.52			C	1.132	2.738	0.68	−4.26	6.53
		E	2.517	3.048	0.41	−3.49	8.52			D	−7.000*	2.727	0.011	−12.37	−1.63
	C	A	−1.282	3.349	0.702	−7.88	5.31								
		B	−3.649	3.059	0.234	−9.67	2.38								
		D	−8.132*	2.738	0.003	−13.53	−2.74								
		E	−1.132	2.738	0.68	−6.53	4.26								

KEYWORDS

- **sustainable marketing**
- **eco-friendly products**
- **customer perception**
- **ecological awareness**
- **advertising**

REFERENCES

Aslihan Nasir, V.; Karakaya, F. Consumer Segments in Organic Foods Market. *J. Consum. Mark.* **2014,** *31* (4), 263–277.

Bergkvist, L.; Bech-Larsen, T. Two Studies of Consequences and Actionable Antecedents of Brand Love. *J. Brand Manag.* **2010,** *17,* 504–518.

Bodur, H. O.; Gao, T.; Grohmann, B. The Ethical Attribute Stigma: Understanding When Ethical Attributes Improve Consumer Responses to Product Evaluations. *J. Bus. Ethics* **2014,** *122,* 167–177.

Chawla, U.; Choudhary, S.; Mishra, V. 4 Young Consumers' Green Purchasing Behavior with Reference to Green Marketing. *Sustain. Mark. Customer Value* **2022,** 59.

Choi, G.; Parsa, H. G. Green practices II: Measuring Restaurant Managers' Psychological Attributes and Their Willingness to Charge for the "Green Practices". *J. Foodser. Bus. Res.* **2007,** *9* (4), 41–63.

Cornelissen, G.; Pandelaere, M.; Warlop, L.; Dewitte, S. Positive Cueing: Promoting Sustainable Consumer Behavior by Cueing Common Environmental Behaviors as Environmental. *Int. J. Res. Mark.* **2008,** *25* (1), 46–55.

Cronin, J. J.; Smith, J. S.; Gleim, M. R.; Ramirez, E.; Martinez, J. D. Green Marketing Strategies: An Examination of Stakeholders and the Opportunities They Present. *J. Acad. Mark. Sci.* **2011,** *39,* 158–174.

Dangelico, R. M.; Pujari, D. Mainstreaming Green Product Innovation: Why and How Companies Integrate Environmental Sustainability. *J. Bus. Ethics* **2010,** *95,* 471–486.

Ellison, B.; Duff, B. R.; Wang, Z.; White, T. B. Putting the Organic Label in Context: Examining the Interactions Between the Organic Label, Product Type, and Retail Outlet. *Food Qual. Prefer.* **2016,** *49,* 140–150.

Eurobarometer, S. Attitudes of European Citizens Towards the Environment. *European Commission* **2008,** *295.*

Franceschini, S.; Faria, L. G.; Jurowetzki, R. Unveiling Scientific Communities About Sustainability and Innovation. A Bibliometric Journey Around Sustainable Terms. *J. Clean. Prod.* **2016,** *127,* 72–83.

Gleim, M. R.; Smith, J. S.; Andrews, D.; Cronin Jr, J. J. Against the Green: A Multi-Method Examination of the Barriers to Green Consumption. *J. Retail.* **2013,** *89* (1), 44–61.

Gleim, M.; J. Lawson, S. Spanning the Gap: An Examination of the Factors Leading to the Green Gap. *J. Consum. Mark.* **2014,** *31* (6/7), 503–514.
Grankvist, G.; Biel, A. The Importance of Beliefs and Purchase Criteria in the Choice of Eco-labeled Food Products. *J. Environ. Psychol.* **2001,,** *21* (4), 405–410.
Griskevicius, V.; Tybur, J. M.; Van den Bergh, B. Going Green to be Seen: Status, Reputation, and Conspicuous Conservation. *Jo. Pers. Soc. Psychol.* **2010,** *98* (3), 392.
Haghjou, M.; Hayati, B.; Pishbahar, E.; Mohammad, R. R.; Dashti, G. *Factors Affecting Consumers'potential Willingness to Pay for Organic Food Products in Iran: Case Study of Tabriz*. 2013.
Han, H. Theory of Green Purchase Behavior (TGPB): A New Theory for Sustainable Consumption of Green Hotel and Green Restaurant Products. *Bus. Strateg. Environ.* **2020,** *29* (6), 2815–2828.
Hardi, P. *Making Sustainability Work: Best Practices in Managing and Measuring Corporate Social, Environmental, and Economic Impacts, MJ Epstein*; Greenleaf Publishing: Sheffield, UK (2008), 2009; p 288.
Holloway, L.; Kneafsey, M.; Venn, L.; Cox, R.; Dowler, E.; Tuomainen, H. Possible Food Economies: A Methodological Framework for Exploring Food Production–consumption Relationships. *Sociol. Rural.* **2007,** *47* (1), 1–19.
Janßen, D.; Langen, N. The Bunch of Sustainability Labels–Do Consumers Differentiate?. *J. Clean. Prod.* **2017,** *143,* 1233–1245.
Jedynak, P.; Bąk, S. *Risk Management in Crisis: Winners and Losers During the COVID-19 Pandemic*. Taylor & Francis, 2021; p 252.
Kannan, D.; Moazzeni, S.; mostafayi Darmian, S.; Afrasiabi, A. A hybrid Approach Based on MCDM Methods and Monte Carlo Simulation for Sustainable Evaluation of Potential Solar Sites in East of Iran. *J. Clean. Prod.* **2021,** *279,* 122368.
Kemp, E.; Bui, M.; Chapa, S. The Role of Advertising in Consumer Emotion Management. *Int. J. Advert.* **2012,** *31* (2), 339–353.
Kim, S.; Seock, Y. K. Impacts of Health and Environmental Consciousness on Young Female Consumers' Attitude Towards and Purchase of Natural Beauty Products. *Int. J. Consum. Stud.* **2009,** *33* (6), 627–638.
Luchs, M. G.; Naylor, R. W.; Irwin, J. R.; Raghunathan, R. The Sustainability Liability: Potential Negative Effects of Ethicality on Product Preference. *J. Mark.* **2010,** *74* (5), 18–31.
Manaktola, K.; Jauhari, V. Exploring Consumer Attitude and Behavior Towards Green Practices in the Lodging Industry in India. *Int. J. Contemp. Hosp. Manag.* **2007,** *19* (5), 364–377.
McDonald, S.; Oates, C. J. Sustainability: Consumer Perceptions and Marketing Strategies. *Bus. Strateg. Environ.* **2006,** *15* (3), 157–170.
Mourad, M.; Serag Eldin Ahmed, Y. Perception of Green Brand in an Emerging Innovative Market. *Eur. J. Innov. Manag.* **2012,** *15* (4), 514–537.
Nielsen, N. V. Global Consumers are Willing to Put Their Money Where Their Heart is When it Comes to Goods and Services from Companies Committed to Social Responsibility. *June, New York* 2014.
Polonsky, M. J.; Rosenberger III, P. J. Reevaluating Green Marketing: A Strategic Approach. *Bus. Horiz.* **2001,** *44* (5), 21–21.
Rex, E.; Baumann, H. Beyond Ecolabels: What Green Marketing can Learn from Conventional Marketing. *J. Clean. Prod.* **2007,** *15* (6), 567–576.
Rockström, J.; Steffen, W.; Noone, K.; Persson, Å.; Chapin, F. S.; Lambin, E. F.;... Foley, J. A. A Safe Operating Space for Humanity. *Nature* **2009,** *461* (7263), 472–475.

Shazmin, S. A. A.; Sipan, I.; Sapri, M. Property Tax Assessment Incentives for Green Building: A Review. *Renew. Sustain. Energy Rev.* **2016,** *60,* 536–548.
Shi, Q.; Zuo, J.; Huang, R.; Huang, J.; Pullen, S. Identifying the Critical Factors for Green Construction–an Empirical Study in China. *Habitat Int.* **2013,** *40,* 1–8.
Sondhi, S.; Chawla, U.; Iqbal, H. Relationship Between Social Cause, Environment Conservation and Environmental Attitude, Towards Promoting Green Purchasing Behavior. *Serb. J. Manag.* **2023,** *18* (1), 27–43.
Testa, F.; Iraldo, F.; Vaccari, A.; Ferrari, E. Why Eco-labels can be Effective Marketing Tools: Evidence from a Study on Italian Consumers. *Bus. Strateg. Environ.* **2015,** *24* (4), 252–265.
Tjärnemo, H.; Södahl, L. Swedish Food Retailers Promoting Climate Smarter Food Choices—trapped Between Visions and Reality? *J. Retail. Consum. Serv.* **2015,** *24,* 130–139.
Tomej, K.; Liburd, J. J. Sustainable Mobility at the Interface of Transport and Tourism. *J. Sustain. Tour.* **2020,** *28* (2), 129–143.
Wang, Y. H.; Tsai, C. F. The Relationship Between Brand Image and Purchase Intention: Evidence from Award Winning Mutual Funds. *Int. J. Bus. Finance Res.* **2014,** *8* (2), 27–40.
Watts, D. C.; Ilbery, B.; Maye, D. Making Reconnections in Agro-food Geography: Alternative Systems of Food Provision. *Prog. Hum. Geogr.* **2005,** *29* (1), 22–40.
Wong, I. A.; Ruan, W. J.; Cai, X.; Huang, G. I. Green-Induced Tourist Equity: The Cross-level Effect of Regional Environmental Performance. *J. Sustain. Tour.* **2021,** *29* (7), 1043–1062.
Wu, S.; Chen, Y. The Impact of Green Marketing and Perceived Innovation on Environmentally Conscious Consumer Behavior. *Int. J. Market. Stud.* **2014,** *5* (5), 24–30.
Xu, F.; Huang, L.; Whitmarsh, L. Home and Away: Cross-contextual Consistency in Tourists' Pro-environmental Behavior. *J. Sustain. Tour.* **2020,** *28* (10), 1443–1459.
Yadav, R.; Pathak, G. S. Determinants of Consumers' Green Purchase Behavior in a Developing Nation: Applying and Extending the Theory of Planned Behavior. *Ecol. Econ.* **2017,** *134,* 114–122.
Zsóka, Á.; Szerényi, Z. M.; Széchy, A.; Kocsis, T. Greening Due to Environmental Education? Environmental Knowledge, Attitudes, Consumer Behavior and Everyday Pro-environmental Activities of Hungarian High School and University Students. *J. Clean. Prod.* **2013,** *48,* 126–138.

CHAPTER 5

Influence of Digital Voice Assistance on Consumer Purchase Intention

SAKSHI DHIMAN[1], JEANNE POULOSE[1], SANJIB BHATTACHARJEE[2], VINOD SHARMA[3], and MANOHAR KAPSE[3]

[1]*School of Business and Management, Christ (Deemed to be University), Delhi, India*

[2]*School of Management, Presidency University, Bengaluru, India*

[3]*Symbiosis Center for Management and Human Resource Development (SCMHRD), Symbiosis International (Deemed University), Pune, India*

ABSTRACT

The focus of this research is to analyze how digital voice assistants (DVAs) influence the buying decisions of consumers when it comes to online shopping in the Delhi-NCR region. The study involves surveying 225 online shoppers using a purposive sampling method to collect data on their perceptions and experiences with DVAs in online shopping. To study consumer purchase intention, we conducted a data analysis that involved a structural equation model, which focused on the perceived ease of use and perceived usefulness of DVAs. The paper highlights the crucial role of DVAs in shaping consumer purchase intention and influencing purchase decisions in the context of e-commerce/online shopping. The study has significant implications for e-commerce companies and marketers. To promote their adoption, they should think about integrating DVAs into their online purchasing platforms, grow DVA trust, and explain their advantages. Additionally, businesses ought to spend money creating more complex DVAs that can offer tailored advice and recommendations based on client preferences and previous purchases.

Agile Business Transformations: Priorities, Lessons, and Practices. Satyajit Chakrabarti, Subrata Chattopadhyay, Udit Chawla, Sundeep Singh Sondhi, & Arunava Dalal (Eds.)

5.1 INTRODUCTION

The way we engage with technology has been revolutionized by voice assistants, which have made it simpler than ever to complete things without using your hands. Online shopping is one industry that has benefited greatly from this technology. Customers can simply order goods, check prices, and track delivery using speech assistants such as Amazon's Alexa, Google Assistant, or Apple's Siri. As e-commerce continues to grow, voice assistants offer a convenient and accessible way to shop without having to navigate through multiple screens or devices. While there are concerns about privacy and security, the ease and simplicity of using voice assistants for online shopping make it a trend that is likely to continue to gain popularity in the coming years.

A virtual assistant, sometimes called a digital voice assistant (DVA), is a piece of AI-powered software that reacts to human voice instructions. These programs can be used to set reminders, send messages, make phone calls, play music, and provide information on a variety of subjects, such as the weather, all while understanding natural language. In smartphones, smart speakers, and other smart devices, DVAs are frequently employed. Apple's Siri, Amazon's Alexa, Google Assistant, and Microsoft's Cortana are a few examples of well-known DVAs.

In 2020, around 150 million individuals bought products online in India, a rise from the 135 million in the previous year. The increase can be attributed to the shift in consumer shopping behavior caused by the COVID-19 pandemic, as well as the growth of the e-commerce industry in India (Statista, 2021). According to a survey conducted by YouGov in 2020, about 74% of urban Indian internet users had used an online shopping app in the past 12 months, while 26% had not. Another survey conducted by Kantar IMRB in 2018 found that around 56% of urban Indian consumers used shopping apps on a weekly or monthly basis. This has led to a growing interest in understanding the influence of DVAs on consumer purchase intention. Research on this topic is still in its early stages, but several theoretical perspectives can provide insight into the potential influence of DVAs on consumer purchase intention. One of these perspectives is the technology acceptance model (TAM).

With the increasing integration of DVAs into our daily lives, it is essential to explore the potential impact they may have on consumers' purchase intentions. According to TAM, a technology's acceptability and adoption depend on how beneficial and simple people find it to use. In the case of DVAs, users may find them more valuable if they can offer quick and easy access to information, goods, and services. Additionally, if DVAs are easy to use through voice commands, users may perceive them as easy to use. Therefore, by improving the perceived value and usability of the goods or services they recommend, DVAs may have a favorable effect on consumer purchase intention.

The purpose of this research paper is to explore the impact of DVAs. This study focuses on the effect of voice assistants on consumers' intention to make purchases online. It aims to investigate how characteristics of DVA, such as technological anxiety, individual innovativeness, perceived usefulness (PU), and ease of use, influence consumer purchase intention.

5.2 LITERATURE REVIEW

The integration of DVAs into our day-to-day lives has brought a significant change in the way we communicate and perform tasks. With the rise of e-commerce, the use of DVAs for online shopping has gained momentum. The purpose of conducting this literature review is to provide a comprehensive understanding of the existing body of knowledge on the topic. The detailed review helped to identify the key theories, concepts, and variables that are relevant to the research. Additionally, it also enabled us to critically evaluate and synthesize the findings of previous studies to identify gaps, inconsistencies, and areas for further research.

The researchers used the TAM created by Davis (1989) to determine how well the digital assistant described in this study was received. TAM is frequently used in Literature and is valued for its ease of use and practicality (Chacko Punnoose, 2012), even though there are other theoretical models for evaluating the adoption and use of new technologies, such as the service robot acceptance model (sRAM) by Wirtz et al. (2018) and the unified theory of acceptance and use of technology (UTAUT) by Venkatesh et al. (2003).

The purpose of the TAM is to examine how users' perspectives and opinions regarding new information and communication technologies impact their choice to embrace or decline these technologies (Yang, 2005). PU and perceived ease of use (PEOU) are the two main constructs that are used to predict utilization. Studies of new technologies in tourism (Tavitiyaman et al., 2020), healthcare (Kuo et al., 2009; Park and Chen, 2007), and organizational decision-making (Cao et al., 2021) commonly make use of these categories.

Studies show that customers are more likely to adopt innovative shopping technologies that offer a fun and enjoyable shopping experience, are perceived as useful, and easy to use, and are influenced by their social environment (Ylilehto et al., 2019). More studies propose that PU, PEOU, trust, and perceived risk are the main factors that affect the acceptance of consumers of online shopping. These studies suggest that PU and PEOU are the most important factors in driving online shopping acceptance (Zhou et al., 2007). Studies have identified several factors that can impact consumer online shopping behavior, including consumer attitudes, perceptions of risk and trust, and the usability of the website. The findings of such studies suggest that trust and security concerns are grave factors that can influence consumer online shopping behavior. The authors also highlight the position of website strategy and usability in lashing consumer behavior (Li et al., 2002).

Some studies explore the impact of AI voice assistants on various aspects of consumer behavior, such as information search, choice, and postpurchase evaluation. They also highlight potential challenges that may arise from the use of these assistants, including issues related to privacy, trust, and control (Dellaert et al., 2020).

Studies discuss the potential benefits and challenges of voice AI in digital commerce, including its ability to enhance personalization and convenience while also posing privacy and security risks. The authors also suggest future research directions, such as investigating the impact of voice AI on different types of products and consumers with varying levels of technological proficiency (Sun et al., 2021). Studies suggest the potential benefits and challenges of using voice assistants in the context of brand management, including its ability to enhance brand engagement and loyalty while also posing risks related to brand dilution and commoditization. They also highlight the importance of understanding consumer behavior and preferences when designing and implementing voice assistant strategies for brands (Mari, 2019). Studies show that consumers' PU and PEOU of voice assistants positively influence their intention to use them for shopping. Additionally, it is also found that trust and privacy concerns are important factors that affect consumers' usage of voice assistants (Muthukumaran and Vani, 2020).

Researchers argue that human-like voice assistants can increase consumer engagement, trust, and satisfaction, ultimately leading to higher adoption and usage rates of voice commerce. They explore the potential mechanisms underlying this effect, such as the use of conversational cues and emotional expressions in voice interactions (Reinkemeier et al., 2020). The examination of how emotional voice assistants impact consumers' shopping attitudes and behavior is the main focus of this study. It has been found that emotional voice assistants have a positive impact on consumer attitudes and behavior, as they are perceived as more trustworthy and satisfying than their non-emotional counterparts (Kaiser et al., 2022).

Researchers have examined the mediating role of psychological power in the interaction between consumers, and voice assistants, using the example of ordering pizza through Amazon's Alexa. It was found that when consumers gave a command to Alexa to order a pizza, they perceived an increase in psychological power, which in turn led to higher satisfaction with the interaction and increased intention to repeat the behavior. Additionally, the study showed that perceptions of psychological power were stronger when the voice assistant was anthropomorphized, suggesting that the design of voice assistants can impact the psychological effects of the interaction (Tassiello et al., 2020). Empirical studies have examined the impact of three dimensions of perceived quality (i.e., functional, technical, and service quality) on perceived trust. They also explore the moderating role of consumers' privacy concerns in this relationship. The authors find that all three dimensions of perceived quality have a positive impact on perceived trust, and privacy concerns weaken the relationship between service quality and perceived trust (Liu et al., 2021). A study conducted by (Park and Kim, 2019) examined the impact of voice assistants on consumer behavior. The results indicated that the use of voice assistants positively influenced consumers' purchase intentions toward products. The study also found that the PU and ease of use of voice assistants were important factors that contributed to their adoption. In another study, (Kim and Lee, 2019) examined the influence of voice assistants on consumers' online shopping behavior. According to research, the use of voice assistants has a positive impact on consumers' intention to make a purchase. The primary factor that influences the adoption of these assistants is the PU they provide.

Studies have explored how AI-powered smart speakers, such as Amazon's Alexa, are changing the way people consume and prefer digital content, particularly movies. It discusses the convenience and accessibility of using voice commands to search and purchase movies, as well as the potential impact on traditional movie distribution channels. It also examines how AI speakers can personalize content recommendations based on user preferences and behavior (Son and Oh, 2019). Authors have argued that voice assistants can serve as a persuasive technology to encourage individuals to engage in charitable giving, volunteering, and other prosocial activities. They discuss the theoretical foundations of this argument and present preliminary evidence from a survey-based study to support their claims (Mohanty et al., 2021).

Schultz and Brüggemann (2021) investigate the reception of DVAs for grocery shopping. They explore the impact of various factors, such as PU, ease of use, and privacy concerns, on consumers' intention to adopt this new shopping method. It was found that PU is the most important factor that influences consumers' acceptance of DVAs for grocery shopping, followed by ease of use and privacy concerns. Farahbakhsh et al. (2021) explored the influence of individual consumer characteristics on the acceptance of digital assistants for grocery shopping. It was found that consumers with higher levels of technology acceptance and prior experience with digital assistants were more likely to adopt them for grocery shopping.

Rase and Ormaza Cuadra (2018) examine the use of personal voice assistants in the context of retail digitalization. Research shows that customers view voice assistants positively in the retail sector, but they also worry about privacy and data security. Studies have pinpointed five crucial elements that impact online shopping habits: personal creativity, perceived simplicity, PU, subjective norms, and trust. They argue that understanding these factors and their interrelationships can help businesses design effective online shopping experiences that meet the needs and preferences of consumers (Venkatesh et al., 2022)

5.3 RESEARCH METHODOLOGY

This research aimed to determine the influence of digital voice assistance on consumer purchase intention toward online shopping. The underlying study of this research study is the TAM. The constructs were identified from previously conducted research on the same concept. The approach which is adopted was quantitative in nature. Residents of Delhi-NCR who use DVAs for online shopping were the subject of this study and a questionnaire was floated among them.

5.3.1 HYPOTHESES

H1: Individual innovativeness has an influence on PEOU.

H2: Individual innovativeness has an influence on PU.

H3: Technological anxiety has an influence on PEOU.

H4: Technological anxiety has an influence on PU.

H5: Age has an influence on PU.

H6: Education has an influence on PU.

H7: Age has an influence on PEOU.

H8: Education has an influence on PEOU.

H9: PEOU has an influence on behavioral intention.

H10: PU has an influence on behavioral intention.

H11: Individual innovativeness has an influence on behavioral intention mediated through PEOU.

H12: Individual innovativeness has an influence on behavioral intention mediated through PU.

H13: Technological anxiety influences behavioral intention mediated through PU.

H14: Technological anxiety influences behavioral intention mediated through PU.

H15: Age has an influence on behavioral intention mediated through PU.

H16: Age has an influence on behavioral intention mediated through PEOU.

H17: Education has an influence on behavioral intention mediated through PU.

H18: Education has an influence on behavioral intention mediated through PEOU.

5.3.2 SAMPLE SIZE AND POPULATION

We collected a total of 225 responses in the Delhi-NCR region. Out of the 225 responses, 200 respondents used DVAs for online shopping and the remaining 25 did not use DVAs for online shopping. Primary data was used to identify the variables of this study. The variables of the study were identified using exploratory research and descriptive research for data analysis using structural equation modeling (SEM).

5.3.3 RESEARCH INSTRUMENT

The study included a total of 225 participants, and a five-point Likert scale was employed for the survey. All questions in the questionnaire were measured with a 5-point Likert scale ranging from 1 (lowest) to 5 (highest). The questionnaire was divided into multiple sections. The first section focused on gathering socio-demographic information such as the respondent's name, age, and educational background. The questionnaire also included a qualifying question to categorize the data into two groups—respondents who use DVAs for online shopping and those who do not.

The questionnaire was divided into the following five sections:

1. Individual innovativeness was measured using four items taken from Kim et al. (2010), Lu (2014), Yang (2005), and Yi et al. (2006).
2. Technological anxiety was measured using five items adapted from Davis (1989).
3. PEOU was measured using nine items adapted from Davis (1989).
4. PU was measured using seven items adapted from Davis (1989).
5. Behavioral intention was measured using three items adapted from Filieri and McLeay (2018) and Hosany and Witham (2010).

5.3.4 DATA COLLECTION

In this study, purposive and convenience sampling was used to gather data from participants. The primary method used for data collection in this study was an online questionnaire. The questionnaire was created using Google Forms and was distributed among private, deemed-to-be universities of Delhi-NCR, especially among participants who are most likely to use these DVAs. In addition to that, the survey was shared on social media platforms such as WhatsApp and Instagram through personal chats and direct messages.

5.4 DATA ANALYSIS

SEM is a statistical method that allows researchers to test complex relationships between variables in a model. It is a versatile and powerful tool that can be used to test hypotheses about relationships among variables, as well as to explore the underlying structure of a data set. SEM was done to check whether the relationship described between the variables in the underlying theory holds good for the current study too.

The SEM analysis provides information on the goodness of fit of the model, which is a statistical technique that examines the relationships between multiple variables. The chi-square statistic (CMIN) is an important indicator of model fit, and in this case, it has a value of 7.788 with 4 degrees of freedom, suggesting that the model does not fit the data well. However, this statistic can be sensitive to sample size, and the model may still be a good fit with a large sample size.

TABLE 5.1 Fitness Indicators.

Fitness Indicators	Extracted values	Threshold limit
CMIN	7.788	
DF	4	
Sig	0.000	< 0.05
CMIN/DF	1.947	< 5.0
Standardized RMR	0.048	< 0.06
Goodness of fit index (GFI)	0.989	> 0.9
Adjusted goodness of fit index (AGFI)	0.924	> 0.9
Normed fit index (NFI)	0.983	> 0.9
Comparative fit index (CFI)	0.992	> 0.9
RMSEA	0.069	< 0.06

The standardized root mean squared residual (standardized RMR), which has a low value of 0.048 and indicates a strong fit, is one of the other measures of model fit. The adjusted goodness of fit index (AGFI) has a value of 0.924, showing that the model fits the data well, while the goodness of fit index (GFI) has a value of 0.989, indicating an excellent fit. In comparison to a baseline model with no correlations between the variables, the model appears to fit well, according to both the normed fit index (NFI), and comparative fit index (CFI). Finally, a low value of 0.069 for the root mean square error of approximation (RMSEA) indicates a satisfactory fit.

Overall, while the chi-square statistic suggests some discrepancies between the model and data, other indicators such as the standardized RMR, GFI, AGFI, NFI, CFI, and RMSEA suggest that the model is a good fit. Therefore, the information obtained from the SEM model suggests that the model fits the data reasonably well.

H1: Individual innovativeness has an influence on PEOU

This research hypothesis suggests that there is a significant relationship between individual innovativeness and PEOU. A low significance level of .000 indicates that the observed relationship is unlikely to be due to chance. The results provide strong evidence to support the hypothesis that individual innovativeness has an influence on PEOU. Further research could explore potential mediators or moderators of this relationship.

TABLE 5.2 Direct Effects.

			Estimate	S.E.	C.R.	P-Value
IN	→	PEU	.209	.052	3.400	***
IN	→	PU	.269	.055	4.667	***
TA	→	PEU	.496	.056	8.077	***
TA	→	PU	.495	.060	8.590	***
Age	→	PU	.019	.009	.322	.747
Education	→	PU	.100	.055	1.704	.088
Age	→	PEU	-.049	.009	-.778	.436
Education	→	PEU	.029	.051	.462	.644
PEU	→	BI	.150	.072	2.774	.006
PU	→	BI	.644	.063	11.951	***

H2: Individual innovativeness has an influence on PU

This research analysis examines whether there is a significant relationship between individual innovativeness and PU, with a significance level of .000 indicating a low chance of chance. The hypothesis suggests that there may be a positive relationship between innovativeness and PU, and the results provide strong evidence to support this hypothesis.

H3: Technological anxiety has an influence on PEOU

The research analysis tests the hypothesis that technological anxiety has an influence on PEOU, with a significance level of .000 indicating a low probability of chance influencing the results. The hypothesis suggests that individuals with higher levels of technological anxiety may find new technologies more difficult to use. The results provide strong evidence to support the hypothesis, indicating that strategies to reduce technological anxiety may improve the PEOU and increase adoption rates.

H4: Technological anxiety has an influence on PU

The significance level (P) is set at .000, indicating a very low probability of a chance relationship. The hypothesis proposes that there may be a relationship between technological anxiety and PU. The significance level of .000 suggests strong evidence to support this hypothesis.

H5: Age has an influence on PU

This research tests the null hypothesis that age has no influence on PU, with a significance level (P) of .747, indicating a high probability of a chance relationship. The hypothesis suggests that technology's benefits may be perceived similarly across age groups, and no significant relationship exists between age and PU. The high significance level indicates no evidence to reject the null hypothesis, suggesting that age has no significant impact on PU.

H6: Education has an influence on PU

This research tests the hypothesis that education has no effect on PU, with a significance level (P) set at .088, indicating a relatively low probability of obtaining the observed relationship by chance alone. The hypothesis suggests that there may be no relationship between education level and PU. While the significance level of .088 indicates some evidence that education may have a small influence on PU, it is not strong enough to reject the null hypothesis, suggesting that education has no significant impact on PU.

H7: Age has an influence on PEOU

This research tests the hypothesis that education has no effect on PU, with a significance level (P) set at .088, indicating a relatively low probability of obtaining the observed relationship by chance alone. The hypothesis suggests that there may be no relationship between education level and PU. While the significance level of .088 indicates some evidence that education may have a small influence on PU, it is not strong enough to reject the null hypothesis, suggesting that education has no significant impact on PU.

H8: Education has an influence on PEOU

The research analysis tests the hypothesis that education has no influence on PEOU, with a significance level of .644 indicating a relatively high probability of obtaining the observed relationship by chance alone. The hypothesis suggests that the ease of use of technology may be perceived equally across different levels of education. The analysis finds no significant evidence to reject the null hypothesis, indicating that education has no significant influence on PEOU.

H9: PEOU has an influence on behavioral intention

This research analysis tests the hypothesis that PEOU has an influence on behavioral intention. The very low significance level of .006 indicates strong evidence to reject the null hypothesis, suggesting that PEOU does have a significant influence on behavioral intention.

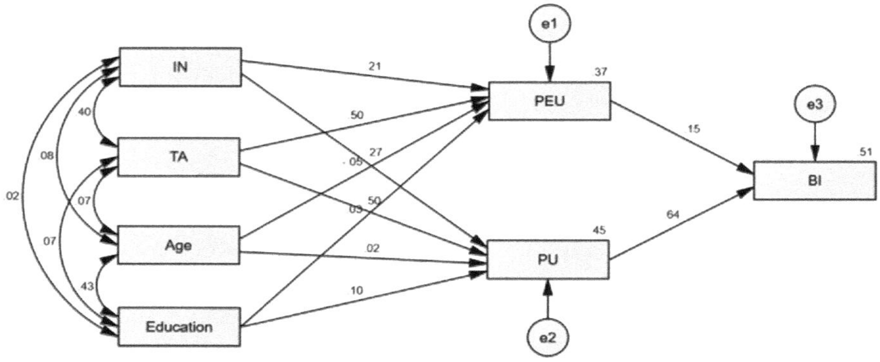

FIGURE 5.1 Structural model.

H10: PU has an influence on behavioral intention

This research tests the hypothesis that PU has an influence on behavioral intention. The hypothesis suggests that an individual's intention to use technology may be influenced by their perception of how useful it is. The significance level for this hypothesis is set at .000, indicating a strong suggestion to reject the null hypothesis and suggesting that PU has a significant influence on behavioral intention.

H11: Individual innovativeness has an influence on behavioral intention mediated through PEOU

The significance level is set at 0.023, indicating a weak relationship between individual innovativeness, PEOU, and behavioral intention. These findings suggest that individual innovativeness may not be a significant factor when designing and marketing technology.

H12: Individual innovativeness has an influence on behavioral intention mediated through PU

The result suggests that there is a statistically significant relationship between individual innovativeness, PU, and behavioral intention, with a P value of 0.001. This means that the observed relationship is unlikely to have occurred by chance alone, providing strong evidence to reject the null hypothesis. The findings indicate that individual innovativeness influences behavioral intention indirectly through PU. In other words, individuals who perceive technology as users are more likely to have the intention to use it, and this relationship is partially mediated by their level of innovativeness.

TABLE 5.3 Direct Effects.

Indirect path	Unstandardized estimate	Lower	Upper	P-Value	Standardized estimate
IN –> PEU –> BI	0.035	0.008	0.083	0.023	0.031*
IN –> PU –> BI	0.195	0.103	0.305	0.001	0.173***
TA –> PEU –> BI	0.091	0.020	0.181	0.028	0.074*
TA –> PU –> BI	0.392	0.288	0.509	0.001	0.319**
Age –> PU –> BI	0.002	–0.010	0.014	0.696	0.012
Age –> PEU –> BI	–0.001	–0.007	0.000	0.146	–0.007
Education –> PU –> BI	0.071	0.003	0.151	0.086	0.064†
Education –> PEU –> BI	0.005	–0.010	0.032	0.525	0.004

H13: Technological anxiety influences behavioral intention mediated through PEOU

According to the statistics, it seems that behavioral intention, PEOU, and technological anxiety are all related. The P value for the hypothesis is 0.028, which is less significant than the 0.05 threshold for normal significance. This indicates that the variables are significantly related to one another. The results imply that there is a causal relationship between behavioral purpose and PEOU, which in turn influences technological fear. This implies that those with high levels of technological anxiety can find it challenging to use a particular device. They may be less likely to use it as a result.

H14: Technological anxiety influences behavioral intention mediated through PU

The P value for this hypothesis is 0.001, which is a very low probability, indicating strong evidence to reject the null hypothesis. This result suggests that there is a significant relationship between technological anxiety and users' behavioral intention to use technology and that this relationship is mediated by how useful they perceive the technology to be. In other words, users who experience technological anxiety may be less likely to intend to use technology, but this effect can be mitigated if they perceive the technology to be useful.

H15: Age influences behavioral intention mediated through PU

There is no statistically significant relationship between age and PU on behavioral intention. The P value of 0.696 is greater than the commonly used threshold of 0.05, indicating that the observed relationship is likely due to chance and is not statistically significant. Therefore, we cannot conclude that age is a significant predictor of PU and behavioral intention.

H16: Age influences behavioral intention mediated through PEOU

The P value of 0.146 suggests that there is no statistically significant relationship between age, PEOU, and behavioral intention to use technology. In other words, age is not a significant predictor of how easy an individual perceives technology to be to use, and this perception does not significantly influence their intention to use technology.

H17: Education influences behavioral intention mediated through PU

The significance level (P) for this hypothesis is 0.086, which is higher than the conventional level of 0.05, indicating that the observed relationship may be due to chance. In other words, the results are not statistically significant enough to reject the null hypothesis. The analysis suggests that there is insufficient evidence to support the idea that education influences behavioral intention to use a technology mediated through PU.

H18: Education influences behavioral intention mediated through PEOU

The P value of 0.525 for the relationship between education, PEOU, and behavioral intention suggests that there is no statistically significant relationship between these variables. This means that education level may not have a significant impact on an individual's perception of the ease of use of technology, and in turn, may not strongly influence their intention to use it.

5.5 DISCUSSION AND CONCLUSION

The research paper examines several hypotheses and concludes that there are significant connections between an individual's innovativeness, technological anxiety, PEOU, PU, and willingness to use technology.

According to the research analysis, individual innovativeness has a significant impact on how people perceive the ease of use and usefulness of technology. This means that those who are more innovative tend to find technology more comfortable to use and more helpful. These findings are important for businesses and marketers who want to target potential customers. Based on the results, companies should focus on attracting innovative individuals as they are more likely to find technology-based products and services easier to use and more valuable.

Apart from this, we observe that individual innovativeness influences behavioral intention mediated through PEOU and PU, respectively. The findings of the study suggest that there is a weak to moderate relationship between individual innovativeness, PEOU, PU, and behavioral intention. The results indicate that more innovative people tend to perceive technology as easier to use and more useful, and therefore, they are more likely to adopt it. Companies and marketers can target more innovative consumers with products that are perceived to be easy to use and useful, which may lead to higher adoption rates.

Another factor, technological anxiety influences PEOU and PU, respectively. People who experience higher levels of technological anxiety may find technology less comfortable to use and less useful. This suggests that designers and developers of technology should consider the emotional and psychological factors that affect users' perception of technology when designing new products. It is important to create products that are easy to use and that reduce users' anxiety levels, especially for those who are less comfortable with technology.

This study examines how technological anxiety affects behavioral intention through PEOU and PU. The results indicate that individuals with higher levels of technological anxiety may be less inclined to adopt technology, even if they consider it simple to use and beneficial. Technology providers may need to focus on designing and providing user-friendly and easily understandable interfaces to reduce anxiety and increase comfort in technology usage.

Demographic factors such as age and education, respectively, have no influence on PU. This implies that technology designers and marketers should focus on creating and promoting technology that is easy to use and provides clear benefits, rather than targeting specific age or education demographics. Age and education, respectively, also had no influence on PEOU. This suggests that age may not be a significant factor in determining PEOU, but education may have a slight influence. Individuals with higher levels of education may find technology easier to use and may require less training or assistance compared to those with lower levels of education.

In this study, the impact of age and education on behavioral intention was examined, with a focus on how PU and PEOU mediate this relationship. The results indicate that age and education may not have a significant effect on determining behavioral intention. In other words, people of any age or educational level are more likely to adopt technology if they perceive it as easy to use and useful. Therefore, it is important for technology companies to focus on developing products that are user-friendly and meet the needs of consumers, rather than targeting specific age or educational groups.

Lastly, we studied the influence of PEOU and PU, respectively, on behavioral intention to use technology. The findings suggest that people who find technology easier to use and more users are more likely to adopt it. This implies that if technology developers can design products that are easy to use and provide clear benefits to users, then users are more likely to adopt and use the technology.

The findings suggest that individual innovativeness, technological anxiety, PEOU, PU, and behavioral intention are interrelated and play a significant role in determining technology adoption and usage behavior. The results have important implications for businesses and organizations that develop and market technology products and services. The findings suggest that companies should focus on designing technology products and services that are easy to use and address user concerns related to technological anxiety. Additionally, the results suggest that companies should target innovators and early adopters who are more likely to adopt new technology.

5.5.1 LIMITATIONS

The study had a small sample size of 225 participants and was only conducted in Delhi-NCR, which may limit its relevance to larger populations or other regions. The study also relied on self-reported data, which can be biased. Participants in a study may report higher levels of ease of use, usefulness, and intention to use technology than they would in real-life situations. However, the study did not take into account other important factors that could affect online shopping behavior, such as trust, security, and privacy concerns. Considering these variables could provide a more complete understanding of consumer behavior toward online shopping.

KEYWORDS

- **digital voice assistants**
- **consumer purchase intention**
- **perceived ease of use**
- **perceived usefulness**
- **technological anxiety**
- **individual innovativeness**

REFERENCES

Davis, F. D. Perceived Usefulness, Perceived Ease of Use, and User Acceptance of Information Technology. *MIS Quart.* **1989,** *13* (3), 319–340.

Dellaert, B. G. C.; Shu, S. B.; Arentze, T. A.; Baker, T.; Diehl, K.; Donkers, B.; Fast, N. J.; Häubl, G.; Johnson, H.; Karmarkar, U. R.; Oppewal, H.; Schmitt, B. H.; Schroeder, J.; Spiller, S. A.; Steffel, M. Consumer Decisions with Artificially Intelligent Voice Assistants. *J. Mark.* **2020,** *84* (4).

Farahbakhsh, M.; Rijsdijk, S. A.; Boënne, M. J. The Influence of Individual Consumer Characteristics on the Acceptance of Digital Assistants: A Grocery Shopping Examination. *J. Retail. Consum. Serv.* **2021,** *63*, 102731.

Grewal, D.; Noble, S. M.; Roggeveen, A. L.; Nordfalt, J. The Future of In-Store Technology. *J. Acad. Mark. Sci.* **2019,** *47* (4), 595–616.

Hansen, T.; Cumberland, F.; Solgaard, H. S. Determinants of Consumers' Adoption of Online Grocery Shopping. In *E - European Advances in Consumer Research*; Ekstrom, K. M.; Brembeck, H., Eds.; Association for Consumer Research: Goteborg, Sweden, 2005; pp 276–277.

Kaiser, C.; Schallner, R. In *The Impact of Emotional Voice Assistants on Consumers' Shopping Attitude and Behavior*, Wirtschaftsinformatik 2022 Proceedings, 2022; vol *10*.

Li, N.; Zhang, P. In *Consumer Online Shopping Attitudes and Behavior: An Assessment of Research*, AMCIS 2002 Proceedings, 2002; vol *74*.

Liu, Y.; Gan, Y.; Song, Y.; Liu, J. What Influences the Perceived Trust of a Voice-Enabled Smart Home System: An Empirical Study. *Sensors* **2021**.

Lixăndroiu, R.; Cazan, A. M.; Maican, C. I. An Analysis of the Impact of Personality Traits towards Augmented Reality in Online Shopping. *Symmetry* **2021,** *13*, 416.

Mari, A. In *Voice Commerce: Understanding Shopping-Related Voice Assistants and their Effect on Brands*, IMMAA Annual Conference, Northwestern University in Qatar, Doha, Oct 4–6, 2019; IMMAA, 2019.

Mari, A.; Algesheimer, R. The Role of Trusting Beliefs in Voice Assistants during Voice Shopping. *J. Interact. Mark.* **2021,** *55*, 68–82.

Mohanty, S.; Paul, I.; Bond, S. Alexa, I Want to Do Good: The Role of Voice Assistants in Encouraging Greater Prosocial Behavior. In *NA - Advances in Consumer Research*; Bradford, T. W., Keinan, A., Thomson, M. M. Eds.; Association for Consumer Research: Duluth, MN, 2021; vol *49*, pp 430–430.

Moriuchi, E. Okay, Google! An Empirical Study on Voice Assistants on Consumer Engagement and Loyalty. *J. Retail. Consum. Serv.* **2020,** *54*, 102020.

Muthukumaran, A. P. K.; Vani, H. Optimizing the Usage of Voice Assistants for Shopping. *Indian J. Sci. Technol.* **2020,** *13* (43), 4407–4416.

Park, E.; Cho, Y.; Han, J.; Kwon, S. J. Comprehensive Approaches to User Acceptance of Internet of Things in a Smart Home Environment. *IEEE Access* **2017,** *5*, 15859–15867.

Poushneh, A. Humanizing Voice Assistant: The Impact of Voice Assistant Personality on Consumers' Attitudes and Behaviors. California State University-Bakersfield, School of Business and Public Administration, Management and Marketing Department, USA, n.d.

Reinkemeier, F.; Gnewuch, U.; Toporowski, W. Can Humanizing Voice Assistants Unleash the Potential of Voice Commerce? *J. Bus. Res.* **2020,** *109*, 338–347.

Schultz, C. D.; Brüggemann, P. In *Acceptance of Digital Voice Assistants for Grocery Shopping*, Proceedings of the European Marketing Academy, 50th, (94494), 2021.

Son, Y.; Oh, W. "Alexa, Buy Me a Movie!": How AI Speakers Reshape Digital Content Consumption and Preference. *J. Promot. Manag.* **2019,** *25* (5), 707–722.

Sun, C.; Shi, Z. (J.); Liu, X.; Ghose, A.; Li, X.; Xiong, F. The Effect of Voice AI on Digital Commerce. *J. Mark.* **2021,** *85* (4), 1–19.

Tassiello, V.; Tillotson, J. S.; Rome, A. S. "Alexa, Order Me A Pizza!": The Mediating Role of Psychological Power in the Consumer–Voice Assistant Interaction. *J. Bus. Res.* **2020,** *113*, 339–349.

Venkatesh, V.; Speier-Pero, C.; Schuetz, S.W. "Why Do People Shop Online? A Comprehensive Framework of Consumers' Online Shopping Intentions and Behaviors," Information Technology & People, 2022, Forthcoming.

Yildiz, O.; Kitapçi, H. Exploring Factors Affecting Consumers' Adoption of Shopping via Mobile Applications in Turkey. *J. Int. Trade Logist. Law* **2019,** *5* (1), 19–35.

Ylilehto, M.; Komulainen, H.; Ulkuniemi, P. The Critical Factors Shaping Customer Shopping Experiences with Innovative Technologies. Department of Marketing, University of Oulu, Oulu, Finland, 2019.

Ysabelle, R.; Andrea, O. C. The Use of Personal Voice Assistants in the Context of Retail Digitalization: An Empirical Study of Consumers' Attitude and Privacy Concerns. Louvain School of Management, Université catholique de Louvain; Prom.: de Moerloose, Chantal, 2018.

Zhou, L.; Dai, L.; Zhang, D. Online Shopping Acceptance Model—A Critical Survey of Consumer Factors in Online Shopping. *J. Electron. Comm. Res.* **2007**.

CHAPTER 6

Farmers' Perception of the Ecologically Intensive Farming: Evidence from Bangladesh

SADIA ISLAM

Department of Environmental and Resource Economics, Dhaka School of Economics, Dhaka, Bangladesh

ABSTRACT

The main attempt of this study was to learn about farmer's considerations toward organic farming and to identify the factors that can play an important role in selecting organic farming instead of conventional farming. This research focuses on the case of Bangladesh. A sample survey has been conducted for the study. The geographic areas for data collection were selected by exploiting a multistage random sampling procedure. The survey covers all of the eight divisions of Bangladesh. Among the total 440 mixed crop farming farmers sample respondents, only 269, or 61.14%, agreed to select organic farming, but 171, or 38.86%, respondents did not agree to select organic farming. The results of the study have shown that the socioeconomic characteristics were significantly connected with the consent to select organic farming decisions. Moreover, this study also reported that the farmers' idea consciousness and perceptions related to organic farming were significantly associated with the decision to select organic farming. Therefore, these factors should be taken into consideration when formulating policy to relate to organic or ecologically intensive farming in Bangladesh.

Agile Business Transformations: Priorities, Lessons, and Practices. Satyajit Chakrabarti, Subrata Chattopadhyay, Udit Chawla, Sundeep Singh Sondhi, & Arunava Dalal (Eds.)

6.1 INTRODUCTION

Agricultural growth is extremely important for poverty alleviation, food security, and economic growth. To meet the increasing food demands of the growing population, agricultural growth is very essential. By 2050, the world's population will be nine billion and to feed them, the world needs to increase food production by 70% (Barkhan and Newell, 2015). However, the unplanned growth of the agriculture sector is creating a catastrophe for the environment and resources (Verger and Boobis, 2013). One-fifth of all greenhouse gas is emitted by the agricultural sector and 68% of the global freshwater is consumed by this sector (UNDP, 2019). Moreover, this sector is highly responsible for changes in climate variability. Therefore, to ensure the responsible use of resources and a balanced agriculture system, it is essential to change our existing production pattern. Considering these issues, it is high time the world needs to promote sustainable agriculture practices. Sustainable agriculture invokes the production of healthy foods without ignoring the ability of future generations to do the same and it also ensures the effective use of a farm's inner resources (Pretty, 1995). Furthermore, agricultural sustainability demands ecological balance, social admissibility, and economic accuracy (Yunlong and Smith, 1994).

Nowadays, organic farming or ecologically intensive farming is considered one of the most effective measures to ensure sustainable agriculture (Eyhorn et al., 2019). Organic farming is an agricultural process that invokes an environmentally, socially, and economically balanced production system (Singh, 2004). If we compare organic farming with the conventional inorganic farming system, then we will find that conventional inorganic farms have higher yields than the ecological intensive farmland, thus conventional inorganic farms are more profitable (Seufert et al., 2012). But these inorganic farming practices are mainly responsible for topsoil depletion, excessive use of fertilizers, ground, and surface water contamination; production of lower nutritional level foods, and use of excessive pesticides, and all of these things create an adverse effect on the environment and human health (Garnett et al., 2013; Tilman et al., 2011).

Therefore, globally a special need has been created for organic farming to make the agriculture system eco-friendlier and more sustainable (Hansen, 1996). Organic farming provides not only eco-friendly production but also ensures nutritional foods with less use of pesticides and fertilizers (Kennedy et al., 2013; Reganold and Wachter, 2016). Moreover, this ecologically intensive farming system helps to maintain soil quality, yields, and biodiversity

(Pimetel et al., 2005). Thus, it can be claimed that, to achieve sustainable agriculture, promoting organic production is a must.

This research work focuses on the case of Bangladesh, a country which is mainly an agricultural country. There is no alternative for Bangladesh to improve its economic enhancement and food security by expanding its agricultural sectors. So, it is essential to expand an environment-friendly agricultural system to achieve long-term food security in the country. Moreover, farmers are the heart of the agricultural sector and their knowledge about organic farming is very important, related to long-term sustainable production in Bangladesh. Farmers in developing countries such as Bangladesh, India, and Pakistan normally have very few ideas on the issues of ecologically intensive farming or organic farming (Houbraken et al., 2016). Therefore, the main objective of this study is to learn about the farmer's knowledge, consciousness, and perception toward organic farming and sustainable agricultural practices, and the socioeconomic factors connected with farmer's consent to select the organic farming related to the sustainable agricultural issues to help formulate a long-term policy for sustainable agriculture in Bangladesh.

6.2 LITERATURE REVIEW

Bangladesh is an intensive agricultural country that covers roughly 9.1 million hectares. Nearly 70% of the country's land area has been used as agricultural land and the GDP contribution from agriculture was 13.3% in 2018–2019 (BBS, 2020). Almost 87% of the rural peoples' income is related to agricultural activities (World Bank, 2016). Furthermore, approximately 99% of the agricultural lands are small scale, which means farms with very few assets and operating in less than two hectares of cropland (BBS, 2016). Bangladesh is a densely populated country. Due to high population growth, an increased demand for land has been created for the purpose of nonagricultural uses such as houses, roads, industries, and other man-made activities (Rahman and Thapa, 1999). Due to this scarcity of land, farmers were encouraged to increase food production by intensifying the use of land, chemical fertilizers, and pesticides (Hossain, 1988). However, this production-intensive agricultural practice is responsible for creating adverse effects on human health and the environment (Hossain and Kashem, 1997).

According to the ILO (2010), agriculture is one of the most dangerous occupations in the world because every year a huge number of agricultural workers are affected by different diseases such as respiratory diseases, hearing problems, different types of cancers (stomach, colon, lung, and skin), chemical toxicity, and heat-related health problems (Paenez and Shahriar, 2018). Moreover, there are different evidences showing that there is high connectivity between agricultural practice and environmental degradation (Sarkar et al., 2012; Travisi et al., 2006; Ahmed et al., 2002). Considering the health and environmental risks of the recent unbalanced conventional inorganic agricultural practices, different initiatives have been already taken by the government, NGOs, and international organizations to improve the behavior of the farmers. But the results come from those interventions are not satisfactory (Dasgupta et al., 2005; Stadlinger et al., 2013) However, farmers' attitudes can be affected by various factors such as level of knowledge or idea (Yang et al., 2014), perceptions (Ahmed et al., 2011; Hashemi and Damalas, 2011; Mohanty et al., 2013; Khan et al., 2015), socioeconomic variables such as gender (Atreya, 2007) and age (Ahmed et al., 2011). Therefore, understanding a farmer's knowledge and perception toward organic farming and the socio-economic factors associated with a farmer's willingness to select organic farming related to sustainable agriculture issues is thus critical to the formulation and implementation of public policies.

6.3 METHODS

This study looks at the consciousness of the rural farmers of Bangladesh toward ecologically intensive farming and their willingness to choose an organic farming system. This work is mainly based on primary data.

A sample survey has been conducted for the study. The geographic areas for data collection were selected by using a multistage random sampling procedure. The survey covers all of the eight divisions of Bangladesh. Among these eight divisions, we have collected data from 16 districts. The households were selected randomly from the villages of different upazillas and districts with the consultations of the Department of Agricultural Extension (DAE), Bangladesh. We have picked the farmers with the help of the information obtained from the Sub-Assistant Agricultural Extension Officer (SAAO) of DAE. A total of 440 active farmers have been surveyed from 16 districts. The farmers were above 18 years old and all of them were the head of the farmland.

The primary data were collected via face-to-face interviews. The time period of the data collection was from November 2022 to March 2023. The survey questionnaire was of three parts. Different socioeconomic variables (age, gender, education, income, and land ownership pattern) were collected in the initial part of the questionnaire. The middle part of the questionnaire asked about the farmers' knowledge, consciousness, and perceptions about organic farming. The ultimate part of the survey questionnaire illustrates a short description of the importance of organic farming. Then, the farmers were asked about his or her decision to choose ecologically intensive farming/ organic farming to promote sustainable agriculture. In the end, the respondents who refused to switch to the organic farming system were surveyed on the reason why they didn't want to choose ecologically intensive farming/ organic farming.

TABLE 6.1 List of Selected Geographic Areas and Respondents for the Study.

Division	District	Upazila	Number of farmers interviewed
Dhaka	Dhaka	Keranigang	30
	Narsigndi	Monahardi	35
Chattogram	Chattrogram	Boalkhali	25
	Brahmonbaria	Nasirnagar	30
Barishal	Patuakhli	Dumki	30
	Bhola	Charfassion	35
Khulna	Khushtia	Daulatpur	20
	Jeshore	Chaudhasa	15
Mymensing	Mymensing	Fulbari	20
	Sherpur	Sherpur Sadar	25
Rajshahi	Rajshahi	Mohanpur	40
	Joypurhat	Joypurhat Sadar	45
Rangpur	Nilfhamari	Sayedpur	30
	Lalmonirhat	Lalmonirhat Sadar	15
Sylhet	Mouluvibazar	Sreemongal	20
	Sunamganj	Sunamganj Sadar	25

Source: Compiled by the author.

This study used descriptive statistical methods for inferences. This study used the chi-square test to find out the relationship between the categorical variables. It can be argued that finding out the association between categorical variable chi-square tests is one of the most common and well-accepted methods.

Agree to select (ATS) organic farming was considered as the dependent variable. A total of eight independent variables—gender, age, land ownership, education, income, idea, consciousness, and perception were used to find out the factors associated with the farmers' consent to select organic farming for formulating policy inputs in Bangladesh.

6.4 RESULTS AND DISCUSSION

This work tries to analyze how the socio-economic factors and farmers' knowledge, consciousness, and perceptions are related to the farmer's agreement to select the organic farming production system. Among the total 440 sample respondents, only 269, or 61.14%, agreed to select organic farming, but 171, or 38.86%, respondents did not agree to select organic farming.

Table 6.2 first presents the gender variation of the sample farmers from the total sample of 440 out of which 378, or 85.90%, of the respondents were male and the remaining 62, or 14.09%, were female respondents. The *P* value of the chi-square test shows that there is no significant relationship between the categorical variable genders of the farmers and agree to select organic farming. This showed that gender difference is not an influential factor in choosing organic farming decisions.

Table 6.2 presents the association between the independent variables and a dependent variable ATS. It presents the age of the farmers as a socioeconomic independent variable. The average age of the farmer was estimated to be 44 Years with a maximum of 70 and a minimum of 18 years. There is a statistically significant relationship found between agreeing to select an organic farming process and the age of the farmers. It is found that younger farmers are more interested in selecting the organic farming process rather than older farmers. Maybe older farmers don't want to change their traditional patterns of farming. Therefore, it can be argued that age difference is an important variable in the decision-making related to organic farming.

Socioeconomic variable land ownership was divided into three categories for this survey—own land, shared land, and rented land. Among the 440 sample households, 131, or 29.77%, respondents had their own land and from these 131 respondents 115 were found they be interested in organic farming and only 16 did not agree to select organic farming. Out of 125, or 28.40%, respondents who have shared the land among them, 80 respondents agreed to select organic farming and 45 were not ready. Moreover, 185, or 42.04%, percent respondents were from rented land. It was observed from these 185 respondents only 74 were found that they are interested in organic farming and the remaining 111 were not agreed to select organic farming.

TABLE 6.2 Description of the Variables and the Results.

	Description of the variables	Percentage	P value ($\chi 2$ from test)	Comments
Dependent variable	Agree to select the organic/ ecologically intensive farming **(ATS)**			Out of 440 sample respondents, 61.14% agreed to select the organic farming process whereas the remaining 38.86% rejected to select organic farming system.
	Yes	61.14		
	No	38.86		
Independent variable	Sex of the respondent **(Sex)**[a]		.602	Association between the dependent variable ATS and independent variable sex is not statistically significant.
	Male	85.90		
	Female	14.09		
	Age of the respondent **(Age)**[b]		.000	A statistically significant statistical relationship exists between the dependent variable ATS and age.
	Land ownership pattern of the farmer **(Land ownership)**[a]		.000	A statistically significant relationship exists between the dependent variable ATS and land ownership.
	Owned land	29.77		
	Shared land	28.40		
	Ranted land	42.04		
	Farmer's education level **(Education)**[a]		.000	Association between the dependent variable ATS and independent variable education is statistically significant.
	Elementary education	23.41		
	Primary education	16.36		
	Secondary education	60.23		
	Monthly income of the family from all sources **(Income)**[a]		.000	A statistically significant relationship ATS and income.
	Low income (below $200)	25.00		
	Medium income (above $200–$400)	58.64		

TABLE 6.2 *(Continued)*

Description of the variables	Percentage	P value ($\chi 2$ from test)	Comments
High income (above $400)	16.36		
Have knowledge about organic farming system **(Knowledge)**[a]		.000	Association between the dependent variable ATS and independent variable knowledge is statistically significant.
Yes	83.2		
No	16.8		
Consider current Agricultural production pattern is not sustainable in the Bangladesh **(Consciousness)**[a]		.000	Association between the dependent variable ATS and independent variable consciousness is statistically significant.
Yes	70.1		
No	29.9		
Consider farmers can play important role for ensuring organic farming **(Perception)**[a]		.000	Statistically significant relationship exists between the categorical dependent variable ATS and independent variable perception.
Yes	64.09		
No	35.90		

[a]*Stands for categorical variable.*

[b]*Stands for continuous variable.*

Source: Compiled by the author from the primary survey.

Therefore, from the different types of land ownership patterns, it can be claimed from the survey that 87.78% of farmers who own land agreed to select organic farming whereas only 12.22% of respondents were rejected to select organic farming. On the other hand, 60.0% of farmers who have rented land disagreed with selecting organic farming. It can be claimed that maybe farmers, those who have their land feel more secure than the others to switch from their traditional production system. However, from the *P* value it is found that there is a significant association between land ownership pattern and the farmer's consent to select organic farming.

Farmers' education level was surveyed for this study to learn about the association between the education level and agree to select organic farming. The education level was segregated into three categories—elementary education (only literacy), primary education (from class one to five), and secondary education (above class five).

Among the respondents, 103, or 23.41%, completed only elementary education and from these respondents, only 30 farmers, or 29.13%, respondents were agreed to choose organic farming and the rest of the 73 farmers, or 70.87%, respondents were not interested to select organic farming. A total of 72, or 16.36 respondents had completed primary education among this group 36, or 50.00%, respondents agreed to choose an organic production system, on the other hand, 36, or 50.00%, respondents were not showing their interest in organic farming. Of the entire 440 sample respondents, only 265, or 60.23%, farmers have completed their secondary education. Among these secondary educated farmers, 179, or 67.55%, farmers agreed to select organic farming whereas only 86, or 32.45%, farmers were not interested in choosing the organic farming production system. From the survey, it is found that education is a very effective variable for farmers' decision-making related to organic farming. The result of the *P* value also indicates that there is a positive association between categorical variable education and agreement to select an organic farming system.

For this survey, income was divided into three categories—low income (below $200), medium income ($201–$400), and high income (above $400). From the survey, we find that out of 440 sample respondents, 110, or 25%, belonged to the low-income group, 258, or 58.64%, were in the medium-income group and only 72, or 16.36%, were in the high-income group. From these three groups, it is found that low-income respondents were not interested in selecting an organic farming system; only 20, or 18.188%, on the other hand, medium-income and high-income respondents showed great interest in organic farming; 185, or 71.76%, and 64, or 88.88%, farmers were ready to select organic farming process, respectively. So, from this survey, it can be claimed that income is an influential factor for decision-making related to organic farming. The result of the *P* value also indicates that there is an association between categorical variable income and agreement to select an organic farming system.

Furthermore, to learn about farmers' knowledge and perception toward organic farming for ensuring a sustainable agricultural system, there were three independent variables were used for this survey. These are farmer's knowledge about the organic farming system (Knowledge), considering the current agricultural production system is not sustainable (Consciousness), considering farmers can play an important role in ensuring organic farming (Perception).

Among the 440 sample respondents, 83.20% respondents mentioned that they have an idea about organic farming/ecologically intensive farming and only 16.80% of respondents said they didn't have any knowledge about organic farming/ecologically intensive farming. The result shows that there was a significant association between the variables knowledge and willingness to select the organic farming process. That means farmers who have knowledge about organic farming; they are more interested rather than those who don't have any idea.

Moreover, 330, or 70.1%, sample farmers considered that the current agricultural production system is not sustainable and only 110, or 29.9%, were not in the same thinking. Some respondents considered the current agricultural production system not sustainable' among them, 235, or 71.21%, mentioned that they were willing to select an organic farming system and only 95, or 28.78%, farmers were not interested in organic farming. Thus, from the findings of the data it can be claimed that the respondents who are more conscious about sustainable farming are more interested in choosing organic farming than the others. From the results of the *P* value, it is found that there is a statistically significant relationship between agreement to select organic farming and the farmers' consciousness related to the production pattern.

However, 282, or 64.09%, respondents mentioned that farmers can play an important role in implementing the organic farming system. Among these 282 farmers, 211, or 74.82%, respondents agreed to select an organic farming system and only 71, or 25.18%, did not agree. The result of the *P* value also shows that there is a significant association between the selection of the organic farming decision and the perception of the farmer can play an important role. Therefore, from the findings of the data it can be claimed that farmers' perceptions are highly important for deciding organic farming.

TABLE 6.3 Reason for Not Ready to Choose Organic Farming.

Reason for not ready to choose organic farming	Freq.	Percentage
Conventional agricultural system is more profitable	75	43.86
Lack of strong marketing linkage	37	21.64
Customer demand for organic food is not mentionable in the domestic market	50	29.24
Any other reason	09	5.26
Total	171	100

Source: Compiled from the primary survey.

Table 6.3 presents the reasons mentioned by the sample respondents who did not agree to select organic farming. According to the 171 sample respondents who are not ready for sustainable consumption, about 75, or 43.86%, and 37, or 21.64%, of the households were not ready to choose because they mentioned that the conventional agricultural system is more profitable and lack of strong marketing linkage relatively. Whereas, about 50, or 29.24%, respondents thought that customer demand for organic food is not mentionable in the domestic market, and the remaining 9, or 5.26%, were not agreed to select organic farming for any other reasons.

6.5 CONCLUSIONS

This study indicated that socioeconomic characteristics (age, land ownership, education, and income) were significantly associated with the decision of the farmers to select the organic farming process. Thus, if we want to promote organic farming system in Bangladesh than socioeconomic characteristics can play a great role and are essential to be considered for policy inputs. Furthermore, this study also found that farmer's knowledge, consciousness, and perception also can play important roles in their decision related to organic farming. If farmers have a proper idea about the benefits of ecologically intensive farming then they may become more interested in choosing organic farming. Therefore, to promote organic farming, the country needs to take some potential steps for increasing farmer's knowledge and consciousness related to sustainable agriculture.

Moreover, this study also tries to find out the reasons why don't some of the respondents want to choose the organic farming process. From the survey, it is found that some of the farmers claim that the conventional agricultural system is more profitable than organic farming. Furthermore, some farmers also mentioned that there is a lack of strong marketing demand and customer demand for organic farming in Bangladesh. Therefore, for an effective policy related to organic farming in Bangladesh, it is also important to consider these issues that have been mentioned by the farmers. At last, it can be expected that the findings from this study can serve as a policy input related to organic farming.

KEYWORDS

- **agriculture**
- **organic farming**
- **perception**
- **sustainable**
- **socioeconomic**

REFERENCES

Ahmed, N.; Islam, Z.; Hasan, M.; Kamal, N. Q. Effect of some Commonly used Insecticides on Yellow Stem Borer Egg Parasitoids in Bangladesh. *Bangladesh J. Entomol.* **2002,** *12* (1), 37–46.

Ahmed, N.; Englund, J. E.; Ahman, I.; Lieberg, M.; Johansson, E. Perception of Pesticide use by Farmers and Neighbors in Two Periurban Areas. *Sci. Total Environ.* **2011**, *412* (77), 77–86. 10.1016/j.scitotenv.2011.10.022

Atreya, K. Pesticide use Knowledge and Practices: A Gender Differences in Nepal. *Environ. Res.* **2007,** *104* (2), 305–311. DOI: 10.1016/j.envres.2007.01.001

Bangladesh Bureau of Statistics (BBS). Yearbook of Agricultural Statistics; Ministry of Planning, Government of Bangladesh, Dhaka, 2016.

Bangladesh Bureau of Statistics (BBS). *Gross* Domestic Product of Bangladesh at Current Prices, 2015–16 to 2018–19; Ministry of Planning, Government of Bangladesh, Dhaka, 2020.

Barkhan, P.; Newell, C. In 2050 there will be 9 Billion People on Earth. How Will We Feed Them?–Visualization. *The Guardian*, 2015. https://www.theguardian.com/environment/2015/oct/13/agriculture-farming-food-addiction-meat-harvest-hungry-world

Dasgupta, S.; Meisner, C.; Haq, M. Health Effects and Pesticide Perception as Determinants of Pesticide Use: Evidence from Bangladesh. *World Bank Policy Research Working Paper*, 3776, 2005.

https://papers.ssrn.com/sol3/papers.cfm?abstract_id=872759

Eyhorn, F.; Muller, A.; Reganold, J. P.; Frison, E.; Herren, H. R.; Luttikholt, L.; Mueller, A.; Sanders, J.; Scialabba, N.; Seufert, V.; Smith, P. Sustainability in Global Agriculture Driven by Organic Farming. *Nat. Sustain.* **2019,** *2*, 253–255. https://doi.org/10.1038/s41893-019-0266-6

Hansen, J. W. Is Agricultural Sustainability a Useful Concept? *Agric. Syst.* **1996,** *50* (2), 117–143. https://doi.org/10.1016/0308-521X(95)00011-S

Hashemi, S. M.; Damalas, C. A. Farmers' Perceptions of Pesticide Efficacy: Reflections on the Importance of Pest Management Practices Adoption. *J. Sustain. Agric.* **2011,** *35* (1), 69–85. https://doi.org/10.1080/10440046.2011.530511

Hossain, M. Nature and Impact of the Green Revolution in Bangladesh, International Food Policy Research Institute & Bangladesh Institute of Development Studies Joint Study; IFPRI, Washington, DC, 1988.

Hossain, S. M. A.; Kashem, M. A. Agronomic Management to Combat Declining Soil Fertility in Bangladesh. Paper Presented in the 6th Biennial Conference of the Bangladesh Society of Agronomy, 1997.

Houbraken, M.; Bauweraerts, I.; Fevery, D.; Van Labeke, M. C.; Spanoghe, P. Pesticide Knowledge and Practice Among Horticultural Workers in the Lâm Đồng Region, Vietnam: A Case Study of Chrysanthemum and Strawberries. *Sci. Total Environ.* **2016,** *550*, 1001–1109. http://hdl.handle.net/1854/LU-7173795

ILO (International Labour Organization). Code of Practice on Safety and Health in Agriculture. Meeting of Experts to Adopt a Code on Safety and Health in Agriculture, Geneva, Switzerland, 2010.

http://www.ilo.org/wcmsp5/groups/public/-dgreports/-dcomm/publ/documents/publication/wcms159457.pdf

Kennedy, C. M.; Lonsdorf, E.; Neel, M. C.; Williams, N. M.; Ricketts, T. H.; Winfree, R.; et al. A Global Quantitative Synthesis of Local and Landscape Effects on Wild Bee Pollinators in Agroecosystems. *Ecol. Lett.* **2013,** *16*, 584–599. https://doi.org/10.1111/ele.12082

Khan, M.; Mahmood, H. Z.; Damalas, C. A. Pesticide use and Risk Perceptions Among Farmers in the Cotton Belt of Punjab, Pakistan. *Crop Prot.* **2015,** *67*, 184–190.

http://dx.doi.org/10.1016%2Fj.cropro.2014.10.013

Mohanty, M. K.; Behera, B. K.; Jena, S. K.; Srikanth, S.; Mogane, C.; Samal, S.; Behera, A. Knowledge Attitude and Practice of Pesticide use Among Agricultural Workers in Puducherry, South India. *J. Forensic Legal Med.* **2013,** *20* (8), 1028–1031. https://doi.org/10.1016/j.jflm.2013.09.030

Paenez, S. M.; Shahriar, M. M. Agricultural Farm-Related Injuries in Bangladesh and Convenient Design of Working Hand Tools. *J. Healthc. Eng.* **2018,** *3*, 1–10. DOI: 10.1155/2018/4273616.

Pimentel, D.; Hepperly, P.; Hanson, J.; Douds, D.; Seidel, R. Environmental, Energetic, and Economic Comparisons of Organic and Conventional Farming Systems. *Bioscience* **2005,** *55*, 573–582. DOI: 10.1641/0006-3568(2005)055[0573:EEAECO]2.0.CO;2

Pretty, J. N. In *Regenerating Agriculture: Policies and Practice for Sustainability and Self-Reliance*; Earthscan Publications Limited: London, 1995.

Rahman, S.; Thapa, G. B. Environmental Impacts of Technological Change in Bangladesh Agriculture: Farmers' Perceptions and Empirical Evidence. *Outlook Agric.* **1999,** *28* (4), 233–238. https://doi.org/10.1177/003072709902800406

Reganold, J. P.; Wachter, J. M. Organic Agriculture in the Twenty-First Century. *Nat. Plants* **2016,** *3* (2), 15–221. DOI: 10.1038/nplants.2015.221

Sarkar, A.; Aronson, K. J.; Patil, S.; Hugar, L. B.; vanLoon, G. W. Emerging Health Risks Associated with Modern Agriculture Practices: A Comprehensive Study in India. *Environ. Res.* **2012,** *115*, 37–50. DOI: 10.1016/j.envres.2012.03.005

Seufert, V.; Ramankutty, N.; Foley, J. A. Comparing the Yields of Organic and Conventional Agriculture. *Nature* **2012,** *485*, 229–232. DOI: 10.1038/nature11069

Singh, S. Marketing of Indian Organic Products: Status, Issues, and Prospects. IIMA Working Papers, India, 2004. http://www.iimwhd.ernet.in/publications/data/2004-10-01.pdf

Stadlinger, N.; Mmochi, M. J.; Kumblad, L. Weak Governmental Institutions Impair the Management of Pesticide Import and Sales in Zanzibar. *Ambio* **2013,** *42* (1), 72–82. DOI: 10.1007/s13280-012-0338-6

Travisi, C. M.; Nijkamp, P.; Vindigni, G. Pesticide Risk Valuation in Empirical Economics: A Comparative Approach. *Ecol. Econ.* **2006,** *56*, 455–474.

UNDP. Global-Innovation-Initiative-Sustainable-Agriculture, 2019. https://www.undp.org/press-releases/global-innovation-initiative-sustainable-agriculture

Verger, P.; Boobis, A. Reevaluate Pesticides for Food Security and Safety. *Science* **2013,** *341* (6147), 717–718. DOI: 10.1126/science.1241572

Yang, X. M.; Wang, F.; Meng, L.; Zhang, W. S.; Fan, L. X.; Geissen, V.; Ritsema, C. J. Farmer and Retailer Knowledge and Awareness of the Risks from Pesticide Use: A Case Study in the Wei River Catchment, China. *Sci. Total Environ.* **2014,** *497* (498), 172–179. DOI: 10.1016/j.scitotenv.2014.07.118

Yunlong, C.; Smith, B. Sustainability in Agriculture: A General Review. *Agric. Ecosyst. Environ.* **1994,** *49* (3), 299–307. https://doi.org/10.1016/0167-8809(94)90059-0

World Bank. Bangladesh: Growing the Economy through Advances in Agriculture, 2016. https://www.worldbank.org/en/results/2016/10/07/bangladesh-growing-economy-through-advances-in-agriculture

CHAPTER 7

Critical Success Factors of Sustainable Marketing Strategy: A Comprehensive Study of Green Businesses

SOURAV MONDAL, ABHISHEK KUMAR, and SAUMYA SINGH

Department of Management Studies and Industrial Engineering, IIT(ISM) Dhanbad, Jharkhand, India

ABSTRACT

Sustainable marketing gives green entrepreneurs a competitive edge, more profits, a better brand image, and a business that is good for the environment by doing the right thing for society and making a profit. Hence, the objective of this study is to develop a comprehensive framework by identifying and analyzing the critical success factors (CSFs) of sustainable marketing strategies that help green entrepreneurs achieve sustainable development. This empirical study has identified 11 CSFs from literature and expert opinions. A hybrid methodology, that is, a case study of Indian businesses and "interpretive structural modeling" (ISM), was used to recognize and establish a contextual relationship. Further, "Matrice d'Impacts Croisés Multiplication Appliquée á un Classment" was used to cluster the identified CSF with respect to "driving power" and "dependence power." Result shows "aligning entrepreneurship goals with marketing goals for sustainability," and "integrating sustainability into product design and development" have the highest "dependent power" whereas "consumer behavior and market demand," "innovation and creativity," "social and environmental responsibility," and "supportive regulatory bodies and government support" have the highest "driving power." The findings of this study would aid in the formulation of

Agile Business Transformations: Priorities, Lessons, and Practices. Satyajit Chakrabarti, Subrata Chattopadhyay, Udit Chawla, Sundeep Singh Sondhi, & Arunava Dalal (Eds.)

policies and strategic decisions that allow green entrepreneurs, managers, and policymakers to identify and comprehend the critical elements of sustainable marketing strategy.

7.1 INTRODUCTION

In recent years, sustainable marketing has emerged as a vital aspect of business strategy for green businesses. The idea of sustainable marketing is to create a marketing strategy that focuses on long-term sustainability and social responsibility (Hansen et al., 2020). A sustainable marketing strategy involves incorporating environmental, social, and economic considerations into the marketing process. As the world becomes more aware of the negative impacts of traditional marketing practices, the demand for sustainable marketing strategies has increased. The success of a sustainable marketing strategy depends on several CSFs that must be identified and addressed to achieve the desired outcomes (Mio et al., 2022).

Numerous studies have investigated the implementation and measurement of sustainable marketing strategies (Zhang et al., 2021). Ofor et al. (2021) studied the opportunities and challenges of green marketing. Another study by Wood et al. (2018) studied sustainable marketing from a financial perspective. Melović et al. (2020) studied sustainable marketing strategy in the context of agricultural business development. Whereas Rudawska (2019); Daifen (2022); Khawand et al. (2022) perform their study on sustainable marketing from different perspectives. Begum et al. (2023), Mio et al. (2022), and Putri et al. (2020) studied green businesses in other situations. Sarkar et al. (2021) studied drivers of green business.

From the literature review, there is no study on critical success factor (CSF) for sustainable marketing. Furthermore, no study has looked at the CSF from the perspective of MSMEs. In past literature, it is also clear that there are limited studies that discuss green business; however, no studies link green business with sustainable marketing. Despite the importance of a sustainable marketing strategy, there is a lack of comprehensive research on the CSF that drives its effectiveness. In addition to the aforementioned, no study discusses how factors of sustainable marketing strategy help develop green business strategies in manufacturing MSMEs. However, implementing sustainable marketing strategies can be challenging for businesses, particularly those in the green sector, as they face unique challenges and opportunities. Hence, the "research objective" (RO) of this study is

- RO1: To recognize the CSF of sustainable marketing strategy that manufacturing MSMEs require to develop green businesses
- RO2: To establish their interrelationship and level-wise structural model among the identified CSFs
- RO3: To cluster the CSFs with respect to their "driving power" and "dependence power"

This research will provide valuable insights into the key factors that are necessary for developing and implementing a sustainable marketing strategy for green businesses. This will be particularly beneficial for small and medium-sized green businesses, which often lack the resources and expertise needed to develop effective marketing strategies. This study helps existing literature on sustainable marketing strategies by identifying the CSFs that contribute to the success of sustainable marketing strategies for green businesses. The findings promote their products and services but also contribute to the sustainability of the environment.

7.2 LITERATURE REVIEW

7.2.1 SUSTAINABLE MARKETING

Sustainable marketing is the process of promoting products or services in a way that supports environmental and social well-being. It involves creating a balance between economic growth, societal well-being, and environmental impact (Sheth and Parvatiyar, 2021; Speckemeier and Tsivrikos, 2022). Sustainable marketing aims to create long-term value for customers, society, and the environment while also meeting the business objectives of the organization. Sustainable marketing plays a crucial role in promoting sustainable development for manufacturing MSMEs by aligning their business practices with environmental and social responsibility, building brand reputation and consumer loyalty, creating a competitive advantage, and driving innovation toward environmentally friendly products and processes (Quaye and Mensah, 2019; Sheth and Parvatiyar, 2021).

7.2.2 RELATIONSHIP OF GREEN BUSINESS WITH SUSTAINABLE MARKETING STRATEGY

Green business and sustainable marketing strategies are closely related, as green businesses rely on sustainable marketing strategies to communicate their environmentally friendly practices and products to their target market, build brand reputation and consumer trust, and create a competitive advantage in the marketplace (Ottman, 2011). Sustainable marketing strategies ensure that green businesses can effectively promote their environmental and social responsibility and, in turn, contribute to the broader goal of sustainable development (Rudawska, 2019). In the manufacturing MSME sector, green business and sustainable marketing strategies are essential for promoting sustainable development by integrating environmentally friendly practices and products into the production process and effectively communicating the value of these practices to consumers. Sustainable marketing strategies for green businesses in manufacturing MSMEs can include initiatives such as green product labeling, eco-friendly packaging, and promoting environmentally responsible production processes, which can help build brand reputation and consumer loyalty and support the broader goal of sustainable development in the industry.

7.2.3 CSF OF SUSTAINABLE MARKETING STRATEGY

The CSF of a sustainable marketing strategy for manufacturing MSMEs for green business development is important because it enables the business to effectively promote its environmental and social responsibility, build consumer trust and loyalty, and contribute to the broader goal of sustainable development. By integrating sustainable practices and products throughout the production process, understanding consumer values and preferences, and continually innovating to improve sustainability, green businesses can enhance their competitiveness and achieve long-term success. Building strong partnerships with suppliers and stakeholders who share a commitment to sustainability and implementing transparent and credible sustainability reporting also helps to enhance the reputation and credibility of the business, which can further support its growth and success.

The discussion of the “CSF” of sustainable marketing strategy is detailed in Table 7.1.

7.3 METHODOLOGY

7.3.1 INTERPRETIVE STRUCTURAL MODELING

Interpretive structural modeling (ISM) is a methodology used to analyze complex systems, organizations, or situations by identifying the relationships

TABLE 7.1 The Discussion of Factors.

CSF	Descriptions	Code	References
Aligning entrepreneurship goals with marketing goals for sustainability	Aligning entrepreneurship goals with marketing goals is crucial for creating a sustainable marketing strategy that supports green business practices and drives the long-term success of a manufacturing SME.	CSF1	Stubbs (2017)
Sustainable marketing orientations	A sustainable marketing orientation for a green manufacturing SME involves incorporating environmentally conscious practices throughout the entire marketing strategy, from product development to promotion and distribution, with a focus on long-term sustainability and positive impact on society and the environment.	CSF2	Habib et al. (2020)
Green motives	A manufacturing SME can adopt sustainable marketing strategies that prioritize green motives, such as promoting eco-friendly production practices, using environmentally friendly materials, and emphasizing the sustainability benefits of their products and services.	CSF3	Li et al. (2020)
Innovation and creativity	Innovation and creativity are crucial for developing effective and sustainable marketing strategies that can help green manufacturing SMEs.	CSF4	Awan et al. (2019)
Social and environmental responsibility	Incorporating social and environmental responsibility into sustainable marketing strategies can enhance the reputation of green manufacturing SMEs, build trust with consumers, and contribute to a more sustainable future.	CSF5	Hansen et al. (2020)
Supportive regulatory bodies and government support	Supportive regulatory bodies and government initiatives can incentivize sustainable practices and provide resources for green manufacturing SMEs to develop effective marketing strategies that align with sustainability goals.	CSF6	Warbroek and Hoppe (2017)
Sustainable environment and social behaviors	Effective sustainable marketing strategies for a green manufacturing SME should integrate environmentally sustainable practices and socially responsible behaviors to promote a sustainable environment and positive social impact.	CSF7	Risitano et al. (2022)
Integrating sustainability into product design and development	Incorporating sustainability into product design and development is essential for sustainable marketing strategies of a green manufacturing SME to create environmentally responsible and innovative products.	CSF8	Habib et al. (2020); Risitano et al. (2022)

TABLE 7.1 *(Continued)*

CSF	Descriptions	Code	References
Using new technology and creativity as a strategic tool for sustainable marketing	Leveraging new technologies and creative solutions is a key strategic tool for sustainable marketing in a green manufacturing SME to communicate their commitment toward sustainability and innovation.	CSF9	Interview
Consumer behavior and market demand	Understanding consumer behavior and market demand is crucial for developing effective sustainable marketing strategies that meet the needs of consumers and promote green products in a manufacturing SME.	CSF10	Yousaf et al. (2021)
Input from regulatory authority	Incorporating input from regulatory authorities is important for creating sustainable marketing strategies in a green manufacturing SME that align with environmental policies and regulations.	CSF11	Narbón-Perpiñá and De Witte (2018)

and hierarchy among the various factors or elements involved. ISM helps in understanding the interdependencies and influences among the various factors or elements and the hierarchical structure among them (Agi and Nishant, 2017). It is a useful tool for decision-making, problem-solving, and developing action plans. It can be applied in a variety of domains, including business, engineering, social sciences, and public policy. ISM can help decision-makers better understand the complex systems they are dealing with, identify the key factors that influence the system, and develop effective strategies for achieving their goals. This methodology has several advantages over other "multicriteria decision-making" (MCDM) approaches, like the "analytic hierarchy process" (AHP) or "technique for order preference by similarity to an ideal solution" (TOPSIS). The advantages are that it develops a hierarchical structure, focuses on the development of contextual relationships, considers all expert input, and has flexibility and transparency.

7.3.2 MICMAC ANALYSIS

MICMAC analysis, also known as "Matrice d'Impacts Croisés-Multiplication Appliquée à un Classement," is a technique used in strategic management to analyze the interactions and dependencies between different factors or variables in a system (Agi and Nishant, 2017). The MICMAC analysis involves creating a matrix of impacts that shows the relationships and dependencies between the variables. The matrix is created by asking experts to rate the degree of influence that each variable has on every other variable in the system. This rating is then multiplied by the rating of the variable being impacted, resulting in a score that represents the impact of the variable. The matrix is then divided into four categories based on the level of influence and dependence of each variable. These categories are "autonomous variables," "dominant variables," "linkage variables," and "dependent variables." Once the variables are categorized, they can be used to develop strategies for managing the system. For example, the autonomous and dominant variables may be targeted for control or manipulation, while the linkage and dependent variables may be monitored or managed as part of a broader strategy. MICMAC analysis can be a useful tool for strategic management in a variety of contexts, including business, government, and environmental management. It provides a structured way to analyze complex systems and identify key factors for strategy development.

7.4 RESULT AND DISCUSSIONS

7.4.1 ISM OUTCOME

7.4.1.1 SSIM MATRIX

To create the "structural self-interaction matrix" (SSIM) matrix, we must demonstrate the relationship between the CSFs and the represented VAXO (Table 7.2). This was developed based on the responses obtained from industry experts. The relationship of "VAXO" is shown below. In addition, the SSIM matrix is shown in Table 7.3.

TABLE 7.2 Symbols.

Symbol	i → j	j → i	(i,j) th Value	(j,i) th value
V	"Yes"	"No"	1	0
A	"No"	"Yes"	0	1
X	"Yes"	"Yes"	1	1
O	"No"	"No"	0	0

TABLE 7.3 SSIM Matrix.

	CSF11	CSF10	CSF9	CSF8	CSF7	CSF6	CSF5	CSF4	CSF3	CSF2	CSF1
CSF1	O	O	O	X	A	O	O	O	O	A	–
CSF2	A	O	A	V	X	O	O	O	A	–	
CSF3	O	O	O	O	V	A	A	O	–		
CSF4	O	X	O	O	O	V	V	–			
CSF5	O	A	V	O	O	X	–				
CSF6	V	A	V	O	O	–					
CSF7	A	O	A	V	–						
CSF8	O	O	O	–							
CSF9	O	O	–								
CSF10	O	–									
CSF11	–										

7.4.1.2 REACHABILITY MATRIX (RM)

The RM has two phases: the "initial reachability matrix" (IRM) and the "final reachability matrix" (FRM). The IRM is obtained by substituting the value of "VAXO" as presented in Table 7.2 (see Table 7.4). Whereas the "final reachability matrix" is obtained by using the "transitivity rule" (see Table 7.5).

TABLE 7.4 IRM Matrix.

	CSF1	CSF2	CSF3	CSF4	CSF5	CSF6	CSF7	CSF8	CSF9	CSF10	CSF11
CSF1	1	0	0	0	0	0	0	1	0	0	0
CSF2	1	1	0	0	0	0	1	1	0	0	0
CSF3	0	1	1	0	0	0	1	0	0	0	0
CSF4	0	0	0	1	1	1	0	0	0	1	0
CSF5	0	0	1	0	1	1	0	0	1	0	0
CSF6	0	0	1	0	1	1	0	0	1	0	1
CSF7	1	1	0	0	0	0	1	1	0	0	0
CSF8	1	0	0	0	0	0	0	1	0	0	0
CSF9	0	1	0	0	0	0	1	0	1	0	0
CSF10	0	0	0	1	1	1	0	0	0	1	0
CSF11	0	1	0	0	0	0	1	0	0	0	1

TABLE 7.5 FRM Matrix.

	CSF1	CSF2	CSF3	CSF4	CSF5	CSF6	CSF7	CSF8	CSF9	CSF10	CSF11
CSF1	1	0	0	0	0	0	0	0	0	0	0
CSF2	1	1	0	0	0	0	1	1	0	0	0
CSF3	1*	1	1	0	0	0	1	1*	0	0	0
CSF4	0	0	1*	1	1	1	0	0	1*	1	1*
CSF5	0	1*	1	0	1	1	1*	0	1	0	1*
CSF6	0	1*	1	0	1	1	1*	0	1	0	1
CSF7	1	1	0	0	0	0	1	1	0	0	0
CSF8	1	0	0	0	0	0	0	1	0	0	0
CSF9	1*	1	0	0	0	0	1	1*	1	0	0
CSF10	0	0	1*	1	1	1	0	0	1*	1	1*
CSF11	1*	1	0	0	0	0	1		0	0	1

7.4.1.3 LEVEL PARTITIONING

CSF's hierarchical structure develops through level partitioning. Table 7.6 shows the partitioning level in detail.

TABLE 7.6 Level Partitioning of CSF.

	Dependency power	Driving power	Level
CSF1	7	2	I
CSF2	7	4	II
CSF3	5	5	III
CSF4	2	7	V
CSF5	4	7	IV
CSF6	4	7	IV
CSF7	7	4	II
CSF8	7	2	I
CSF9	5	5	III
CSF10	2	7	V
CSF11	5	5	III

We derived a five-level structure from the level partitioning, as shown in Figure 7.1. The reciprocal interaction among the CSFs is collected from the FRM and joined by directed lines to form the structural model. A unidirectional arrow linking nodes "A" and "B" implies that "A" travels to "B." A bidirectional line linking "A" and "B" nodes shows "A" and "B" mutually guiding each other. Figure 7.1 illustrates an ISM digraph of CSFs. Figure 7.1 shows the ISM digraph.

7.4.1.4 MICMAC ANALYSIS

This analysis investigates the "driving" and "dependent power" of sustainable marketing strategies. The "horizontal axis" represents the "dependence on the power" of a sustainable marketing strategy, while the Y-axis represents the "driving force." Following plotting, we divided the important enablers of a sustainable marketing strategy into four clusters, as shown in Figure 7.2, namely "autonomous," "driving," "dependence," and "linkage."

7.4.1.4.1 Findings from MICMAC Analysis

Cluster 1: Autonomous CSFs of sustainable marketing strategy: This coordinate CSFs have weak "driving" as well as weak "dependence power." This study no CSFs of sustainable marketing strategy falls under this category.

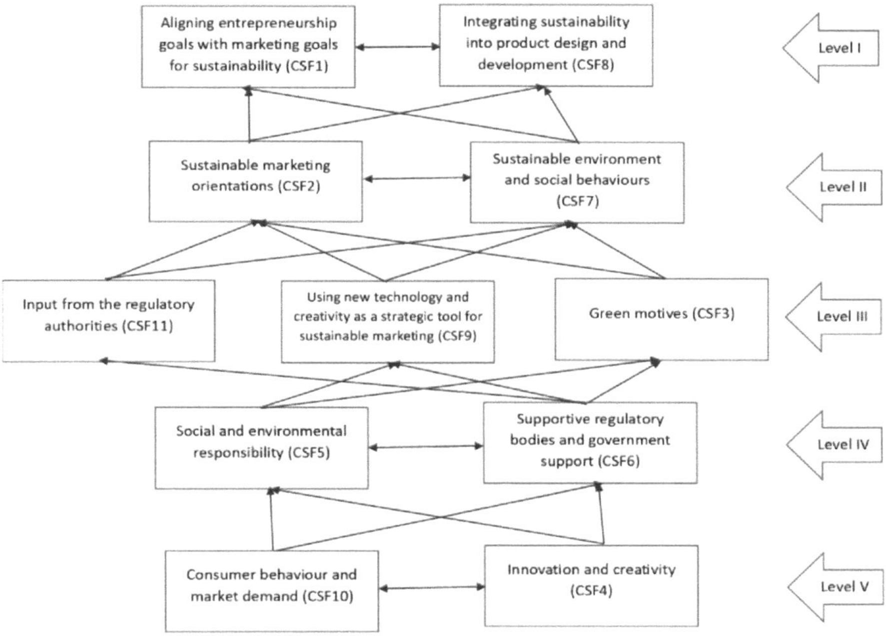

FIGURE 7.1 ISM result-level partitioning.

- Cluster 2: Driving CSFs of sustainable marketing strategy: This coordinate CSFs has weak dependence and strong driving power. Four CSFs, that is, innovation and creativity (CSF4), social and environmental responsibility (CSF5), supportive regulatory bodies and government support (CSF6), and consumer behavior and market demand (CSF10), are falling into this cluster.
- Cluster 3: Linkage CSFs of sustainable marketing strategy: This cluster has strong "driving" and strong "dependence powers." The five CSFs, that is, sustainable marketing orientations (CSF2), green motives (CSF3), sustainable environment and social behaviors (CSF7), using new technology and creativity as a strategic tool for sustainable marketing (CSF9), and input from the relevant regulatory authorities (CSF11), fall under this category.
- Cluster 4: Dependent CSFs of sustainable marketing strategy: This cluster has strong dependent power but weak driving power. Aligning entrepreneurship goals with marketing goals for sustainability (CSF1), and integrating sustainability into product design and development (CSF8) belong to this group.

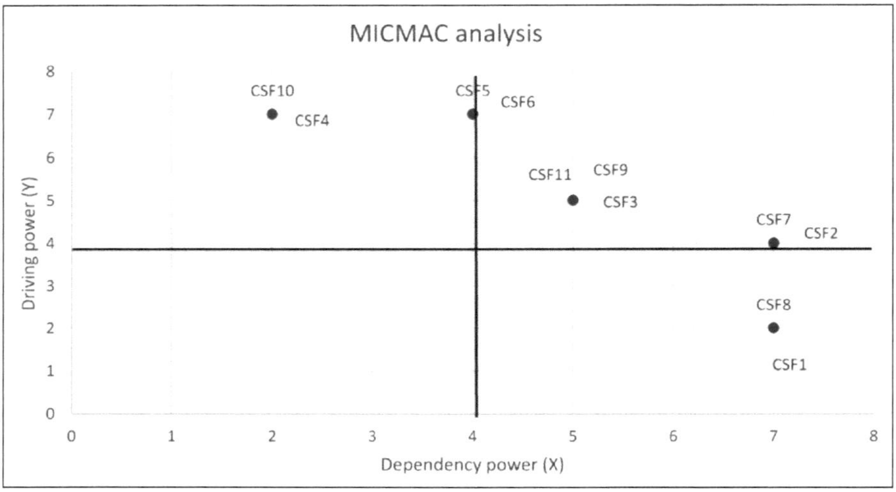

FIGURE 7.2 Plotting of position coordinates of CSF of sustainable marketing strategy.

7.5 CONCLUSIONS

In this paper, an attempt has been made to study and identify the CSFs of sustainable marketing strategy that are required to develop for Indian manufacturing small and medium enterprises. There are several types of CSFs that are required for business positivity, competitive advantage, and sustainable development. Using the past literature and experts from the industry, this study identified 11 CSFs. In conclusion, this comprehensive study of green businesses has highlighted several CSF for a sustainable marketing strategy. The findings show that "aligning entrepreneurship goals with marketing goals for sustainability," and "integrating sustainability into product design and development" have the highest "dependent power" whereas "consumer behavior and market demand," "innovation and creativity," "social and environmental responsibility," and "supportive regulatory bodies and government support" have the highest "driving power." The findings suggest that a customer-centric approach, along with a clear understanding of the target audience, is crucial for businesses to succeed in the green market. Additionally, businesses need to develop a comprehensive and authentic green strategy that aligns with their values and goals to build trust and credibility among consumers. Moreover, this study emphasizes the importance of a holistic and integrated approach to sustainable marketing strategy that considers environment, social, and economic aspects of the business. The results have significant implications for businesses that aspire to become more sustainable and environmentally responsible and can help them develop effective marketing strategies that resonate with their customers and contribute to a more sustainable future.

7.6 IMPLICATIONS, LIMITATIONS, AND FUTURE RECOMMENDATIONS

7.6.1 IMPLICATIONS

The implications show green businesses should prioritise the integration of sustainability into their marketing strategies to achieve a competitive edge and improve their brand image. The study emphasises the importance of aligning entrepreneurship goals with marketing goals for sustainability to achieve long-term business objectives while fulfilling social and environmental responsibilities. To effectively implement sustainable marketing strategies, green businesses should continuously monitor consumer behavior and market demand and innovate products and services to align with sustainability goals. Regulatory bodies and governments should create policies that support sustainable marketing and provide support to green businesses to develop sustainable business models.

Further, the research contributes to the works on sustainable marketing by identifying CSF and establishing mutual relationships between them. The use of ISM and MICMAC analysis provides a unique approach to identifying CSF for sustainable marketing strategies. In addition, the study highlights the importance of considering sustainability as a critical element in marketing strategy development and implementation. Furthermore, the findings of this study can help green businesses develop effective sustainable marketing strategies by identifying the CSF and prioritizing them accordingly. The study emphasizes the importance of considering customer needs and preferences when developing sustainable marketing strategies, which can improve customer satisfaction and loyalty. Governments and regulatory bodies can use the findings helps to develop policies that support sustainable marketing and green businesses. In addition to this, the study focuses specifically on green businesses, providing unique insights into the CSF for sustainable marketing in this sector. The use of ISM and MICMAC analysis provides a unique approach to identifying CSF for sustainable marketing strategies that can be applied to other sectors as well. The study highlights the importance of aligning entrepreneurship goals with marketing goals for sustainability, a unique perspective that has not been extensively studied in the literature.

7.6.2 LIMITATIONS AND FUTURE RECOMMENDATIONS

This research recognizes several limitations in its identification of 19 CSF to smart sustainable logistics based on previous literature. Future studies might build on this study by finding other factors via a more thorough literature analysis. The ISM was used in this research to make the relationship with the CSF and identify the best options. Alternative methodologies, such as the "fuzzy best worst method" (FBWM), might be used in future research to give a more genuine picture of decision-makers' viewpoints by considering their inherent uncertainty and confusion. Although fourteen experts took part in this study, future research might benefit from a broader selection of experts from many domains. This allows for the incorporation of a greater range of information and ideas, resulting in a more thorough understanding of the subject matter. This early study has undoubtedly provided the ground-work for additional research on the topic. It has highlighted the possibility for future studies to dive further into the complexity of smart sustainable logistics, opening up new possibilities for R&D.

KEYWORDS

- **critical success factors**
- **sustainable marketing strategy**
- **green entrepreneurship**
- **ISM**
- **MICMAC**

REFERENCES

Agi, M. A. N.; Nishant, R. Understanding Influential Factors on Implementing Green Supply Chain Management Practices: An Interpretive Structural Modelling Analysis. *J. Environ. Manag.* **2017,** *188*, 351–363.

Awan, U.; Sroufe, R.; Kraslawski, A. Creativity Enables Sustainable Development: Supplier Engagement as a Boundary Condition for the Positive Effect on Green Innovation. *J. Clean. Prod.* **2019,** *226*, 172–185.

Begum, S.; Ashfaq, M.; Asiaei, K.; Shahzad, K. Green Intellectual Capital and Green Business Strategy: The Role of Green Absorptive Capacity. *Bus. Strategy Environ.* **2023,** 1–17.

Daifen, T. Evaluate the Sustainable Marketing Strategy to Optimal Online Leasing of New Energy Vehicles under the Background Big Data Economy. *J. Enterp. Inf. Manag.* **2022,** 35(4–5), 1409–1424.

Habib, M. A.; Bao, Y.; Ilmudeen, A. The Impact of Green Entrepreneurial Orientation, Market Orientation and Green Supply Chain Management Practices on Sustainable firm Performance. *Cogent Bus. Manag.* **2020,** *7* (1).

Hansen, D. J.; Deacon, J. H.; Pascal, V.; Sethna, Z. The Future is in the Past: A Framework for the Marketing-Entrepreneurship Interface (MEI). *J. Bus. Res.* **2020,** *113*, 198–208.

Khawand, S.; Ghasemi, M.; Sahranavard, S. A. Employee Involvement and Socialization as an Example of Sustainable Marketing Strategy and Organization's Citizenship Behavior: Empirical Evidence from Beirut Hotel Sector. *Sustainability* **2022,** *14* (14).

Li, W.; Bhutto, T. A.; Xuhui, W.; Maitlo, Q.; Zafar, A. U.; Ahmed Bhutto, N. Unlocking Employees' Green Creativity: The Effects of Green Transformational Leadership, Green Intrinsic, and Extrinsic Motivation. *J. Clean. Prod.* **2020,** *255*, 120229.

Melović, B.; Cirović, D.; Backovic-Vulić, T.; Dudić, B.; Gubinova, K. Attracting Green Consumers as a Basis for Creating Sustainable Marketing Strategy on the Organic Market-Relevance for Sustainable Agriculture Business Development. *Foods* **2020,** *9* (11), 1–25.

Mio, C.; Costantini, A.; Panfilo, S. Performance Measurement Tools for Sustainable Business: A Systematic Literature Review on the Sustainability Balanced Scorecard Use. *Corp. Soc. Resp. Environ. Manag.* **2022,** *29* (2), 367–384.

Narbón-Perpiñá, I.; De Witte, K. Local Governments' Efficiency: A Systematic Literature Review—Part I. *Int. Trans. Oper. Res.* **2018,** *25* (2), 431–468.

Ofori, D. Opportunities and Challenges of Green Marketing. In *Green Marketing in Emerging Markets: Strategic and Operational Perspectives*, 2021; pp 251–276.

Ottman, J. A. In *The New Rules of Green Marketing: Strategies, Tools, and Inspiration for Sustainable Branding*; Berrett-Koehler Publishers, 2011.

Putri, V. W.; Ridloah, S.; Wijaya, A. P. In *Strategy for Increasing Green Economic Performance of Small and Medium Enterprises Based on Green Business Management*, IOP Conference Series: Earth and Environmental Science, 2020; vol *485* (1).

Quaye, D.; Mensah, I. Marketing Innovation and Sustainable Competitive Advantage of Manufacturing SMEs in Ghana. *Manag. Decis.* **2019,** *57* (7), 1535–1553.

Risitano, M.; Romano, R.; Rusciano, V.; Civero, G.; Scarpato, D. The Impact of Sustainability on Marketing Strategy and Business Performance: The Case of Italian Fisheries. *Bus. Strategy Environ.* **2022,** *31* (4), 1538–1551.

Rudawska, E. Sustainable Marketing Strategy in Food and Drink Industry: A Comparative Analysis of B2B and B2C SMEs Operating in Europe. *J. Bus. Ind. Mark.* **2019,** *34* (4), 875–890.

Sarkar, A.; Qian, L.; Peau, A. K.; Shahriar, S. Modeling Drivers for Successful Adoption of Green Business: An Interpretive Structural Modeling Approach. *Environ. Sci. Pollut. Res.* **2021,** *28* (1), 1077–1096.

Sheth, J. N.; Parvatiyar, A. Sustainable Marketing: Market-Driving, Not Market-Driven. *J. Macromark.* **2021,** *41* (1), 150–165.

Speckemeier, L.; Tsivrikos, D. Green Entrepreneurship: Should Legislators Invest in the Formation of Sustainable Hubs? *Sustainability (Switzerland)* **2022,** *14* (12).

Stubbs, W. Characterising B Corps as a Sustainable Business Model: An Exploratory Study of B Corps in Australia. *J. Clean. Prod.* **2017,** *144*, 299–312.

Warbroek, B.; Hoppe, T. Modes of Governing and Policy of Local and Regional Governments Supporting Local Low-Carbon Energy Initiatives; Exploring the Cases of the Dutch Regions of Overijssel and Fryslân. *Sustainability (Switzerland)* **2017,** *9* (1), 1–36.

Wood, L. C.; Wang, J. X.; Duong, L. N. K.; Reiners, T.; Smith, R. Stock Market Reactions to Auto Manufacturers' Environmental Failures. *J. Macromark.* **2018,** *38* (4), 364–382.

Yousaf, Z.; Radulescu, M.; Sinisi, C. I.; Serbanescu, L.; Paunescu, L. M. Harmonization of Green Motives and Green Business Strategies Towards Sustainable Development of Hospitality and Tourism Industry: Green Environmental Policies. *Sustainability (Switzerland)* **2021,** *13* (12).

Zhang, Y.; Xu, S.; Zhang, L.; Yang, M. Big Data and Human Resource Management Research: An Integrative Review and New Directions for Future Research. *J. Bus. Res.* **2021,** *133*, 34–50.

CHAPTER 8

Factors Affecting Sustainable Practices of Digital Entrepreneurs for Social Tourism by Using Digital Platforms: A Study

ABHISHEK KUMAR, SOURAV MONDAL, and SAUMYA SINGH

Indian Institute of Technology (Indian School of Mines), Dhanbad, Jharkhand, India

ABSTRACT

The tourism industry has expanded at an unprecedented rate in recent years, with social tourism gaining popularity due to increased demand for responsible and sustainable travel. The rise of social tourism may largely be attributed to the ability of digital entrepreneurs to provide unique and tailor-made experiences via the use of online platforms. However, the use of digital platforms by entrepreneurs to integrate sustainable practices into social tourism has been limited. As a consequence, there is an adverse effect on society and the environment. By identifying the main motivators and obstacles for these entrepreneurs' implementation and adoption of sustainable practices, this research aims to fill a knowledge vacuum in this area. Complex relationships among the factors affecting sustainable practices were analyzed using the "interpretive structural modeling" (ISM) methodology. The findings showed that while perceived value, perceived attitude, government backing, and individual motivation have great driving power, regulatory and financial factors have strong dependent power. These conclusions can serve as a roadmap for academics, digital entrepreneurs, and governments who want to promote sustainable social tourism practices.

Agile Business Transformations: Priorities, Lessons, and Practices. Satyajit Chakrabarti, Subrata Chattopadhyay, Udit Chawla, Sundeep Singh Sondhi, & Arunava Dalal (Eds.)

8.1 INTRODUCTION

The tourism industry has been undergoing swift expansion, and social tourism has surfaced as a popular form of travel due to the escalating need for conscientious and sustainable tourism practices (Frey and George, 2010). The expansion of social tourism has been significantly facilitated by digital platforms, which have empowered digital entrepreneurs to provide customized travel experiences to tourists (Milwood and Maxwell, 2020). The incorporation of sustainable measures in social tourism through digital platforms by entrepreneurs has been restricted, resulting in adverse consequences for both the environment and society (Carr et al., 2016; Gössling and Michael Hall, 2019). This study intends to close a knowledge gap by identifying the key factors that influence the adoption and implementation of environmentally friendly solutions by digital entrepreneurs working in the realm of social tourism. The research problem is limited to the insufficient incorporation of sustainable measures in social tourism by digital entrepreneurs through digital platforms, potentially resulting in adverse consequences for the environment and society. The literature reveals a research gap in regard to the factors that influence entrepreneurs' implementation and adoption of sustainable practices. The objective of this research is to focus on the aforementioned research void by zeroing in on the aforementioned variables in an effort to find a solution. Hence, this study seeks to address the following questions: What are the key barriers and drivers to the implementation and adoption of sustainable practices by digital entrepreneurs in social tourism? How do these factors relate to each other? What are the implications of these findings for policymakers, academics, and digital entrepreneurs in promoting sustainable practices in social tourism? Therefore, the following are the objectives of this research:

- To ascertain the key factors that affect the adoption and implementation of sustainable practices by digital entrepreneurs in social tourism
- To conduct an analysis of the interrelationships among these factors utilizing the interpretive structural modeling (ISM) methodology

The study's importance lies in its potential to provide guidance to policymakers, academics, and digital entrepreneurs in advancing sustainable practices within the realm of social tourism. The study's scope includes identifying the key drivers and barriers to sustainable practices by digital entrepreneurs in social tourism using ISM methodology. This study incorporates several fundamental definitions and concepts, such as social tourism, sustainable practices, digital platforms, entrepreneurship, regulatory and financial factors, perceived value, perceived attitude, government support, and personal motivation. The literature review section of this article is dedicated to the examination of the relevant literature, which will offer both a comprehensive overview and an explanation of the aforementioned terminology.

8.2 LITERATURE REVIEW

8.2.1 OVERVIEW OF SUSTAINABLE PRACTICES IN SOCIAL TOURISM

Sustainable tourism has become a key issue for governments, corporations, and travelers worldwide due to the growing knowledge of the detrimental effect of tourism on the native inhabitants and environment (Kapera, 2018). Responsible and sustainable tourism aims to reduce negative impacts while maximizing positive outcomes for local communities and the environment (Budeanu, 2005). For local communities to benefit economically, culturally, and socially from tourism, it must be characterized by social inclusivity (Risteskia et al., 2012). Previous research (Budeanu et al., 2016) on sustainable practices in tourism has identified various drivers and barriers, including regulatory frameworks, financial incentives, consumer demand, and collaboration with stakeholders.

However, it is worth noting that the existing literature on the relationship between digital entrepreneurship and the advancement of sustainable practices in social tourism is limited, with only a few studies (Budeanu et al., 2016; Cavalcante et al., 2021) explicitly focusing on this subject. Therefore, this research endeavor assumes particular importance as it significantly contributes to the current academic discourse. This study assumes a critical role in addressing a notable gap in the existing literature by meticulously uncovering and delineating the key factors that influence the adoption and implementation of sustainable practices within the domain of social tourism, particularly among digital entrepreneurs who operate through digital platforms.

8.2.2 THE ROLE OF DIGITAL PLATFORMS IN SOCIAL TOURISM

The tourism industry has undergone a significant transformation due to the advent of digital platforms, which have facilitated the provision of customized and engaging travel experiences to customers by entrepreneurs

(Buhalis et al., 2023). Digital platforms have the potential to enhance accessibility to cost-effective and comprehensive travel opportunities for disadvantaged and economically challenged demographics in social tourism. This can contribute to the advancement of social integration and the mitigation of inequality (Moreno de la Santa, 2020). The utilization of digital platforms in the context of social tourism has given rise to apprehensions regarding the sustainability of tourism practices and their influence on indigenous communities.

8.2.3 ENTREPRENEURSHIP IN SOCIAL TOURISM

Entrepreneurship plays a crucial role in social tourism, as entrepreneurs can identify new market opportunities and offer innovative and sustainable tourism products and services (Antunes et al., 2023). Social entrepreneurs, in particular, focus on social and environmental goals while generating profits (Bauwens et al., 2020). However, the success of social entrepreneurship in tourism depends on various factors, including government policies, access to funding and resources, and collaboration with local communities.

8.2.4 PREVIOUS RESEARCH ON FACTORS AFFECTING SUSTAINABLE PRACTICES IN SOCIAL TOURISM

The influences on the adoption and application of sustainable practices in tourism have been the subject of several studies (Babu et al., 2018; Bauwens et al., 2020). Numerous factors, such as legislative frameworks, financial incentives, consumer demand, and stakeholder engagement, have been identified as drivers and barriers in this research. Few studies (Baig et al., 2022; Constantin and Kavoura, 2022; Deb et al., 2022), however, have particularly examined the function of digital entrepreneurship in encouraging environmentally friendly practices in social tourism.

8.2.5 CONCEPTUAL FRAMEWORK

The ISM technique is used in this study to determine the key drivers and barriers to sustainable social tourism practices by digital entrepreneurs employing digital platforms (Mishra et al., 2017; Shafiee et al., 2022). This study's conceptual framework comprises of regulatory and financial factors as dependent factors, while perceived value, perceived attitude, government support, and personal motivation are considered as the driving variables. The framework aims to offer an understanding of the complex relationships among these factors and their influence on sustainable practices in the field of social tourism.

8.3 METHODOLOGY

8.3.1 RESEARCH DESIGN AND APPROACH

This study employs the ISM methodology in an effort to understand the multifaceted relationships that shape a given phenomenon. Using ISM, this study seeks to identify and analyze the key drivers and barriers influencing the adoption of sustainable practices among digital entrepreneurs operating in the social tourism sector. Creating a hierarchical framework of the factors affecting sustainable practices is part of the ISM methodology. After that, the factors are analyzed using the method MICMAC—Matrice d'Impacts Croisés Multiplication Appliquée à un Classement.

The MICMAC analysis is then used to assess the factors which classify the factors into the following four categories: autonomous, dependent, linkage, and insignificant (Singh et al., 2015). This method is used to analyze complex systems or relationships among variables to comprehend their hierarchical structure and interdependencies. There are multiple steps involved, which are listed as follows:

- **Identify the variables:** Determine which factors or variables are pertinent to the system or problem under consideration. These factors, concepts, components, or elements may be interconnected and have an impact on one another.
- **Define the relationship matrix:** Create a matrix that represents the relationships between the identified variables. Typically, this matrix is square, with the cells denoting the strength of the relationships between the rows, columns, and variables. The relationships can be binary (indicating the presence or absence of a relationship) or can be represented by numbers indicating the strength or intensity of the relationship.
- **Assess the relationship strength:** Analyze the interdependence of the variables in the relationship matrix and assess the quality of the relationships between them. There are a variety of ways to do this,

including the use of expert Judgement, surveys, and in-person interviews. It's possible to use a qualitative scale (weak, moderate, strong) or a quantitative scale (ranging from 1 to 5) to describe the closeness of the relationship.

TABLE 8.1 Relationship Matrix.

Variables	Financial support	Regulatory support	Government support	Personal motivation	Perceived attitude	Perceived value
Perceived value	O	O	O	A	X	–
Perceived attitude	O	O	O	A	–	
Personal motivation	A	A	A	–		
Government support	O	X	–			
Regulatory support	X	–				
Financial support	–					

- **Construct the reachability matrix:** The measured strengths of relationships are used to build a reachability matrix, which is then used to identify the interrelationships and impacts among variables. Table 8.2 presents a reachability matrix where variables are assigned binary values that represent whether or not they can exert direct or indirect control over another variable. If there is a possible effect, a "1" will be entered into a matrix cell; otherwise, a "0" will be entered. Table 8.4 can be used to gain a better understanding of the level partitioning. Table 8.3 depicts the final reachability matrix that can be generated from the initial reachability matrix. It depicts the interdependencies between variables in a way that is both intuitive and accurate. In the final reachability matrix, the binary values assigned to each cell represent the degree of direct or indirect interaction between variables.
- **Derive the digraph:** A directed graph or digraph can be constructed from the reachability matrix. In the digraph, the variables are represented as nodes or vertices, and their connections are shown as directed edges or arcs. Those variables with no outgoing edges are the most independent, whereas those with no incoming edges are the most dependent. Review the digraph analysis: The digraph's analysis

can reveal the variable levels' hierarchical structure. Methods such as level partitioning, level intersection, and level ranking can be used for this purpose. Generally speaking, the variables with greater influence or greater reachability will be placed higher in the hierarchy, while the less influential or less reachable variables will be placed lower.

TABLE 8.2 Reachability Matrix.

Variables	1	2	3	4	5	6	Driving power
Perceived value	1	1	0	0	0	0	2
Perceived attitude	1	1	0	0	0	0	2
Personal motivation	1	1	1	0	0	0	3
Government support	0	0	1	1	1	0	3
Regulatory support	0	0	1	1	1	1	4
Financial support	0	0	1	0	1	1	3
Dependence power	3	3	4	2	3	2	

TABLE 8.3 Final Reachability Matrix.

Variables	1	2	3	4	5	6	Driving power
Perceived value	1	1	0	0	0	0	2
Perceived attitude	1	1	0	0	0	0	2
Personal motivation	1	1	1	0	0	0	3
Government support	1*	1*	1	1	1	1*	6
Regulatory support	1*	1*	1	1	1	1	6
Financial support	1*	1*	1	1*	1	1	6
Dependence power	6	6	4	3	3	3	25

Note: The asterisk (*) symbol indicates a transitive relationship among obstacles. This means that if factor "A" affects factor "B," and factor "B" affects factor "C," we can infer that factor "A" will also affect factor "C."

- **Validate the model:** To ensure the ISM model accurately represents the real-world system or problem being analyzed, it is important to validate it by gathering input from domain experts or other stakeholders. Make any necessary adjustments to the model depending on feedback received. Figure 8.1 explains the three-tiered hierarchical structure.
- **Interpret the results:** Finally, we need to understand the ISM analysis results to learn anything useful about the system or problem

you started with. The ISM model can help with this by providing insight into the hierarchical structure of the variables, highlighting feedback loops and crucial routes, and informing the development of strategies and interventions. Figure 8.2 displays the results of a MICMAC study as a plot.

TABLE 8.4 Level Partitioning.

Elements (Mi)	Reachability set R(Mi)	Antecedent set A(Ni)	Intersection set R(Mi)∩A(Ni)	Level
Iteration I				
1	1, 2,	1, 2, 3, 4, 5, 6,	1, 2,	1
2	1, 2,	1, 2, 3, 4, 5, 6,	1, 2,	1
3	1, 2, 3,	3, 4, 5, 6,	3,	
4	1, 2, 3, 4, 5, 6,	4, 5, 6,	4, 5, 6,	
5	1, 2, 3, 4, 5, 6,	4, 5, 6,	4, 5, 6,	
6	1, 2, 3, 4, 5, 6,	4, 5, 6,	4, 5, 6,	
Iteration II				
3	3,	3, 4, 5, 6,	3,	2
4	3, 4, 5, 6,	4, 5, 6,	4, 5, 6,	
5	3, 4, 5, 6,	4, 5, 6,	4, 5, 6,	
6	3, 4, 5, 6,	4, 5, 6,	4, 5, 6,	
Iteration III				
4	4, 5, 6,	4, 5, 6,	4, 5, 6,	3
5	4, 5, 6,	4, 5, 6,	4, 5, 6,	3
6	4, 5, 6,	4, 5, 6,	4, 5, 6,	3

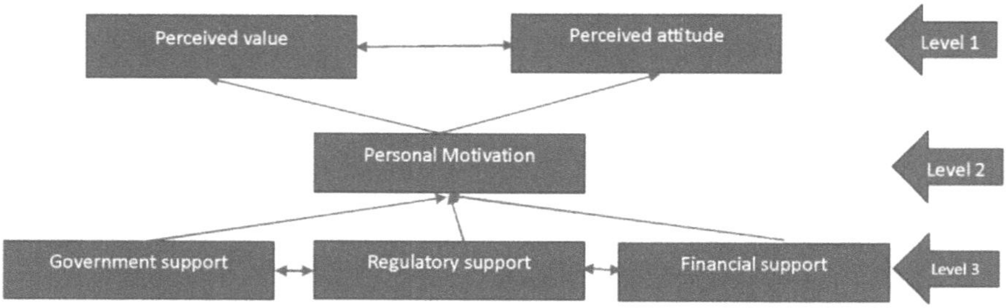

FIGURE 8.1 ISM digraph.

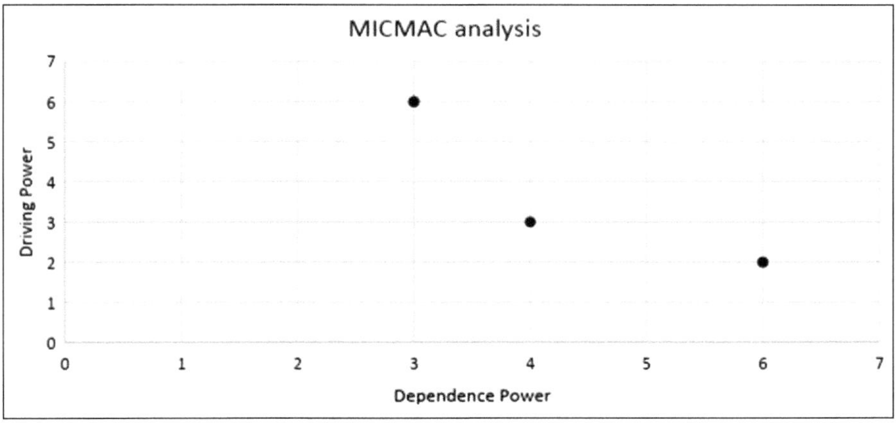

FIGURE 8.2 Plot of MICMAC analysis.

Understanding the hierarchical structure and interdependencies among variables in a complex system or problem necessitates a methodical approach that entails identifying variables, assessing their relationships, constructing a reachability matrix, deriving a digraph, analyzing the digraph, validating the model, and interpreting the results. Policy formulation (Avinash et al., 2018), risk management (Cherrafi et al., 2017; Wu et al., 2015), product development (Kaswan and Rathi, 2019), organizational analysis (Kumar and Goel, 2021), and technological innovation (Sharma et al., 2022) are just some of the many areas where ISM has been applied. It's a helpful resource for navigating complicated systems, making informed decisions, and resolving issues in a wide range of contexts.

8.4 RESULTS AND DISCUSSIONS

The research uncovered a number of variables that influence the rate at which digital entrepreneurs using digital platforms adopt and implement sustainable practices in social tourism. The regulatory and financial reasons, the perceived value and attitude, the government assistance, and the personal motivation categories were identified. Governmental mandates, tariffs, and financial incentives for eco-friendly methods all played a role (Pan et al., 2018). Customer preferences, market demand, and the digital entrepreneurs' opinions of the relevance of sustainability were all included in the value and attitude categories (Al-Ansi and Han, 2019). The federal government provided cash, as well as policies and programs, to encourage ecotourism. To succeed, digital entrepreneurs need to be personally motivated to embrace and implement sustainable practices.

According to the findings, digital entrepreneurs in social tourism see regulatory and financial considerations as the most significant obstacles to the adoption and implementation of sustainable practices (Lutfi et al., 2022). The government's rules, taxes, and monetary incentives for sustainable practices were all interconnected and crucial. However, digital entrepreneurs viewed these factors as crucial drivers of sustainable practices in social tourism due to their high levels of driving power: perceived value and attitude, government backing, and personal motivation. Customers' preferences, market demand, and digital business owners' views on the issue of sustainability all factored into their evaluation of the venture's worth and attitude. The federal government provided cash, as well as policies and programs, to encourage ecotourism. To succeed, digital entrepreneurs need to be personally motivated to embrace and implement sustainable practices.

The findings were interpreted, and the links between the factors affecting sustainable practices in social tourism by digital entrepreneurs were identified, using the MICMAC analysis. Regulatory and financial reasons were found to be the most significant inhibitors, while perceived value and attitude, government backing, and personal motivation were found to be the most significant drivers of sustainable practices. The research also found that the two most important variables in encouraging digital businesses to practice sustainable social tourism were government backing and personal drive. All of these factors were highly influential and interconnected. However, regulatory and financial concerns exhibited high dependent power and were interrelated, suggesting that they would need to be addressed through a concerted effort by all relevant parties. The purpose of this research was to use ISM methodology to identify the most important drivers and constraints to the implementation and adoption of sustainable practices by digital entrepreneurs in social tourism.

The findings of this study can be utilized by policymakers, researchers, and digital entrepreneurs to promote eco-friendly social tourism practices. It was discovered that perceived value, perceived attitude, government support, and personal motivation are potent drivers, whereas regulatory and financial variables are dependent. In addition to government support and personal motivation, the research indicates that digital entrepreneurs must understand the significance of sustainable practices and have a positive attitude towards them. The findings of this study regarding legal and financial obstacles to the sustainability of digital entrepreneurs highlight the need for policymakers to cultivate an environment that is conducive to the adoption of such practices. The results of employing the ISM method and MICMAC analysis to the hierarchical structure are depicted in Figure 8.2.

8.5 IMPLICATIONS

The implications of the study's findings for academics, policymakers, and digital entrepreneurs are numerous. The study highlights the necessity for policymakers to establish a regulatory and financial environment that encourages digital businesses to implement sustainable social tourism practices. This may involve providing financial incentives, developing regulations that promote sustainable practices, and training and assisting entrepreneurs. The study illuminates for academics the intricate relationships between the factors influencing sustainable practices in social tourism. The methods utilized in this study can be used to various contexts in order to identify the drivers and barriers to sustainable practices in other contexts. The study underlines the significance of understanding the value of sustainable practices and having a favorable attitude toward them for digital entrepreneurs. Government support and personal motivation were also identified as important factors This knowledge can help entrepreneurs prioritize sustainable practices in their business models and seek support from stakeholders and policymakers.

8.6 LIMITATIONS AND FUTURE RESEARCH DIRECTIONS

In accordance with the ethos of scholarly inquiry, it is imperative to acknowledge that this study, like all endeavors of intellectual exploration, is not exempt from certain limitations that need careful consideration. To start with, the study was executed within a particular setting and may lack generalizability to other contexts. The study's methodology was based on the subjective perceptions and opinions of its participants, which could potentially be influenced by various biases. Future research may overcome these limitations by employing a more extensive sample size and incorporating quantitative data to supplement the qualitative data. Further studies may delve into the specific sustainable practices that digital entrepreneurs can adopt and the means by which they can be assimilated into their operational frameworks. Future research could look into the impact of sustainable tourism practices on the financial performance of digital entrepreneurs operating in the area of social tourism.

Finally, the study may potentially investigate the impact of engaging in collaborative efforts with local communities and other stakeholders toward the advancement of sustainable practices in the realm of social tourism.

8.7 CONCLUSION

The study aimed to identify the factors affecting the adoption and implementation of sustainable practices by digital entrepreneurs in social tourism using ISM methodology. Qualitative analysis is applied to the data collected from semistructured interviews to decipher its meaning. The analysis involves identifying and categorizing the variables that emerge from the interviews. The variables are then used to develop a hierarchical structure of the factors affecting sustainable practices by digital entrepreneurs in social tourism. The results are presented in the form of a diagram that depicts the complex relationships among the factors affecting sustainable practices.

According to the findings of this study, regulatory and financial factors have strong dependent power, whereas perceived value, perceived attitude, government support, and personal motivation have strong driving power. This study considerably contributes to the current scholarly discourse by providing a thorough examination of the determining factors that influence the implementation and adoption of sustainable practices within the domain of social tourism, particularly among digital entrepreneurs. This research contributes to the advancement of knowledge in this field by providing a deeper understanding of the complexities and dynamics underlying the promotion of sustainable practices in social tourism. These findings can be utilized by policymakers, academics, and digital entrepreneurs to promote sustainable social tourism practices. The research has practical implications for policymakers, academics, and digital entrepreneurs.

Policymakers can use the findings of this study to develop regulatory frameworks and financial incentives to promote sustainable practices in social tourism. Academics can use these findings to further research in this area and to develop training programs for digital entrepreneurs to promote sustainable practices in social tourism. Digital entrepreneurs can use these findings to develop strategies to integrate sustainable practices into their business operations, thereby improving the sustainability of social tourism.

KEYWORDS

- **tourism**
- **entrepreneurship**
- **ISM**
- **MICMAC**

REFERENCES

Al-Ansi, A.; Han, H. Role of Halal-Friendly Destination Performances, Value, Satisfaction, and Trust in Generating Destination Image and Loyalty. *J. Destin. Mark. Manag.* **2019,** *13*, 51–60. https://doi.org/10.1016/j.jdmm.2019.05.007

Antunes, M.; Dias, Á.; Gonçalves, F.; Sousa, B.; Pereira, L. Measuring Sustainable Tourism Lifestyle Entrepreneurship Orientation to Improve Tourist Experience. *Sustainability* **2023,** *15* (2), 1201. https://doi.org/10.3390/su15021201

Avinash, A.; Sasikumar, P.; Murugesan, A. Understanding the Interaction Among the Barriers of Biodiesel Production from Waste Cooking Oil in India- An Interpretive Structural Modeling Approach. *Renew. Energy* **2018,** *127*, 678–684. https://doi.org/10.1016/j.renene.2018.04.079

Babu, D. E.; Kaur, A.; Rajendran, C. Sustainability Practices in Tourism Supply Chain: Importance Performance Analysis. *Benchmarking* **2018,** *25* (4), 1148–1170. https://doi.org/10.1108/BIJ-06-2016-0084

Bahadori, M.; Teymourzadeh, E.; Tajik, H.; Ravangard, R.; Raadabadi, M.; Hosseini, S. M. Factors Affecting Strategic Plan Implementation using Interpretive Structural Modeling (ISM). *Int. J. Health Care Qual. Assur.* **2018,** *31* (5), 406–414. https://doi.org/10.1108/IJHCQA-05-2017-0075

Baig, U.; Hussain, B. M.; Meidute-Kavaliauskiene, I.; Davidavicius, S. Digital Entrepreneurship: Future Research Directions and Opportunities for New Business Model. *Sustainability (Switzerland)* **2022,** *14* (9), 1–16. https://doi.org/10.3390/su14095004

Bauwens, T.; Huybrechts, B.; Dufays, F. Understanding the Diverse Scaling Strategies of Social Enterprises as Hybrid Organizations: The Case of Renewable Energy Cooperatives. *Org. Environ.* **2020,** *33* (2), 195–219. https://doi.org/10.1177/1086026619837126

Budeanu, A. Impacts and Responsibilities for Sustainable Tourism: A Tour Operator's Perspective. *J. Clean. Prod.* **2005,** *13* (2), 89–97. https://doi.org/10.1016/j.jclepro.2003.12.024

Budeanu, A.; Miller, G.; Moscardo, G.; Ooi, C. S. Sustainable Tourism, Progress, Challenges and Opportunities: An Introduction. *J. Clean. Prod.* **2016,** *111*, 285–294. https://doi.org/10.1016/j.jclepro.2015.10.027

Buhalis, D.; Leung, D.; Lin, M. Metaverse as a Disruptive Technology Revolutionising Tourism Management and Marketing. *Tour. Manag.* **2023,** *97*, 104724. https://doi.org/10.1016/j.tourman.2023.104724

Carr, A.; Ruhanen, L.; Whitford, M. Indigenous Peoples and Tourism: The Challenges and Opportunities for Sustainable Tourism. *J. Sustain. Tour.* **2016,** *24* (8–9), 1067–1079. https://doi.org/10.1080/09669582.2016.1206112

Cavalcante, W. Q. de F.; Coelho, A.; Bairrada, C. M. Sustainability and Tourism Marketing: A Bibliometric Analysis of Publications between 1997 and 2020 using Vosviewer Software. *Sustainability (Switzerland)* **2021,** *13* (9). https://doi.org/10.3390/su13094987

Cherrafi, A.; Elfezazi, S.; Garza-reyes, J. A.; Benhida, K. The Management of Operations Barriers in Green Lean Implementation: A Combined Systematic Literature Review and Interpretive Structural Modelling Approach Barriers in Green Lean Implementation: A Combined Systematic Literature Review and. *Prod. Plan. Control* **2017,** *7287*, 1–14. https://doi.org/10.1080/09537287.2017.1324184

Constantin, F.; Kavoura, A. Digital Entrepreneurship via Sustainable Online Communication of Dentistry Profession, Oradea, Romania: A Longitudinal Analysis. *Sustainability (Switzerland)* **2022,** *14* (2), 1–20. https://doi.org/10.3390/su14020802

Deb, S. K.; Nafi, S. M.; Valeri, M. Promoting Tourism Business through Digital Marketing in the New Normal Era: A Sustainable Approach. *Eur. J. Innov. Manag.* **2022.** https://doi.org/10.1108/EJIM-04-2022-0218

Frey, N.; George, R. Responsible Tourism Management: The Missing Link between Business Owners' Attitudes and Behavior in the Cape Town Tourism Industry. *Tour. Manag.* **2010,** *31* (5), 621–628. https://doi.org/10.1016/j.tourman.2009.06.017

Gössling, S.; Michael Hall, C. Sharing Versus Collaborative Economy: How to Align ICT Developments and the SDGs in Tourism? *J. Sustain. Tour.* **2019,** *27* (1), 74–96. https://doi.org/10.1080/09669582.2018.1560455

Kapera, I. Sustainable Tourism Development Efforts by Local Governments in Poland. *Sustain. Cities Soc.* **2018,** *40*, 581–588. https://doi.org/10.1016/j.scs.2018.05.001

Kaswan, M. S.; Rathi, R. Analysis and Modeling the Enablers of Green Lean Six Sigma Implementation using Interpretive Structural Modeling. *J. Clean. Prod.* **2019,** *231*, 1182–1191. https://doi.org/10.1016/j.jclepro.2019.05.253

Kumar, R.; Goel, P. Exploring the Domain of Interpretive Structural Modelling (ISM) for Sustainable Future Panorama: A Bibliometric and Content Analysis. *Arch. Comput. Methods Eng.* **2021,** *0123456789*. https://doi.org/10.1007/s11831-021-09675-7

Lim, M. K.; Tseng, M. L.; Tan, K. H.; Bui, T. D. Knowledge Management in Sustainable Supply Chain Management: Improving Performance through an Interpretive Structural Modelling Approach. *J. Clean. Prod.* **2017,** *162*, 806–816. https://doi.org/10.1016/j.jclepro.2017.06.056

Lutfi, A.; Alsyouf, A.; Almaiah, M. A.; Alrawad, M.; Abdo, A. A. K.; Al-Khasawneh, A. L.; Ibrahim, N.; Saad, M. Factors Influencing the Adoption of Big Data Analytics in the Digital Transformation Era: Case Study of Jordanian SMEs. *Sustainability (Switzerland)* **2022,** *14* (3), 1–17. https://doi.org/10.3390/su14031802

Milwood, P. A.; Maxwell, A. A Boundary Objects View of Entrepreneurial Ecosystems in Tourism. *J. Hosp. Tour. Manag.* **2020,** *44*, 243–252. https://doi.org/10.1016/j.jhtm.2020.06.008

Mishra, N.; Singh, A.; Rana, N. P.; Dwivedi, Y. K. Interpretive Structural Modelling and Fuzzy MICMAC Approaches for Customer Centric Beef Supply Chain: Application of a Big Data Technique. *Prod. Plan. Control* **2017,** *28* (11–12), 945–963. https://doi.org/10.1080/09537287.2017.1336789

Moreno de la Santa, J. G. S. Tourism as a Lever for a More Inclusive Society. *Worldw. Hosp. Tour. Themes* **2020,** *12* (6), 731–738. https://doi.org/10.1108/WHATT-07-2020-0071

Pan, S. Y.; Gao, M.; Kim, H.; Shah, K. J.; Pei, S. L.; Chiang, P. C. Advances and Challenges in Sustainable Tourism Toward a Green Economy. *Sci. Total Environ.* **2018,** *635*, 452–469. https://doi.org/10.1016/j.scitotenv.2018.04.134

Ranjan Debata, B.; Sree, K.; Patnaik, B.; Sankar Mahapatra, S. Evaluating Medical Tourism Enablers with Interpretive Structural Modeling. *Benchmarking Int. J.* **2013,** *20* (6), 716–743. https://doi.org/10.1108/BIJ-10-2011-0079

Risteskia, M.; Kocevskia, J.; Arnaudov, K. Spatial Planning and Sustainable Tourism as Basis for Developing Competitive Tourist Destinations. *Procedia Soc. Behav. Sci.* **2012,** *44*, 375–386. https://doi.org/10.1016/j.sbspro.2012.05.042

Shafiee, S.; Ghatari, A. R.; Hasanzadeh, A.; Jahanyan, S. Developing a Model for Smart Tourism Destinations: An Interpretive Structural Modelling Approach. In *Information Technology and Tourism*; Springer: Berlin Heidelberg, 2022; vol *24* (4). https://doi.org/10.1007/s40558-022-00236-7

Sharma, K.; Jain, M.; Dhir, S. Analysing the Impact of Artificial Intelligence on the Competitiveness of Tourism Firms: A Modified Total Interpretive Structural Modeling (m-TISM) Approach. *Int. J. Emerg. Mark.* **2022,** *17* (4), 1067–1084. https://doi.org/10.1108/IJOEM-05-2021-0810

Singh, S.; Kumar, R.; Kumar, U. Modelling Factors Affecting Human Operator Failure Probability in Railway Maintenance Tasks: An ISM-Based Analysis. *Int. J. Syst. Assur. Eng. Manag.* **2015,** *6* (2), 129–138. https://doi.org/10.1007/s13198-014-0255-0

Wu, W. S.; Yang, C. F.; Chang, J. C.; Château, P. A.; Chang, Y. C. Risk Assessment by Integrating Interpretive Structural Modeling and Bayesian Network, Case of Offshore Pipeline Project. *Reliab. Eng. Syst. Saf.* **2015,** *142*, 515–524. https://doi.org/10.1016/j.ress.2015.06.013

CHAPTER 9

Sustainable Synergy: Exploring the Relationship Between Environmental Marketing and Green Entrepreneurship for Business

MANJARI SHARMA[1], ANUGU HARSHAVARDHAN REDDY[2], and ZIDAN KACHHI[3]

[1]*School of Commerce, Finance & Accountancy, CHRIST (Deemed To Be University), Pune Lavasa Campus, India*

[2]*School of Business & Management, CHRIST (Deemed To Be University), Pune Lavasa Campus, India*

[3]*School of Commerce, Finance & Accountancy, CHRIST (Deemed To Be University), Pune Lavasa Campus, India*

ABSTRACT

Environmental marketing and green entrepreneurship have emerged as vital approaches for businesses to integrate sustainability principles into their operations. This study explores the relationship between environmental marketing and green entrepreneurship as a sustainable approach for businesses. The methodology adopted for this study involves an exploratory literature review, which includes a review of scholarly articles on environmental marketing and green entrepreneurship. The sample description included a wide range of literature from diverse sources, covering various aspects of environmental marketing and green entrepreneurship. Literature was analyzed using qualitative thematic analysis, which involves identifying recurring themes, patterns, and insights from the literature. The results reveal that environmental

Agile Business Transformations: Priorities, Lessons, and Practices. Satyajit Chakrabarti, Subrata Chattopadhyay, Udit Chawla, Sundeep Singh Sondhi, & Arunava Dalal (Eds.)

marketing and green entrepreneurship are closely interconnected with the themes that emerged. The discussion revolves around the conclusions drawn from the results, including the implications for businesses, consumers, and society, and the potential benefits of integrating environmental marketing and green entrepreneurship as a sustainable approach. The study provides insights for businesses, policymakers, and other stakeholders on the importance of environmental marketing and green entrepreneurship in driving sustainable business practices and fostering environmental sustainability.

9.1 INTRODUCTION

In today's global corporate environment, sustainability has emerged as a crucial problem, with increasing concerns about environmental degradation and social responsibility. Government and International bodies have raised environmental concerns from time to time and are working continuously to overcome environmental-related issues and create sustainably solutions to various problems like the usage of plastics, waste management, air and water pollution, and many more.

Various organizations are mandated to adopt sustainable practices and strategies to mitigate their environmental and societal impacts. In response, the ideas of environmental marketing and green entrepreneurship have emerged as important concepts that businesses can leverage to promote environmentally responsible products, services, and practices. Based on empirical evidence and existing literature, this chapter discovers the association between environmental marketing and green entrepreneurship as a sustainable business approach.

Environmental marketing is a strategic approach that uses marketing strategies to advertise eco-friendly goods and services and to convey a business' commitment to sustainability (Peattie and Charter, 2003). It includes a range of tactics, including developing green product development, branding, pricing, distribution, and communication (Polonsky and Rosenberger, 2001). On the other side, green entrepreneurship is creating and managing firms built on ecologically sustainable concepts and practices (Schaper et al., 2014). According to Schaltegger and Wagner (2011), green entrepreneurs are distinguished by their proactive and creative approach to addressing environmental concerns through their business strategies, products, and practices.

A study by Molinillo et al. (2018) discovered that green entrepreneurs use a variety of environmental marketing strategies, such as green branding and green communication, to sell their sustainable goods and services to consumers. These strategies help green entrepreneurs stand out from the competition and lure in customers that care about the environment and respect sustainability. Similarly, Baumann et al. (2017) found that green entrepreneurs might convey their commitment to sustainability through environmental marketing and establish a positive reputation, which can increase customer loyalty and trust in their brands.

Environmental marketing also allows green business owners to inform customers about environmental concerns and encourage pro-environmental behavior. For instance, Peattie and Charter (2003) revealed that environmental marketing initiatives can increase customers' awareness of environmental issues and inspire them to engage in more sustainable habits, such as recycling or cutting back on energy use. This shows that environmental marketing may do more than just advertise goods or services; it can also influence social change by fostering ethical customer behavior.

Environmental marketing has effects on businesses, consumers, and society as a whole in addition to its advantages for green business owners. First, companies can use environmental marketing as a tactic to stand out from the competition and achieve a competitive edge. Consumer preference for environmentally friendly goods and services is growing, according to a study by Ottman et al. (2006). Companies that successfully market their sustainability initiatives to consumers can win their business and increase customer loyalty. Additionally, environmental marketing can support businesses' long-term success.

This chapter's objective is to explore the relationship between green entrepreneurship and environmental marketing as a sustainable approach for business. The paper intends to uncover the interconnectedness between environmental marketing and green entrepreneurship and highlight the implications for businesses, consumers, and society by going through a comprehensive literature review and qualitative theme analysis. The chapter also aims to give firms, governments, and other stakeholders insights into the significance of integrating environmental marketing and green entrepreneurship in promoting environmentally sustainable business practices.

9.2 METHODOLOGY

This research has adopted an exploratory research method of study. The study has undergone several research papers in the past, from 2015 to 2023. The discovered papers during the selected period were categorized based on various themes and scopes.

The research databases Google Scholar, Semantic Scholar, and Social Science Research Network were used to search for relevant studies using the keywords environmental marketing, green entrepreneurship, sustainable business, green product, etc.

If a paper included the variables environmental marketing, green entrepreneurship, and sustainable business in relation to each other, they were included in the present study. Literature that did not fulfill these criteria were rejected.

The authors found 64 a number of studies, out of which 32 studies were used for the categorization of themes based on the inclusion criteria.

9.3 FINDINGS AND DISCUSSION

The review of the literature revealed that many studies are increasing, including variables related to environment-conscious business frameworks. Most methods being used to study these areas include theoretical conceptualization models, reviews, and empirical research. These studies seem to be ultimately contributing to the analysis of present policies and the formation of fresh ones. They also address the challenges, opportunities, and benefits of green entrepreneurship in the context of society and communities. Many investigations are integrating the creation of business models while studying internal factors such as motivation, intention, orientation, resilience, and many more. Common broader themes that emerged during the review include innovation, integration of technology, eco-entrepreneurship, sustainable development, green economic development, social entrepreneurship, environmental marketing, and consumer contribution.

9.3.1 RESEARCH IMPLICATIONS

The outcomes of the study can be applied to understand the current policies in effect in various organizations and how these policies can be modified to accommodate green initiatives within their framework. Additionally, this study can also be used to sensitize students and create awareness about environmental marketing and green entrepreneurship. To motivate first-generation entrepreneurs, the findings can inculcate in them a greater comprehension of the importance of green practices in their business processes. Shaping consumer intentions to buy environmentally conscious products and services.

TABLE 9.1 Literature Analysis from 2015 to 2023.

Reference	Aim	Method	Results	Scope/Theme
Schaper et al. (2014)	This paper aims to provide an introduction to the special issue on green entrepreneurship and environmental marketing, highlighting the importance of the topic.	Literature review	Explored the motivations, obstacles, and advantages of green entrepreneurship and focused on the influence of ideological elements, such as environmental ideals and beliefs, on this behavior.	Green entrepreneurship and environmental marketing
Prakash and Potoski (2015)	This paper aims to explore the concept of environmental entrepreneurship and investigate the role of corporations in addressing environmental issues.	Qualitative analysis of case studies	Through entrepreneurship, corporations may play a vital role in tackling environmental challenges.	Environmental entrepreneurship, corporations
Valliere and Peterson (2015)	This paper aims to provide a synthesis, overview, and research agenda for green marketing, including environmental marketing.	Literature review	Outlines the field of green marketing, including environmental marketing, and its research objectives.	Green marketing, environmental marketing
George and Bock (2015)	This paper aims to discover the notion of business models in the context of entrepreneurship research, including green entrepreneurship.	Conceptual analysis	Examines how business models may have an impact on entrepreneurship research, especially green entrepreneurship.	Business models, entrepreneurship research, green entrepreneurship
Zott and Amit (2015)	This paper targets to provide an outline of recent developments and future research directions related to business models, including those in the context of green entrepreneurship.	Literature review	Provides a summary of current research directions and recent breakthroughs in business models, including green entrepreneurship.	Business models, green entrepreneurship
Wüstenhagen and Schaltegger (2016)	This paper aims to investigate the role of eco-entrepreneurship in innovation policy, using empirical data from the start-up sector in Germany.	Empirical analysis of start-up data	Eco-entrepreneurship can support environmental innovation and government objectives.	Eco-entrepreneurship, innovation policy, Germany

TABLE 9.1 *(Continued)*

Reference	Aim	Method	Results	Scope/Theme
Hockerts and Wüstenhagen (2016)	To propose a conceptual framework, the "green innovation cascade," for understanding the process of green entrepreneurship and innovation from invention to transition.	Conceptual analysis and framework development	conceptual framework that incorporates the creation, commercialization, dissemination, and transition stages of green innovation and emphasizes the contribution of entrepreneurs in bridging the gaps between them.	Scope: Green entrepreneurship and the innovation cascade
Hart (2017)	This paper aims to explore the contribution of entrepreneurship to sustainability, social inclusion, and the common good, including green entrepreneurship.	Literature review	Discusses how entrepreneurship, particularly green entrepreneurship, may help with sustainability, social inclusion, and the common good.	Entrepreneurship, sustainability, social inclusion, common good, green entrepreneurship
Díaz-García and González-Moreno (2017)	To conduct a systematic literature review on social entrepreneurship in the environmental sector.	Systematic literature review	Research gaps and potential future approaches were found after analyzing the conceptualization, motives, methods, outcomes, and problems of the existing literature on social entrepreneurship in the environmental domain.	Scope: Social entrepreneurship in the environmental sector
Jayawarna et al. (2017)	To investigate the role of green entrepreneurship in the sharing economy, specifically in the context of sharing economy platforms for sustainable consumption	Empirical study using qualitative interviews	Examined the goals, tactics, and difficulties faced by green business owners in the sharing economy and identified critical elements, such as community involvement, resource accessibility, and regulatory backing, which either promote or obstruct their success.	Scope: Green entrepreneurship in the sharing economy

TABLE 9.1 *(Continued)*

Reference	Aim	Method	Results	Scope/Theme
Dean et al. (2017)	This paper aims to explore the role of social entrepreneurship in building community resilience, including in the context of environmental and green entrepreneurship.	Qualitative analysis of interviews	By tackling social and environmental issues, social entrepreneurship can help build community resilience.	Social entrepreneurship, community resilience, environmental entrepreneurship
Polonsky (2018)	This paper aims to identify the impediments and opportunities for transformative green marketing, including environmental marketing.	Literature review	Outlines the challenges and potential for innovative green marketing, including environmental marketing.	Green marketing, environmental marketing
Sudin and Mostafa (2018)	To examine the relationship between green marketing, environmental responsibility, and business outcomes in the context of Malaysia.	Survey and quantitative analysis	Green marketing has been found to have a favorable impact on company results through environmental responsibility. This relationship's mediating aspects include the quality of green products, customer trust, and competitive advantage.	Green
Kang et al. (2018)	To review the literature on the linkages between green marketing and green entrepreneurship, and provide empirical evidence and future research directions in this area.	Literature review and conceptual analysis	Examined the body of knowledge already available on green marketing and green entrepreneurship, pointed out the connections between these two ideas, and suggested a study agenda for future investigations into the connections, workings, and results of green marketing and green entrepreneurship.	Green marketing, green entrepreneurship, and research directions

TABLE 9.1 *(Continued)*

Reference	Aim	Method	Results	Scope/Theme
Wijewardena and Gamage (2018)	To conduct a literature review on sustainable entrepreneurship and environmental marketing.	Literature review	Reviewed the literature on sustainable entrepreneurship and environmental marketing, including its conceptualizations, inspirations, plans, results, and difficulties, and found areas that needed further study as well as potential.	Sustainable entrepreneurship and environmental marketing
Schaltegger et al. (2018)	To analyze the co-evolutionary dynamics of business models for sustainability, including sustainable entrepreneurship, innovation, and transformation.	analysis and framework development	Developed a conceptual framework that integrates various sustainability-related aspects of business models, for instance value proposition, value creation, value seizure, and value delivery, and emphasises the co-evolutionary interactions between these dimensions as well as the entrepreneur role in promoting innovations and transformation of business models.	Business models for sustainability, entrepreneurship, innovation, and transformation
Carrigan and Attalla (2019)	To investigate consumers' motivations for using sharing services in the context of a "post-growth" society, where sustainability and environmental concerns are prominent.	Empirical study using quantitative survey	Identified various motivations for using sharing services, including environmental concerns, social connectedness, economic affordability, and convenience, and found that environmental motivations significantly influence consumers' intention to use sharing services, particularly in a "post-growth" societal context.	Sharing economy, consumers' motivations, and environmental concerns

TABLE 9.1 *(Continued)*

Reference	Aim	Method	Results	Scope/Theme
Hörisch and Freeman (2018)	This paper aims to explore the relationship between business models, normativity, and entrepreneurial agency, including in the context of green entrepreneurship.	Conceptual analysis	Examines the connection between entrepreneurial agency, normativity, and business models, notably in the context of green entrepreneurship.	Business models, normativity, entrepreneurial agency, green entrepreneurship
Deutz and Glasbergen (2018)	This paper aims to provide a review on the state of the art of greening the entrepreneur, including in the context of green entrepreneurship and environmental marketing, and proposes a research agenda for future studies.	Literature review	Gives a thorough analysis of "greening the entrepreneur" and suggests a study agenda for further investigations.	Green entrepreneurship, environmental marketing, greening the entrepreneur
Schaltegger et al. (2018)	To analyze the co-evolutionary dynamics of business models for sustainability, including sustainable entrepreneurship, innovation, and transformation.	Conceptual analysis and framework development	Developed a conceptual framework that integrates different dimensions of business models for sustainability, including value proposition, value creation, value seizure, and value delivery, and highlights the co-evolutionary interactions among these dimensions, and the entrepreneur role in driving business exemplary innovation and change for sustainability.	Scope: Business models for sustainability, entrepreneurship, innovation, and transformation
Andreini et al. (2019)	This paper aims to conduct a systematic literature review on green marketing and sustainable entrepreneurship, including the relationship between environmental marketing and green entrepreneurship.	Systematic literature review	Analysis of the connections between green entrepreneurship, sustainable entrepreneurship, and marketing for the environment.	Green marketing, sustainable entrepreneurship, green entrepreneurship

TABLE 9.1 *(Continued)*

Reference	Aim	Method	Results	Scope/Theme
Gast et al. (2019)	This paper aims to investigate the relationship between environmental marketing and the resource-based view in the context of the German manufacturing industry.	Empirical analysis of survey data	Environmental marketing can enhance a company's capabilities and resources and provide it a competitive advantage.	Environmental marketing, resource-based view, German manufacturing industry
Hall et al. (2019)	This paper aims to review the past contributions of sustainable entrepreneurship research and provide future directions for the field.	Literature review and conceptual analysis	Outlines the major research areas, offers suggestions for future research, and provides a thorough assessment of the literature on sustainable entrepreneurship.	Sustainable development, entrepreneurship, literature review
Lüdeke-Freund and Dembek (2019)	This paper aims to explore the motivations of environmentally and socially motivated individuals to start sustainable businesses, including green entrepreneurship.	Literature review and empirical analysis	Identifies the drivers of sustainable entrepreneurship and emphasizes the significance of social and environmental considerations	Sustainable entrepreneurship, green entrepreneurship, motivations
Wang and Lin (2019)	This paper aims to investigate the influence of entrepreneurial orientation on environmental marketing strategy, and the mediating role of green marketing capability.	Empirical analysis of survey data	Green marketing expertise has a mediating function in the favorable influence of entrepreneurial attitude on environmental marketing strategy.	Entrepreneurial orientation, environmental marketing strategy, green marketing capability
Rehman et al. (2020)	This paper aims to investigate the green entrepreneurial intention of individuals by integrating the Theory of Planned Behavior and Social Cognitive Career Theory, focusing on environmental entrepreneurship.	Empirical analysis of survey data	Identifies elements that affect the purpose of green entrepreneurs and emphasizes the importance of environmental attitudes and self-efficacy	Green entrepreneurial intention, Theory of Planned Behavior, Social Cognitive Career Theory, environmental entrepreneurship

TABLE 9.1 *(Continued)*

Reference	Aim	Method	Results	Scope/Theme
Shahbaz et al. (2020)	This paper aims to explore the nexus between green marketing, environmental entrepreneurship, and sustainable development, and highlights the potential contribution of green marketing and environmental entrepreneurship toward sustainable development.	Conceptual analysis	Highlights the potential contribution to sustainable development and discusses the connections between green marketing, environmental entrepreneurship, and sustainable development.	Green marketing, environmental entrepreneurship, sustainable development
Jiao et al. (2021)	This paper aims to investigate the relationship between environmental orientation and performance in green entrepreneurship and the intermediating role of green innovation capability.	Empirical analysis of survey data	Through the mediating function of green innovation potential, environmental orientation promotes green entrepreneurship performance in a favorable manner.	Environmental orientation, green entrepreneurship, green innovation capability
Zarei et al. (2021)	This paper aims to explore the entrepreneurial opportunities and barriers in green entrepreneurship through qualitative analysis.	Qualitative analysis of interviews	Identifies green entrepreneurship's business prospects and obstacles, such as those linked to regulations, finances, and markets.	Green entrepreneurship, entrepreneurial opportunities, barriers
Wang et al. (2022)	To conceptualize how ecopreneurship and green technological innovation play a role in the effects of green economy policies on sustainable economic development.	Theoretical framework	Green entrepreneurs can propose novel green technology and sustainability-driven business models in an environment that is conducive to "green" incorporation in public policy.	sustainable economic development
Mia et al. (2021)	To examine the significance of university students' entrepreneurial purpose to advance social change through eco-entrepreneurship in connection to the AMO hypothesis.	Partial Least Square Structural Equation Model (PLS-SEM)	AMO theory has an impact on the entrepreneurship education, incentives, and predictor variables, and these abilities are statistically relevant for green entrepreneurship.	green entrepreneurship and social change

TABLE 9.1 *(Continued)*

Reference	Aim	Method	Results	Scope/Theme
Genoveva and Tanardi (2021)	To assess the desire of millennials in Indonesia to become environmentally conscious entrepreneurs and investigate their future behavior once they become entrepreneurs	Online questionnaire, PLS-SEM	Greener awareness and understanding could result in more environmentally concerned business people.	Green entrepreneurship

9.3.2 CONCLUSION AND RECOMMENDATIONS

In conclusion, green entrepreneurship and environmental marketing are crucial elements of a sustainable business strategy in the current global economic environment. Green business owners can promote their environmentally friendly goods and services, educate clients about environmental issues, and promote environmentally friendly behavior by utilizing environmental marketing techniques. Environmental marketing can also aid green business owners in obtaining funding and building a solid reputation that will improve client loyalty and brand trust. Businesses can gain a competitive edge and long-term success by integrating sustainable practises and strategies into their operations as demand from customers for eco-friendly goods and services continues to develop. To encourage environmental responsibility and contribute to a more sustainable future, firms must embrace environmental marketing and green entrepreneurship.

Future research in the areas of green entrepreneurship and environmental marketing may fill a number of research gaps identified in the publications analyzed in Table 9.1. First of all, there is a need for more long-term research that looks at how green entrepreneurship performs over time and what effects it has on social, economic, and environmental spheres. This might help us comprehend the impact and long-term feasibility of green entrepreneurial endeavors. Second, future studies ought to concentrate on context-specific factors that influence green entrepreneurial practises and tactics. To fully comprehend the distinctive potential and limitations of green entrepreneurship and environmental marketing, this may include researching certain businesses, sectors, regions, or countries. Thirdly, more research needs to be done on how stakeholders may affect and promote green entrepreneurial initiatives. It may be possible to gain insight into how to advance and maintain green entrepreneurship ventures by comprehending stakeholder dynamics and interactions. Fourthly, there has to be more study on the psychological and behavioral characteristics of green business owners and consumers. This could entail examining the factors, such as environmental values, attitudes, risk perceptions, and decision-making processes, that affect green consumer and entrepreneur behaviors. Last, but not the least, investigating the links between social identities and green entrepreneurship may illuminate the challenges faced by disadvantaged groups and offer solutions for fostering inclusivity and diversity in the sector. Such a strategy could aid in the growth of a green entrepreneurship industry that is more equal and inclusive.

KEYWORDS

- **environmental marketing**
- **green entrepreneurship**
- **sustainability**
- **business perspectives**

REFERENCES

Andreini, D.; Ciappei, C.; De Marco, A. Green Marketing and Sustainable Entrepreneurship: A Systematic Literature Review. *Corp. Soc. Resp. Environ. Manag.* **2019,** *26* (3), 645–660.

Baumann, S.; Kunze, F.; Kowalski, P. Promoting Green Entrepreneurship: A Conceptual Framework for Achieving Environmental and Economic Sustainability. *J. Bus. Ventur. Insights* **2017,** *8,* 86–93.

Carrigan, M.; Attalla, A. The Sharing Economy and a "Post-Growth" Society: An Examination of Consumers' Motivations for Using Sharing Services. *J. Bus. Ethics* **2019,** *160* (3), 775–788.

Dean, M. A.; Raiborn, C.; Yohn, T. L. Social Entrepreneurship as a Path to Community Resilience: Voices from the Grassroots. *J. Entrep. Public Policy* **2017,** *6* (1), 87–110.

Deutz, P.; Glasbergen, P. Greening the Entrepreneur: A Review on the State of the Art and a Research Agenda. *Small Bus. Econ.* **2018,** *50* (2), 335–359.

Díaz-García, C.; González-Moreno, Á. Social Entrepreneurship in the Environmental Sector: A Systematic Literature Review. *Sustainability* **2017,** *9* (6), 999.

Gast, J.; Gundolf, K.; Kraus, S. Environmental Marketing and the Resource-Based View: Insights from the German Manufacturing Industry. *Bus. Strateg. Environ.* **2019,** *28* (3), 360–374.

Genoveva, G.; Tanardi, J. Green Entrepreneurship: A New Paradigm for Millennials in Indonesia. International Journal of Innovation, *Creat. Change* **2021,** *15* (6), 288–305.

George, G.; Bock, A. J. The Business Model in Practice and its Implications for Entrepreneurship Research. *Entrep. Theory Pract.* **2015,** *39* (1), 83–111.

Hall, J. K.; Daneke, G. A.; Lenox, M. J. Sustainable Development and Entrepreneurship: Past Contributions and Future Directions. *J. Bus. Ventur.* **2019,** *34* (5), 647–663.

Hart, S. L. Entrepreneurship's Contribution to Sustainability, Social Inclusion, and the Common Good. *Acad. Manag. Perspect.* **2017,** *31* (3), 236–254.

Hockerts, K.; Wüstenhagen, R. Green Entrepreneurship and the Green Innovation Cascade: Bridging the Gap between Invention and Transition. *J. Clean. Prod.* **2016,** *127,* 418–431.

Hörisch, J.; Freeman, R. E. Business models, Normativity, and Entrepreneurial Agency: The Promise of a Philosophy of Entrepreneurship. *J. Bus. Ethics* **2018,** *150* (1), 1–15.

Jayawarna, D.; Jones, O.; Macpherson, A. Green Entrepreneurship in the Sharing Economy: An Empirical Investigation. *Int. Small Bus. J.* **2017,** *35* (1), 44–59.

Jiao, H.; Li, Y.; Yuan, X. The Relationship Between Environmental Orientation and Performance in *green entrepreneurship*: The Mediating Role of Green Innovation Capability. *Sustainability* **2021,** *13* (1), 43.

Kang, K. H.; Lee, S.; Huh, C. Green Marketing and Green Entrepreneurship: Linkages, Empirical Evidence, and Future Research Directions. *Sustainability* **2018,** *10* (8), 2804.

Lüdeke-Freund, F.; Dembek, K. Sustainable Entrepreneurship in Organizations: What Motivates Environmentally and Socially Motivated Individuals to Start Sustainable Businesses? *Organ. Environ.* **2019,** *32* (1), 6–28.

Mia, M. M.; Rizwan, S.; Zayed, N. M.; Nitsenko, V.; Miroshnyk, O.; Kryshtal, H.; Ostapenko, R. The Impact of Green Entrepreneurship on Social Change and Factors Influencing AMO Theory. *Sustainability* **2021,** *13* (6), 3566.

Molinillo, S.; Vidal-Suárez, M.; Frías-Jamilena, D. M. The Influence of Green Marketing on Environmental Entrepreneurial Intention: The Mediating Role of Environmental Attitude. *J. Clean. Prod.* **2018,** *171,* 522–530.

Ottman, J. A.; Stafford, E. R.; Hartman, C. L. Avoiding Green Marketing Myopia: Ways to Improve Consumer Appeal for Environmentally Preferable Products. *Environ. Sci. Policy Sustain. Dev.* **2006,** *48* (5), 22–36.

Peattie, S.; Charter, M. Ready to Fly Solo? Reducing Social Marketing's Dependence on Commercial Marketing Theory. *Marketing Theory* **2003,** *3* (3), 333–355.

Peattie, S.; Peattie, I. Ready to Fly Solo? Self-Initiated Single Market Entry by International Environmental Non-Governmental Organizations. *Int. Mark. Rev.* **2003,** *20* (2), 192–213.

Polonsky, M. J. Transformative Green Marketing: Impediments and Opportunities. *Australasian Mark. J. (AMJ)* **2018,** *26* (4), 311–320.

Polonsky, M. J.; Rosenberger III, P. J. Reevaluating Green Marketing: A Strategic Approach. *Business Horizons* **2001,** *44* (5), 21–30

Prakash, G.; Potoski, M. Environmental Entrepreneurship: Can Corporations Save the Planet? *Bus. Soc.* **2015,** *54* (2), 157–193.

Rehman, A. U.; Ali, R.; Abbas, J. Green Entrepreneurial Intention: An Integration of Theory of Planned Behavior and Social Cognitive Career Theory. *Corp. Soc. Resp. Environ. Manag.* **2020,** *27* (5), 2110–2121.

Schaltegger, S.; Wagner, M. Sustainable Entrepreneurship and Sustainability Innovation: Categories and Interactions. *Bus. Strateg. Environ.* **2011,** *20* (4), 222–237.

Schaltegger, S.; Hansen, E. G.; Lüdeke-Freund, F. Business Models for Sustainability: A Co-Evolutionary Analysis of Sustainable Entrepreneurship, Innovation, and Transformation. *Organ. Environ.* **2018,** *31* (4), 336–354.

Schaltegger, S.; Hansen, E. G.; Lüdeke-Freund, F. Business Models for Sustainability: A Co-evolutionary Analysis of Sustainable Entrepreneurship, Innovation, and Transformation. *Organ. Environ.* **2018,** *31* (4), 336–354.

Schaper, M. T.; Volery, T.; Weber, P. C.; Gibson, B. Entrepreneurship and Green Business: An Overview and Future Research Directions. *Organ. Environ.* **2014,** *27* (2), 109–139.

Shahbaz, M.; Amjad, R.; Javed, M. A. Green Marketing, Environmental Entrepreneurship and Sustainable Development: Exploring the Nexus. *Corp. Soc. Resp. Environ. Manag.* **2020,** *27* (6), 2823–2833.

Sudin, S.; Mostafa, M. M. Green Marketing, Environmental Responsibility, and Business Outcomes: Evidence from Malaysia. *Bus. Strateg. Environ.* **2018,** *27* (8), 1450–1462

Valliere, D.; Peterson, R. T. Green Marketing: A Synthesis, Overview and Research Agenda. *J. Acad. Mark. Sci.* **2015,** *43* (1), 1–18.

Wang, D.; Lin, Z. The Influence of Entrepreneurial Orientation on Environmental Marketing Strategy: The Mediating Role of Green Marketing Capability. *Front. Bus. Res. China* **2019,** *13* (1), 1–27.

Wang, X.; Javaid, M. U.; Bano, S.; Younas, H.; Jan, A.; Salameh, A. A. Interplay Among Institutional Actors for Sustainable Economic Development—Role of Green Policies, Ecoprenuership, and Green Technological Innovation. *J. Clean. Prod.* **2022,** *332,* 130202.
Wijewardena, H.; Gamage, S. Sustainable Entrepreneurship and Environmental Marketing: A Review of Literature. *Int. J. Manag. Sustain.* **2018,** *7* (4), 27–38.
Wüstenhagen, R.; Schaltegger, S. The Role of Eco-entrepreneurship in Innovation policy: Empirical Insights on the Start-up Sector in Germany. *Ecol. Econom.* **2016,** *126,* 112–122.
Zarei, B.; Azadi, M.; Hosseininia, G.; Teixeira, R. Entrepreneurial Opportunities and Barriers in Green Entrepreneurship: A Qualitative Study. *Sustain. Prod. Consump.* **2021,** *28,* 1038–1053.
Zott, C.; Amit, R. The Business Model: Recent Developments and Future Research. *J. Manag.* **2015,** *43* (1), 76–107.

CHAPTER 10

The Effectiveness of Vlogging as a Tool for Sustainable Travel Education: Evidence from Luxury Travel Vloggers in Dubai

RAJESH MOHNOT[1], SHUBHAM KUMAR SHAW[2], DEBOLINA MITRA[3], VISHAL CHOUDHARY[4], and RAUNAK PANDEY[5]

[1]*Department of Finance, Ajman University, Ajman, United Arab Emirates*

[2]*Techno India University, Kolkata, West Bengal, India*

[3]*Academic Associate, Indian Institute of Management, Bangalore, India*

[4]*The Heritage Academy, Kolkata, West Bengal, India*

[5]*The Calcutta Anglo Gujarati College, Kolkata, West Bengal, India*

ABSTRACT

Purpose: The rise of ecotourism has highlighted how important it is to educate tourists on how to travel sustainably. In this study, a case study of luxury travel vloggers in Dubai is utilized to assess the potential of using vlogging as a tool for sustainable travel education.

The survey revealed that the vloggers' fans believed that vlogging was an effective way to teach others about environmental friendly travel. They believed that vlogging might promote eco-friendly travel destinations and experiences, encourage visitors to engage in eco-friendly behaviors, and spread awareness of eco-friendly travel options. Overall, our study suggests that vlogging, especially among young people with high levels of education and financial resources, may be an effective method for teaching them about sustainable travel. Luxury travel vloggers in Dubai may use their platform to

Agile Business Transformations: Priorities, Lessons, and Practices. Satyajit Chakrabarti, Subrata Chattopadhyay, Udit Chawla, Sundeep Singh Sondhi, & Arunava Dalal (Eds.)

promote environmentally responsible travel and educate their audience about its benefits. However, vloggers need to make sure that their messages on sustainability are factually correct, trustworthy, and backed up by research. Future research may look at the effectiveness of vlogging as a method for teaching different types of travelers about sustainable travel in different contexts. It may examine how social media apps like Instagram and TikTok support the promotion of environmentally friendly travel strategies and destinations. In the end, this research could contribute to the development of sustainable tourist policies that are both favorable commercially and environmentally.

Design/methodology: Structured questionnaires were used to conduct this research. Men and women from diverse age groups, economic ranges, and work-related circumstances, together with business, service, and others, provided the study's principal sources of data. Each survey parameter was estimated on a measure of 5 points, ranging from 1 for "strongly disagree" to 5 for "strongly agree."

Findings: The study found that luxury travel vloggers in Dubai may successfully disseminate information about eco-friendly travel via their blogs. The viewers of the vloggers had an interest in sustainability and saw vlogging as a way to disseminate information and promote eco-friendly travel alternatives.

10.1 INTRODUCTION

Tourism has always been a major contributor to the global economy, with its growth showing no signs of slowing down. However, with this growth comes the pressing issue of sustainability, as the environmental and social impact of tourism activities can have long-term consequences on destinations and communities (Ontiveros, 2016). In this context, sustainable travel education has become an increasingly important topic of discussion among industry professionals, policymakers, and tourists themselves (Li et al., 2017). Travel has also become one of the most popular leisure activities in the world, with more than 1.5 billion international tourist arrivals in 2019 (UNWTO, 2021). However, the growth of tourism has also led to negative impacts on the environment, economy, and society in many destinations (Huang, 2021). As a result, sustainable tourism has emerged as a new paradigm that aims to balance the economic, environmental, and social aspects of tourism development (Sheppard and Fennell, 2019). Sustainable travel education is a critical element of sustainable tourism, as it can raise awareness among tourists about the impacts of their travel and encourage them to make responsible choices (Pike and Page, 2014).

One of the emerging tools for sustainable travel education is vlogging, which refers to the practice of creating and sharing video content on social media platforms. Vlogging has gained popularity in recent years, as it allows travelers to share their experiences with a global audience, build their brands, and monetize their content (Yang et al., 2022). Luxury travel vloggers are a particular type of vlogger who focuses on high-end travel experiences and cater to affluent audiences (Balleys et al., 2020). Dubai is a popular destination for luxury travel, known for its opulent hotels, shopping malls, and entertainment venues (Alrawadieh et al., 2020). Therefore, this research paper aims to examine the effectiveness of vlogging as a tool for sustainable travel education, using luxury travel vloggers in Dubai as a case study.

This research paper will focus specifically on luxury travel vloggers in Dubai, exploring the effectiveness of vlogging as a tool for sustainable travel education. Dubai is an interesting case study, as it is a city that has seen rapid growth in its tourism industry but has also made significant efforts toward sustainability in recent years (Fred, 2015). By analyzing the content of luxury travel vlogs produced in Dubai, this study seeks to offer proof of the impact of vlogging on tourists' sustainable travel education.

To accomplish this, the paper will draw on a range of theoretical frameworks and concepts, including the tourist experience, authenticity, social media, and electronic word-of-mouth (Arpornpisal, 2018). The tourist experience will be used as a lens to understand the role of vlogs in shaping tourists' perceptions of destinations and sustainability practices, while authenticity will be examined as a key factor in determining the credibility and effectiveness of vlogs (Zhang and Chikwaya, 2018). Social media's effects on tourism and hospitality, including its role in disseminating sustainable travel education, will also be explored. Finally, electronic word-of-mouth, or the sharing of information and opinions about travel experiences online, will be considered a potential outcome of vlogging.

This paper will build on the existing literature on tourism and sustainability by providing empirical evidence on the effectiveness of vlogging as a tool for sustainable travel education (Werenowska and Rzepka, 2020). It will also contribute to the emerging field of luxury travel vlogging, which has received little attention in academic research to date (Chu, 2020). By analyzing the content of luxury travel vlogs produced in Dubai, this research intends to provide light on how vlogging can be used to promote sustainable travel practices in a luxury travel context.

The following sections of the paper will evaluate the available research on vlogging, sustainable travel education, and luxury travel in Dubai, followed by a summary of the study methodology and data analysis. The results of the study will then be presented, and the paper will conclude followed by a discussion of the results' implications for the tourism industry and future research directions.

10.2 LITERATURE REVIEW

Vlogging has become a possible tool for improving the visitor experience, which is a crucial component of sustainable travel education. This review of the literature looks at the efficacy of vlogging in Dubai in promoting sustainable travel education among luxury travel vloggers, with a particular emphasis on the influence on the visitor experience.

According to Northern Arizona University, Parks and Recreation Management, a good tourist experience can be an outcome of a collection of industries, services, and activities that delivers a travel experience, including transportation, accommodation, eating and drinking establishments, retail shops, entertainment business, hospitality services, and activity facilities provided for tourists traveling to places away from home (Chawla and Sengupta, 2017). Over time, the number of researchers and their studies has increased, resulting in a more current and rigorous understanding of the nature of tourists (Sondhi et al., 2023).

Numerous studies have shown how vlogging may improve the visitor experience. For instance, Arica et al. (2022) discovered that vlogs offer a more participatory and engaging experience than traditional tourist promotion, resulting in a greater emotional tie to the location. Chen et al. (2022) also showed how vlogs might improve the authenticity and distinctiveness of the visitor experience.

Vlogs have been demonstrated to be successful in modifying tourists' attitudes and behavior when it comes to promoting sustainable tourism education. Customers who are happy search for a memorable experience and spirited service where it matters. Satisfied and happy customers are loyal customers (Das et al. 2017). According to Li et al. (2022), vlogs can raise tourists' understanding of sustainable tourism practices and encourage more responsible behavior. Service quality and tourist satisfaction are strong determinants in tourist retention (Chawla and Sengupta, 2017). Additionally, Mirasol and Cunanan (2017) showed how vlogs might encourage sustainable tourism practices by disseminating accurate knowledge on environmental preservation and community development. Therefore, satisfaction or dissatisfaction results from experiencing a service quality encounter and comparing that encounter with what was expected (Das et al. 2017).

Numerous studies have shown how vlogging may improve the authenticity of the travel experience. Vlogs offer a more genuine and all-encompassing experience than conventional tourism promotion, claim Kim and Kim (2021). Similarly to this, Li et al. (2017) discovered that vlogs let travelers research a location before going there, which can improve their trip experience. A sense of camaraderie among travelers has also been demonstrated to be fostered via vlogs (Kozinets, 2015).

Authenticity is essential for encouraging sustainable tourist practices. According to Ooi et al. (2012), vloggers can affect visitors' behavior by sharing accurate information about eco-friendly habits including minimizing plastic usage and aiding local communities. Similarly, to this, Zhumadilova (2016) showed how real vlogs might raise visitors' understanding of sustainable tourism strategies and encourage more responsible behavior.

Numerous studies have emphasized the capability of social media as an instrument for advancing education on sustainable tourism. As an illustration, Buhalis and Amaranggana (2013) discovered that social media may significantly improve sustainable tourism practices by raising tourists' awareness and understanding of such practices. Similarly to this, Cheng et al. (2020) showed how social media may be a powerful tool for promoting sustainable tourist practices by disseminating factual data on environmental preservation and neighborhood development.

Social media vlogging has been proven to be successful in enhancing visitors' travel experiences by making them more engaging and participatory. Nhon and Thu, (2014) discovered, for instance, that social media vlogging might raise a greater emotional connection to the place is produced by the perception of authenticity in the visitor experience.

The potential of eWOM in fostering sustainable tourism education has been emphasized by several research. For instance, Li et al. (2017) discovered that eWOM had a considerable impact on visitors' perceptions of sustainable tourism, with positive eWOM resulting in greater perceptions of sustainability. Similarly to this, Kim and Kim (2021) showed how eWOM may help promote sustainable tourism practices by raising visitors' awareness of and familiarity with such practices.

Numerous studies have examined the efficacy of vlogging as a technique for eWOM and found that it can be a useful method for producing positive eWOM. Arora and Lata (2020), for instance, discovered that travel vlogs can raise visitors' intentions to visit a location by improving the perception of the location's authenticity. Similarly to this, Tanford and Montgomery (2015) showed how to travel vlogs may effectively promote sustainable tourism practices by offering accurate information on environmental protection and community development. Industries and enterprises have been compelled to adapt to rapid environmental change (Sondhi et al., 2023). Overall, this literature review suggests that vlogging can be an effective tool for generating positive eWOM and promoting sustainable tourism education, particularly among luxury travel vloggers in Dubai.

With a focus on luxury travel vloggers in Dubai, this review of the literature looked at the current research on using vlogging as a tool for sustainable travel education. The usefulness of vlogging as a method for teaching about sustainable travel has been examined, along with the roles played by the tourist experience, authenticity, social media, and electronic word-of-mouth. The research we have looked at indicates that luxury travel vloggers may offer immersive and genuine visitor experiences that help raise knowledge and appreciation of sustainable tourism. Furthermore, electronic word-of-mouth and social media may be effective instruments for promoting eco-friendly travel strategies. To successfully promote sustainable tourism practices, future studies should concentrate on creating best practices for luxury travel vloggers in Dubai.

10.3 THEORETICAL BACKGROUND

Authenticity in vlogging is crucial for gaining the audience's trust and commitment (Chapple and Cownie, 2017). This entails being sincere, truthful, and open in your relationships and content production. Being genuine contributes to the development of trust, which increases viewer commitment, loyalty, and engagement (Vivek et al., 2012). Vloggers should provide material that is consistent with their values, beliefs, and personalities if they want to build genuine relationships with their audience (Wellman et al., 2020).

The term "tourist experience" describes how viewers feel about travel and tourism-related videos as a whole (Moscardo, 2010). It covers the feelings, sensory sensations, and educational materials that vloggers deliver (Wang and Picone, 2022).

In the context of vlogging, the term "social media " refers to internet platforms like Facebook, YouTube, Instagram, and TikTok where vloggers may engage with their audience by publishing videos, photographs, and anecdotes (Gholamhosseinzadeh, 2023). Since social media enables direct communication between vloggers and their audience, it is crucial for fostering trust and loyalty (Uzunoğlu and Kip, 2014). It enables vloggers to establish and maintain relationships with and loyalty toward their followers, which results in long-lasting support from their audience (Pedroni and Pofi, 2018).

The spreading and exchanging of information and viewpoints on vloggers via online platforms are referred to as electronic word-of-mouth (Sotiriadis and Van Zyl, 2013). This includes consumer evaluations, remarks, and viewer interactions. Viewers' behavior and engagement with the vlogger's material are influenced by how committed and trustworthy they are to the vlogger. It affects the vlogger's popularity, credibility, and reputation as well (Ladhari et al., 2020).

10.4 OBJECTIVE OF THE STUDY

To develop a theoretical framework to understand the elements that impact vloggers' presenting attitude on sustainable travel education through vlogging in Dubai.

10.5 RESEARCH METHODOLOGY

In total, 368 responses have been gathered from Dubai using an organized questionnaire and unintended contacts with the customer. People of varied ages, genders, occupations, and economic levels provided the data. Using a five-point scale, the survey's parameter studies were each calculated (from 1-strongly disagree, to 5-strongly agree). For the investigation, convenient sampling was employed.

10.6 FINDINGS AND ANALYSIS

TABLE 10.1 KMO and Bartlett's Test.

Kaiser–Meyer–Olkin Measure of Sampling Adequacy.		**0.875**
Bartlett's Test of Sphericity	Approx. Chi-Square	2469.699
	df	105
	Sig.	0

In terms of Kaiser–Meyer–Olkin (KMO) measurements of sample adequacy (which span the 0–1), values closer to one are preferred while values lower than 0.5 are seen to be sufficient. We may continue with the factor analysis since the KMO value in the table above is 0.875, which is higher than 0.5. Similarly, Bartlett's Test of Sphericity shows how strongly the variables are related to one another. The significance of Bartlett's Test of Sphericity may be observed from the table, where the significant result is less than 0.05 (0.000). The Kaiser–Meyer–Olkin Measure of Sampling Adequacy (KMO) and Bartlett's Test are both included in Table 10.1. Bartlett's Test of Sphericity: 0.875 Together, Chi-Square 2469.699 df 105 Sig..000. The tests offer the minimal requirements that must be met before doing a factor analysis.

TABLE 10.2 Total Variance Explained.

Component	Initial eigenvalues			Extraction sums of squared loadings		
	Total	% of Variance	Cumulative %	Total	% of Variance	Cumulative %
1	6.025	40.168	40.168	6.025	40.168	40.168
2	1.673	11.157	51.325	1.673	11.157	51.325
3	1.313	8.757	60.081	1.313	8.757	60.081
4	0.822	5.478	65.559			
5	0.79	5.269	70.828			
6	0.733	4.887	75.715			
7	0.609	4.06	79.775			
8	0.583	3.89	83.665			
9	0.502	3.346	87.01			
10	0.468	3.12	90.131			
11	0.37	2.47	92.601			
12	0.345	2.301	94.902			
13	0.293	1.954	96.856			
14	0.25	1.669	98.525			
15	0.221	1.475	100			

Total Variance Explained table, under the title "Total of Initial Eigenvalues," each factor presents itself as a proper value known as an eigenvalue. Frameworks with several eigenvalues, which solely represent actual value, are measured for future research.

The observation states that Factor 1 (Tourist experience) consists for a variation of 6.025 that is 40.168% of the total variances, likewise, Factor 2 (Authenticity) consists for a variance of 1.673 which is 11.157 % of the total variance, Factor 3 (social media content) consists for a variation of 1.313 that is 8.757% of the total variation and as a result, the first three factors account for 60.081% of the total.

TABLE 10.3 Exploratory Factor Analysis.

Constructs	Items	Tourist experience	Authenticity	Social Media Content
TE1	Luxury travel vlogs have provided me with practical tips on how to travel sustainably.	0.803		
TE2	Your desire to go to eco-friendly locations has grown as a result of watching luxury travel vlogs.	0.722		
TE3	Luxury travel vlogs have made you more aware of your vacation's impact on the environment.	0.705		
TE4	Your total vacation experience has been enhanced by luxury travel vlogs.	0.692		
TE5	You have been encouraged to adjust your travel habits to be more environmentally friendly by watching luxury travel vlogs.	0.671		
TE6	Watching luxury travel vloggers in Dubai has increased your interest in sustainable travel.	0.593		
TE7	Sustainable travel should be a primary focus of luxury travel vloggers.	0.532		
AT1	Luxury travel vloggers in Dubai provide authentic information about sustainable travel practices.		0.841	
AT2	Vlogging is an effective tool for educating people about sustainable travel.		0.817	
AT3	Luxury travel vloggers in Dubai exclusively highlight the advantages of eco-friendly travel, which gives off a misleading picture of sustainability.		0.761	
AT4	The authenticity of a vlogger's sustainable travel practices is important when evaluating the effectiveness of their education efforts.		0.506	
SM1	Social media is an effective tool for promoting sustainable travel education through vlogging.			0.831
SM2	The use of social media to promote sustainable travel education can have a significant impact on reducing carbon emissions from tourism.			0.802
SM3	Social media platforms like Instagram and YouTube should do more to promote sustainable travel content and support sustainable travel vloggers.			0.726
SM4	The use of social media to promote sustainable travel education through vlogging is an innovative and effective approach to sustainable tourism.			0.576

H0: B1 = 0

The null hypothesis indicates that there is no direct relationship between the vloggers' presenting attitude and the factors, "Tourist experience," "Authenticity," and "social media content."

H1: B1! = 0

The alternative hypothesis indicates that there is a relationship between the vloggers' presenting attitude and the factors, "Tourist experience," "Authenticity," and "social media content."

TABLE 10.4 Model Summary.

Model	R	R Square	Adjusted R Square	Std. Error of the Estimate
1	0.807[a]	0.651	0.648	0.6761

A regression model's model summary indicates how well it matches the data. Numerous correlation coefficients quantify the accuracy of the dependent variable's prediction in a model summary. According to the above table's R-square value of 0.651, the independent variables "Tourist experience," "Authenticity," and "Social media content" can account for 65.1% of the total variation in the dependent variable, vloggers' presenting attitude.

TABLE 10.5 ANOVA.[a]

Model		Sum of squares	df	Mean square	F	Sig.
1	Regression	310.912	3	103.637	226.723	.000[b]
	Residual	166.845	365	0.457		
	Total	477.756	368			

From Table 10.5, we can see that the regression model significantly and accurately predicts the dependent variable, and that the value of the dependent variable is statistically significant because the p-value is less than 0.05 (or 0.000). Thus, H1 is rejected, whereas H0 is accepted.

10.6.1 STATISTICALLY SIGNIFICANT AT 0.05 LEVEL

Vloggers' presenting attitude = 3.537 *(Constant) + 0.916*(Tourist experience) +0.162*(social media content)

TABLE 10.6 Coefficients[a].

Model		Unstandardized coefficients		Standardized coefficients	t	Sig.
		B	Std. error	Beta		
1	(Constant)	3.537	0.035		100.482	0
	Tourist experience	0.916	0.035	0.803	25.976	0
	Authenticity	-0.054	0.035	-0.047	-1.519	0.13
	Social media content	0.262	0.035	0.154	1.762	0.029

The impact on vloggers' presenting attitude is found to be high toward tourist experience and social media content and has significant influence.

10.7 CONCLUSION

This study sought to determine if luxury travel vloggers in Dubai are effective at using vlogging as a tool for sustainable travel education. The findings of this investigation suggest that vlogging may be a potent and useful technique for informing visitors about eco-friendly travel strategies. The study demonstrated that using vlogs to provide real and reliable information that is presented in an interesting and accessible way may improve the visitor's experience.

The study also discovered that social media websites like YouTube and Instagram can help spread sustainable travel messaging via electronic word-of-mouth. Social media usage may foster a feeling of community among visitors and motivate them to engage in eco-friendly travel practices.

However, it is crucial to remember that the vlogger's authority and sincerity determine how effective vlogging is as a method for educating others about sustainable travel. When luxury travel vloggers are viewed as credible and genuine, their followers are more likely to embrace sustainable travel practices.

This study emphasizes the potential of vlogging as a method for educating about sustainable travel and stresses the use of social media, authenticity, and trustworthiness in promoting sustainable travel practices. Future activities and regulations encouraging sustainable tourism that encourage responsible travel can be informed by the study's findings.

KEYWORDS

- **travel vloggers**
- **travel behavior**
- **sustainable travel education**
- **sustainable tourism**
- **tourism industry**

REFERENCES

Alrawadieh, Z.; Guttentag, D.; Aydogan Cifci, M.; Cetin, G. Budget and Midrange Hotel Managers' Perceptions of and Responses to Airbnb: Evidence from Istanbul. *Int. J. Contemp. Hosp. Manag.* **2020,** *32* (2), 588–604.

Arica, R.; Cobanoglu, C.; Cakir, O.; Corbaci, A.; Hsu, M. J.; Della Corte, V. Travel Experience Sharing on Social Media: Effects of the Importance Attached to Content Sharing and What Factors Inhibit and Facilitate it. *Int. J. Contemp. Hosp. Manag.* 2022.

Arora, N.; Lata, S. YouTube Channels Influence on Destination Visit Intentions. *J. Indian Bus. Res.* 2020. https://doi.org/10.1108/JIBR-09-2019-0269

Arpornpisal, C. Tourism Elements Influence the Decision Making in Traveling to Visit Phra Pathom Chedi, Nakhon Pathom, Thailand. 2018. https://papers.ssrn.com/sol3/papers.cfm?abstract_id=3190064

Balleys, C.; Millerand, F.; Thoër, C.; Duque, N. Searching for Oneself on YouTube: Teenage Peer Socialization and Social Recognition Processes. *Soc. Media Soc.* **2020,** *6* (2), 20563051 20909474.

Buhalis, D.; Amaranggana, A. In *Smart Tourism Destinations*, Information and Communication Technologies in Tourism 2014: Proceedings of the International Conference in Dublin, Ireland, January 21–24, 2014; Springer International Publishing, 2013, pp 553–564.

Chapple, C.; Cownie, F. An Investigation Into Viewers' Trust in and Response Towards Disclosed Paid-for Endorsements by YouTube Lifestyle Vloggers. *J. Promot. Commun.* **2017,** *5* (2).

Chawla, U.; Sengupta, K. S. Factors Affecting Customers' Accommodation Satisfaction and Service Quality in the Hotel Industry of Rural West Bengal. *LBS J. Manag. Res.* **2017,** *15* (1), 34–47.

Chen, Y.; Tingchi Liu, M.; Liu, Y.; Chang, A. W. Y.; Yen, J. The Influence of Trust and Relationship Commitment to Vloggers on Viewers' Purchase Intention. *Asia Pac. J. Mark. Logist.* **2022,** *34* (2), 249–267.

Cheng, Y.; Wei, W.; Zhang, L. Seeing Destinations Through Vlogs: Implications for Leveraging Customer Engagement Behavior to Increase Travel Intention. *Int. J. Contemp. Hosp. Manag.* **2020,** *32* (10), 3227–3248.

Chu, J. Sustainable travel on YouTube. Discussion and Perception: How do YouTube Travel Vlogs Discuss Sustainable Travel? *How are They Perceived?* 2020.

Das, D.; Chawla, U.; Ray, S. Factors affecting Customer Satisfaction and Service Quality in the Boutique Hotel Industry of Kolkata, West Bengal. *Int. J. Manag. (IJM)* **2017,** *8* (6).

Fred, B. The Factors Influencing the Choice of Tourist Destinations and Attraction Sites Among International Tourists 2015. http://scholar.mzumbe.ac.tz/

Gholamhosseinzadeh, M. S. Theorizing Vloggers' Approaches and Practices in Travel Vlog Production Through Grounded Theory. *J. Hosp. Mark. Manag.* **2023,** *32* (2), 196–223.

Huang, H. W. Effects of Smartphone-Based Collaborative Vlog Projects on EFL Learners' Speaking Performance and Learning Engagement. *Australas. J. Educ. Technol.* **2021,** *37* (6), 18–40.

Kim, I.; Kim, J. J. Emotional Attachment, Age and Online Travel Community Behavior: The Role of Parasocial Interaction. *Curr. Issues Tourism* **2021,** *24* (24), 3466–3488.

Kozinets, R. V. The Post-human Future of Brands. *Strong Brands Strong Relationships* **2015,** *1,* 149–158.

Ladhari, R.; Massa, E.; Skandrani, H. YouTube Vloggers' Popularity and Influence: The Roles of Homophily, Emotional Attachment, and Expertise. *J. Retail. Consum. Serv.* **2020,** *54,* 102027.

Li, S. C.; Robinson, P.; Oriade, A. Destination Marketing: The Use of Technology Since the Millennium. *J. Destin. Mark. Manag.* **2017,** *6* (2), 95–102

Li, W.; Kim, Y. R.; Scarles, C.; Liu, A. Exploring the Impact of Travel Vlogs on Prospect Tourists: A SOR Based Theoretical Framework. In *ENTER22 e-Tourism Conference*, Springer International Publishing: Cham, 2022; pp 486–491.

Mirasol, R. G.; Cunanan, M. E. R. R. Attitudes Towards Travel Blogs and its Effect Over Tour Related Decisions. *Int. J. Educat. Res.* **2017,** *5* (5), 203–210.

Moreno-Luna, L.; Robina-Ramírez, R.; Sánchez, M. S. O.; Castro-Serrano, J. Tourism and Sustainability in Times of COVID-19: The case of Spain. *Int. J. Environ. Res. Public Health* **2021,** *18* (4), 1859.

Moscardo, G. The Shaping of Tourist Experience: The Importance of Stories and Themes. *The Tourism and Leisure Experience: Consumer and Managerial Perspectives.* **2010,** *44,* 43–58.

Nhon, H.; Thu, N.(Factors Affecting Travel-decision Making: A Study of the Credibility of Online Travel-related Information in Vietnam 2014.

Ontiveros, J. The Impact of Travel Blogs in Destination Experience: An E-Ethnographic Investigation 2016. http://arno.uvt.nl/show.cgi?fid=135452

Ooi, N.; Laing, J.; Mair, J. In *The Impact of Mountain Resort Tourism Development on Ranching Culture and Identity within the Rocky Mountain West: A Case Study of Steamboat Springs, Colorado*, CAUTHE 2012: The New Golden Age of Tourism and Hospitality; Book 2; Proceedings of the 22nd Annual Conference; La Trobe University: Melbourne, Vic., 2012, (pp. 454–457).

Pedroni, M.; Pofi, M. P. Commodifying the Followers Or Challenging the Mainstream? The Two-sided Potential of Curvy Fashion Bloggers. *Observatorio (OBS*)* **2018,** *12* (SPE1), 05–27.

Pike, S.; Page, S. J. Destination Marketing Organizations and Destination Marketing: A Narrative Analysis of the Literature. *Tour. Manag.* **2014,** *41,* 202–227.

Sheppard, V. A.; Fennell, D. A. Progress in Tourism Public Sector Policy: Toward an Ethic for Non-human Animals. *Tour. Manag.* **2019,** *73,* 134–142.

Sondhi, S.; Chawla, U.; Iqbal, H. Relationship Between Social Cause, Environment Conservation and Environmental Attitude, Towards Promoting Green Purchasing Behavior. Serbian *J. Manag.* **2023,** *18* (1), 27–43.

Sotiriadis, M. D.; Van Zyl, C. Electronic Word-of-mouth and Online Reviews in Tourism Services: The Use of Twitter by Tourists. *Electronic Commerce Research* **2013,** *13,* 103–124.

Tanford, S.; Montgomery, R. The Effects of Social Influence and Cognitive Dissonance on Travel Purchase Decisions. *J. Travel Res.* **2015,** *54* (5), 596–610.

Uzunoğlu, E.; Kip, S. M. Brand Communication Through Digital Influencers: Leveraging Blogger Engagement. *Int. J. Inform. Manag.* **2014,** *34* (5), 592–602.

Vivek, S. D.; Beatty, S. E.; Morgan, R. M. Customer Engagement: Exploring Customer Relationships Beyond Purchase. *J. Mark. Theory Pract.* **2012,** *20* (2), 122–146.

Wang, X.; Picone, I. Mobilized, Negotiated and Balanced: Chinese School Vloggers' Platform Engagements and Layered Identity Construction on Bilibili. *J. Youth Stud.* **2022,** 1–17.

Wellman, M. L.; Stoldt, R.; Tully, M.; Ekdale, B. Ethics of Authenticity: Social Media Influencers and the Production of Sponsored Content. *J. Media Ethics* **2020,** *35* (2), 68–82.

Werenowska, A.; Rzepka, M. The Role of Social Media in Generation Y Travel Decision-making Process (case Study in Poland). *Information* **2020,** *11* (8), 396. https://doi.org/10.3390/info11080396

Yang, T.; Yang, F.; Men, J. The Impact of Danmu Technological Features on Consumer Loyalty Intention Toward Recommendation Vlogs: A Perspective from Social Presence and Immersion. *Inform. Technol. Peopl.* **2022,** *35* (4), 1193–1218.

Zhang, Y.; Chikwaya, T. Commerce & Friendship: A Qualitative Study of New Value Streams Created by Beauty Vloggers Through Relationship Building on Social Media 2018.

Zhumadilova, A. The Impact of TV Shows and Video Blogs on Tourists' Destination Choice. *Tourism Today* **2016,** *16,* 148–166.

CHAPTER 11

Gig Workers' Motivation Regarding Online Food Delivery Sector in Kolkata: A Qualitative Exploration

CYNTHIA SAHA and SUMANTA DUTTA

Postgraduate and Research Department of Commerce, St. Xavier's College (Autonomous), Kolkata, India

ABSTRACT

Purpose: In India, there are many food delivery apps which hire people as "delivery partners." They are a part of the gig economy and belong to the population of gig workers. Millions of drivers have been employed by the online food delivery sector, who sell their labor as platform employees. The purpose of this study is to throw a light on the "new economy" namely the gig economy particularly the online food delivery sector of South Kolkata. In the context of gig economy, it is contract-based short-term jobs that are currently generating a huge number of employment opportunities to the people all over the world, thereby reducing unemployment of developing countries like India. This research topic was selected to identify why and how the gig workers of the online food delivery industry of South Kolkata are motivated to take up such jobs, complete their task, and earn money to sustain their needs and families despite not having a concrete brick and mortar structure of organization.

Design/Methodology/Approach: The online food delivery gig workers of Zomato and Swiggy that are the two most popular food delivery platforms of South Kolkata have been studied for the purpose of this paper. This is a qualitative research based on the phenomenological approach to understand

Agile Business Transformations: Priorities, Lessons, and Practices. Satyajit Chakrabarti, Subrata Chattopadhyay, Udit Chawla, Sundeep Singh Sondhi, & Arunava Dalal (Eds.)

the "lived experiences" of the online food delivery gig workers. This study employed thematic analysis because it is congruent with the phenomenological research analysis of studying the experiences and meaning of life via the participant's personal experience.

Research limitations/implications: For this study, two online food delivery companies, Zomato and Swiggy, were taken into consideration and this study is based on South Kolkata only. The present study can be conducted in various places in India and can include gig workers of other online food delivery platforms.

Originality/value: Limited research has been conducted to identify the driving force or the motivation of the gig workers (delivery partners) to take up such contractual short time jobs in the online food delivery sector of India, and no study has been undertaken till date in the city of South Kolkata related to this issue of gig economy.

11.1 INTRODUCTION

The whole world was facing a volatile situation after the economic crisis of 2008. People were losing jobs, and there was a situation of unequal employment opportunities resulting in a rise in unemployment and underemployment.[1] In this context, there was a growing demand of part-time temporary jobs, which resulted in the emergence of a new type of economy, "The Gig Economy."[2] The gig economy provides employment that is limited and temporary in nature, such as freelancing and other "non-permanent" jobs (Gleim et al., 2019). However, nowadays, to achieve work–life balance, many people are choosing to work as gig workers, as it is part time and flexible in nature. People choose contract or 'gig work' that is project-or task-based because it gives them more independence, pays them according to their task completed, and favors a short-term working relationship with the customers (Manyika et al., 2016).

In India, there are many food delivery apps that hire people as 'delivery partner'. They are a part of the gig economy and belong to the population of gig workers. Millions of drivers have been employed by the platform food delivery sector, who sell their labor as platform employees (Huang, 2022). They work for flexible hours and receive payments according to the number

[1]What is the Gig Economy? how has It Changed the Way we Work? N26. (n.d.) [Online]. https://n26.com/en-eu/blog/gig-economy (accessed Mar 19, 2023).

[2]Gig Economy—A labor market characterized by the prevalence of short-term contracts or freelance work as opposed to permanent jobs.

of orders they have delivered to the customers plus they get tips and incentives, and ratings are given to them according to their performance by the customers. Certain criterions that are considered by the online apps while hiring gig workers are—they must have smartphones with good Internet service, and they should possess vehicles according to the need of the jobs. Criterions like education qualification, family background, race, gender, and income are not considered by the apps while recruiting. They should know the common languages particularly Hindi and other regional languages. These online service-based apps generate a large amount of employment opportunities for the mass especially during festivals like Durga Puja, Diwali, Holi, Christmas, etc., thereby reducing unemployment rate and poverty. Some popular online food delivery apps that provide services of ordering readymade foods from various restaurants across the states of India are Zomato, Swiggy, Dunzo, TravelKhana, Box8, FreshMenu, Eat.Fit, EatSure, MagicPin, and Voosh.[3] Each app has their own different mission and vision and promises the customers to deliver readymade food from the restaurants in less time, so they do not have to wait for the food for longer hours to get delivered. The apps charge commission from restaurants ranging from 25 to 30% for business generation (Nensee, 2022). Customers place (and pay for) orders through the app, which are then delivered to the partner restaurant. Riders deliver food that customers have ordered from a restaurant through the apps of their choice as promptly as they can, regardless of the time of day or the weather (Popan, 2021).

11.2 LITERATURE REVIEW

González (2022) highlighted the difference between online food delivery platform companies and the conventional full-time food delivery companies with respect to quality of service and consumer satisfaction provided by them. The study initially stated that there exists a negative relation between online food delivery services and the quality of service provided by them. The researcher adopted a mix approach study on gig workers and did a thematic analysis of the consumer reviews using 'KH Coder', and it was found that consumers do not find the service of the online food delivery unsatisfactory.

Lord et al. (2022) conducted a literature-based study to examine the sustainability issue related to the online food delivery workers who form the part of the gig economy. This study throws a light on how the new increasing

[3]Online food delivery apps that hire gig workers for their services.

online last mile delivery service of food and grocery items impacts the logistics and transportation system, thereby questioning environmental sustainability. A qualitative study has been undertaken using the conflict model of sustainability proposed by Campbell and Systems Thinking to analyze and prove the presence of sustainability in the gig economy, and it was found that in a broader aspect there exists a negative relationship between sustainability and work of online food delivery workers.

Pereira et al. (2022) conducted an exploratory study to understand how 'gamification' can be used by organizations to increase the gig workers' engagement and their level of performance. The study is based on an empirical analysis of 532 responses to a set of questionnaires, sent to HR managers of firms hiring the gig workers, for a period of one month. The primary data collected is tested by using 'Common Method Bias' and theories of 'Swift Trust' and 'Psychological Contracts.' The study concluded that there exists a positive relation between performance, 'swift trust' and gig workers engagement and task performed moderates the link between 'swift trust' and gig workers' engagement.

Mahato et al. (2021) first examined the potential effects of closing the distinction between conventional methods of work and the gig work on the 'blended workforce' but lastly using the theoretical concepts it was concluded that the 'blended workforce' was anticipated to have a significant role in generating new employment prospects, enhancing job satisfaction, and lowering expenses while raising businesses' productivity. The study is qualitative in nature, and it is done based on the Indian context by using theoretical models such as 'SORT (skillset, openness, rise and trace) model, Youth Leadership Programme (YLP) and 3-Strike fit technique'.

Nath (2020) conducted a literature-based descriptive study to find out the existence of trust among the gig economic workers. The study showed that the management platform companies should support and protect the gig workers when they encounter discriminations during their interaction with the customers in the market. The study concluded that building trust can be greatly aided by formalizing the methods through which platform businesses interact with gig economy workers, and to ensure that gig economy workers are covered by labor laws and to preserve their fundamental interests, regulatory changes are necessary.

Jabagi et al. (2019) conducted a study to find out how the gig workers are motivated to work and enhance engagement and complete their set tasks despite having a proper brick and mortar structure. Therefore, the study stated the various ways used by online platforms to encourage, help, or support and motivate the gig economy workers in the absence of human efforts to do so. The study is qualitative in nature, and it pointed out how the theory of self-determination and theory of job characteristics evokes motivation within the gig workers. Social media technologies like social networking and social badging help gig workers communicate with other gig workers which has a positive impact on their competence level and enhances motivation to complete their tasks.

Prabhat et al. (2019) conducted an empirical study for a period of seven months to analyze the life of the 133 gig workers, which is the sample size of this study, with special reference to the Uber drivers. The study that is qualitative in nature pointed out the opportunities, struggles, and challenges faced by the Uber drivers while working for ridesharing application and the motivational force behind taking up such jobs as a career option in a developing country like India.

Flanagan (2017) conducted a literature-based study and observed that gig economy is a concept of workplace fissure. He stated that gig economy is not something which is new, but it is the revival of old procedures of extraction of labor. Like every other workplace, gig economy has uneven distribution of powers among the platform company's management system and requires attentive administration to make sure that all the people of Australia are working either in online platforms or somewhere else and earning enough to lead a standard life.

11.3 RESEARCH GAP

To commence with the thesis titled, 'A Perception Study on The Motivation and Sustainability of The Gig Workers of The Online Food Delivery Sector in South Kolkata', we have reviewed 15 papers. From this reviewed literature we have found that much research has been done on:

1. The basic framework of the gig economy pertaining to different sectors of the economy (Pereira et al., 2022; Nath, 2020).
2. The effect of gig economy in the generation of employment all over the world and change in the traditional work style (Mahato et al., 2021; Flanagan, 2017).
3. The working of the gig workers who are a part of the digital platform organizations (Prabhat et al., 2019).
4. The work life, success, and motivation of the gig workers in online food delivery platform in foreign countries (Gonz´alez, 2022; Lord et al., 2022; Jabagi et al., 2019).

We have noticed that very few research have been conducted to identify the driving force or the motivation of the gig workers to take up such contractual short time, especially the job of the online food delivery gig workers, and we can see that no study has been undertaken till date in the city of South Kolkata related to this issue of gig economy. We will try to look deep into these issues and explore more with the help of this qualitative study.

11.4 RESEARCH OBJECTIVES

From the research gap identified above, the following research objectives have been set for the paper, 'A Perception Study on The Motivation and Sustainability of The Gig Workers of The Online Food Delivery Sector in South Kolkata': to identify the factors affecting the motivation of the gig workers of the online food delivery sector in South Kolkata.

11.5 RESEARCH METHODS

11.5.1 TYPE OF STUDY

This study employs a qualitative research technique based on a phenomenological approach to understand the "lived experiences" of the online food delivery gig workers and thematic analysis because it is congruent with the phenomenological research strategy of studying the experiences and meaning of life via the participant's personal experience (Lebar, 2017).

11.5.2 PERIOD OF STUDY

The location of this study is Kolkata, and the delivery partners have been interviewed for a period of three months starting from December 2022 till March 2023.

11.5.3 SAMPLING METHOD

In this study, the snowball sampling technique is applied. This technique of sampling method is generally used when it is difficult to identify the members of the desired population. According to this, the initial group of respondents is selected at random. After being interviewed, these respondents are asked to identify others who belong to the same targeted population, and here in our study the targeted group is the gig workers of food delivery companies of Zomato and Swiggy of South Kolkata.

11.5.4 SAMPLE SIZE

For our study, about 10 delivery partners from Zomato and Swiggy were interviewed using the snowball technique to collect data needed to undertake the phenomenological analysis. These participants have been assigned the codes GW1 through GW10 to preserve individual anonymity.

11.5.5 SAMPLING TOOLS

Using the qualitative data analysis programme NVivo, the interviews were coded and analyzed. Topics and groups were created based on the major keywords identified through word, paragraph, and overall meaning structure analysis of verbatim transcripts (Rahman et al., 2022). Using the same programme, the codes were then utilized to create word clouds (Ganguly et al., 2022).

11.6 ANALYSIS AND INTERPRETATIONS

This study has been undertaken to understand what motivates the gig workers of online delivery food platforms to take up such jobs. For our study we have interviewed the gig workers of only Swiggy and Zomato[4], the two most popular online food delivery apps of South Kolkata.

11.7 PARTICIPANT'S PROFILE

Table 11.1 depicts the demographics of the participants in this study.

Participant's Details: This study includes 10 participants, both male and female. The participants have been assigned the codes of GW1 to GW10 to preserve individual anonymity. The analytical results show that 8 participants

[4]Popular online food delivery apps operating in India.

TABLE 11.1 Demographics of the Participants.

Participants	Age (years)	Gender	Hometown	Education level	Marital status	Online food delivery platform	Part-time/ full-time
GW1	30	Male	Kolkata	Up to class 12	Married	Zomato	Full-time
GW2	28	Male	Kolkata	Graduate	Married	Swiggy	Full-time
GW3	51	Male	Kolkata	Graduate	Married	Zomato	Full-time
GW4	26	Male	Kolkata	Up to class 12	Married	Zomato	Part-time
GW5	24	Male	Kolkata	Up to class 12	Single	Swiggy	Full-time
GW6	24	Male	Kolkata	Graduate and pursuing ITI	Single	Swiggy	Full-time
GW7	28	Male	Kolkata	Up to class 8	Single	Zomato	Full-time
GW8	21	Male	Kolkata	Up to class 12	Single	Zomato	Part-time
GW9	23	Female	Sundarban	Pursuing post graduation	Single	Zomato	Part-time
GW10	27	Female	Kolkata	Graduate	Married	Swiggy	Part-time

are male and 2 are female participants. Nine participants of this study are from Kolkata and 1 female participant is from Sundarban area who has shifted to Kolkata for her studies.

Age: The participants in the research varied in age from 21 to 51 years old.

Education Qualification: One male participant of this study has education qualification up to class 8, 4 male participants have education qualification up to class 12, and the remaining 4 participants are graduated, and one female candidate is pursuing postgraduation.

Marital Status: The study includes both married and unmarried individuals in terms of marital status. Individuals who are married have one child each.

Online Food Delivery Platform: Six participants work in Zomato out of which three participants work as full-time delivery partners and three participants work as part-time delivery partners. Four participants work in Swiggy out of which two participants work as full-time delivery partners and one participant works as a part-time delivery partner.

11.8 DATA INTERPRETATION

NVivo software was used to analyze the collected data, and word clouds were created by using the codes assigned to the transcribed document of the recorded interviews. The interpretations for each research objectives are as follows:

OBJECTIVE 1: To identify the factors affecting the motivation of the gig employees of the online food delivery sector in South Kolkata.

Discussion: Our study aims to identify the factors affecting motivation of the gig workers behind taking up jobs as delivery partners in the online food delivery platforms, Zomato and Swiggy. Figure 11.1. is a word cloud depicting the most frequently used words by the participants when they were asked about the motivating factors and reasons to work as online food delivery gig workers.

The ERG theory of motivation can be connected to delivery partners working for food delivery firms such as Swiggy or Zomato in the following ways:

1. **Existence Needs:** Existence needs are connected to fundamental physiological requirements such as food, housing, and safety for delivery partners. Food delivery services like Swiggy and Zomato provide delivery partners with a source of revenue to help them fulfil

their necessities. Food delivery firms, for example, might assist their delivery partners in meeting their survival needs by providing flexible work hours, safe working conditions, and regular reimbursements.

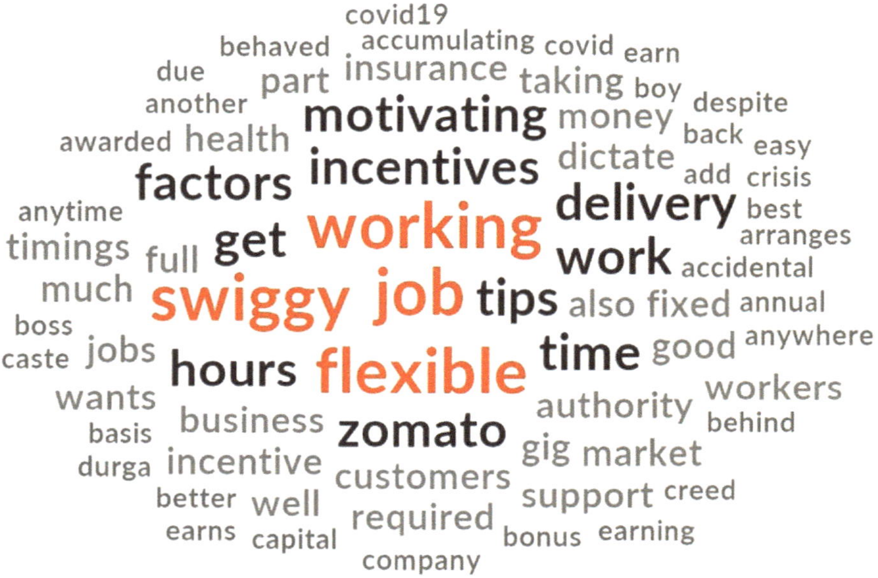

FIGURE 11.1 Word Cloud of interviews for delivery partners relating to motivational factors.
Source: Researcher's own computation generated from NVivo software.

2. **Relatedness Needs:** Relatedness requirements are connected to delivery partners' desire for social engagement and connections. Meal delivery services can help to build a sense of relatedness. Relatedness demands are connected to delivery partners' desire for social engagement and connections. By planning social events and giving chances for contact and feedback, food delivery firms may develop a feeling of community and belonging among their delivery partners. Food delivery organizations can assist delivery partners in meeting their relatedness demands by establishing a pleasant work culture.
3. **Growth Needs:** Growth requirements of delivery partners are tied to their desire for personal and professional development. Food delivery firms may help their delivery partners improve by offering training and development programmes, performance-based rewards, and prospects for advancement. Food delivery firms may assist fulfil

their growth objectives by investing in the growth and development of their delivery partners.

Ultimately, the ERG theory of motivation emphasizes the significance of meeting the different demands of delivery partners employed by food delivery firms. Food delivery organizations may assist their delivery partners feel motivated, engaged, and devoted to their work by addressing their requirements for existence, relatedness, and growth.

Following are some motivational factors that could be identified:

1. **Incentives**—The delivery partners of both Zomato and Swiggy receive incentives when they work for more than 14 h a day and deliver food via bike and during special occasions like Durga Puja, Christmas, and New Year's Eve. This was mentioned by GW8 who works in Zomato which is—"*Incentives are received during occasions like on Holi, Durga Puja, Christmas, I get an incentive of ₹2700 if I complete 24 orders per day.*" This was confirmed by GW9 who also works in Zomato—"*I get incentives when there is any special occasion or on national holidays.*"

   GW2 who works in Swiggy said that—"*During Durga Puja or any other festival I receive incentive of ₹800 per day from Swiggy which is higher than what Zomato pays their delivery workers. Swiggy offers more incentives than Zomato.*" Additionally, he mentions that "*delivery partners who use bike to deliver food gets more incentive than the bicycle riders*" and this was confirmed by GW6 who said—"*I deliver food via bicycle, so I do not get incentive. I only get incentive by working 16 hours long per day.*"

   GW7 mentioned that—"*If I earn ₹400 by delivering orders, then I get an extra ₹100 as incentive.*"

   GW4 said that—"*Delivery boys who login from night 7 pm onwards they get heavy incentives, so I do not get....*"

2. **Tips and Bonus**—The delivery partners receive tips from customers for fast delivery and good behavior, and they receive joining bonus as well. This was stated by GW6 "*.... but whenever there is a Cash on Delivery order, I get ₹50 to ₹100 tips by chance if the order value is ₹3000 or more*" and confirmed by GW2 who mentioned that—"*it is a difficult to earn incentives now because maximum orders are prepaid and only when there is Cash on Delivery order, I might expect tips.*"

   GW8 said that—"*customers give tips of ₹20 or ₹30 when I go to deliver food.*"

FIGURE 11.2 Picture of respondent GW4.

Source: Clicked by researcher.

GW4 pointed out that—"*There is a Zomato scheme of joining bonus of ₹400 which one can get within a month after completing delivery of 100 orders…*"

3. **Flexibility of Working Hours**—There exists flexibility of working hours as the delivery partners can work anytime; they want to work in part-time or full-time. GW9 mentioned that—"*I work as a part-time delivery partner and I have no fixed working hours; in the morning I login for 2 hours and then I go to college and spend time studying and going to tuitions and then again when I am free, I start working especially at night.*"

   GW8 stated that—"*…. a part time job for me and I am doing it for time pass. I work whenever I want to specially when I get an off or on weekends as I am working as a full-time tele caller in a BPO in Salt lake area.*"

   GW10 who works for Swiggy and is a mother said that—"*I work as a part time delivery woman. I start my shift around 10 am in the morning after dropping my daughter to her school and continue to work till 3 pm in the afternoon until my daughter comes home from school.*"

   GW2 stated that—"*This is a full-time job for me. My shift timings are from 12 noon till 4 pm and again from 6 pm till 11.30 pm. There is a non-pick hour from 4pm to 6pm and I can login in that time also which signifies there's no fixed time. I can login whenever I wish to."*

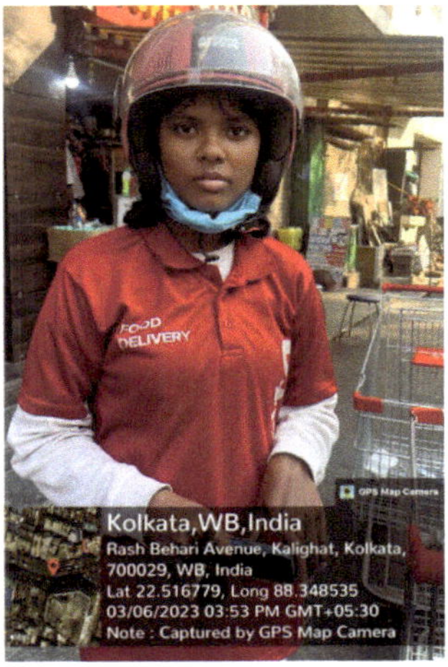

FIGURE 11.3 Picture of respondent GW9.

Source: Clicked by researcher.

4. **Company Benefits**—Both the companies, Zomato and Swiggy, give their deliver partners health insurance and accidental insurance. This is evident when GW1 who works in Zomato addressed in the interview that—"*I have received an insurance of ₹10,00,000 for death coverage and outdoor accidental insurance of ₹50,000 which I can claim if I face any accident while working*" and the same was confirmed by GW4 who also works in Zomato.

   GW7 stated that—"*Zomato has introduced a new scheme where the workers get ₹500 per day on showing proper medical proof if they are sick and unable to work.*"

   GW2 mentioned that—"*Swiggy has given me an accident insurance of ₹3,00,000 and death insurance of ₹5,00,000. As I work for full-time, weekly I get one day off on any weekdays but not weekends because rush is maximum in weekends. Swiggy also organises award function where award is given to delivery partner who has the record of highest orders delivered.*"

   GW10 mentioned that—"*Last year September, I faced an accident and when I informed the team leader, he sent two people to take me to hospital where I underwent treatment, and all the expenses were borne by Swiggy. The hospital bill was submitted to Swiggy, and the company reimbursed the full amount...*"

GW2 said that—"*In Swiggy there is a rule that if any delivery boy who is working for them for more than 6 years, they are hired to work in Swiggy's back office and work as team leader and guide other delivery boys. The experienced ones are only hired because they have the first hand on road experience.*"

FIGURE 11.4 Picture of respondent GW5.

Source: Clicked by the researcher.

5. **Customer Feedbacks**—Behavior of the customers, their positive feedbacks, and high ratings and tips also motivate the delivery partners to work. GW2 said that—"*I have good customer experience. There are some "royal customers" those who order food frequently. I have very good relationship with them, and the customers know me. During summer when I go to deliver food, the customer first gives me water or any drink and tells me to relax for 5 mins and then takes the order and gives me ₹100 tips.*"

   GW10 mentioned that—"*Once it has happened that I delivered an order way before the time that was showing in the Zomato app, so the customer got happy and send me extra ₹150 in my Gpay account and gave me a 5-star rating.*"

GW9 mentioned that—"*80% customers are good. But some people are very rude and behave badly with me.*"

GW6 stated that—"*Most of the customers give me 5-star ratings.*"

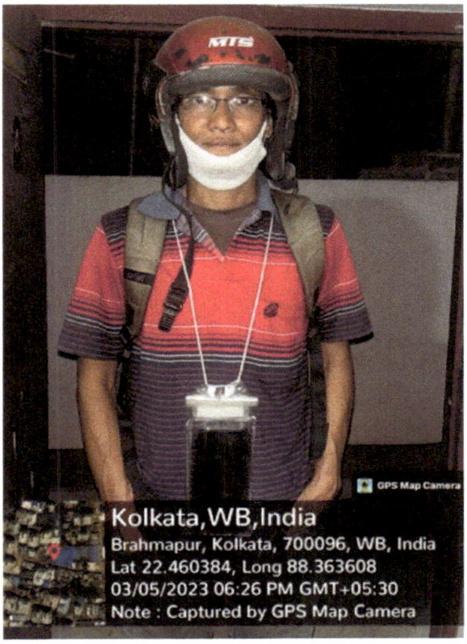

FIGURE 11.5 Picture of respondent GW3.

Source: Clicked by the researcher.

5. **Lack of Availability of Jobs**—Due to the pandemic of Covid-19, many people have lost their jobs because the company they were working in got shut down, and after that there is a lack of availability of job and this was confirmed by GW1 who said that—"*I have taken up this job in Zomato because the last company where I used to work got shut down due to the pandemic of Covid-19. I have searched for other jobs that time and even now but did not get any or were not paying me a decent salary.*"

   Even GW3 said the same thing—"*I lost my job during the pandemic of Covid-19, so I started working as a Swiggy delivery boy to support my family financially. I have been looking for other jobs but not getting a suitable one. I earn more in this job than what the other companies are offering me.*"

GW2 mentioned that—"*I have taken up this job in Swiggy to support my family financially in this time of crisis post Covid-19 when the economy is growing and there are very less job opportunities in the market.*"

GW7 said that—"*.... because I am not getting job vacancy anywhere. Previously I used to work as a salesman but due to lockdown the company got shut down.*"

GW6 stated that—"*I have taken up this job of Swiggy delivery partner because in market there is no job despite being a graduate. Everywhere political power and support is required to get a job in the private sector.*"

11.9 CONCLUSION

Our study titled, 'A Perception Study on The Motivation and Sustainability of The Gig Workers of The Online Food Delivery Sector in South Kolkata,' aimed to identify the factors affecting the motivation of the gig employees of the online food delivery sector in South Kolkata. From the given data analysis and interpretations, we can conclude that delivery partners from Swiggy and Zomato are motivated by a variety of factors, including financial incentives, flexibility, and autonomy. A good relationship between delivery partners and consumers is critical for social sustainability as it leads to positive feedback and word of mouth, higher trust, and loyalty, better working conditions and better communication. A good relationship between delivery partners of Swiggy and Zomato and good relationship between delivery partners and team leaders of Swiggy and Zomato is essential for achieving social sustainability because it leads to more efficient operations, increased safety, improved working conditions, and collaboration and learning, greater support for delivery partners and more accurate feedback and evaluation.

KEYWORDS

- **gig workers**
- **motivation**
- **online food delivery platforms**
- **phenomenological analysis**

REFERENCES

Flanagan, F. Symposium on Work in the 'Gig' Economy: Introduction. *Econ. Labour Relat. Rev.* **2017,** *28* (3), 378–381.

Ganguly, A.; Joseph, J.;.; Dutta, S.; Dey, K. op.cit, 13.

Gleim, M. R.; Johnson, C. M..; Lawson, S. J. Sharers and Sellers: A Multi-Group Examination of Gig Economy Workers' Perceptions. *J. Bus. Res.* **2019,** *98,* 142–152.

Gonz´alez, S. M. Gig Economy Delivery Services versus Professional Service Companies: Consumers' Perceptions of Food-Delivery Services. *Technol. Soc.* **2022,** *69.*

Huang, H. Riders on the Storm: Amplified Platform Precarity and the Impact of COVID-19 on Online Food-delivery Drivers in China. *J. Contemp. China.* **2022,** *31* (135), 351–365.

Jabagi, N.; Croteau, A.-M.; Audebrand, L. K..; Marsan, J. Gig-Workers' Motivation: Thinking Beyond Carrots and Sticks. *J. Manag. Psychol.* **2019,** *34* (1).

Lebar, O. *Penyelidikan Kualitatif: Pengenalan Kepada teori Dan Metod*; Universiti Pendidikan Sultan Idris; 2012.

Lord, C.; Bates, O.; Friday, A.; McLeod, F.; Cherrett, T.; Martinez-Sykora, A..; Oakey, A. The Sustainability of the Gig Economy Food Delivery System (Deliveroo, UberEATS and Just-Eat): Histories and Futures of Rebound, Lock-in and Path Dependency. *Int. J. Sustain. Transport.* **2022.**

Mahato, M.; Kumar, N..; Jena, L. Re-Thinking Gig Economy in Conventional Workforce Post-COVID 19: A Blended Approach for Upholding Fair Balance. *J. Work Appl. Manag.* **2021,** *13* (2), 261–276.

Manyika, J.; Lund, S.; Bughin, J.; Robinson, K.; Mischke, J.;.; Mahajan, D. Independent work: Choice, Necessity, and the Gig Economy. *McKinsey.* **2016,** Retrieved.

Nath, P. Trust in Gig Economy. *NHRD Netw. J.* **2020,** *13* (4), 480–486.

Nensee, K. How Much Commission do Food Delivery Apps like Zomato and Swiggy Charge [Online] July 14, 2022. StartupTalky. https://startuptalky.com/food-delivery-apps-charges/ (accessed Mar 19, 2023).

Papon, C. Embodied Precariat and Digital Control in the "Gig Economy": The Mobile Labor of Food Delivery Workers. *J. Urban Technol.* **2021**.

Pereira, V.; Behl, A.; Jayawardena, N.; Laker, B.; Dwivedi, Y..; Bhardwaj, S. The Art of Gamifying Digital Gig Workers: A Theoretical Assessment of Evaluating Engagement and Motivation. *Prod. Plan. Control* **2022,** 1–17.

Prabhat, S.; Nanavati, S..; Rangaswamy, N. India's "Uberwallah": Profiling Uber Drivers in the Gig. *Assoc. Comp. Mach.* **2019,** *43,* 1–5.

Rahman, R. H. A.; Hamid, M. A. A.; Patah, S. A.; Zaini, F.;.; Mohyedin, A. S. M. op.cit, 13.

CHAPTER 12

Regenerative Farming: A Comprehensive and Holistic Approach to Food and Agriculture in Nigeria

KIRTI P. SHARMA[1], SAHIL SHAW[1], MOIN REZA[1], and ABHIJIT KUMAR GUPTA[2]

[1]*Techno India, Kolkata, India*

[2]*D Empressa Pvt. Ltd, India*

ABSTRACT

Purpose: The restoration and improvement of the soil's condition, diversification, and natural ecosystems are key components of regenerative farming, a regular share to agricultural and food production. This agricultural approach places an emphasis on cooperating with the environment instead of battling it and blends existing knowledge with contemporary understanding of science. Regenerative farming provides a viable answer to the problems the farming sector is confronting in Nigeria, including soil erosion, water shortages, and global warming. Regenerative farming practises put an emphasis on enhancing soil quality, wildlife, water management, livestock incorporation, and community involvement. Farmers may improve the bounty and production of their farmland even while generating wholesome food for their local residents by implementing regenerative farming techniques. The long-term viability of agricultural systems depends on ecosystem services including fertilization, pest management, and biogeochemical cycles, all of which may be supported by regenerative farming. A much more inclusive and neighborhood-focused food system might be developed through restorative farming. Regenerative farming can aid in the creation of an increasingly

Agile Business Transformations: Priorities, Lessons, and Practices. Satyajit Chakrabarti, Subrata Chattopadhyay, Udit Chawla, Sundeep Singh Sondhi, & Arunava Dalal (Eds.)

sustainable food supply chain that really is more capable of adapting to shifting environmental circumstances through fostering partnerships between landowners, customers, and other partners. Regeneration agriculture is a potential method of food production that helps both producers and consumers as a whole. Regeneration farming may contribute to the development of a more resilient and environmentally friendly food system by repairing and enhancing soil health, fostering biodiversity, saving water, incorporating animals, and involving communities. This strategy has the ability to enhance farmers' livelihoods and supply wholesome food for everyone in Nigeria and even beyond.

Findings: The following factors emerged from the investigation, which has been "Perceived Soil Quality," "Perceived Water Quality," "Perceived Seed Quality," and "Climatic Change." It has also been discovered that the factors "Perceived Soil Quality" and "Climatic Change" have a major impact on community engagement.

Design/Methodology: This research is done with the help of structured questionnaires. The primary data for the study was collected from different demographic factors. 1 (strongly disagree) to 5 (strongly agree), five points were used to compute each parameter studied for the survey.

12.1 INTRODUCTION

In demand to advance and restore the integrity of grounds, environments, and societies, regeneration agriculture is an improved farming system. Using a thorough and holistic approach, the interdependence of land, groundwater, wildlife, and population health is highlighted with over 70% of total of the workforce employed and a GDP contribution of over 22%, agriculture is a crucial part of the economy (FAO, 2020). Yet, there are a number of issues the Nigerian agricultural sector must deal with, including poor productivity, degraded soil, and the effects of climate change. Absolute poverty, instability, and rural–urban migration are all made worse by these issues. The environment is undesirably obstructed by humans' irresponsible behavior, which also has a significant negative impact on the world's ecological arrangement and results in the destruction of readily available natural resources, an increase in climatic variability, increasing temperatures, and irradiation (Sondhi et al., 2023).

By addressing their root causes, restorative farming offers a potential solution to these problems. Improved soil health can lead to higher production, less soil erosion, and better nutrient recycling. Regenerative farming focuses on these benefits. It also promotes ecosystem services and biodiversity, which can increase the system's resistance to changing climate and other stressors (Wallace, 2018). Regenerative farming also improves the health of the land and its inhabitants while generating a variety of nutritious crops and livestock, which in turn contributes to nutritional and food security (Pretty et al., 2018). Regenerative agricultural practises are still not widely used in Nigeria, mostly due to an absence of information, funding, and support from the government (Talabi et al., 2020). In order to encourage the use of regenerative farming within Nigeria along with other nations that are developing, study and policy projects are thus required.

By addressing their root causes, restorative farming offers a potential solution to these problems. Improved soil health can lead to higher production, less soil erosion, and good nutrient recycling. Regenerative farming focuses on these benefits (Wallace, 2018). Organizations should work to strengthen consumers' perceptions of an environmental brand's technology rather than focusing just on environmentally friendly innovations developed from the management' perspective in order to adoptive brand trustworthiness (Sondhi et al., 2023).

As a sustainable farming strategy to solve issues with food and nutrition security, regeneration farming techniques have gained popularity in Nigeria. Many studies have shown that these techniques have a positive impact on biodiversity, agricultural production, and soil health. For instance, research by Sogbesan and Adetunji (2021) found that tropical forests, which integrate trees with crops or animals, can boost nutrient cycling, improve soil organic matter, and aid in the prevention of pests and diseases in Nigeria. The possibility of cover crops and intercropping to enhance soil health and boost crop production in Nigeria was underlined in another research by Adekunle et al. (2021).

The importance of regenerative agricultural techniques has also been highlighted in recent legislative changes in Nigeria. To encourage sustainable livestock farming and improve eating grass management strategies nationwide, the Nigerian government unveiled the National Livestock Transformation Plan (NLTP) in 2019. The strategy gives priority to regenerative farming practises like silvopastoralism, which integrates forests into animal agriculture systems to improve soil quality and provide a host of benefits to producers and the ecosystem (Federal Government of Nigeria, 2019). A project to advance Nigeria's farming automation and industrialization was also started by the government and is known as the Green Imperative Program. In order to increase agricultural output and the country's food security, the initiative emphasizes sustainable farming methods including regenerative farming

(Federal Ministry of Agriculture and Rural Development, 2018). Businesses have created their own competence in environmentally conscious advertising depending on their objectives, liability concerns, and practicality because there is not a widely accepted definition of the term (Sondhi et al., 2023).

Furthermore, current research has emphasized the capacity of regenerative farming to encourage climate resilience in Nigeria. Faluyi et al.'s (2021) research displayed that agroforestry practices could enhance water use efficiency, decrease greenhouse gas emissions, and promote soil carbon sequestration in Nigeria. Another study by Amole and Alabi (2021) found that regenerative agriculture practices can improve adaptive capacity and promote resilience among smallholder farmers in Nigeria. As a whole, these latest discoveries and research show the value of regenerative farming methods in Nigeria and reinforce the demand for additional funding, information sharing, and government encouragement to encourage their implementation. Regenerative farming may improve Nigeria's nutrition, sustainability in the environment, and capacity for adaptability through fostering sustainable practises in agriculture.

12.2 LITERATURE REVIEW

A more contemporary definition of soil health is provided by the Intergovernmental Technical Panel on Soils (ITPS), which states that it is "the soil's capacity to support the productivity, variety, and ecological services of agricultural ecosystems" (ITPS 2020). Removal of soil organic carbon (SOC) is one of the foremost issues contributing to soil degradation. Aeration, water infiltration, soil structure, fertility, and nutrient availability have all been found to benefit from SOC (Robertson et al., 2015). In recent years, it has also been considered as a means of reducing climate change (Chabbi et al., 2017). Numerous studies have looked into how farmers' opinions of the soil's quality relate to their readiness to use regenerative farming techniques. For instance, an investigation by Gbandi et al. (2021) discovered that farmers were less inclined to embrace regenerative farming techniques compared to those who regarded their soil to be of excellent quality. Adisa et al. (2020) also found that farmers were more likely to use regenerative farming techniques when they had a favorable opinion of the quality of their soil. Socioeconomic variables including access to knowledge, educational attainment, and agricultural experience can also have an impact on how well-suited the soil is viewed to farming.

Research by Adeoye et al. (2021) found that farmers who had accessibility to agricultural extension programs are often more probable to have a favorable opinion of soil quality and use regenerative farming techniques. Also, a report by Oyekale et al. (2019) showed that farmers with greater farming experience seem to be more likely to evaluate their soil quality as excellent and use regenerative farming approaches.

By altering soil characteristics, stomatal conductance, and hydraulic conductance, among other ways, AM fungi promote water uptake. Hyphae are still thought to play a small part in water uptake, according to certain research (Püschel et al., 2020), while others argue that they do play a role at all. The origins of AM plants are able to switch between multiple water transport channels and boost apoplastic water flow when there is a lack of moisture (Bárzana et al., 2012). In a recent study, Kakouridis et al. (2022) showed that additional cytoplasmic water transport occurs in AM fungus, and their findings showed that AM fungi are responsible for 46.2% of the water discharged by AM plants. According to studies, a farmer's impression of the quality of their water can have a big impact on how likely they are to use regenerative farming techniques. Research by Adesina et al. (2020) discovered that farmers who regarded their water to be of bad quality were less likely to employ regenerative farming techniques than those who thought their water to be of excellent quality. Similar findings were found in research by Oyedele et al. (2019) which found that farmers were more likely to embrace regenerative farming methods if they had a favorable impression of the quality of their water. Being able to access water supplies, the presence of contaminants, and water treatment procedures are just a few examples of the many variables that might affect how people perceive the quality of their water. Adeyemi et al. (2021) discovered that farmers with access to fresh-water sources were even more likely to think highly of their water quality and use regenerative agricultural techniques. Similar to this, Ogunwole et al. (2018) study found that farmers who used water treatment techniques were more likely to think well of their water quality and use regenerative farming techniques.

Research has demonstrated that a farmer's assessment of the quality of their seed can have a big impact on whether or not they choose to use regenerative farming methods. For instance, research by Fawole et al. (2020) found that farmers were less inclined to embrace regenerative farming approaches compared to those who felt their seed quality was good if they evaluated their seed quality as being poor. Similar to this, research by Olayemi et al. (2021) showed that farmers who believed their seeds were of high quality were more willing to use regenerative farming techniques. It indicates a sense of responsibility for the environment on the side of customers as well as a personal dedication to environmental conservation (Chawla et al., 2022). Many variables, including seed source, seed care, and seed germination rates, might affect how good seeds are perceived to be. For instance, Adetunji et al. (2019) indicated that farmers who utilized seeds that were certified are more inclined to think highly of their seed quality and apply regenerative farming methods. Similar findings were found in a study by Babalola et al. (2021) which found that farmers who utilized seed treatments like seed priming were significantly more inclined to view their seed as having a high quality and apply regenerative farming techniques.

12.3 THEORETICAL BACKGROUND

Perceived soil quality for farming is a subjective assessment made by farmers regarding the quality of their soil. This assessment is important in the context of adopting regenerative practices. The term is used in the Innovation Resistance Theory (IRT) (Dimitrova et al., 2022) paradigm and considers factors such as compatibility, compared benefits, variety, accessibility, and threat. By understanding how farmers perceive their soil quality through IRT, efforts can be directed toward overcoming resistance and promoting the use of regenerative farming methods for environmentally friendly and sustainable agricultural systems (Mani and Chouk, 2018). Perceived water quality for regenerative farming refers to how farmers personally evaluate the condition and suitability of water resources when using regenerative practices. This evaluation includes factors such as agreement with their principles, perceived benefits compared to traditional methods, difficulty implementing regenerative practices, noticeable improvements in water quality, and concerns about potential negative outcomes (Rhodes, 2017; Newton et al., 2020). Innovation Resistance Theory can help us understand farmers' perspectives on water quality, which can then be used to overcome resistance and promote the use of regenerative farming methods that enhance water quality and support sustainable agriculture (Burns, 2021).

The perceived quality of seeds in regenerative farming is how farmers individually assess the characteristics and usefulness of seeds when using regenerative practices. This includes factors like how well the seeds align with their principles and goals, the perceived benefits of using renewable grains, the difficulty in selecting and supervising seeds, the visible improvements in crop yield and resilience, and concerns about potential negative effects.

To promote the widespread adoption of regenerative farming practices that prioritize high-quality, locally appropriate, and genetically diverse seeds for sustainable agriculture, it is crucial to understand farmers' opinions on seed quality using Innovation Resistance Theory (Hutchison et al., 2007; Krupke et al., 2017). Increasing carbon dioxide (hereinafter CO_2) and greenhouse gas (hereafter GHGs) outputs are the cause of climate change, which is increasing and poses an imminent danger to the entire planet (Shaheen et al., 2020). Over the past ten years, CO_2 and GHG emissions have reached historic levels throughout the world (Mohsin et al., 2021). Therefore, climate change is a worrying and scary issue for all countries throughout the world. It has caused problems in the social and economic spheres in a number of countries and posed a greater risk to life and the environment (Ahmed et al., 2019). Therefore, a quick change in weather patterns or growing CO_2 levels are two signs of climate change's negative effects (Malhi et al., 2021).

12.4 OBJECTIVE OF THE STUDY

To understand the factors influencing farmers community engagement through regenerative farming as an alternative to traditional ways in Nigeria.

12.5 METHODOLOGY

This research is done with the help of structured questionnaires. 216 responds were collected in total. The primary data for the study was collected from men and women of different age groups, belonging to different income brackets, from various occupation backgrounds like business, service, and others. Each parameter study for the survey was calculated using five points like a scale (from 1—strongly disagree, to 5—strongly agree).

12.6 FINDING AND ANALYSIS

TABLE 12.1 KMO and Bartlett's Test.

Kaiser–Meyer–Olkin Measure of Sampling Adequacy		0.911
Bartlett's Test of Sphericity	Approx. Chi-Square	1822.26
	df	190
	Sig.	0

In terms of Kaiser–Meyer–Olkin (KMO) measurements of the quantity of samples (which range from 0 to 1), values nearer to one are preferred while values lower than 0.5 are seen to be sufficient. We may continue with the factor analysis since the KMO value in Table 12.1 is 0.911, which is higher than 0.5. Similarly, Bartlett's Test of Sphericity shows how strongly the variables are related to one another. The significance of the Bartlett's Test of Sphericity may be observed from the table, where the significant result is less than 0.05 (0.000).

TABLE 12.2 Total Variance Explained.

Component	Initial eigenvalues			Extraction sums of squared loadings		
	Total	% of Variance	Cumulative %	Total	% of Variance	Cumulative %
1	7.773	38.865	38.865	7.773	38.865	38.865
2	1.618	8.091	46.957	1.618	8.091	46.957
3	1.187	5.934	52.89	1.187	5.934	52.89
4	1.026	5.132	58.023	1.026	5.132	58.023
5	0.936	4.679	62.702			
6	0.861	4.303	67.005			
7	0.768	3.839	70.844			
8	0.688	3.44	74.284			
9	0.644	3.219	77.503			
10	0.568	2.84	80.343			
11	0.535	2.673	83.016			
12	0.5	2.501	85.517			
13	0.485	2.424	87.941			
14	0.462	2.312	90.253			
15	0.397	1.984	92.237			
16	0.38	1.9	94.136			
17	0.344	1.72	95.856			
18	0.315	1.575	97.432			
19	0.272	1.358	98.79			
20	0.242	1.21	100			

Every factor expresses a quality score, termed as eigenvalue, under the heading "Total" of "Initial eigenvalues " (Table 12.2). Since they only represent genuine value, parameters with eigenvalues larger than 1 are taken into consideration for further research.

TABLE 12.3 Rotated Component Matrix[a].

Constructs		Component			
		Perceived soil quality	**Perceived water quality**	**Perceived seed quality**	**Climatic change**
PSQ1	Regenerative farming prioritizes soil health and is a more sustainable approach to food and agriculture than conventional farming.	0.7			
PSQ2	Regenerative farming practices, such as crop rotation and cover cropping, can help improve soil health and enhance nutrient cycling	0.66			
PSQ3	Promoting biodiversity in agricultural ecosystems, such as by planting a diversity of crops, can improve soil health and increase the resilience of farming systems	0.61			
PSQ4	Cover cropping and crop rotation can help to improve soil quality and fertility.	0.58			
PSQ5	Regenerative farming is less efficient and more labor-intensive than conventional farming practices, making it less feasible for large-scale agriculture.	0.53			
PSQ6	Soil health is the foundation of all agricultural systems, and regenerative farming practices are essential for the long-term viability of our food systems.	0.52			
PSQ7	Farmers often rely on their own knowledge and experience to select seeds that will produce high yields and thrive in local conditions.	0.5			
PSQ8	Soil quality influences agricultural decisions and environmental stewardship	0.48			
PWQ1	The increased use of regenerative farming practices can help mitigate the negative impacts of climate change on water availability and quality		0.78		
PWQ2	Regenerative farming practices can help reduce the use of harmful chemicals and pesticides that can contaminate water supplies.		0.74		
PWQ3	Water quality is a critical factor in regenerative farming in Nigeria, as it affects the health of the soil, the growth and quality of crops, and the overall sustainability of the agricultural system.		0.64		

TABLE 12.3 *(Continued)*

Constructs		Component			
		Perceived soil quality	Perceived water quality	Perceived seed quality	Climatic change
PWQ4	Farmers have access to clean and healthy water sources, it is important to invest in policies and practices that protect and improve water quality, including reducing pollution, promoting sustainable water use, and conserving natural water resources.		0.63		
PRS1	Farmers often rely on their own knowledge and experience to select seeds that will produce high yields and thrive in local conditions.			0.66	
PRS2	Regenerative farming practices and improving seed quality as it is possible to increase agricultural productivity, enhance food security, and reduce the negative impact of agriculture on the environment.			0.64	
PRS3	The use of high-quality seeds can also provide economic benefits to farmers, by reducing input costs and increasing yields, as well as improving the quality and marketability of their crops			0.62	
PRS4	The use of high-quality seeds that are well-suited to the local climate and soil conditions.			0.56	
PRS5	To promote the use of high-quality seeds in regenerative farming, there is a need for greater investment in seed research and development.			0.55	
CLC1	The promotion of crop diversity in regenerative farming can improve ecosystem resilience to changing climate conditions in Nigeria.				0.77
CLC2	Regenerative farming in Nigeria can foster climate-smart agriculture, providing a more adaptive and sustainable approach to food production amid changing climate conditions.				0.74
CLC3	Regenerative farming practices that focus on building soil health can enhance the resilience of crops to climate-related stresses, such as droughts and floods.				0.59

It can be seen that factor 1 (“perceived soil quality”) accounts for a variance of 7.773 which is 38.865% of the total variance, Factor 2 (“perceived water quality”) accounts for a variance of 1.618 which is 8.091% of the total variance, Factor 3 (“perceived seed quality”) accounts for a variance of 1.187 which is 5.931% of the total variance, Factor 4 (“climatic change”) accounts for a variance of 1.026 which is 5.132% of the total variance and thus, the first four aspects together are responsible for 58.023%.

H0: B1 = 0 the null hypothesis implies that there is no linear relationship between community engagement and the factors, “Perceived Soil Quality,” “Perceived Water Quality,” “Perceived Seed Quality,” and “Climatic Change”

H1: B1! = 0 the alternative hypothesis implies that there is a relationship, positive or negative, between community engagement and the factors, “Perceived Soil Quality,” “Perceived Water Quality,” “Perceived Seed Quality,” and “Climatic Change.”

TABLE 12.4 Model Summary.

Model	R	R Square	Adjusted R Square	Std. Error of the Estimate
1	.792[a]	0.627	0.62	0.7198

A regression model’s model summary describes how well it matches the data. Multiple correlation coefficients are used in a model summary Ror to scale how well the dependent variable may be predicted. According to the above table’s R-square (Table 12.4) value of 0.627, the independent variables “perceived soil quality,” “perceived water quality,” “perceived seed quality,” and “climatic change” may account for 62.7% of the total variance in the dependent variable, overall adaptability.

TABLE 12.5 ANOVA[a].

Model		Sum of squares	df	Mean Square	F	Sig.
1	Regression	183.932	4	45.983	88.746	.000[b]
	Residual	109.328	211	0.518		
	Total	293.259	216			

We can see from the ANOVA table in Table 12.5 that the regression model successfully forecasts the dependent variable, and the outcome is considered significant because the p-value is less than 0.05 (or 0.000). As a result, H1 is disapproved whereas H0 is approved.

TABLE 12.6 Coefficients[a].

Model		Unstandardized coefficients		Standardized coefficients	t	Sig.
		B	Std. error	Beta		
1	(Constant)	3.352	0.049		68.436	0
	Perceived soil quality	0.819	0.049	0.701	16.676	0
	Perceived water quality	0.121	0.049	0.103	2.456	0.015
	Perceived seed quality	0.271	0.049	0.232	5.516	0
	Climatic change	0.312	0.049	0.267	6.358	0

12.6.1 STATISTICALLY SIGNIFICANT AT 0.05 LEVEL

Community Engagement = 3.724 + 0.701* (perceived soil quality) + 0.103* (perceived water quality) + 0.232* (perceived seed quality) + 0.267* (climatic change)

The component has been shown to have a strong impact on community involvement and has an important effect on perceived soil quality, perceived seed quality, and climate change.

12.7 CONCLUSION

Regenerative farming is a thorough and all-encompassing method of food and agricultural production in Nigeria that emphasizes enhancing soil health, water resource conservation, and seed quality. Regenerative farming techniques may improve the fertility of the ground, increase water penetration and preservation, and boost the establishment of seeds and plant development, as shown by the analysis of perceived soil health, observed the quality of water, as well as perceived seed quality. The achievement of food security, the mitigation of environmental damage, and the enhancement of the rural economy in Nigeria depend on these advantages.

The report emphasizes the need for producers and politicians in Nigeria to become more cognizant of and implement regenerative agricultural practises. To promote regenerative farming's wider acceptance, additional study is required to determine its benefits for society and the economy. Farmers also need to be informed about the fundamentals of regenerative agriculture and given the resources and instruction they need to put these practises into practise.

The agricultural sector in Nigeria has a tremendous deal of potential with regenerative farming. It is a more all-encompassing and ecologically responsible kind of farming that may boost soil health, save water, and increase seed quality. The study highlights how crucial it is to use techniques for regenerative agriculture in Nigeria in order to accomplish food security and preservation of the environment.

KEYWORDS

- **sustainable agriculture**
- **soil health**
- **biodiversity**
- **food security and holistic approach**

REFERENCES

Adekunle, A.; Adegbite, O.; Adeoye, I. Regenerative Agriculture for Sustainable Development in Nigeria. *Int. J. Agric. Sustain.* **2021,** *19* (1), 66–81.

Adeoye, G. O.; Adeoye, B. W.; Olagunju, F. I.; Ojediran, J. O. The Impact of Agricultural Extension Services on Farmers' Perception of Soil Health and Adoption of Sustainable Land Management Practices in Nigeria. *Land Use Policy* **2021,** *101,* 105146.

Adesina, F. A.; Ayinde, O. E.; Ogunbode, E. E. Farmers' Perception of Water Quality and its Influence on the Adoption of Sustainable Land Management Practices in Nigeria. *Environ. Sci. Pollut. Res.* **2020,** *27* (29), 36684–36694.

Adetunji, M. T.; Ogunwole, J. O.; Afolayan, R. A. Influence of Seed Quality on Adoption of Sustainable Land Management Practices Among Maize Farmers in Ogun State, Nigeria. *J. Agric. Environ. Sci.* **2019,** *8* (1), 40–47.

Adisa, R. S.; Akintoye, H. A.; Adewumi, M. O.; Oyekale, T. O. Determinants of Farmers' Adoption of Regenerative Agriculture Practices in Southwest Nigeria. *J. Agric. Ext.* **2020,** *24* (2), 91–102.

Ahmed, N.; Thompson, S.; Glaser, M. Global Aquaculture Productivity, Environmental Sustainability, and Climate Change Adaptability. *Environ. Manage.* **2019,** *63,* 159–172. doi: 10.1007/s00267-018-1117-3

Amole, A. F.; Alabi, M. O. Regenerative Agriculture and Climate Change Adaptation Among Smallholder Farmers in Nigeria. *Clim. Dev.* **2021,** *13* (3), 232–243.

Babalola, A. A.; Ayinde, O. E.; Fakayode, S. B. Effect of Seed Priming on Perceived Seed Quality and Adoption of Sustainable Land Management Practices Among Maize Farmers in Oyo State, Nigeria. *J. Plant Nutr.* **2021,** *44* (7), 1052–1064.

Badawy, S. M. Optimization of Reaction Time for Detection of Organophosphorus Pesticides by Enzymatic Inhibition Assay and Mathematical Modeling of Enzyme Inhibition. *J. Environ. Sci. Health, Part B* **2021,** *56* (2), 142–149. doi:10.1080/03601234.2020.1853455.

Bárzana, G.; Aroca, R.; Paz, J. A.; Chaumont, F.; Martinez-Ballesta, M. C.; Carvajal, M.; Ruiz-Lozano, J. M. Arbuscular Mycorrhizal Symbiosis Increases Relative Apoplastic Water Flow in Roots of the Host Plant Under both Well-watered and Drought Stress Conditions. *Ann. Bot.* **2012,** *109* (5), 1009–1017. doi:10.1093/aob/mcs007

Burns, E. A. Placing Regenerative Farming on Environmental Educators' Horizons. *Austral. J. Environ. Educ.* **2021,** *37,* 29–39. doi: 10.1017/aee.2020.21

Chabbi, A.; Lehmann, J.; Ciais, P.; Loescher, H. W.; Cotrufo, M. F.; Don, A.;... Rumpel, C. Aligning Agriculture and Climate Policy. *Nat. Clim. Change* **2017,** *7* (5), 307–309. doi: 10.1038/nclimate3286

Chawla, U.; Choudhary, S.; Mishra, V. 4 Young Consumers' Green Purchasing Behavior with Reference to Green Marketing. *Sustain. Mark. Custom. Value* **2022,** 59.

Crippa, M.; Solazzo, E.; Guizzardi, D.; Monforti-Ferrario, F.; Tubiello, F. N.; Leip, A. J. N. F. Food Systems are Responsible for a Third of Global Anthropogenic GHG Emissions. *Nat. Food* **2021,** *2* (3), 198–209. doi:10.1038/s43016-021-00225-9

Dimitrova, I.; Öhman, P.; Yazdanfar, D. Barriers to bank customers' intention to fully adopt digital payment methods. *Int. J. Qual. Serv. Sci.* **2022,** *14,* 16–36. doi: 10.1108/IJQSS-03-2021-0045

Faluyi, O. A. et al. Agroforestry as a Climate-resilient Agricultural System in Nigeria. *J. Agric. Sci.* **2021,** *159* (2), 123–135.

Fawole, O. P.; Ayinde, O. E.; Adejumo, B. A. Perception of Seed Quality and Adoption of Sustainable Land Management Practices Among Cassava Farmers in Oyo State, Nigeria. *Sustain. Agric. Res.* **2020,** *9* (3), 1–11.

Federal Government of Nigeria. National Livestock Transformation Plan. 2019. Retrieved from https://www.fmard.gov.ng/national-livestock-transformation-plan-nltp/

Federal Ministry of Agriculture and Rural Development. The Green Imperative. 2018. Retrieved from https://fmard.gov.ng/green-imperative

Gbandi, E. C.; Amusa, T. A.; Akintola, J. O. Assessment of Factors Influencing Farmers' Adoption of Regenerative Agriculture Practices in Nigeria. *J. Agric. Rural Dev. Trop. Subtrop.* **2021,** *122* (1), 33–44.

Hutchison, W. D.; Burkness, E.; Moon, R.; Leslie, T.; Fleischer, S.; Abrahamson, M.; Hamilton, K.; Steffey, K.; Gray, M.In *Evidence for Regional Suppression of European corn Borer Populations in Bt Maize in the Midwestern US: Analysis of Long-term time Series' from Three States*; XVI International Plant Protection Congress: Glasgow, Scotland, 2007. 512–513.

ITPS. Towards a Definition of Soil Health. 2020. Retrieved from https://www.fao.org/documents/card/fr/c/cb1110en/

Kakouridis, A.; Hagen, J. A.; Kan, M. P.; Mambelli, S.; Feldman, L. J.; Herman, D. J.; . . . Firestone, M. K. Routes to Roots: Direct Evidence of Water Transport by Arbuscular Mycorrhizal Fungi to Host Plants. *New Phytol.* **2022,** *236* (1), 210–221. doi:10.1111/nph.18281

Krupke, C. H.; Holland, J. D.; Long, E. Y.; Eitzer, B. D.Planting of Neonicotinoid-treated maize Poses Risks for Honey Bees and Other Non-target Organisms over a Wide Area Without Consistent Crop Yield Benefit. *J. Appl. Ecol.,* 2017 Epub ahead of print May 22 2017

Malhi, G. S.; Kaur, M.; Kaushik, P. Impact of Climate Change on Agriculture and its Mitigation Strategies: a Review. *Sustainability* **2021,** *13,* 1318. doi: 10.3390/su13031318

Mani, Z.; Chouk, I. Consumer Resistance to Innovation in Services: Challenges and Barriers in the Internet of Things Era. *J. Product Innov. Manag.* **2018,** *35,* 780–807. doi: 10.1111/jpim.12463

Mohsin, M.; Kamran, H. W.; Nawaz, M. A.; Hussain, M. S.; Dahri, A. S. Assessing the Impact of Transition from Nonrenewable to Renewable Energy Consumption on Economic Growth-Environmental Nexus from Developing Asian economies. *J. Environ. Manage.* **2021,** *284,* 111999. doi: 10.1016/j.jenvman.2021.111999

Newton, P.; Civita, N.; Frankel-Goldwater, L.; Bartel, K.; Johns, C. What is Regenerative Agriculture? A Review of Scholar and Practitioner Definitions Based on Processes and Outcomes. *Front. Sust. Food Syst.* **2020,** *4,* 194. doi: 10.3389/fsufs.2020.577723

Nurzhanova, A.; Pidlisnyuk, V.; Abit, K.; Nurzhanov, C.; Kenessov, B.; Stefanovska, T.; Erickson, L. Comparative Assessment of Using Miscanthus × Giganteus for Remediation of Soils Contaminated by Heavy Metals: A Case of Military and Mining Sites. *Environ. Sci. Pollut. Res.* **2019,** *26* (13), 13320–13333. doi:10.1007/s11356-019-04707-z.

Ogunwole, J. O.; Akinbile, L. A.; Oloyede, O. T. Perceived Water Quality and Adoption of Sustainable Land Management Practices Among Maize Farmers in Oyo State, Nigeria. *J. Environ. Manag.* **2018,** *223,* 224–233.

Olayemi, O. J.; Adekoya, A. A.; Adetunji, M. T. Effect of Seed Quality on Adoption of Sustainable Land Management Practices Among Maize Farmers in Southwest Nigeria. *J. Crop Improv.* **2021,** *35* (2), 141–154.

Oyekale, A. S.; Adeyemo, R.; Ogunlade, I. Perceptions of Soil Fertility and Management Practices Among Cassava Farmers in Southwest Nigeria. *Heliyon* **2019,** *5* (11), e02855.

Pretty, J.; Benton, T. G.; Bharucha, Z. P.; Dicks, L. V.; Flora, C. B.; Godfray, H. C. J.; . . . Wratten, S. Global Assessment of Agricultural System Redesign for Sustainable Intensification. *Nat. Sustain.* **2018,** *1* (8), 441–446. doi:10.1038/s41893-018-0114-0

Püschel, D.; Bitterlich, M.; Rydlová, J.; Jansa, J. Facilitation of Plant Water Uptake by an Arbuscular Mycorrhizal Fungus: A Gordian Knot of Roots and Hyphae. *Mycorrhiza* **2020,** *30* (2–3), 299–313. doi:10.1007/s00572-020-00949-9, PubMed: 32253570

Rhodes, C. J. The Imperative for Regenerative Agriculture. *Sci. Prog.* **2017,** *100,* 80–129. doi: 10.3184/003685017X14876775256165

Robertson, F.; Armstrong, R.; Partington, D.; Perris, R.; Oliver, I.; Aumann, C.;. . . Rees, D. Effect of Cropping Practices on Soil Organic Carbon: Evidence from Long-term Field Experiments in Victoria, Australia. *Soil Res.* **2015,** *53* (6), 636–646. doi:10.1071/SR14227

Shaheen, A.; Sheng, J.; Arshad, S.; Muhammad, H.; Salam, S. Forecasting the Determinants of Environmental Degradation: A Gray Modeling Approach. *Energy Sources Part A Recov. Utiliz. Environ. Effects*. **2020,** 1–21. doi: 10.1080/15567036.2020.1827090 [Epub ahead of print].

Sogbesan, O. A.; Adetunji, M. T. Agroforestry for Soil and Crop Health Improvement: A Review of Practices and Challenges in Nigeria. *J. Agric. Ext.* **2021,** *25* (1), 1–12.

Sondhi, S.; Chawla, U.; Iqbal, H. Relationship Between Social Cause, Environment Conservation and Environmental Attitude, Towards Promoting Green Purchasing Behavior. *Serb. J. Manag.* **2023,** *18* (1), 27–43.

Talabi, A. O.; Olusegun, E. O.; Adeyemi, O. 2020.

Wallace, R. Regenerative Agriculture: A Practical Solution to Global Warming. *J. Soil Water Conserv.* **2018,** *73* (5), 121A–125A.

CHAPTER 13

Predicting Sustainable Working Capital Requirement for Firms by Using Dynamic Panel Data System Generalized Method of Moment

PINKU PAUL

Management Development Institute, Murshidabad, West Bengal, India

ABSTRACT

The research aimed to unveil the key drivers of working capital (WC) in non-financial firms in India. A comprehensive dataset of 1818 organizations from 2011 to 2021 was meticulously gathered from the CMIE database. The variables explored the intricate link between working capital requirement (WCR) and key determinants such as profit, leverage, asset composition, size, and sales growth. Employing a robust methodology of dynamic panel data-System GMM for model estimation, the study established the relationship between these factors with confidence. The findings highlight the pivotal role of a company's asset composition and earnings in predicting its WCR while revealing that leverage was not a significant factor. Furthermore, the study uncovered a compelling inverse relationship between the company's size and the working capital needed to manage its operations effectively.

13.1 INTRODUCTION

The firm's survival and growth largely depend on how efficiently it manages its funds. The firm's continuity and performance depend on how efficiently

Agile Business Transformations: Priorities, Lessons, and Practices. Satyajit Chakrabarti, Subrata Chattopadhyay, Udit Chawla, Sundeep Singh Sondhi, & Arunava Dalal (Eds.)

it manages its daily operations and maintains a better equilibrium between liquidity and profitability requirements (Aktas et al., 2015). The difficulty lies in identifying the optimal working capital requirement and its drivers (Lamberson, 1995). Both long-term and short-duration financing choices are important for the firm. Capital management for the long horizon has an objective to enhance the firm's worth (Samiloglu and Demirgunes, 2008), and short-term investment decision influences the profitability of the firm (Smith, 1987). Both are equally important for the survival of the organization. Many of the studies on working capital management (WCM) have been done for developed economies, whereas for developing economies like India, there has been limited research conducted (Saravanan et al., 2017). Also, research carried out in the WCM context was more in terms to understand the association of WCM with the profitability and value of the organization.

The working capital (WC) contributing factors are also known as the liquidity factors responsible for appropriate WCM. The working capital requirement (WCR) can be predicted in terms of the sales growth of the firms (Beaver, 1966). The current assets investment decisions are considered important factors of WCM. It was discovered that the firm's cash conversion cycle (CCC) was adversely related to its ROA. Moreover, inventory conversion and receivable conversion have a positive association with the return on assets of manufacturing firms. Therefore, managing the current assets of the firms becomes important for the managers to make certain an easy flow of operation and maintain the profitability of the firm (Nimalathasan, 2010). Some of the significant factors affecting the liquidity decision of the firms were size, asset tangibility, age, profitability, firm status, and growth at different quantile levels (Wasiuzzaman, 2018). Now understanding the working capital requirement and predicting the same is a major concern area for the firm's survival and growth. Understanding the relevance of working capital for sustainability and long-term future prospect, the researcher attempted to predict the WCR of the firms in the nonfinancial sector of India by identifying the crucial issues. And later, the association of these determinants with the WCR of the firms was analyzed. Efficient utilization will lead to better management of funds and later the profitability of the firms. Per the best understanding of the researcher, the paper will contribute to understanding the WCR in the Indian context considering not only the short-period variables but also the long-period variables impacting the overall business of the company. Although such types of studies have been conducted for developed and some developing economies.

The study is structured as a review of literature for identifying the determinants of WCR followed by the estimation of the empirical model in the second and third segments, respectively. The impact of determinants on the WCR is presented in the fourth segment. The last segment concluded the study with the future scope of research.

13.2 LITERATURE REVIEW

Earlier research works have indicated that the shareholders' value creation can be done through a proper equilibrium between the profitability and liquidity of the firm in WCM (Aktas et al., 2015). The WCM of the firms was explained and elaborated by the researchers with the help and use of different types of ratios (Chiou et al., 2006; Nazir and Afza, 2009; Paul and Mitra, 2018). It was also observed that the collapse of the small- and medium-scale firms was particularly due to the improper administration of the short-term funds in the organization operations reported for developed economies such as the USA and the UK (Peel and Wilson, 1996).

The financial ratios have been one of the crucial indicators to understand and predict the well-being of the business. It not only helps to understand the strengths but also highlights the weakness of the firms (Beaver, 1966). The organizations should hold back a suitable amount of working cash to ensure the smooth functioning of daily business operations. For this reason, the company should keep enough current assets to cover its ongoing obligations. Additionally, the firms' effective working capital utilization needs to be measured. This was accomplished by calculating the percentage of working capital needed to produce sales for the company. To measure the WCM's effective decision-making and implementation, the networking capital turnover ratio was used (Wasiuzzaman, 2018). The WC turnover ratio is a gauge of the effective use of the WC. A higher turnover ratio shows that the company is making the most use of its current assets and liabilities to increase sales and company growth. To determine the variables influencing the company's WCR prediction, a thorough literature review was done.

13.2.1 ASSET COMPOSITION

The manufacturing firms are basically capital-intensive in nature. According to the researcher, working capital investment was significantly influenced by the proportion of fixed asset investments (Kwenda, 2014). For the company's smooth operation, WCR focuses on maintaining an appropriate level of current assets. Understanding the right proportion of current and non-current assets in a company will be made easier with the assets' composition. The productive assets utilized by the company to ensure its smooth operation are represented by the firm's non-current assets. Firms invest in long-term assets with high growth potential, indicating that they rely more on short-term debt than long-term debt to fund WC (Baños-Caballero et al., 2010).

13.2.2 PROFITABILITY

Profitability was employed as a metric to comprehend how effectively the company managed its assets to generate profit as Return on Assets (Kamal and MohdZulkifli, 2004). There is an opposite association between profitability and liquidity. Aggressive WCR demonstrated higher profitability (Jose et al., 1996). The research focused on the reduction of the CCC, and the organization's improved performance. The CCC was used to represent liquidity, and profitability was described by ROA and ROE (Wang, 2002). Additionally, several studies from various countries show that liquidity has a negative influence on profitability (Deloof, 2003; Falope and Ajilore, 2009; Gill et al., 2010; Lazaridis and Tryfonidis, 2006; Shin and Soenen, 1998). The impact of WCR on profitability was determined by examining 127 textile industry organizations in Pakistan for the period 2001–2012. The variables used in the study, economic growth rate, assets outstanding, net WC, average days of collection, current liabilities to total assets, firm debt levels, and WC to operating income, were negatively associated with firm profitability. Variables such as sales growth, company size, debt, inventory turnover days, CCC, and working capital to total assets were significantly positively correlated with company profitability; on the other hand, it is not solely dependent on the company's profit (Tahir and Anuar, 2016). DuPont's model breaks down profitability measures, ROE and ROA, into a combination of several factors, such as asset turnover, profit margin, and firm leverage (Paul, 2021).

13.2.3 LEVERAGE

Fund management has become the most important element of corporate sustainability. WC financing has a huge influence on overall WCR and a company's bottom line. Previous research has shown that an organization's financing pattern of its working capital needs has influenced its management and performance (Nazir and Afza, 2009; Baños-Caballero et al., 2010; Bei and Wijewardana, 2012). The pecking order theory of capital composition states that organizations with less debt tend to have more debt. The researcher conducted research on companies in India and China. The study showed that Chinese companies in a saturation scenario are paying down their debt because they have more short-period debt in their capital structure. In India, on the other hand, saturated firms are not making up for the extreme dent in the capital composition (Bhama et al., 2019). Financing is therefore always an important decision-making criterion for companies. An optimal capital structure has a significant impact on company value and company survival.

Companies that adopt conservative policies to fund their WC needs can create value for their companies, while companies that adopt aggressive policies create more value in the stock market (Nazir and Afza, 2009). There is an opposite relationship between WC funding and corporate performance. When a business is in financial difficulty, short-term loans can be used to meet its working capital needs. The WCR decision involves working capital financing, as short-period debt is a crucial component of financing (Altaf and Ahmad, 2019).

13.2.4 FIRMS' SIZE

Earlier research has established that there exists an opposite association between size and liquidity (Nazir and Afza, 2009; Kwenda, 2014; Hill et al., 2010). Larger businesses required less liquidity because they had a more diverse business and a larger customer base. It was also supported by (Nazir and Afza, 2009) that higher cash and credit sales turnover are correlated with a more satisfied customer base for larger firms and can manage with less liquidity while smaller businesses required more liquidity.

13.2.5 SALES GROWTH

The growth of sales had no considerable influence on the need to invest in WC (Kwenda, 2014). The increasing sales turnover necessitates greater current assets in terms of inventory level (Moussawi et al., 2006). The higher sales growth demands less focus on liquidity and working capital requirements (Chiou et al., 2006; Hill et al., 2010). Thus, to survive and flourish, the company should retain the maximum number of current assets.

A vacuum has been found in the literature, as a result, in the explanation of the association between the WC use of the enterprises and factors affecting liquidity management. There was evidence from earlier research about the connection between WCR and the profitability and performance of the enterprises; however, the Indian perspective did not show an association between factors on WCR of the firms. Hence, the current research aims to close this gap by identifying the factors that affect working capital and firms' WCR and then evaluating the implications of those factors.

13.3 RESEARCH METHODOLOGY

13.3.1 DATA

To understand the impact of the determinants of WC, data from the firms was obtained from the electronic database CMIE Prowess IQ. The financial information of 1818 nonfinancial firms of India enrolled at the BSE Stock Exchange for a span of ten years (2011–2021) has been collected for the study. A systemic method was adopted to reach the sample, where the firms with missing data, nonavailability of compatible financial information, and full information were dropped from the sample.

13.3.2 VARIABLES

After conducting an in-depth literature review, the determinants and the variable used for model estimation were identified. Table 13.1 enlists the determinants and the variables.

13.3.3 MODEL ESTIMATION

For certain periods and many individuals with a direct operational association and with the explained variable is dynamic, i.e., dependent on its own previous comprehensions with also autonomous or the predictor variables connected with previous and possibly current realizations of the error, the system generalized method of moment (System GMM) in dynamic panel regression is used (Arellano and Bond, 1991; Arellano and Bover, 1995; Blundell, and Bond, 1998). This method also takes care of the fixed specific effects, heteroskedasticity, and autocorrelation with one another but not through them. Therefore, to understand the influence of the factors for understanding the WCR by using the system generalized method of the moment with the effect on time and across firms.

TABLE 13.1 Determinants and Variables Used in Model Estimation.

Variables	Calculation	Literature support
Working capital requirement (wtr)	Log (Current assets− Current liabilities)	Beaver, 1966; Beaver, 1966
Profit (profit)	Log profit after tax	Kamal and MohdZulkifli, 2004; Wang, 2002; Deloof, 2003; Falope and Ajilore, 2009; Gill et al., 2010
Leverage (lev)	Log long term liabilities	Nazir and Afza, 2009; Altaf and Ahmad, 2019
Asset composition (atcomp)	Log non-current assets	Kwenda, 2014; Baños-Caballero et al., 2010; Kamal and MohdZulkifli, 2004
Firms' size (size)	Log of total assets	Nazir and Afza, 2009; Paul and Mitra, 2018
Sales growth (salesgr)	Log sales turnover	Kwenda, 2014; Hill et al., 2010

Source: Authors' compilation

$$y_{mn} = \beta_0 + \beta_1 x_{mn-1} + \beta_2 y_{mn-1} + \alpha_i + \varepsilon_{mn} \qquad (13.1)$$

And to check the variables uncorrelated with the future error term, no autocorrelated error, the first differentiation is done. The model estimated as per is as follows:

$$y_{mn} - y_{mn-1} = \beta_0 + \beta_1 (x_{mn-1} - x_{mn-2}) + \beta_2 (y_{mn-1} - y_{mn-2}) + (\varepsilon_{mn} - \varepsilon_{mn-1}) \qquad (13.2)$$

The model estimation uses the past understanding of the explained variable i.e., WCR and the predictor variables profit, leverage, asset composition, size, and sales growth of the firm. The explained variable (wtr_{mn}) stands for the WCR of the organization 'm' at the time 'n.' Similarly, the predictor variables with the control variables were also considered for the organization 'm' at the time 'n' for the model estimation.

$$\begin{aligned} wtr_{mn} - wtr_{mn-1} &= \beta_0 + \beta_1 (profit_{mn-1} - profit_{mn-2}) + \beta_2 (lev_{mn-1-} - lev_{mn-2}) \\ &+ \beta_3 (atcomp_{mn-1} - atcomp_{mn-2}) + \beta_4 (size_{mn-1} - size_{mn-2}) \\ &+ \beta_5 (salesgr_{mn-1} - salesgr_{mn-2}) + \beta_6 (wtr_{mn-1} - wtr_{mn-2}) + (\varepsilon_{mn} - \varepsilon_{mn-1}) \end{aligned} \qquad (13.3)$$

13.4 RESULTS

13.4.1 ANALYSIS OF DESCRIPTIVE STATISTICS

The detailed measurements of the explained and predictor with the control variables used in the model estimation are condensed in Table 13.2. The maximum value for wcr was 192.567 and the minimum was −1830.96, with the mean value of −0.4510 and Std. Dev. value of 22.83. The profit of the firms has a Max value of 69.338 and a Min value of –5.7096. The Std. Dev. of profit was 0.7618 and a mean value of 0.0390. The average of lev of the firms over the year was reported as 0.1811 and for atcomp, it was 0.3508. The average salesgr was 8.6812.

TABLE 13.2 Results of descriptive statistics.

Variables	Mean	Std. Dev.	Min	Max
wcr	–0.4510	22.8273	–1830.96	192.567
profit	0.0390	0.7618	–5.7096	69.338
lev	0.1811	0.3964	–0.7100	14.002
atcomp	0.3508	0.1802	0.00009	0.9926
size	7.7509	1.9406	1.1314	16.086
Salesgr	8.6812	1.9609	–1.6094	15.633

Source: Authors' calculations.

13.4.2 CORRELATIONS ANALYSIS AND VIFS

Subsequently, the Pearson correlation test and variance of factors (VIFs) were conducted to check the multicollinearity problem. Pearson correlation coefficients were computed to understand the association among the variables used in the Model. The findings are captured in Table 13.3. The variable wcr had a significant relation between lev, size, and salesgr, wherein with lev and size had a positive relation with salesgr. The variable profit has a definite and statistically substantial association with lev.

TABLE 13.3 Results of Correlations Analysis and VIFs.

	wcr	Profit	lev	Atcomp	size	salesgr	VIFs
wcr	1.000						–
Profit	0.0132	1.000					1.02
lev	–0.0360*	0.0917*	1.000				1.03
atcomp	–0.0133	0.0089	0.1334*	1.000			1.02
size	–0.0216*	–0.0166	–0.1356*	0.0752*	1.000		7.42
salesgr	0.0528*	0.0066	–0.1736*	–0.0048	0.9256*	1.000	7.49

*Significant at 5%, VIFs: variance of factors.

Source: Authors' calculation.

Similarly, the variable lev had a statistically significant relationship with atcomp, size, and salesgr. The atcomp had a positive relation with lev but the size and salesgr had a negative relationship with lev. The variable atcomp has a positive relation with size. The variable size had a sincere relationship with salesgr (positive). All the correlation coefficients of the variables were within the limit of 0.8 except salesgr and size. So further, VIFs were calculated for all independent and control variables, and it was found that the VIFs values for the variables were below 10. Therefore, it can be concluded that there was no serious multicollinearity problem.

13.4.3 DYNAMIC PANEL DATA-SYSTEM GMM

The outcomes of dynamic panel data with two step system GMM outcomes are presented in Table 13.4. In the model, Lnprofit and Lnsize have a positive impact on the wcr, whereas Lnatcomp and Lnsalesgr has negative impact on wcr. The findings reveal that there is no substantial impact of Lnlev on the wcr. The coefficient of the Lnwcr was reported to be 0.506 which estimates the effect of the WCR of the previous period on the current period which is reported as positive and statistically substantial at 5% level as per the dynamic estimator used in the model. The adjustment of the real WCR to the predicted WCR is 0.494. Thus, it is inferred that in one year about 49.4% difference between the predicted and the real is adjusted. This is the WCR gap reported by the model. The nonfinancial firms in one year can close the WCR to 49.4% as per the outcomes of the study. This signifies a considerable impact of the current year WCR on the previous year WCR.

TABLE 13.4 Dynamic Panel Data with Two-Step System GMM.

Lnwcr	Coefficient (B)	Std. error	p-Value
		Lnwcr	
L.1	0.506	0.043	0.000*
Lnprofit	0.148	0.119	0.000*
Lnlev	–0.13	0.007	0.063
Lnatcomp	–0.271	0.025	0.000*
Lnsize	0.583	0.064	0.000*
Lnsalesgr	–0.019	0.022	0.000*
Constant	–0.197	0.104	0.058

*Significant at 5% level.

Source: Authors' calculations.

13.4.4 TEST OF ROBUSTNESS

To test the condition of nonexistence of correlation in the error term, the Arellano and Bond assessment is used (Cameron and Trivedi, 2009). The Arellano-Bond assessment for AR(1) in first differences is normally found to be significant.at 5% level. The Arellano-Bond assessment for AR(2) in first differences is conducted and the results are presented in Table 13.5. As the p-value is greater than 0.05, the null hypothesis is not rejected and it can be interpreted as the, the errors terms are not serially correlated.

The outcomes of the instrument validity test are described in Table 13.6, where the sargen test validates the instrument used in the model (Roodman, 2009). As the p-value is higher than 0.05, the instruments in the model estimation are valid. For two-step estimations, the Hansen test is used. As the p-value is greater than 0.05 and less than 0.8, it is an optimal fit and rejects the null hypothesis (Roodman, 2009).

TABLE 13.5 Results of Autocorrelation Test.

Arellano–Bond test	p-Value
AR(1) in first differences	0.000*
AR(2) in first differences	0.831

*Significant at 5% level.

Source: Authors' calculations

TABLE 13.6 Results of Instrument Validity Test.

	p-Value
Sargan test	0.063
Hansen test	0.214

*Significant at 5% level.

Source: Authors' calculations.

13.5 DISCUSSIONS

The empirical model was developed by applying the dynamic panel data-system GMM. The study's findings demonstrated that the firm-specific variables employed in the analysis had an impact on the WCR of the companies. The previous year WCR has impact on the current year WCR which has been reported as 49.4%. The firm's earnings and asset mix were significantly positively correlated with WCR. The size of the business and WCR were inversely related. WC consumption rises with increasing firm size, and vice versa (Nazir and Afza, 2009; Hill et al., 2010). The model also indicated that the WCR is significantly impacted by profitability (Wang, 2002). According to research by Banos-Caballero et al., the asset mix has an inverse effect on the WCR because nonfinancial enterprises, which are typically capital intensive, spend significantly more in non-current assets than in current assets (2010). The outcomes of study support the idea that the model's increased sales have a detrimental effect on the WCR (Chiou et al., 2006; Hill et al., 2010). As a result, it can be said that the nonfinancial enterprises' profit, asset composition, and firm size were the key drivers for predicting WCR. Leverage and sales growth, however, had little to no impact on the enterprises' WCR. The micro factors that are unique to the firm's overall WCR play a significant role. The organization should focus on the improvement of the profitability and the structure of the assets maintained in the organization with respect to fixed assets as well as the current assets to improve the WC position. The impact of borrowings has a significant opposite impact on the WCR of the organization. In the same spirit the sales growth also shows a reverse association with the WCR of the organization. Therefore, the management should keep in mind the factors affecting the WCR while predicting it for a certain period of the organization.

13.6 CONCLUSIONS

The intent of the study was to discover the contributing elements of WC of nonfinancial firms in India. For this reason, a dataset of 1818 organizations from 2011–2021 was obtained by using the CMIE database. Variables used to show the association between WCR and its determinants as a set of predictor variables such as profit, lev, atcomp, size, and salesgr. Thus, it is concluded that the composition of the assets and earnings of a company can be used to predict the WCR of companies. And leverage was not a significant factor in predicting WCR. At the same time, the size of the organization had an inverse association with the requirement of WC to manage the company's operations.

To the author's understanding, this research is one of the attempts to forecast the WC of nonfinancial corporations in the Indian context.

Previous investigations have been performed to examine the association between organizations' performance and factors affecting WC in the Indian context. Therefore, the study provides one more dimension to understanding corporate WCR in the Indian context for nonfinancial firms and endogeneity issues were addressed using a systemic GMM model. The study had certain limitations regarding the number of variables used to understand WC needs. Hence, it is proposed that potential research may include more variables to improve understanding. The time was limited to ten years only according to the availability of data.

KEYWORDS

- **working capital**
- **dynamic panel data-System-GMM**
- **profit**
- **leverage**
- **asset composition**
- **size**
- **sales growth**

REFERENCES

Aktas, N.; Croci, E.; Petmezas, D. Is Working Capital Management Value-enhancing? Evidence from Firm Performance and Investments. *J. Corp. Financ.* **2015,** *30* (1), 98–113.

Altaf, N.; Ahmad, F. Working Capital Financing, Firm Performance, and Financial Constraints: Empirical Evidence from India. *Int. J. Manag. Financ.* **2019,** *15* (4), 464–477.

Arellano, M.; Bond, S. Some Tests of Specification for Panel Data: Monte Carlo Evidence and An Application to Employment Equations. *Rev. Econ. Stud.* **1991,** *58* (2), 277–297.

Arellano, M.; Bover, O. Another Look at the Instrumental Variable Estimation of Error Components Models. *J. Econom.* **1995,** *68* (1), 29–51.

Baños-Caballero, S.; García-Teruel, P. J.; Martínez-Solano, P. Working Capital Management in SMEs. *Account. Financ.* **2010,** *50* (3), 511–527.

Beaver, W. Financial Ratios as Predictors of Failure. *J. Account. Res.* **1966,** *4,* 71–111.

Bei, Z.; Wijewardana, W. P. Working Capital Policy Practice: Evidence from Sri Lankan Companies. *Proc.-Soc. Behav. Sci.* **2012,** *40,* 695–700.

Bhama, V.; Jain, P. K.; Yadav, S. S. Pecking Order Test at Varying Debt Levels: A Comparative Study of Indian and Chinese Firms. *J. Emerg. Mark. Financ.* **2019,** *18* (2), 237–261.

Blundell, R.; Bond, S. Initial Conditions and Moment Restrictions in Dynamic Panel Data Models. *J. Econom.* **1998,** *87* (1), 115–143.

Cameron, A. and Trivedi, P. *Microeconometrics using Stata.* Stata Press College Station: Texas, United States, 2009.

Chiou, J.-R.; Cheng, L.; Wu, H.-W. The Determinants of Working Capital Management. *J. Am. Acad. Bus.* **2006,** *10* (1), 149–155.

Deloof, M. Does Working Capital Management Affect Profitability of Belgian Firms? *J. Bus. Financ. Account.* **2003,** *30* (3/4), 573–588.

Falope, O. I.; Ajilore, O. T. Working Capital Management and Corporate Profitability: Evidence From Panel Data Analysis of Selected Quoted Companies in Nigeria. *Res. J. Bus. Manag.* **2009,** *3* (3), 73–84.Gill, A.; Biger, N.; Mathur, N. The Relationship Between Working Capital Management and Profitability: Evidence from the United States. *Bus. Econ. J.* **2010,** *10* (1), 1–9.

Hill, M. D.; Kelly, G. W.; Highfield, M. J. Net Operating Working Capital Behavior: A First Look. *Financ. Manag.* **2010,** *39* (2), 783–805.

Jose, M.; Lancaster, C.; Stevens, J. Corporate Returns and Cash Conversion Cycles. *J. Econ. Financ.* **1996,** *20* (1), 33–46.

Kamal, N.; MohdZulkifli, M. Determinants of Corporate Performance of Malaysian Companies, Accepted for Presentation at the Fourth Asia Pacific Interdisciplinary Research in Accounting Conference, 4 to 6, July, 2004.

Kwenda, F. Determinants of Working Capital Investment in South Africa: Evidence from Selected JSE-Listed Firms. *J. Econ. Behav. Stud.* **2014,** *6* (7), 569–580.

Lamberson, M. Changes in Working Capital of Small Firms in Relation to Changes in Economic Activity. *Am. J. Bus.* **1995,** *10* (2), 45–50.

Lazaridis, I.; Tryfonidis, D. Relationship Between Working Capital Management and Profitability of Listed Companies in the Athens Stock Exchange. *J. Financ. Manag. Anal.* **2006,** *19* (1), 26–35.

Moussawi, R.; LaPlante, M.; Kieschnick, R.; Baranchuk, N. Corporate Working Capital. 2006. Management: Determinants and Consequences, Baylor University, TX.

Nazir, M. S.; Afza, T. Impact of Aggressive Working Capital Management Policy on Firms' Profitability. *IUP J. Appl. Financ.* **2009,** *15* (8), 19–30.

Nimalathasan, B. Working Capital Management and its Impact on Profitability: A Study Listed Manufacturing Companies in Sri Lanka. *J. Manag.* **2010,** *8* (1), 76–83.

Paul, P. and Mitra, P. Analysis of the Effect of Working Capital Management on Profitability of the Firm: Evidence from Indian Steel Industry *Asia-Pacific J. Manag. Res. Innov.* **2018,** *14* (1–2), 32–38.

Paul, P. A Study of Multilayered Profitability Analysis by Using DuPont Model: Evidence from Indian Pharmaceutical Industry. *Glob. Bus. Rev.* **2021,** Online first on March 21, 2021, https://doi.org/10.1177/0972150921993056.

Peel, M. J.; Wilson, N. Working Capital and Financial Management Practices in the Small Firm Sector. *Int. Small Bus. J.* **1996,** *14* (2), 52–68.

Roodman, D. A Note on the Theme of Too Many Instruments'. *Oxford B. Econ. Stat.* **2009,** *71* (1), 135–158.

Roodman, D. How to do xtabond2: An Introduction to Difference and System GMM in Stata. *Stata J.:* **2009,** *9* (1), 86–136.

Samiloglu, F.; Demirgunes, K. The Effect of Working Capital Management on Firm Profitability: Evidence from Turkey. *Int. J. Appl. Econ. Financ.* **2008,** *2* (1), 44–50.

Saravanan, P.; Sivasankaran, N.; Srikanth, M.; Shaw, T. S. Enhancing Shareholder Value Through Efficient Working Capital Management: An Empirical Evidence from India. *Financ. India* **2017,** *31* (3), 851–871.
Shin, H. H.; Soenen, L. Efficiency of Working Capital Management and Corporate Profitability. *Financial Pract. Educat.* **1998,** *8* (2), 37–45.
Smith, J. K. Trade Credit and Informational Asymmetry. *J. Financ.* **1987,** *42* (4), 863–872.
Tahir, M.; Anuar, M. B. A. The Determinants of Working Capital Management and Firm's Performance of Textile Sector in Pakistan. *Qual. Quant.* **2016,** *50* (2), 605–618.
Wang, Y. J. Liquidity Management, Operating Performance, and Corporate Value: Evidence from Japan and Taiwan. *J. Multinati. Financ. Manag.* **2002,** *12* (2), 159–169.
Wasiuzzaman, S. Determinants of Liquidity in Malaysian SMEs: A Quantile Regression Approach. *Int. J. Prod. Perfor. Manag.* **2018,** *67* (9), 1566–1584.

CHAPTER 14

Exploring the Authenticity of Food Tourism Experiences: An Examination of Tourist Expectations and Perceptions in Saudi Arabia

CYNTHIA SIMON EL HAJJ[1], AMAAN SINGH[2], HARSH VIKRAM SINGH[2], ADITYA VIKRAM SINGH[3], and ANKITA SINGH[3]

[1]*Business Administration, Holy Spirit University of Kaslik (USEK), Lebanon*

[2]*Techno India University, Kolkata, West Bengal, India*

[3]*Jagdish Sheth School of Management (JAGSoM), Bangalore, India*

ABSTRACT

Purpose: Food tourism is on the rise, as travelers look for new and exciting culinary experiences. Saudi Arabia is a popular destination for this type of tourism, but little is known about the validity of culinary experiences in the country. This study's objective is to look at how visitors rate the authenticity of their food tourism experiences in Saudi Arabia.

The study also aims to examine how tourists' views of the authenticity of their culinary tourism experiences relate to their expectations and desires, and to determine how these aspects affect how satisfied tourists are with their experiences as a whole. By focusing on these issues, the study aims to advance knowledge of the elements that influence visitor satisfaction in the context of food tourism in Saudi Arabia and to offer insights that can guide the creation of more effective marketing plans for this expanding area of the travel and hospitality industry.

Agile Business Transformations: Priorities, Lessons, and Practices. Satyajit Chakrabarti, Subrata Chattopadhyay, Udit Chawla, Sundeep Singh Sondhi, & Arunava Dalal (Eds.)

This study provides insights into the authenticity of food tourism experiences in Saudi Arabia, and underscores the importance of meeting the varied expectations and views of visitors. This information may be used to help create food tourism experiences that accurately portray Saudi Arabia's rich culinary history.

Design/methodology: Structured questionnaires were used to conduct this research. Men and women from diverse age groups, economic ranges, and occupational backgrounds—including business, service, and others—were used to gather the study's primary data. From 1 (strongly disagree) to 5 (strongly agree), five points were used to compute each parameter studied for the survey.

Findings: The findings of the study show that Saudi Arabian tourists are particularly demanding when it comes to the authenticity of their culinary tourism experiences. They believe that the availability of real food is an important factor in choosing a destination for culinary tourism, and that a number of other factors, including the standard of the cuisine, the dishes' cultural and historical relevance, and the level of engagement with locals, also affect tourists' impressions of the authenticity of their experiences.

14.1 INTRODUCTION

As tourism becomes a gradually important part of the economy, food tourism is an increasingly important concern for destination managers, researchers, and marketers. Tourists frequently engage in considerable social, cultural, and economic activities when they visit new locations. These journeys may have either personal or professional purposes. The experiences and relationships that people have while traveling are the major focus of tourism (Chawla and Sengupta, 2017). This is because food is one of the fundamental components of a tourist's experience, and can often be a key factor in whether or not someone decides to visit a destination (Henderson, 2009; Robinson and Getz, 2014). Since food has always been a major attraction for travelers, several locations have made an effort to provide unique culinary experiences to visitors (Cohen and Avieli, 2004; Tsai and Wang, 2017). Local cuisine may help a place's reputation since it reflects many national, regional, and individual characteristics (Chang et al., 2010; Henderson, 2009).

According to research by Mak et al. (2017), it is important for destination planners to take into account the preferences and interests of tourists in order to influence where they choose to visit. Various studies have found that tourists are more likely to enjoy and prefer eating local cuisine when visiting a new destination (Cohen and Avieli, 2004; Robinson and Getz, 2016; Sharples and Hall, 2004). Benefits of eating local cuisine include emotional satisfaction, practicality, epistemology, and social relationships. This encourages tourists to return or recommend a region to others. The diversity and promotion of a location's restaurants affect how desirable it is. Food quality has a tremendous impact on consumer happiness and loyalty. The capacity of hotels and tourist destinations to provide enticing meals at reasonable rates across a range of price points also has an impact on visitor satisfaction (Das et al., 2017).

Recent studies have suggested that the quality of the cuisine when tourists are traveling can affect how satisfied they are with their vacation (Ramkissoon and Uysal, 2011; Lego Muñoz and Wood, 2009). For travelers' food consumption experiences, quality aspects of food tourism, such as cuisine, service, and the ambience, are just as important as authenticity. Both can contribute to a great travel experience (Antun et al., 2010; Richards, 2012; Ha et al., 2010). Local eateries serve as conduits for tourists and regional food (Cohen and Avieli, 2004). Restaurants promote local food in appropriate ways so that tourists will eat it. The standard and variety of hotel rooms and services play a significant role in the overall health of the tourism sector. The availability and quality of hotel alternatives directly affect the tourism industry's success, making it vital to carefully choose the best lodging options for its ongoing growth and development (Chawla and Sengupta, 2017).

Food tourism has become increasingly popular, resulting in increased visits to restaurants and food establishments (Okumus et al., 2018). Culinary, gastronomic, and gourmet tourism are terms used to characterize food tourism (Ellis et al., 2018). Food tourism is a type of tourism that focuses on experiencing food and culinary culture. It can provide visitors with memorable experiences that are distinct from general tourism (Chen and Huang, 2018).

The Middle East is a region that is growing quickly in tourism due to its many attractions and unique culture (UNWTO, 2012b). The Middle East is forecast to become one of the most competitive regions in the world, with a rich infrastructure and many services that are of interest to tourists from around the world (Deloitte, 2010). The majority of Middle Eastern locations have been adversely affected by social and political unrest in recent years. Saudi Arabia has also been affected.

Heritage food is an important part of a place's identity and culture. It is getting more popular, especially among tourists, because it is a unique experience (Quintero-Angel et al., 2022; Timothy, 2015). Tourists seeking out unique or excellent gastronomic experiences are drawn to heritage food

(Cohen and Avieli, 2004; Hall and Mitchell, 2007; Kim et al., 2019; Quan and Wang, 2004). The popularity of tourist-friendly culinary traditions among travelers may lead to greater appreciation of these traditions and even to preservation efforts. This tradition-specific cuisine incorporates intangible components like dining etiquette, service methods, speciality ingredients, and cooking techniques.

Productive families are another form of FSE in the catering industry, with families often working from their homes (ALosaimi et al., 2020; Juera, 2020; Ministries, 2019). In Saudi Arabia, a productive family (home-based catering) is referred to as a family of one or more people who live in a single home and prepare food for local consumption, such as traditional cuisine (Ministries, 2019). Many women in Saudi Arabia cook traditional foods for weddings and large feasts, which is why they are successful. They offer more individualized services at a lower price than hotels and restaurants, which makes them a popular choice (Juera, 2020). Different types of FSEs offer different types of cuisines, but there are significant differences between their clientele, size, menus, and administration.

This article investigates food tourism in Saudi Arabia, looking at how tradition and modernity are balanced throughout the development, promotion, and consumption of culinary experiences. This is done by considering the perspectives of market management staff, food sellers, and customers involved in these processes.

14.2 THEORETICAL BACKGROUND

Perceived affordability is the personal evaluation of how expensive food-related experiences are when traveling (Walker et al., 2010). It accounts for both the real prices of food and dining alternatives as well as how valuable people believe them to be. Travelers who are interested in food frequently think about their budget while also seeking for special culinary experiences (Kivela and Crotts, 2009). Travelers' choices are directly influenced by how much their budget and total trip expenditures contrast with the perceived prices of dining out (Rittichainuwat and Chakraborty, 2009). The hotel industry makes a lot of efforts to comprehend and accommodate the various demands of visitors (Chawla and Sengupta, 2017).

Perceived authenticity is essential in developing trust between visitors and the destination, strengthening the commitment to return and share positive experiences, and fostering emotional and cultural connections between travelers and the places they visit (Alves et al., 2019). Perceived authenticity, or how tourists perceive local cuisine as being representative of the traditions and culture of the area, is a significant aspect of culinary tourism (Ellis et al., 2018).

Regarding food and culinary events, perceived appearance relates to how they are presented visually (Michel et al., 2014). It significantly affects the flavor of food and how fulfilled individuals feel. In culinary tourism, restaurants' and food markets' visual appeal as well as how the food is presented all contribute to drawing customers and enriching their experiences (Chan et al., 2020). People's views and intentions toward consuming new foods and taking part in food-related activities are also influenced by how they perceive their looks (Grunert et al., 2012). The opinion of visitors' capacity to control their behavior can be favorably influenced by delicious and aesthetically pleasing meals, which can also encourage them to taste local cuisine (Tsai, 2016). A tourist might feel content or unsatisfied depending on how their exceptional service corresponds to their initial expectations (Das et al., 2017).

Perceived quality refers to a tourist's personal opinion on the overall quality of their food experiences, including taste, freshness, and service (Muskat et al., 2019). A traveler's views and intentions about tasting new meals and partaking in culinary tourism might be influenced by perceptions of food quality (Ab Karim and Chi, 2010). A place's reputation as a destination for food tourism may be improved by good impressions of the quality of the cuisine, which can result in higher satisfaction, repetitive business, and positive referrals (Zhang et al., 2019). The hospitality sector offers a range of services, including travel, lodging, food and drink, events, and entertainment. Its considerate and ethical treatment of clients defines it (Das et al., 2017).

14.3 OBJECTIVE OF THE STUDY

To investigate tourist expectations and perceptions in order to explore the authenticity of food tourism experiences in Saudi Arabia.

14.4 RESEARCH METHODOLOGY

In Saudi Arabia, 500 samples were gathered using a structured questionnaire and regular interactions with the tourists. People of various ages, genders, occupations, and economic levels were used to collect the data. Using a five-point scale (ranging from 1—strongly disagree to 5—strongly agree), each survey parameter study was determined.

14.5 FINDINGS AND ANALYSIS

14.5.1 MEASUREMENT MODEL

In order to analyze data, confirmatory factor analysis (CFA) is frequently employed in public research. To look at variable variation, both exploratory and CFA approaches are applied. Numerous statistical tools, including chi-square ($\chi 2$), the goodness of fit index (GFI), adjusted goodness of fit index (AGFI), comparative fit index (CFI), and root mean square error of approximation (RMSEA)" are used for this study. By comparing the actual and anticipated covariances, the Chi-Square value was used to assess how well the model fit the data (Hu and Bentler, 1999: 2). The Goodness of Fit Index (GFI) is adjusted depending on the degrees of freedom using a metric called the Adjusted Goodness of Fit Index (AGFI). When more complicated models are utilized, it is related to the GFI and reduces the fit (Tabachnick and Fidell, 2007). The AGFI and GFI are comparable in that both have values between 0 and 1. It is widely agreed that models fit the data well when their values are 0.90 or above. A modified version of the NFI that can correctly evaluate the performance of small sample numbers is called the Comparative Fit Index (CFI) (Tabachnick and Fidell, 2007). A RMSEA of 0.08–0.10 demonstrates an excellent match, whereas 0.08 or less indicates a mediocre fit (MacCallum et al, 1996). Composite reliability (CR) is defined as a measure of the consistency of contented construct pointers. Higher CR indicates that possible variables are reliable; the values should be greater than 0.5.

TABLE 14.1 Goodness of Fit Indices (CFA).

CMIN/DF	P	GFI	AGFI	NFI	TLI	CFI	PCLOSE	RMSEA
2.559	0.000	0.861	0.821	0.843	0.924	0.951	0.02	0.073

From Table 14.1, we can see that we are getting satisfied results for the confirmatory factor analysis.

From Figure 14.1, we can see that we are getting satisfied results for the Structured Equation Modeling. The structural model of FOOD TOURISM (Figure 14.1) suggests that PAF—"PERCEIVED AFFORDABILITY" and PAU—"PERCEIVED AUTHENTICITY" impose a larger impact on tourist's food satisfaction (SATF) as it signifies most important construct as the regression weights are 0.53 and 0.44. The study also signifies that there is also a positive relationship between TFS— "TOURIST FOOD SATISFACTION" and the construct PAF—"PERCEIVED APPEARANCE," construct PQ—"PERCEIVED QUALITY,"

TABLE 14.2 Discriminant Validity.

	Perceived affordability (PAF)	Perceived authenticity (PAU)	Perceived appearance (PAP)	Perceived quality (PQ)
Perceived affordability (PAF)	**0.83**			
Perceived authenticity (PAU)	0.265	**0.82**		
Perceived appearance (PAP)	0.269	0.545	**0.78**	
Perceived quality (PQ)	0.252	0.533	0.589	0.77

TABLE 14.3 Results of the Measurement Model.

Measurement Items	AVE	CR
Perceived affordability (PAF)	0.69	0.91
Perceived authenticity (PAU)	0.68	0.90
Perceived appearance (PAP)	0.61	0.88
Perceived quality (PQ)	0.60	0.87

TABLE 14.4 Goodness of Fitness (SEM).

CMIN/DF	P	GFI	AGFI	NFI	TLI	CFI	PCLOSE	RMSEA
2.45	0.000	0.851	0.811	0.833	0.911	0.940	0.00	0.084

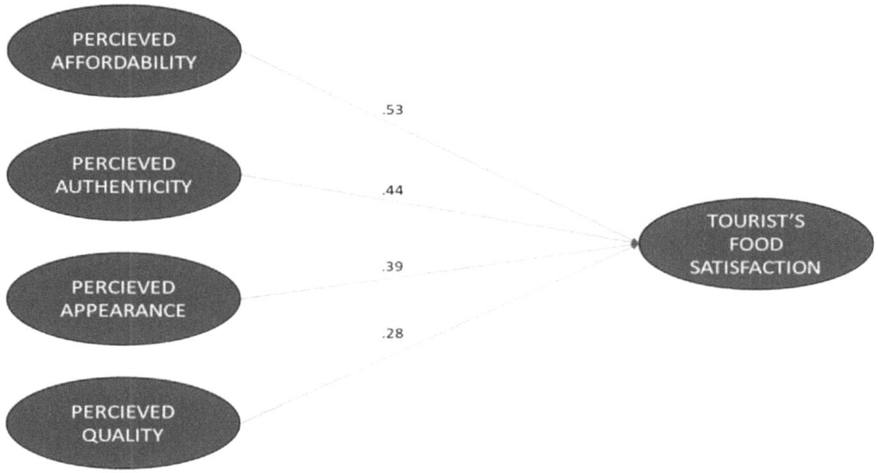

FIGURE 14.1 Structural equation modeling.

as the regression weights are 0.39 and 0.28. Thus, it may be hypothesized that tourists in general consider PAF—"PERCEIVED AFFORDABILITY" and

PAU—"PERCEIVED AUTHENTICITY" play a very important role in determining tourists' food satisfaction.

14.6 CONCLUSION

A growing segment of the worldwide tourist sector is food tourism, which is attracting the interest of marketers, researchers, and destination managers alike. Throughout their journeys, travelers participate in a variety of social, cultural, and commercial activities, with food having a significant role in determining their experiences. Many localities work hard to create distinctive culinary experiences that represent their character and culture since the allure of local food frequently impacts tourists' decisions to visit a location. Tourists like and favor local food, according to research, which increases their emotional well-being and makes them want to return or suggest the area to others. The kind of foods visitors choose to eat and their overall happiness are greatly influenced by variables such as perceived affordability, authenticity, appearance, and quality. In order to create and promote outstanding culinary experiences for guests, venues must work together and find a balance between tradition and modernity as food tourism becomes more and more popular. A varied range of travelers might be drawn in by offering gastronomic experiences that are seen as being affordable. In order to create unique culinary tourism experiences that reflect the culture and history of the area, authenticity is essential. Travelers' perceptions of food offers are greatly influenced by their look. In order to delight visitors and entice them to promote the location, quality is essential. Working with trained chefs, adhering to food safety regulations, and utilizing locally sourced, premium ingredients are all necessary to achieve quality.

KEYWORDS

- **authenticity**
- **food tourism**
- **experiences**
- **tourist expectations**
- **perceptions**
- **local people**

REFERENCES

Ab Karim, S.; Chi, C. G. Q. Culinary Tourism as a Destination Attraction: An Empirical Examination of Destinations' Food Image. *J. Hosp. Mark. Manag.* **2010,** *19* (6), 531–555.'

Alves, H.; Campón-Cerro, A. M.; Hernández-Mogollón, J. M. Enhancing rural Destinations' Loyalty Through Relationship Quality. *Span. J. Mark.-ESIC* **2019,** *23* (2), 185–204.

Antun, J. M.; Frash, R. E. Jr.; Costen, W.; Runyan, R. C. Accurately Assessing Expectations Most Important to Restaurant Patrons: The Creation of the DinEX Scale. *J. Foodserv. Bus. Res.* **2010,** *13,* 360–379. [CrossRef]

Hall, C. M.; Mitchell, R. Gastronomic Tourism: Comparing food and Wine Tourism Experiences. In *Niche Tourism*, Routledge, 2007; pp 87–102.

Chan, G. S. H.; Li, J. Re-Examination of Servicescape Model: Food Expectation and Patronage to Macau's Restaurant from Chinese Visitors' Perspectives. *J. Serv. Sci. Manag.* **2020,** *13* (03), 470.

Chang, R. C.; Kivela, J.; Mak, A. Food Preferences of Chinese Tourists. *Ann. Tour. Res.* **2010,** *37* (4), 989–1011.

Chawla, U.; Sengupta, K. S. Factors Affecting Customers' Accommodation Satisfaction and Service Quality in the Hotel Industry of Rural West Bengal. *LBS J. Manag. Res.* **2017,** *15* (1), 34–47.

Chen, Q.; Huang, R. Local Food in China: A Viable Destination Attraction. *Br. Food J.* **2018,** *120* (1), 146–157.

Cohen, E.; Avieli, N Food in Tourism: Attraction and Impediment. *Ann. Tour. Res.* **2004,** *31* (4), 755–778.

Timothy, D. J. Heritage Cuisines: Traditions, Identities and Tourism. Routledge, 2015.

Das, D.; Chawla, U.; Ray, S. Factors Affecting Customer Satisfaction and Service Quality in the Boutique Hotel Industry of Kolkata, West Bengal. *Int. J. Manag. (IJM)* **2017,** *8* (6).

Deloitte. Tourism, Hospitality & Leisure in the Middle East: Ready to Move to the Next Level. *Report by Deloitte Middle East* 2010.

Ellis, A.; Park, E.; Kim, S.; Yeoman, I. What is Food Tourism? *Tour. Manag.* **2018,** *68,* 250–263.

Grunert, K. G.; Shepherd, R.; Traill, W. B.; Wold, B. Food Choice, Energy Balance and its Determinants: Views of Human Behavior in Economics and Psychology. *Trends in Food Sci. Technol.* **2012,** *28* (2), 132–142.

Ha, J.; Jang, S. Effects of service quality and food quality: The Moderating role of Atmospherics in An Ethnic Restaurant Segment. *Int. J. Hosp. Manag.* **2010,** *29,* 520–529. [CrossRef]

Henderson, J. C. Food tourism reviewed. *Br. Food J.* **2009,** *111* (4), 317–326.

Hu, L. T.; Bentler, P. M. Cutoff Criteria for Fit Indexes in Covariance Structure Analysis: Conventional Criteria Versus New Alternatives. *Struct. Eq. Model.* **1999,** *6* (1), 1–55.

Kivela, J. J.; Crotts, J. C. Understanding Travelers' Experiences of Gastronomy through Etymology and Narration. *J. Hosp. Tour. Res.* **2009,** *33* (2), 161–192.

Lego Muñoz, C.; Wood, N. T. A Recipe for Success: Understanding Regional Perceptions of Authenticity in Themed Restaurants. *Int. J. Cult. Tour. Hosp. Res.* **2009,** *3,* 269–280. [CrossRef]

Quintero-Angel, M.; Mendoza, D.M.; Martínez-Giron, J. Food Fears and Risk of Loss of Food Heritage: A Little-explored Effect of Food Modernity and Times of Pandemic. *Int. J. Gastron. Food Sci.* **2022,**100499.

MacCallum, R. C.; Browne, M. W.; Sugawara, H. M. Power Analysis and Determination of Sample Size for Covariance Structure Modeling. *Psychol. Methods* **1996,** *1* (2), 130–49.

Mak, A. H,; Lumbers, M.; Eves. A.; et al. The Effects of Food-Related Personality Traits on Tourist Food Consumption Motivations. *Asia Pacific J. Tour. Res.* **2017,** *22* (1), 1–20.
Michel, C.; Velasco, C.; Gatti, E.; Spence, C. A taste of Kandinsky: Assessing the Influence of the Artistic Visual Presentation of Food on the Dining Experience. *Flavour* **2014,** *3* (1), 1–11.
Ministries, B. O. E. A. T. C. O. Regulations for the Work of Productive Families, 2019.
Muskat, B.; Hörtnagl, T.; Prayag, G.; Wagner, S. Perceived Quality, Authenticity, and Price in Tourists' Dining Experiences: Testing Competing Models of Satisfaction and Behavioral Intentions. *J. Vacat. Mark.* **2019,** *25* (4), 480–498.
ALosaimi, N. H.; Elzein, N. M.; Tukka, A. M. In *Mobile Application for Productive Families Business*, 2020 3rd International Conference on Computer Applications & Information Security (ICCAIS), IEEE, 2020, pp. 1–4.
Okumus, B.; Koseoglu, M. A.; Ma, F.Food and gastronomy research in tourism and hospitality: a bibliometric analysis. *Int. J. Hosp. Manag.* **2018,** *73,* 64–74.
Ramkissoon, H.; Uysal, M. S. The Effects of Perceived Authenticity, Information Search Behavior, Motivation and Destination Imagery on Cultural Behavioural Intentions of Tourists. *Curr. Issues Tour.* **2011,** *14,* 537–562. [CrossRef]
Richards, G. Food and the Tourism Experience: Major Findings and Policy Orientations. In *Food and the Tourism Experience*; Dodd, D., Ed.; OECD: Paris, France, 2012; pp 13–46.
Rittichainuwat, B. N.; Chakraborty, G. Perceived Travel Risks Regarding Terrorism and Disease: The case of Thailand. *Tour. Manag.* **2009,** *30* (3), 410–418.
Robinson, R.; Getz, D. Profiling Potential Food Tourists: An Australian study. *Br. Food J.* **2014,** *116* (4), 690–706.
Robinson, R. N.; Getz, D. Food Enthusiasts and Tourism: Exploring Food Involvement Dimensions. *J. Hosp. Tour. Res.* **2016,** *40* (4), 432–455.
Kim, S.; Park, E.; Lamb, D. Extraordinary or Ordinary? Food Tourism Motivations of Japanese Domestic Noodle Tourists. *Tourism Manag. Perspect.* **2019,** *29,* 176–186.
Quan, S.; Wang, N. Towards a Structural Model of the Tourist Experience: An Illustration from Food Experiences in Tourism. *Tour. Manag.* **2004,** *25* (3) 297–305.
Sharples, L.; Hall, C. M. The Consumption of Experiences or the Experience of Consumption? An Introduction to the Tourism of Taste. In *Food Tourism Around The World*, Routledge: Abingdon, 2004; pp 13–36.
Tabachnick, B. G.; Fidell, L. S. Using Multivariate Statistics, 5th ed.; Allyn and Bacon: New York, 2007.
Tsai, C.-T. S.; Wang, Y.-C. Experiential Value in Branding Food Tourism. *J. Destin. Mark. Manag.* **2017,** *6* (1), 56–65.
Tsai, C. T. Memorable Tourist Experiences and Place Attachment when Consuming Local Food. *Int. J. Tour. Res.* **2016,** *18* (6), 536–548.
UNWTO. The Middle East Outbound travel Market with Special Insight into the Image of Europe as a Destination. Report by the UNWTO. Madrid: Spain, 2012b.
Juera, W. B. Assessment of Customer Satisfaction on Home-Based Catering Business in Cabadbaran City: Basis for Enhancement Program. *IOER Int. Multidiscip. Res. J.* **2020,** *2* (1).
Walker, R. E.; Keane, C. R.; Burke, J. G. Disparities and Access to Healthy Food in the United States: A Review of Food Deserts Literature. *Health & Place* **2010,** *16* (5), 876–884.
Zhang, T.; Chen, J.; Hu, B. Authenticity, Quality, and Loyalty: Local Food and Sustainable Tourism Experience. *Sustainability* **2019,** *11* (12), 3437.

CHAPTER 15

Trends, Challenges, and Future Directions of Sustainable Tourism: A Systematic Literature Review

SOUMYA MUKHERJEE[1], MANALI CHOWDHURY[2,3,4], and MRINAL KANTI DAS[5]

[1]*Department of Management Studies, Techno India (Hooghly Campus), Chinsurah, West Bengal, India*

[2]*Aliah University, Kolkata, India*

[3]*Institute of Engineering & Management, Kolkata*

[4]*Department of Business Administration, University of Engineering & Management, Kolkata, India*

[5]*Department of Commerce, Kanchrapara College, Kanchrapara, North 24 Parganas, West Bengal, India*

ABSTRACT

This study focuses on the environmental, sociocultural, and economic aspects of sustainable tourism through a systematic literature review of the last 5 years (2018–2023) of research solely focused on sustainability tourism. The findings of the review highlight the significance of a multidimensional approach by outlining key concepts, principles, and frameworks used in sustainable tourism research. The review also identifies emerging research areas, such as the intersection of sustainable tourism with digital transformation, climate change adaptation, and social justice. Further, it explores innovative solutions and technologies that contribute to sustainable practices

Agile Business Transformations: Priorities, Lessons, and Practices. Satyajit Chakrabarti, Subrata Chattopadhyay, Udit Chawla, Sundeep Singh Sondhi, & Arunava Dalal (Eds.)

in tourism. This study offers insights into sustainable practices, community engagement, and economic benefits and challenges. The paper concludes with recommendations for future research directions and useful applications for achieving sustainability in the tourism sector.

15.1 INTRODUCTION

15.1.1 BACKGROUND AND SIGNIFICANCE OF SUSTAINABLE TOURISM

The idea and practice of sustainable tourism have made great progress in the global travel industry recently. The long-term survival of tourism locations is maintained by attempting to balance economic development, socio-cultural preservation, and environmental protection (Hall, 2019; Gössling et al., 2021). Tourism is expanding quickly, thus making it more difficult to disregard the need for sustainable practices.

Tourism has major negative consequences on the ecosystem, including increased carbon emissions, habitat degradation, and resource depletion, as argued by Gössling et al. (2020). In addition, disagreements between tourists and the local populace may arise due to the socio-cultural changes brought about by tourism (Ruhanen et al., 2018). Because of these difficulties, sustainable tourism is becoming recognized to reduce its negative consequences while boosting its positive ones.

15.1.2 IMPORTANCE OF CONDUCTING A SYSTEMATIC LITERATURE REVIEW

Because sustainable tourism is multidisciplinary, a comprehensive literature evaluation is necessary to synthesize present findings, identify research gaps, and offer evidence-based insights. Data from various academic publications may be analyzed and combined using a systematic literature review (Tranfield et al., 2003). By utilizing such a methodical approach, biases are lessened while a thorough comprehension of the area can be gained.

15.1.3 OBJECTIVES AND SCOPE OF THE STUDY

The purpose of this paper is to present a comprehensive literature review on sustainable tourism, with a focus on recent developments and emerging trends. By evaluating a wide range of academic publications, including empirical research, theoretical frameworks, and case studies, we want to provide insight into sustainable tourism.

The three facets of sustainable tourism—environmental, social, and economic—are all covered in this study. We will look at current studies on the consequences of environmental issues, such as reducing climate change, preserving biodiversity, and sustainably managing resources. We will also look at the sociological aspects of sustainable tourism, such as community empowerment, involvement in neighborhood concerns, and cultural preservation. Finally, we will examine the financial rewards, sustainable business strategies, and competitiveness of locales regarding sustainable tourism.

15.2 METHODOLOGY

15.2.1 EXPLANATION OF SYSTEMATIC LITERATURE REVIEW PROCESS

Identifying, deciding, and reviewing important research in an orderly and independent way are all made possible by the systematic literature review process (Tranfield et al., 2003). To guarantee the rigor and quality of the review, we adhered to the Preferred Reporting Items for Systematic Reviews and Meta-Analyses (PRISMA) criteria in this study (Moher et al., 2009).

15.2.2 INCLUSION AND EXCLUSION CRITERIA

To ensure the validity and relevance of the selected research, specific inclusion and exclusion criteria were applied. The inclusion criteria encompassed research articles, conference papers, and book chapters published over the last five years (2018–2023) to ensure the inclusion of recent work. Publications that did not mention it or did not make any empirical or theoretical contributions were excluded and only studies that dealt explicitly with sustainable tourism were considered.

15.2.3 SEARCH STRATEGY AND DATABASES UTILIZED

To retrieve pertinent research papers, an extensive search strategy was performed. Key academic databases like Scopus, Web of Science, and Google Scholar were all thoroughly searched. The searches were conducted using a combination of the keywords "sustainable tourism," "environmental sustainability," "socio-cultural impacts," "economic dimensions," and "tourism development."

15.2.4 DATA EXTRACTION AND ANALYSIS METHODS

To extract pertinent information from the chosen research, data extraction was done. Author(s), publication year, research goals, methodology, major discoveries, and theoretical frameworks used were among the information that was extracted. Thematic analysis was used to organize and synthesize the data, allowing for the discovery of recurring themes, trends, and patterns in the chosen literature (Braun and Clarke, 2006).

15.3 SUSTAINABLE TOURISM: CONCEPTUAL FRAMEWORK

15.3.1 UNDERSTANDING OF SUSTAINABLE TOURISM

Sustainable tourism seeks to maximize destination advantages while minimizing negative impacts on the environment, society, and economy (UNWTO, 2019a, 2019b). To ensure the long-term preservation of tourism destinations, it incorporates environmental conservation, socio-cultural authenticity, and economic viability (Hall, 2021). Sustainable tourism emphasizes community participation, cultural preservation, and equitable economic distribution in addition to environmental conservation (Gössling et al., 2022). It acknowledges the interdependence of environmental, sociocultural, and economic elements and seeks to strike a balance between the requirements of tourists, host communities, and the environment.

15.3.2 DIMENSIONS OF SUSTAINABLE TOURISM

The notion of sustainable development serves as the foundation for the concepts of sustainable tourism, and numerous important aspects, listed as follows, have been noted in the literature (Hall, 2021):

a) Environmental dimension: Focuses on reducing negative environmental impacts through resource conservation, waste management, and biodiversity preservation (Gössling et al., 2022).

b) Socio-cultural component: Promotes the preservation of local customs and traditions, engages, and empowers communities, and respects their socio-cultural values (Hall, 2021; Ruhanen et al., 2020).
c) Economic dimension: Emphasizes equitable distribution of economic benefits, supports local businesses, and enhances the livelihoods of host communities (Buckley, 2019).

15.3.3 FRAMEWORKS OR MODELS USED IN SUSTAINABLE TOURISM RESEARCH

The following models and frameworks have been used for this study:

a) The triple bottom line (TBL) approach: A comprehensive framework that considers environmental, socio-cultural, and economic aspects of sustainable tourism, popularized by Elkington (1997).
b) Tourism area life cycle (TALC) model: This model describes the stages of tourist destinations and emphasizes sustainable planning and management at each stage for long-term success, as proposed by Butler (1980).
c) The framework for destination management organizations (DMO): Focuses on destination-level governance and stakeholder collaboration to achieve sustainable tourism outcomes, highlighting coordination of marketing, planning, and management efforts, as outlined by Pike (2019).

These conceptual and practical frameworks and models offer insights into the intricate dynamics and relationships between the sustainability components as well as conceptual and practical guidelines for research on sustainable tourism.

15.4 TRENDS IN SUSTAINABLE TOURISM RESEARCH

15.4.1 ANALYSIS OF RESEARCH TOPICS AND THEMES

To address the complexities and challenges of sustainability, numerous topics and themes have been studied in the field of sustainable tourism. Recent investigations have covered the following important topics:

a) Climate change and environmental impacts: Investigating the environmental effects of tourism, strategies to mitigate climate change, and the role of sustainable practices (Becken et al., 2021; Gössling et al., 2021)

b) Community engagement and empowerment: Emphasizing the involvement of local communities in decision-making, supporting community-based tourism, and examining socio-cultural impacts on local populations (Ruhanen et al., 2020; Font et al., 2022)
c) Sustainable business models and innovation: Exploring how to promote sustainability in travel and tourism through innovative commercial strategies, such as green certifications and ethical supplier chains (Buckley et al., 2021; Koens et al., 2020)

15.4.2 WIDELY USED RESEARCH TECHNIQUES

Researchers have employed a variety of tools and strategies to investigate the phenomena of sustainable tourism, some of which are listed as follows:

a) Quantitative analysis: Evaluating the financial benefits and liabilities of sustainable tourism using surveys, statistical analysis, and modeling (Gössling et al., 2021; Weaver and Lawton, 2020).
b) Qualitative inquiry: Employing interviews, focus groups, and participant observation to explore socio-cultural dimensions, understand local perspectives, and capture narratives and experiences (Ruhanen et al., 2020; Font et al., 2022).
c) Mixed-methods approaches: Some researchers have used mixed-methods approaches, integrating qualitative and quantitative techniques, to fully comprehend sustainable tourism concerns and triangulate findings (Dredge and Jamal, 2019; Becken et al., 2021).

15.4.3 GEOGRAPHIC FOCUS AND REGIONAL VARIATIONS

Sustainable tourism research has demonstrated regional variations, listed as follows, with different geographic areas receiving attention:

a) Developing countries: Research has concentrated on sustainable tourism in developing countries, addressing poverty alleviation, community empowerment, and sustainable development (Mowforth and Munt, 2015; Gursoy et al., 2019).
b) Urban destinations: The focus on sustainable tourism in urban areas has explored urban regeneration, smart tourism, and sustainability integration in city tourism planning and management (Gössling et al., 2022; Hall and Page, 2019).

c) Ecotourism and protected areas: Studies have examined sustainable tourism practices in environmentally sensitive regions and protected areas, including environmental impacts, tourist management plans, and conservation initiatives (Newsome et al., 2012; Weaver, 2019).

These geographical variations and research trends illuminate the possibilities and issues that might arise in varied situations and deepen our understanding of sustainable tourism.

15.5 ENVIRONMENTAL SUSTAINABILITY IN TOURISM

15.5.1 LITERATURE REVIEW ON ENVIRONMENTAL IMPACTS OF TOURISM

Based on current research, this section offers a thorough analysis of the effects of tourism on the environment. Important research areas include:

a) Carbon and energy footprint: Research has assessed the energy and carbon footprints of various tourism activities, including travel and accommodation (Scott et al., 2021; Gössling et al., 2021).
b) Biodiversity and habitat loss: Studies even figure out that tourism contributes to habitat degradation and biodiversity loss (Higham et al., 2019; Buckley et al., 2021).
c) Water resources and pollution: Researchers have looked at how tourism affects water resources, including water use and wastewater contamination (Hall, 2020; Gössling et al., 2022).

15.5.2 SUSTAINABLE PRACTICES FOR RESOURCE CONSERVATION

Sustainable resource conservation methods have been researched as solutions to environmental problems. The following strategies are highlighted by a recent study:

a) Sustainable energy and efficiency measures: Integration of renewable energy sources and energy-efficient technology reduces carbon emissions and energy consumption in tourism (Becken et al., 2021; Hall and Page, 2019).
b) Waste management and circular economy: Adoption of waste reduction tactics and circular economy concepts minimizes trash creation and promotes resource recovery (Gössling et al., 2022; Weaver, 2019).

c) Sustainable water management: Water conservation techniques and wastewater treatment technology mitigate negative environmental effects on water resources in tourism (Scott et al., 2021; Gössling et al., 2022).

15.6 SOCIO-CULTURAL SUSTAINABILITY IN TOURISM

15.6.1 LITERATURE REVIEW ON SOCIO-CULTURAL IMPACTS OF TOURISM

An overview of current research on the effects of tourism on society and culture is given in this section. Important research areas include:

a) Social and cultural change: Studies have explored the influence of tourism on local communities, including changes in social structures, lifestyles, and cultural practices (Dredge and Jamal, 2015; Nyaupane and Poudel, 2011).
b) Community well-being: Research has looked at how tourism affects local communities' well-being, including economic advantages, job possibilities, and social cohesiveness (Hall and Williams, 2020; Gursoy et al., 2021).
c) Cultural authenticity: Researchers have evaluated how tourism affects the integrity and authenticity of regional cultures and customs (García-Rosell et al., 2019; Salazar, 2018).

15.6.2 COMMUNITY ENGAGEMENT AND EMPOWERMENT

Strategies for community empowerment and involvement have been investigated to improve socio-cultural sustainability in tourism. Recent studies emphasize the following strategies:

a) Community participation: Actively involving local communities in tourism decision-making processes promotes socio-cultural sustainability (Hall, 2020; Jamal and Stronza, 2009).
b) Capacity building and skill development: Initiatives that enhance community members' skills and capacities enable their active participation and benefit from tourism (Mowforth and Munt, 2015; Dredge and Jenkins, 2020).

c) Socio-economic benefits distribution: Fair distribution of tourism-related gains among community members reduces socio-economic inequities (Pereira et al., 2021; Andereck et al., 2018).

15.6.3 CULTURAL PRESERVATION AND HERITAGE MANAGEMENT

Tourism's socio-cultural sustainability depends on the preservation and management of cultural heritage. The following areas were examined in recent studies:

a) Cultural heritage conservation: Research focuses on methods and regulations for safeguarding intangible cultural practices, artifacts, and heritage sites (Gursoy et al., 2019; Richards and Munsters, 2010).
b) Cultural tourism planning: Incorporating cultural heritage into planning processes ensures sustainable and responsible tourist development (Farsari and Sigala, 2021; Leask and Fyall, 2020).
c) Tourism and Indigenous cultures: Studies explore respectful engagement, cultural representation, and protection of Indigenous rights in tourism, addressing challenges and opportunities (Butler and Ruhanen, 2019; Fennell, 2019).

Tourism can help local communities develop sustainably and thrive by recognizing and resolving the socio-cultural effects of the industry, putting community involvement programs into action, and protecting cultural assets.

15.7 ECONOMIC SUSTAINABILITY IN TOURISM

15.7.1 LITERATURE REVIEW ON ECONOMIC ASPECTS OF SUSTAINABLE TOURISM

Recent research on the financial advantages of sustainable tourism is summarized in this section. Investigative focuses include the following:

a) Economic impact assessment: Studies have examined the economic contributions of tourism, including job creation, income generation, and foreign exchange earnings (WTTC, 2021; UNWTO, 2019a, 2019b).
b) Economic leakage and retention: Research has looked at the extent of economic leakage from tourism locations and how to increase the retention of tourism money within local economies (Hall, 2020; Gössling et al., 2012).

c) Economic diversification: Researchers have examined how tourism promotes economic resilience, diversifies local economies, and lessens reliance on a single industry (Brouder et al., 2016; Bramwell et al., 2019).

15.7.2 ECONOMIC BENEFITS AND CHALLENGES OF SUSTAINABLE TOURISM

Economic sustainability requires an understanding of both the benefits and challenges of tourism. The following factors are included in recent research:

a) Economic benefits: Sustainable tourism research highlights improved livelihoods, income distribution, and support for small and medium-sized businesses (SMEs) (Hall and Lew, 2018; Spenceley, 2012).
b) Cost-benefit analysis: Evaluating economic feasibility and return on investment through cost-benefit studies of sustainable tourism projects (Dwyer et al., 2019; Coccossis and Mexa, 2018).
c) Economic challenges: Scholars identify seasonality, infrastructure development costs, and effective destination management as hurdles to achieving economic sustainability (Koens et al., 2018; Hall and Williams, 2020).

15.7.3 SUSTAINABLE BUSINESS MODELS AND STRATEGIES

This section explores sustainable business principles and tourism-related practices:

a) Responsible tourism practices: Fair trade, community participation, and sustainable supply chain management are examples of ethical business practices that have been researched (Font et al., 2021; Gössling et al., 2020).
b) Sustainable destination marketing: Studies focus on innovative marketing strategies that attract eco-friendly tourists and contribute to the local economy (Cater and Cater, 2020; Kieti et al., 2019).
c) Collaboration and partnerships: Scholars emphasize the importance of stakeholder collaboration and partnerships to foster sustainable economic growth in the tourism sector (Bramwell and Lane, 2021; Hall and Lew, 2018).

Destinations can achieve economic sustainability and community welfare by understanding the economic aspects of sustainable tourism, addressing its advantages and challenges, and implementing environmentally responsible business models and strategies.

15.8 CHALLENGES AND BARRIERS TO IMPLEMENTING SUSTAINABLE TOURISM

15.8.1 KEY CHALLENGES AND BARRIERS TO SUSTAINABLE TOURISM

Recent research has highlighted numerous crucial aspects in the analysis of the main obstacles and hurdles to the implementation of sustainable tourism practices (Hall, 2020; Gössling et al., 2020). Environmental pressures are emphasized as a critical problem, comprising the need to successfully regulate environmental consequences, handle resource depletion, and prioritize the preservation of sensitive ecosystems. As stakeholders struggle to strike a balance between economic development and environmental goals, economic factors provide another challenging challenge. This entails figuring out how to handle the apparent trade-off between development and environmental conservation, as well as evaluating the financial viability of sustainable tourist efforts (Buckley et al., 2016; Weaver, 2020). In addition, sociocultural elements add to the difficulties encountered in sustainable tourism. Among these are the necessity to address concerns pertaining to authenticity and cultural appropriation, the preservation of local cultures, the reduction of sociocultural disturbances, and others (Jamal and Stronza, 2009; Nyaupane and Poudel, 2011). The need to implement thorough methods and work together to overcome difficulties and promote sustainable practices in the tourist sector is highlighted by these issues taken together.

15.8.2 GOVERNANCE AND POLICY ISSUES

The successful implementation of sustainable tourism depends heavily on effective governance and policy frameworks. The results of a recent study have clarified several issues in this area. Policy coordination, which comprises the difficulty of developing integrated plans for sustainable tourism by harmonizing laws and regulations across various government levels and sectors, is one of the major problems (Bramwell and Lane, 2021; Hall, 2020). Another issue is stakeholder alignment, since different organizations, including enterprises, communities, and nongovernmental organizations, may have conflicting objectives and interests, making it challenging to come to agreements and work together (Buckley, 2012; Koens et al., 2018). Furthermore, there are difficulties in enforcing and adhering to sustainable tourism practices, including the adoption and oversight of regulations, benchmarks, and certification programs to guarantee adherence to green practices (Richards and Munsters, 2010; Font et al., 2021). The promotion of sustainable practices in the tourist sector and the long-term effectiveness of sustainable tourism projects depend heavily on addressing these governance and policy concerns.

15.8.3 STAKEHOLDER COLLABORATION AND ENGAGEMENT

Effective stakeholder involvement and collaboration are essential for the implementation of sustainable tourism. Numerous issues in this field have been brought to light by recent studies. One such issue is the lack of understanding of sustainable tourism concepts and practices among industry experts, tourists, and locals (Mowforth and Munt, 2015; Cater and Cater, 2020). To address this issue, efforts must be made to raise awareness and understanding through informational outreach and education. The need to eliminate power disparities among stakeholders and ensure equitable participation and meaningful involvement in decision-making processes has been highlighted (Jamal and Stronza, 2009; Hall and Lew, 2018). Likewise, encouraging successful collaboration and cooperation requires managing disputes and resolving tensions caused by competing stakeholder interests (Gursoy et al., 2019; Bramwell and Lane, 2021). To guarantee that sustainable tourism practices are effectively adopted, overcoming these issues calls for joint efforts, the creation of efficient governance structures, and ongoing stakeholder engagement.

15.9 FUTURE DIRECTIONS AND RESEARCH GAPS

15.9.1 EMERGING RESEARCH AREAS AND DIRECTIONS

In the realm of sustainable tourism, recent investigations have revealed a few new study paths and areas. One of these areas focuses on the effects of digital transformation on sustainable tourism practices, visitor experiences, and destination management (Buhalis, 2021; Xiang et al., 2020). The goal of this study is to comprehend how emerging digital technologies, such as blockchain, artificial intelligence, and virtual reality, might improve tourism's sustainability. Tourism and climate change adaptation are two interesting topics for future research. Researchers in this discipline look at novel tactics and solutions to lessen the effects of climate change on tourism locations. (Hall et al., 2021; Gössling et al., 2021). Significant stress is given to creating resilient infrastructure and putting adaptive management techniques into practice. The connection between social justice and ecological tourism is also gaining popularity. In the framework of sustainable tourism, researchers are looking at questions of justice, inclusiveness, indigenous rights, and community empowerment (Gursoy et al., 2020; Novelli et al., 2019). Scientists are interested in learning how sustainable tourism may advance social justice and local communities' chances for success.

15.9.2 INNOVATIVE SOLUTIONS AND TECHNOLOGIES

The promotion of environmentally friendly practices in the tourist sector depends heavily on the adoption of cutting-edge technology and solutions. Sustainable mobility and transportation are one area of emphasis, where researchers investigate solutions like electric cars and effective public transit systems to cut carbon emissions and improve tourist mobility (Gössling et al., 2020; Becken et al., 2019). The creation of smart and sustainable destinations is another crucial factor. Studies show how the Internet of Things (IoT), data analytics, and smart technologies have the potential to assist sustainability at the destination level. These tools can help with efficient resource management, trash minimization, and visitor management, resulting in more environmentally friendly tourist practices (Gretzel et al., 2015; Neuhofer et al., 2020). The idea of a circular economy in the tourist industry also presents exciting research opportunities. To reduce resource consumption and advance a regenerative tourism system, experts are looking at efforts including waste reduction and the creation of sustainable supply chains. These circular economy strategies assist the tourist sector in managing resources sustainably (Hall, 2020; Gössling et al., 2019).

15.9.3 AREAS FOR FUTURE INVESTIGATION

To pave the path for a more sustainable future in the tourist sector, it is critical to identify topics for additional study and research. The industry may make substantial progress by researching these new research disciplines, deploying cutting-edge technologies, and bridging research gaps. The evaluation of sustainable tourism initiatives and the assessment of long-term effects are important research areas. Longitudinal studies and thorough analyses can shed light on how these activities will ultimately affect the environment, the economy, and society (Buckley, 2012; Gössling et al., 2020). Making wise decisions and creating successful policies require an understanding of the long-term effects. Collaboration and stakeholder involvement are essential to the effective implementation of sustainable tourism practices. The implementation of sustainable tourism practices should be supported by the identification of successful methods for involving stakeholders, encouraging cooperation, and creating partnerships (Bramwell and Lane, 2021; Hall and Lew, 2018). Sustainable tourism initiatives may be more inclusive and representative by incorporating a variety of stakeholders, such as local communities, companies, and governmental organizations. The relationship between tourism and the preservation of biodiversity is another area where there is room for improvement, and it is one that is being investigated by the National Geographic Society. To promote sustainable tourism, protected areas must be investigated, and biodiversity conservation must be incorporated into management and planning procedures (Buckley et al., 2016; Honey, 2008).

These considerations are needed to be given importance while examining the effects of tourism on ecosystems. It might be useful to design strategies to reduce negative effects and support conservation efforts within the tourist industry by understanding how tourism and biodiversity conservation interact. The tourism industry may move its sustainability agenda forward by concentrating on these topics for future research. Long-term impact studies, stakeholder engagement initiatives, and biodiversity conservation activities are key steps toward a more sustainable and responsible tourist business.

15.10 CONCLUSION

15.10.1 SUMMARY OF MAIN FINDINGS FROM THE SYSTEMATIC LITERATURE REVIEW

The systematic evaluation of the literature on sustainable tourism has produced significant results that offer insightful information on the topic. First off, it is obvious that sustainable tourism involves a complex understanding that includes environmental, societal, and economic components. The intricacy and interconnection of sustainable tourism principles are highlighted by this thorough approach. Emerging research trends have been found, pointing to new research avenues in the discipline. The convergence of sustainable tourism and social justice, digital transformation, circular economy practices, smart destinations, and sustainable transportation are examples of these. These study fields reflect the changing nature of sustainable tourism as well as the need to address current problems and possibilities. With an emphasis on resource conservation, eco-friendly practices, and efficient environmental management, environmental sustainability emerges as a significant focus. Implementing effective environmental management methods and adopting sustainable practices are necessary to reduce the negative effects of tourism on the environment. The significance of community involvement, cultural preservation, and heritage management is highlighted by the relevance of socio-cultural sustainability, which is another critical component. Approaches that are respectful and inclusive must be used to protect the welfare of host communities and foster real experiences. As a crucial component of sustainable tourism, economic sustainability is highlighted last. For long-term economic viability to be achieved while also supporting sustainable development objectives, it is essential to deploy sustainable business models and strategies.

15.10.2 IMPLICATIONS FOR POLICYMAKERS, PRACTITIONERS, AND RESEARCHERS

For policymakers, practitioners, and academics working on this subject, the results of the extensive literature review on sustainable tourism have important implications. The findings of the evaluation may be used by policymakers to direct their efforts in coordinating policies, including stakeholders, and creating governance frameworks that promote the adoption of sustainable tourism practices. Policymakers may foster an atmosphere that is supportive of sustainable development by integrating their policies with the diverse character of sustainable tourism. The evaluation emphasizes the need to implement sustainable practices for tourism practitioners. Practitioners may use the findings to incorporate eco-friendly technology into their operations, such as smart destination solutions and sustainable transit alternatives. Furthermore, encouraging partnerships with local stakeholders such as communities and companies is critical for boosting sustainable tourism. The evaluation emphasizes the importance of such collaboration in reaching common sustainability goals.

The assessment can help researchers in the subject of sustainable tourism by identifying research gaps and opportunities for additional inquiry. The evaluation highlights developing study themes, such as the confluence of sustainable tourism with social justice and digital transformation and invites scholars to delve deeper into these issues. Furthermore, the evaluation emphasizes the importance of longitudinal studies to measure the long-term consequences of sustainable tourism initiatives, as well as effective stakeholder involvement and cooperation techniques.

15.10.3 SUGGESTIONS FOR FURTHER RESEARCH AND PRACTICAL APPLICATIONS

Based on the findings of this thorough literature review, several recommendations for more study and real-world applications in sustainable tourism may be made. To begin, undertaking longitudinal studies that evaluate the long-term effects of sustainable tourism on many factors, such as the environment, economy, and society, will offer insightful data on the potency and endurance of sustainable practices. The complexity of sustainable tourism may also be addressed and complete solutions can be fostered by embracing multidisciplinary approaches that incorporate viewpoints from other domains, such as environmental science, social sciences, and business management. In addition, it is critical to develop collaboration and knowledge sharing among academics, decision-makers, practitioners, and local communities to effectively implement sustainable practices. This collaboration may promote the exchange of knowledge, experiences, and best practices, resulting in more informed decision-making and the execution of long-term projects. Eventually, case studies and documentation of best practices in sustainable tourism may provide insightful analysis and useful advice for the sector. Practitioners may improve their sustainability efforts by studying effective examples of sustainable tourism initiatives and taking inspiration and knowledge from real-world experiences.

The tourism industry may advance significantly toward a more sustainable and responsible future by filling in these research gaps and using the findings in real-world scenarios. These suggestions promote ongoing study, multidisciplinary cooperation, and the sharing of information and experiences to promote the adoption of sustainable tourism practices at the local, regional, and international levels.

KEYWORDS

- **sustainable tourism**
- **environmental impacts**
- **socio-cultural impacts**
- **economic aspects**
- **emerging research areas**
- **innovative solutions**
- **challenges**

REFERENCES

Andereck, K. L.; Valentine, K. M.; Knopf, R. C.; Vogt, C. A. Residents' Perceptions of Tourism as Indicators of Community Quality of Life. *J. Travel Res.* **2018,** *57* (8), 1111–1124.

Becken, S.; Gossling, S.; Scott, D. In *Tourism and Water*; Channel View Publications, 2019.

Becken, S.; Lennox, J.; Fjällström, M. Measuring Tourism's Carbon Footprint. In *Tourism and Carbon Management: Methods, Practices, and Case Studies*; Gössling, S., Scott, D., Hall, C. M., Eds.; Channel View Publications, 2021; pp 15–30.

Bramwell, B.; Lane, B. In *Tourism Collaboration and Partnerships: Politics, Practice and Sustainability*; Channel View Publications, 2021.

Bramwell, B.; Sharman, A.; Lane, B. In *Tourism and Economic Development: Pathways to Prosperity*, 2nd Ed.; Routledge, 2019.

Braun, V.; Clarke, V. Using Thematic Analysis in Psychology. *Qualit. Res. Psychol.* **2006,** *3* (2), 77–101.

Brouder, P.; Teixeira, R.; Ioannides, D.; Ioannides, D. In *Tourism in City Destinations: New Skills for New Jobs*; Springer, 2016.

Buckley, R. In *Sustainable Tourism: Research and Reality*; Channel View Publications, 2012.

Buckley, R. Sustainable Tourism: Research and Reality. *Ann. Tour. Res.* **2019,** *79*, 102812.

Buckley, R.; Zhong, L.; Chen, Z.; Witt, S. F. In *Tourism Economics and Policy*; Channel View Publications, 2016.

Buhalis, D. Tourism Management in the Digital Economy: Big Data, Analytics, and Digital Transformation; Routledge, 2021.

Butler, R. W.; Ruhanen, L. M. In *Tourism and Indigenous Peoples: Issues and Implications*; Channel View Publications, 2019.

Cater, C.; Cater, E. In *Tourism Destination Marketing: A Collaborative Approach*; Channel View Publications, 2020.

Coccossis, H.; Mexa, A. In *Tourism and Regional Development: New Pathways*; Routledge, 2018.

Dredge, D.; Jamal, T. In *Tourism and Mobilities: Local-global Connections*; Channel View Publications, 2015.

Dredge, D.; Jamal, T. Mixed Methods in Tourism Research: Theoretical, Methodological and Practical Issues. *J. Travel Res.* **2019,** *58* (1), 14–26.
Dredge, D.; Jenkins, J. In *Tourism and Sustainable Development: Principles, Processes, and Policies*; Channel View Publications, 2020.
Dwyer, L.; Edwards, D.; Mistilis, N.; Roman, C.; Scott, N.; Quinn, B.; Livaic, Z. In *Economic Impact Analysis: Methodologies and Applications*; Goodfellow Publishers, 2019.
Elkington, J. In *Cannibals with Forks: The Triple Bottom Line of 21st-Century Business*; Capstone, 1997.
Farsari, Y.; Sigala, M. Cultural Heritage and Tourism: An Introduction. In *Cultural Heritage and Tourism in the Digital Age: Communication and Engagement*; Farsari, Y., Sigala, M., Eds.; Springer, 2021; pp 1–16.
Fennell, D. A. In *Tourism and Indigenous Peoples: Issues and Implications*, 2nd Ed.; Channel View Publications, 2019.
Font, X.; Walmsley, A.; Cogotti, S.; McCombes, L. In *Responsible Tourism: Theory and Practice*; Goodfellow Publishers, 2021.
García-Rosell, J. C.; Koens, K.; Seyfi, S. In *Authenticity and Tourism: Materialities, Perceptions, Experiences*; Channel View Publications, 2019.
Gössling, S.; Scott, D.; Hall, C. M. In *Tourism and Water: Interactions and Impacts*; Channel View Publications, 2012.
Gössling, S.; Scott, D.; Hall, C. M. In *Tourism and Water*; Channel View Publications, 2019.
Gössling, S.; Scott, D.; Hall, C. M. In *Tourism and Water: Interactions, Impacts, and Challenges*; Channel View Publications, 2020.
Gössling, S.; Scott, D.; Hall, C. M. In *Tourism and Water: Climate Change, Sustainability, and Water Resources*; Channel View Publications, 2021.
Gössling, S.; Scott, D.; Hall, C. M. In *Tourism and Sustainability: New Tourism in the Third Millennium*, 3rd Ed.; Channel View Publications, 2022.
Gretzel, U.; Sigala, M.; Xiang, Z.; Koo, C. Smart Tourism: Foundations and Developments. *Electron. Mark.* **2015,** *25* (3), 179–188.
Gursoy, D.; Chi, C. G. Q.; Lu, L. Socio-Cultural Impacts of Tourism: A Systematic Review of the Literature with a Focus on Methodological Issues. *J. Travel Res.* **2020,** 0047287520939424.
Gursoy, D.; Jurowski, C.; Uysal, M. In *Tourism and Societal Impacts: Place, Policy and Perceived Authenticity*; CABI, 2019.
Gursoy, D.; Kim, K.; Uysal, M. Residents' Attitudes towards Tourism Development: A Meta-Analysis. *Ann. Tour. Res.* **2021,** *88*, 103159.
Hall, C. M. In *Tourism and Regional Development: New Pathways*; Routledge, 2019.
Hall, C. M.; Lew, A. A. In *Understanding and Managing Tourism Impacts: An Integrated Approach*; Routledge, 2018.
Hall, C. M.; Page, S. Tourism and Urban Transformations. In *The Routledge Handbook of Tourism Cities*; Hall, C. M., Page, S., Eds.; Routledge, 2019; pp 1–12.
Hall, C. M.; Scott, D.; Gössling, S. In *Tourism and Climate Change: Impacts, Adaptation, and Mitigation*; Channel View Publications, 2021.
Honey, M. In *Ecotourism and Sustainable Development: Who Owns Paradise?*; Island Press, 2008.
Jamal, T. B.; Stronza, A. Collaboration Theory and Tourism Practice in Protected Areas: Stakeholders, Structuring and Sustainability. *J. Sustain. Tour.* **2009,** *17* (2), 169–189.
Kieti, D. M.; Muturi, W.; Kibicho, W. Enhancing Sustainable Destination Marketing through Value Co-creation in Destination Branding. *J. Sustain. Tour.* **2019,** *27* (1), 49–66.

Koens, K.; Papp, B.; Postma, A. Local Community Involvement in Tourism Entrepreneurship: A Literature Review. *J. Sustain. Tour.* **2018,** *26* (8), 1318–1337.

Leask, A.; Fyall, A. In *Managing World Heritage Sites: New Challenges and Issues*; Routledge, 2020.

Moher, D.; Liberati, A.; Tetzlaff, J.; Altman, D. G.; PRISMA Group. Preferred Reporting Items for Systematic Reviews and Meta-Analyses: The PRISMA Statement. *PLoS Med.* **2009,** *6* (7), e1000097.

Mowforth, M.; Munt, I. In *Tourism and Sustainability: Development, Globalisation and New Tourism in the Third World*, 4th Ed.; Routledge, 2015.

Neuhofer, B.; Buhalis, D.; Ladkin, A. Technology as a Catalyst of Change: Enablers and Barriers of the Tourist Experience and their Consequences. In *The Routledge Handbook of Transport Economics*, 2020; pp 1–15.

Novelli, M.; Barnes, J.; Humavindu, M. In *Tourism and Water: Contemporary Tourism Reviews*; Channel View Publications, 2019.

Nyaupane, G. P.; Poudel, S. Linking Community, Tourism Development, and Sustainability: A Case Study of Ghale Gaun, Nepal. *J. Sustain. Tour.* **2011,** *19* (6), 747–764.

Pereira, M.; Andrade, C.; Caldeira, A. Exploring the Role of Community Involvement in Tourism Development and its Impact on Residents' Well-Being. *J. Sustain. Tour.* **2021,** *29* (7), 1024–1041.

Richards, G.; Munsters, W. In *Cultural Tourism Research Methods*; CABI, 2010.

Ruhanen, L.; Weiler, B.; Moyle, B.; McLennan, C. In *Tourism and Resilience: Individual, Organisational and Destination Perspectives*; Channel View Publications, 2018.

Ruhanen, L.; Weiler, B.; Moyle, B.; McLennan, C. In *Tourism and Resilience: Individual, Organisational and Destination Perspectives*, 2nd Ed.; Channel View Publications, 2020.

Salazar, N. B. Tourism Imaginaries: Anthropological Approaches. In *Tourism Imaginaries at the Disciplinary Crossroads: Place, Practice, Media*; Salazar, N. B., Ed.; Routledge, 2018; pp 1–19.

Spenceley, A. In *Responsible Tourism: Critical Issues for Conservation and Development*; Earthscan, 2012.

Tranfield, D.; Denyer, D.; Smart, P. Towards a Methodology for Developing Evidence-Informed Management Knowledge by Means of Systematic Review. *Brit. J. Manag.* **2003,** *14* (3), 207–222.

UNWTO. In *Making Tourism More Sustainable – A Guide for Policy Makers*; World Tourism Organization, 2019a.

UNWTO. In *Tourism Highlights 2019 Edition*; World Tourism Organization, 2019b.

Weaver, D. B. In *Sustainable Tourism: Theory, Policies and Practices*, 2nd Ed.; Channel View Publications, 2019.

Weaver, D. In *Sustainable Tourism*; Goodfellow Publishers, 2020.

Weaver, D. B.; Lawton, L. J. Survey Research in Tourism. In *Routledge Handbook of Tourism Research Methods*; Hall, C. M., Gössling, S., Eds.; Routledge, 2020; pp 91–108.

WTTC. Travel & Tourism Economic Impact 2021: Global Summary. World Travel & Tourism Council, 2021.

Xiang, Z.; Du, Q.; Ma, Y.; Fan, W.; Wang, D. Digital Transformation and Marketing Innovation: The Role of Emerging Information Technology. *Int. J. Inf. Manag.* **2020,** *52*, 101994.

CHAPTER 16

Factors Affecting Decision-Making of New-Age Consumers with Regards to Private-Label Brands: A Conceptual Framework

SUBHANAN DEY and M. RAJKUMAR

ICFAI Management School, ICFAI University, Ranchi, Jharkhand, India

ABSTRACT

Retailers, be it apparel or grocery, have been advocating a private-label strategy for some time now. When we talk of consumers belonging to a certain age group such as the millennials and the Gen-Z, whose consumer behavior is much different from the earlier generations, it becomes all the more critical for the retailer to address their issues The rise of the private-label market provides an alternative solution both for consumers during purchasing as often these products are of equal or better quality. It also provides a sustainable means through which a retailer can survive with their own brands over a longer period. Existing literature on private-label brands has made inroads into significant development of theory and practical suggestions; however, the gaps remain, and the criticality of managing private labels at the stage of demography-wise variations, especially age-wise variations. Reaching out to the millennials and Gen-Z—the two generations that are supposedly not brand loyal, yet make up a chunk of the population buying from retail stores, are the subjects worth researching. In this paper, we seek to propose a framework for understanding the decision-making model influencing the purchase of private-label grocery brands. The intention and

Agile Business Transformations: Priorities, Lessons, and Practices. Satyajit Chakrabarti, Subrata Chattopadhyay, Udit Chawla, Sundeep Singh Sondhi, & Arunava Dalal (Eds.)

behavior of buying private-label brands will be highlighted—the researchers have studied the various models of consumer buying and hence developed a conceptual framework considering the present lifestyle of consumers and their shopping habits.

16.1 INTRODUCTION

As per the reports from the *Retail Industry in India—Indian Retail Sector, Market Size*, the retail market in India has undergone a significant transformation and has witnessed tremendous growth in the last 10 years. India currently has the fourth-largest retail market in the world. Indian retail market recovered from pandemic lows and grew 10% YOY from \$630 billion to reach \$690 billion in 2021. Private-label brands (PLBs), often known as own brands or store brands, are products that a retailer owns, controls, and sells almost exclusively (Baltas and Argouslidis, 2007). Most PLBs have a strong connection to the store, particularly if the company's name is featured on branded items. There has been a significant development in terms of research on in-store branding in line with the rapid growth of the store brands in recent times. Hoch and Banerji (1993) suggested that PLBs have advanced shares in order to offer higher perimeters, and might succeed deliberately in areas where they contend against smaller manufacturer brands who spend lower on advertising. The gap between national brands and PLBs in the level of quality also depends on the technology requirements in manufacturing that vary across categories (Hoch and Banerji, 1993). Research has been more limited on the consumer-level factors that make PLBs differentially successful across product categories. Some researchers studying consumer-level factors for PLB proneness—such as Richardson et al. (1994)—have not studied across-category variations at all.

Previous research on private-label goods made an effort to analyze and determine the demographic factors influencing their purchase. According to Richardson et al. (1994) and Shannon and Mandhachitara (2005), families with more members are more inclined to purchase PLBs. All generations have been impacted by the digital revolution, but especially Gen Y and Gen Z. With the advent of the Internet, smartphones, and social media, people's interactions with one another and their purchasing behavior have transformed (Thangavel et al., 2021). Due to the ongoing political, cultural, and socioeconomic changes that take place in society as a whole, today's youthful generation tends to shop in ways that are significantly different from those of previous generations (Ma et al., 2010). Identification of Gen Z's consuming traits is crucial because recent studies by Puiu (2016), as quoted by Thangavel et al. (2021), found that Gen Z differs from preceding generations in terms of consumer values, interests, and concepts. Although frequently highlighted in the literature, the consumer behavior and habits of millennials represent a unique demographic and psychographic market category (Naumovska, 2017). Members of Gen Y have particular physical characteristics, and as consumers, they have strong brand preferences and specialized buying habits. Gen Y has grown up in an overly brand-conscious and promoted society; therefore, they are knowledgeable about which brands and items to choose (Naumovska, 2017). The generation that is most interested in private brands is the millennial generation, and they anticipate that their connection with private brands will be much higher than it actually is.

Marketers can significantly enhance testing, advertising, and merchandising (Samdani, 2020). However, according to Samdani (2020), millennials' purchase attitudes vary depending on the category of PL products. For example, when it comes to beauty products, customers feel more personal risk and are more likely to buy branded products, which can make it challenging for PL manufacturers to increase market share. Millennials are more likely to purchase at the grocery store and are more likely to favor healthier products, hot sauce, energy drinks, and specialty alcohol, regardless of brand name and cost, which is a deciding factor when selecting convenience goods with store brands or private labels (Samdani, 2020). While buying private-label items, they also stated that food was their first choice and cosmetic products were their second. The last five decades' worth of work on PLBs has been highlighted by Riboldazzi et al. (2021) The research gaps, as had been clearly identified in their paper as follows: value co-creation, new age (Millennial and Gen-Z) customer behavior, and social media marketing adoption are all private-label research topics. Consumer studies with private labels also compare various merchant types, such as by positioning strategy or shop structure. This study aims to identify the factors that contribute to ultimate purchase behavior, particularly with regard to Gen-Z and Millennials, a group whose purchasing habits have not yet been thoroughly studied. If successfully marketed to Zoomers, PLBs with higher margins will have longer shelf lives and be more sustainable. Individuals' purchasing habits have a significant impact on consumer behavior in general.

16.2 REVIEW OF LITERATURE

16.2.1 EXTRINSIC CUES

The cue utilization theory is one of the principal theories that creates a rational framework for assessing customers' opinions of the value of the store brand (Dick et al., 1995). Consumers are more likely to rely on extrinsic factors when judging the quality of a product since they do not have access to the product's intrinsic cues or don't know enough about the things (Brouthers and Xu, 2002). A set of cues for judging the product's quality then emerges from their memories, and they are caused by the prediction or confidence values (Richardson et al., 1994). The confidence value of a cue is the extent to which consumers are confident in their capacity to utilize and evaluate that cue appropriately (Dick and Richardson, 1997). First off, consumers' decisions and perceptions of quality can be greatly influenced by feature distinction (Mishra et al., 2020). Second, by enabling customers to judge products using intrinsic signals rather than extrinsic cues, businesses can use free samples to improve consumers' perceptions of product quality. Third, retailers can improve customers' perceptions of quality by using a variety of extrinsic signals in visual merchandising to create the proper aesthetic image around the store's PLBs (Mishra et al., 2020). Fourth, greater spending on private-label advertising might also be a sign of higher quality (Mishra et al., 2020).

16.2.1.1 ADVERTISING

To set themselves apart from other retailers and compete directly with top manufacturer brands, advanced retailers are now investing in premium store brands. Store brands are promoted and positioned as being of higher quality by these shops (Huang and Huddleston, 2009; Kumar and Steenkamp, 2007). As a result, the significance of promoting shop brands has increased (Levy and Gendel-Guterman, 2012). Since an expensive and extensive advertising campaign is a signal of high quality, extrinsic cues, notably perceived advertising expenditures and advertising innovation, can transmit high quality (Levy and Guterman, 2012).

16.2.1.2 PACKAGING

After first focusing on pricing, PLBs transitioned to a quality positioning and, more recently, a positioning that emphasizes status, benefiting from the reputation of the stores (Vale and Matos, 2015). Companies spend a lot of money on packaging and advertising to create and sustain favorable associations that set their products apart from those of competitors (Aribarg et al., 2014). Numerous studies have shown that the characteristics of the packaging, such as its shape (Folkes et al., 1993; Raghubir and Krishna, 1999), size (Coelho do Vale et al., 2008; Wansink, 1996), and placement of the brand logo (Lans et al., 2008), can influence how consumers assess and select the products. Given that the majority of the competition on the shelves is visual (Lans et al., 2008), packaging plays a crucial part in the decision-making process because many of its characteristics trigger strong brand connections (Vale and Matos, 2015).

16.2.2 PERCEIVED RISK

Perceived risk is a total of several risk factors together (Beneke and Carter, 2015). Arslan et al. (2013) highlighted the various risks as follows: *financial risk*—the potential for financial loss as a result of making an unwise buying decision or losing money by choosing an inferior or unknown brand; *social risk*—a potential perception that purchasing a certain brand or product will result in a loss of status or image; *physical risk*—a consumer's concern that particular products could impair their health or physically harm them; *functional risk*—the worry that a product purchase won't produce the results that customers want; and *psychological risk*—the disappointment a customer feels after choosing a subpar good or service.

16.2.3 PERCEIVED QUALITY

The definition of perceived quality is "the consumer's assessment of a product's overall excellence or superiority" (Rahman and Soesilo, 2018). Park and Namkung (2022) related perceived quality with consumers' overall evaluations of a product and might therefore vary from person to person even when they receive the same good or service. According to numerous studies, there are noticeable discrepancies between national brands and PLBs in terms of perceived quality, showing that customers give national brands' products a higher rating than private-label companies (Rahman and Soesilo, 2018; Batra, 2000). A private label with both a lesser quality variance and a higher quality level might increase its market share (Dick et al., 1996). The perceived quality of private labels is the main factor influencing share

(Sethuraman and Cole, 1999). According to Hoch and Banerji (1993), quality rather than price is the secret to victory in the conflict between national brands and private labels. Evidences were highlighted in the work of Rahman and Soesilo (2018) where in the United Kingdom, store brand product quality and packaging improvements increased the market share of private-label companies. Additionally, some recent studies support the notion that one of the most significant factors influencing consumer purchase intention for private-label goods is perceived quality (Nurafifah Jaafar, 2012).

16.2.4 PERCEIVED RELATIVE PRICE

According to Olson and Jacoby (1972), perceived relative pricing is the price that the client encodes by comparing the cost of the product to the cost of substitute goods. Beneke and Carter (2015) state that customers' perceptions of pricing are critical because they serve as an extrinsic signal and provide one of the most crucial sources of information when making decisions about what to buy. It has been discovered that there is a large inverse link between perceived price and perceived value, which means that a high price reduces purchasing power (Huang and Huddleston, 2009; Desarbo et al., 2001; Beneke et al., 2013). According to Oosthuizen (2015), a product is evaluated based on its perceived relative price in relation to the benefits it offers, what consumers are ready to pay for it, and the trade-off between price and quality to see if it meets their demands. Consumers' purchasing intentions are directly impacted by the perceived relative pricing of a product. If a product's price is viewed as unfair, the perceived value and buying intention of the product are negatively impacted (Beneke et al., 2012; Mathur and Gangwani, 2021a).

16.2.5 PERCEIVED VALUE FOR MONEY

The term "perceived value for money" refers to how consumers rate a product in relation to its cost (Mishra et al., 2021; Mathur and Gangwani, 2021). Consumers are influenced by price, risk, and quality cues to determine the perceived value of PLBs, according to research by Beneke and Carter (2015). While Yee and San (2011) demonstrated clear connections between customers' perceptions of value and their purchasing behavior, they also stated that consumers' intentions to buy a certain product increased with the perceived value of that product (Mathur and Gangwani, 2021). According to Grewal et al. (1998), PV is "a trade-off between the quality or benefits customers experience in the product relative to the sacrifice they perceive by paying the price" (Konuk, 2018).

16.2.6 TRUST

"The expectation held by the customer that the service provider is dependable and can be relied upon to deliver on its commitments" is the definition of trust (Konuk, 2018). Brand love, brand devotion, and brand loyalty are important characteristics for emotionally attached consumers (Grisaffe and Nguyen, 2011). These traits imply that customers who have a "effective emotional attachment" are more likely to remain loyal to the brand for a longer amount of time (Shahid et al., 2022) resulting in a satisfied and trusting customer. The trustworthiness of this alliance significantly affects consumer behavior outcomes and contributes to the long-term profitability of the brand (Thomson et al., 2005; Shahid et al., 2022).

16.2.7 ATTITUDE

The majority of private-label research has focused on "private-label proneness," which refers to attitudes, behaviors, and market segments for private labels (or generic items) in general. Most recent studies look at the causes and effects of a broad private-label mentality (Collins et al., 2015). According to (Lymperopoulos et al., 2010), customers' purchasing intentions and perceptions of their economic status are influenced by their "style of thinking." According to a study, consumers would try to save costs by buying private-label goods during a recession, but once things started to get better, they would go back to their trusted brands (Conroy, 2010; Nurafifah Jaafar, 2012). This is due to the fact that a person will characterize a product in a good way when it is known to them. Retailers should therefore provide customers reason to feel confident about their product in order to increase consumer trust in private-label products (Chaniotakis et al., 2010). Trust in private-label goods is determined by perceived benefits, hence perceived price-quality relationships have an impact on consumer attitudes.

16.2.8 PURCHASE INTENTION

According to Kuo et al. (2009), as cited by Kakkos et al. (2015a), purchase intention is defined as "the likelihood that customers will plan or be willing to purchase a specific product or service in the future" and is the exact first step before engaging in real purchasing action (Kakkos et al., 2015b). Buying intention metrics are employed in sales forecasting because they are low-cost, simple to understand, and indicate future purchasing behavior (Kakkos et al., 2015). Such information is frequently used to forecast consumer demand for new goods, which has an operational impact on production schedule regulation, advertising, distribution, and price policy (Morwitz et al., 2007).

16.3 RESEARCH PROPOSITION AND THEORETICAL MODEL

16.3.1 EXTRINSIC CUES AND TRUST

Better advertisements of in-store brands could result in the trustworthiness of the product. According to Batra and Sinha (2000), store brands' ability to gain market share is hampered by the volume of national brands' advertising. Using extrinsic cues that indicate quality, advertising is a tactic employed by managers to create good brand perception about their products (Levy and Gendel-Guterman, 2012). Based on the aforementioned data, it is predicted that a more favorable extrinsic cues will probably result in customers purchasing more private-label goods. Similarly, an increased positive store image is projected to boost the trustworthiness of private-label goods. Based on this logic, the following assumptions are formulated.

Proposition 1: Private-label extrinsic cues has a positive effect in building trust on the private-label product.

16.3.2 TRUST AND INTENTION

In many commercial decisions including uncertainty and dependency, trust has become crucial. Information regarding the products must be made available for consumers to build trust with the merchants. In fact, some shops advertise goods that might deceive customers, influencing their decision to buy and undermining their confidence in the products (Chinomona and Dubihlela, 2014). Moreover, businesses are constrained by factors such as the physical distance between consumers and sellers, which requires shops to earn customers' trust by being trustworthy (Chinomona and Dubihlela, 2014). According to past empirical data and the trust transfer theory, consumers' trust in the PLB manufacturer brand should translate into trust in PLB. In other words, the degree to which a PLB may be trusted can be inferred from prior experience with the manufacturer brand (Konuk, 2018).

Proposition 2: Trust of consumer influences the intention to go for the PLB.

16.3.3 PERCEIVED RISK AND PERCEIVED VALUE FOR MONEY

Perceived value is defined as "that which is regarded to be fair, just, or merited in relation to the perceived cost of the product, while taking into account appropriate competitor alternatives" in the context of equity theory (Mathur and Gangwani, 2021). In the context of a retail store, perceived value is shown to be one of the antecedents of buy intentions (Mathur and Gangwani, 2021). The most important factor influencing consumers' buying intentions is debatably their perception of value (Ming-Sung Cheng et al., 2007)

Proposition 3: Lesser the perceived risk, better the perceived value for money.

16.3.4 PERCEIVED RISK AND ATTITUDE

When a purchase is made, internal memories from previous purchases and external memories from information acquired both play a part in the decision-making process (Chaniotakis et al., 2010). When people have a bad experience with a product, it will affect their decision to buy it again, but when quality and price are in line, the opposite is true. Also, it is simple to share such an experience with others, which can affect how they decide (Jaafar, 2012). Beneke et al. (2012) observed a negative relationship between perceived psychological, functional, and financial risks and customers' attitude toward PLB, despite Thanasuta (2015) finding no association between Thai consumers and the purchase of PLB (Mostafa and Elseidi, 2018).

Proposition 4: Lesser the perceived risk, better the attitude formation toward buying PLBs.

16.3.5 PERCEIVED QUALITY AND PERCEIVED VALUE FOR MONEY

All product characteristics and features that are accountable for meeting users' needs are supported by quality (Kakkos et al., 2015). Perceived quality is essentially how customers assess a product based on their most recent purchasing history. A crucial factor in product evaluations is perceived quality, which affects consumer behavior and purchasing decisions, and thus, purchase intentions (Kakkos et al., 2015). More particular, goods that match or above consumers' quality expectations strongly encourage repeat purchases and prevent switching (Deng et al., 2010). This ought to be the case for PL items as well, albeit doubts about the calibre of store brands may deter more customers from using them (Gonzalez et al., 2006), as cited by (Kakkos et al., 2015).

Proposition 5: Better the perceived quality, greater the perceived value for money.

16.3.6 PERCEIVED QUALITY AND ATTITUDE

Dick et al. (1996) claim that PLB's market share and purchase level are determined by consumers' perceptions of the product's quality. However, Thanasuta (2015) revealed a negligible correlation between the purchase of PLB and quality-conscious Thai customers (Mostafa and Elseidi, 2018). In the literature on consumer behavior, the link between customer perception and attitude has long been recognized. The earlier discovery refutes the enduring myth that quality-conscious buyers have a bad attitude toward store brands (Veloutsou et al., 2004), as cited by (Mostafa and Elseidi, 2018).

Proposition 6: Better the perceived quality, better the attitude toward buying PLBs.

16.3.7 PERCEIVED RELATIVE PRICE AND PERCEIVED VALUE FOR MONEY

Several studies, such as those by (Varki and Colgate, 2001; Etgar and Malhotra, 1981; Gerstner, 1985) support the idea that perceived relative pricing is also a factor in how well consumers think a product is made and how the perceived value for money is. These studies also found a positive association between the variables (Beneke and Carter, 2015).

Proposition 7: Better the perceived relative price, better the perceived value for money for buying PLBs.

16.3.8 PERCEIVED RELATIVE PRICE AND ATTITUDE TOWARD PLBS

According to the cue utilization theory, customers are said to use price as an extrinsic cue when deciding what to buy (Beneke et al., 2012). PLB customers are frequently described as being price conscious, and price consciousness means that they weigh the relative prices of any brand before considering for purchase (Mostafa and Elseidi, 2018).

Proposition 8: Better the perceived relative price, better the attitude toward buying PLBs.

16.3.9 PERCEIVED VALUE FOR MONEY AND INTENTION TOWARD PLBS

An increase in purchase intention indicates a potential for an increase in purchases, according to (Dodds et al., 1991) cited by (Maharani et al., 2020). When customers are committed to a brand, they are more likely to have favorable purchase intentions and make actual purchases (Maharani et al., 2020). According to Kuo et al. (2009), buying intention refers to the potential for consumers to consider buying, or the consumer's decision to repurchase the product, and it indicates the likelihood that consumers will plan or attempt to buy certain products or services in the future (Maharani et al., 2020).

Proposition 9: Greater the perceived value for money, better the intention toward buying PLBs.

16.3.10 ATTITUDE AND INTENTION TOWARD BUYING PLBS

In order to focus on elements that are likely to shape consumer perceptions around PL branded items, one must first realize that buying decisions can be impacted by a variety of demands, including physiological and/or socio-psychological (e.g., prestige, recognition, comfort) needs (Kakkos et al., 2015), and thus is the basis for the following proposition.

Proposition 10: Better the attitude, better is the intention toward buying PLBs.

16.3.11 INTENTION AND BEHAVIOR TOWARD BUYING PRIVATE LABEL BRANDS

Depending on the product category, private brand attitude is the best predictor of purchase intention and increases the number of shopping trips (Jin and Suh, 2005). While external factors influence the purchasing decisions of consumers who are price-conscious, perceived quality and store image influence purchase intention (Muruganantham and Priyadharshini, 2017).

Proposition 11: Greater the intention, higher the willingness to buy PLBs.

16.4 CONCEPTUAL MODEL

The underpinning theory in the conceptual model for measuring the factors affecting decision making of new-age consumers with regards to PLBs is built on the Theory of Reasoned Action (Song, 2013) and Planned Behavior, Cue Utilization Theory (Hill, 1983), David Aker's Theory of Brand Equity, and Trust Transfer theory. The Theory of Reasoned Action and Theory of Planned Behavior (TPB) created in 1980 were intended to predict an individual's intention by using the elements such as attitude, intention and subjective norms and the intention influence on behavior. The foundation of the cue utilization theory is the observation that the presence of a cue increases the marginal utility that results from consumption. Every time a potential customer chooses a product, they essentially choose one of several cues, such as "the perceived value or the convenience value" or "the intrinsic and extrinsic cue," to understand the product. Cue utilization theory is applied to determine consumer perceptions of store brand quality when it comes to the selection of private-label goods (Richardson et al., 1994). Easterbrook, 1959 propounded the concept of cue utilization to explain how extrinsic and intrinsic cues can be used to build consumer's quality perceptions about an unknown brand (Richardson et al., 2006). It provides a logical framework to assess consumer perceptions of store brand quality (Richardson et al., 1994). According to this theory, a product consists of an array of cues that serve as surrogate indicators of quality to shoppers, as cited by Richardson et al. (1994) on (Cox, 1967). In many situations, consumers do not know the true quality of competing products (or brands) before making their purchase decisions. In such cases, research suggests that consumers are likely to rely on simple heuristics, or cues, the majority of which are product market factors, to assess product quality (Richardson et al., 1994). The cue utilization theory is based on the fact the presence of the cue raises the marginal utility one derives from consumption. Cue utilization was used to gain insights into how consumers make use of cues to form perception and judgment of product quality (Richardson et al., 1994). Findings support a multidimensional measurement model of perceived quality, consisting of salient components – functional attributes, brand personality, after-sales support and perceived costs – that consumers use during their evaluation of perceived quality (Olson and Jacoby, 1972). According to trust transfer theory, trust transfers occur when "the unidentified recipient is being seen as related to the source of the transferred trust"" (Lien et al., 2014) as cited by (Konuk, 2018).

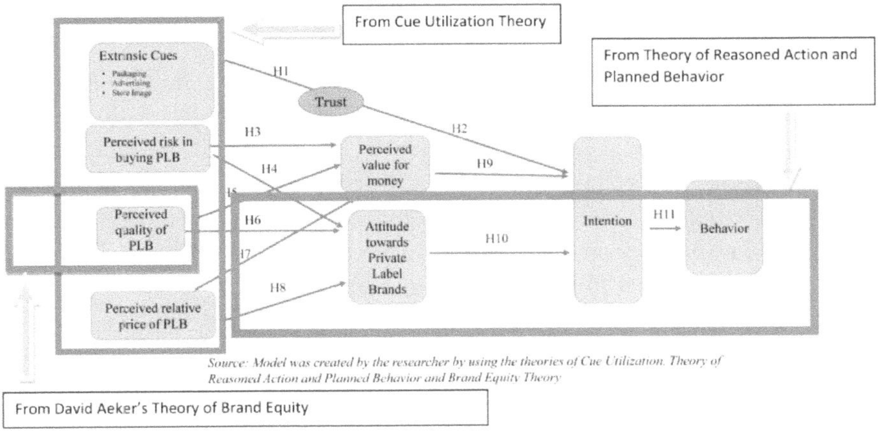

Source: Author

16.5 IMPLICATIONS

Private-label purchases can have several impacts on Gen Z and Millennial consumers, as these consumer groups are often more receptive to private-label products compared to previous generations. Here are a few ways in which private-label purchases can impact Gen Z and Millennial consumers:

1. Cost savings: Gen Z and Millennials are often more price-conscious due to factors such as student loans, high housing costs, and limited job opportunities. Private-label products generally offer lower prices compared to national brands, allowing these consumers to save money on their purchases. This affordability factor can be particularly appealing to young consumers who are budget-conscious.
2. Quality perception: Private-label products have significantly improved in terms of quality over the years. Many retailers now invest in creating high-quality private-label products that are comparable, if not better, than national brand counterparts. As a result, Gen Z and Millennials are more willing to consider private-label purchases without compromising on quality. This shift in perception has made private labels more attractive to these consumer groups.
3. Ethical and sustainable options: Gen Z and Millennials are known for their concern about ethical and sustainable practices. PLBs often have more control over their supply chains and can prioritize environmentally friendly and socially responsible practices. As a result, private-label products may align better with the values of Gen Z and Millennials, who are more likely to support brands that demonstrate a commitment to sustainability and ethics.
4. Brand loyalty shift: Gen Z and Millennials are generally less brand loyal compared to older generations. They prioritize value, quality, and convenience over brand names. Private-label products offer an alternative option that meets these criteria. By providing competitive offerings, private labels can influence younger consumers to switch their loyalty from national brands to private labels, particularly if the products meet their needs and expectations.
5. Product innovation: PLBs are often more agile and responsive to market trends and consumer demands. They have the flexibility to experiment with new product categories, flavors, or packaging, catering to the preferences of Gen Z and Millennials who seek variety and novelty in their purchases. This focus on innovation can be appealing to young consumers looking for unique and trendy options.

It is worth noting that individual preferences and attitudes toward private-label products may vary among Gen Z and Millennials. While some may be enthusiastic supporters, others may still prefer national brands based on personal preferences or specific product categories. Nonetheless, the impact of private-label purchases on these consumer groups is significant and continues to shape their purchasing decisions.

16.6 CONCLUSION

All attempts are being made by PLBs to keep up with the expanding market share that they are gaining. While the consumer tries to purchase the PLBs, several considerations are at play. In particular, the new age consumers, including the Millennials and the Gen-Z, who will make up a sizable portion of the population and try to force their way into buying private-label products, were the focus of this paper's analysis of the key variables that motivate them to go for a PLB purchase. By highlighting the importance of Gen-Z and the Millennials and Private-label branding, this study will contribute to the body of information on consumer behavior. In conclusion, because of their shopping habits, spending power, awareness of products, and interest in products, the new age generation has a greater impact on individual and family purchase behavior. Every marketer needs to understand the mindset because it makes up a sizable portion of the Indian market if they want to distinguish out from the competition in the future. It is now even more crucial for marketers to tailor their communication strategies and platforms to meet the needs of these new-age consumers. This is because consumers' buying habits are changing. Such a client-centered marketing strategy would attract the new-age consumers and aid in long-term sustenance.

KEYWORDS

- **private-label attitudes**
- **extrinsic cues**
- **brand image**
- **personality factors**
- **intention to purchase**
- **perceived quality**
- **perceived value for money**
- **perceived price**

REFERENCES

Aribarg, A.; Arora, N.; Henderson, T.; Kim, Y. Private Label Imitation of a National Brand: Implications for Consumer Choice and Law. *J. Mark. Res.* **2014,** *51* (6), 657–675.

Arslan, Y.; Geçti, F.; Zengin, H. Examining Perceived Risk and Its Influence on Attitudes: A Study on Private Label Consumers in Turkey. *Asian Soc. Sci.* **2013,** *9* (4).
Batra, R. Consumer-Level Factors Moderating The Success Of Private Label Brands. *J. Retail.* **2000,** *76* (2), 175–191.
Batra, R.; Sinha, I. Consumer-Level Factors Moderating the Success of Private Label Brands. *J. Retail.* **2000,** *76* (2), 175–191.
Beneke, J.; Carter, S. The Development of a Consumer Value Proposition of Private Label Brands and the Application thereof in a South African Retail Context. *J. Retail. Consum. Serv.* **2015,** *25*, 22–35.
Beneke, J.; Flynn, R.; Greig, T.; Mukaiwa, M. The Influence of Perceived Product Quality, Relative Price and Risk on Customer Value and Willingness to Buy: A Study of Private Label Merchandise. *J. Prod. Brand Manag.* **2013,** *22* (3), 218–228.
Beneke, J.; Greene, A.; Lok, I.; Mallett, K. The Influence of Perceived Risk on Purchase Intent – The Case of Premium Grocery Private Label Brands in South Africa. *J. Prod. Brand Manag.* **2012,** *21* (1), 4–14.
Brouthers, L. E.; Xu, K. Product Stereotypes, Strategy and Performance Satisfaction: The Case of Chinese Exporters. *J. Int. Bus. Stud.* **2002,** *33* (4), 657–677.
Chaniotakis, I. E.; Lymperopoulos, C.; Soureli, M. Consumers' Intentions of Buying Own-Label Premium Food Products. *J. Prod. Brand Manag.* **2010,** *19* (5), 327–334.
Chinomona, R.; Dubihlela, D. Does Customer Satisfaction Lead to Customer Trust, Loyalty and Repurchase Intention of Local Store Brands? The Case of Gauteng Province of South Africa. *Mediterr. J. Soc. Sci.* **2014,** *5* (9), 23–32.
Coelho do Vale, R.; Verga Matos, P. The Impact of Copycat Packaging Strategies on the Adoption of Private Labels. *J. Prod. Brand Manag.* **2015,** *24* (6), 646–659.
Collins, A. M.; Cronin, J. M.; Burt, S.; George, R. J. From Store Brands to Store Brandscapes: The Emergence of a Time and Money Saving Heuristic. *Eur. J. Mark.* **2015,** *49* (5–6), 894–918.
Desarbo, W. S.; Jedidi, K.; Sinha, I. Customer Value Analysis in a Heterogeneous Market. *Strat. Manag. J.* **2001,** *22* (9), 845–857.
Dick, A.; Jain, A.; Richardson, P. Correlates Private Brand Proneness. *J. Prod. Brand Manag.* **1995,** *4* (4), 15–22.
Dick, A.; Richardson, P. How Consumers Evaluate. *Pric. Strat. Pract.* **1997,** *5* (1), 18–24.
Dodds, W. B.; Monroe, K. B.; Grewal, D. Effects of Price, Brand, and Store Information on Buyers' Product Evaluations. *J. Market. Res.* **1991,** *28* (3).
Etgar, M.; Malhotra, N. K. Determinants of Price Dependency: Personal and Perceptual Factors. *J. Consum. Res.* **1981,** *8* (2).
Gerstner, E. Do Higher Prices Signal Higher Quality? *J. Mark. Res.* **1985,** *22* (2).
Grewal, D.; Monroe, K. B.; Krishnan, R. The Effects of Price-Comparison Advertising on Buyers' Perceptions of Acquisition Value, Transaction Value, and Behavioral Intentions. *J. Mark.* **1998,** *62* (2).
Grisaffe, D. B.; Nguyen, H. P. Antecedents of Emotional Attachment to Brands. *J. Bus. Res.* **2011,** *64* (10), 1052–1059.
Hill, M. R. In *Easterbrook's Hypothesis and Eyewitness Cue Utilization*, 1983.
Hoch, S. J.; Banerji, S. *When Do Private Labels Succeed?*, 1993.
Huang, Y.; Huddleston, P. Retailer Premium Own-Brands: Creating Customer Loyalty through Own-Brand Products Advantage. *Int. J. Retail Distrib. Manag.* **2009,** *37* (11), 975–992.
Jin, B.; Suh, Y. G. Integrating Effect of Consumer Perception Factors in Predicting Private Brand Purchase in a Korean Discount Store Context. *J. Consum. Mark.* **2005,** *22* (2), 62–71.

Johnn Yee, C.; Cheng San, N. Consumers' Perceived Quality, Perceived Value and Perceived Risk Towards Purchase Decision on Automobile. *Am. J. Econ. Bus. Adminis.* **2011,** *3* (1), 47–57.

Kakkos, N.; Trivellas, P.; Sdrolias, L. Identifying Drivers of Purchase Intention for Private Label Brands. Preliminary Evidence from Greek Consumers. *Procedia Soc. Behav. Sci.* **2015,** *175*, 522–528.

Konuk, F. A. The Role of Store Image, Perceived Quality, Trust and Perceived Value in Predicting Consumers' Purchase Intentions Towards Organic Private Label Food. *J. Retail. Consum. Serv.* **2018,** *43*, 304–310.

Kumar, N.; Steenkamp, J. B. E. M. Brand versus Brand. *Int. Comm. Rev.* **2007,** *7* (1), 46–53.

Kuo, Y. F.; Wu, C. M.; Deng, W. J. The Relationships Among Service Quality, Perceived Value, Customer Satisfaction, and Post-Purchase Intention in Mobile Value-Added Services. *Comput. Hum. Behav.* **2009,** *25* (4), 887–896.

Levy, S.; Gendel-Guterman, H. Does Advertising Matter to Store Brand Purchase Intention? A Conceptual Framework. *J. Prod. Brand Manag.* **2012,** *21* (2), 89–97.

Lien, C. H.; Wu, J. J.; Chen, Y. H.; Wang, C. J. Trust transfer and the effect of service quality on trust in the healthcare industry. *Manag. Serv. Qual.* **2014,** *24* (4), 399–416.

Lymperopoulos, C.; Chaniotakis, I. E.; Rigopoulou, I. D. Acceptance of Detergent-Retail Brands: The Role of Consumer Confidence and Trust. *Int. J. Retail Distrib. Manag.* **2010,** *38* (9), 719–736.

Maharani, N.; Helmi, A.; Mulyana, A.; Hasan, M. Factors Influencing Purchase Intention on Private Label Products. *J. Asian Fin. Econ. Bus.* **2020,** *7*(11), 939–945.

Mathur, M.; Gangwani, S. Mediating Role of Perceived Value on the Relationship Among Perceived Risks, Perceived Quality, and Purchase Intention of Private Label Brands. *Int. J. Appl. Manag. Technol.* **2021a,** *20* (1), 4.

Mathur, M.; Gangwani, S. Mediating Role of Perceived Value on the Relationship Among Perceived Risks, Perceived Quality, and Purchase Intention of Private Label Brands. *Int. J. Appl. Manag. Technol.* **2021b,** *20* (1), 71–87.

Ming-Sung Cheng, J.; Shui-Lien Chen, L.; Shih-Tse Wang, E.; Ying-Chao Lin, J. Do Consumers Perceive Differences among National Brands, International Private Labels and Local Private Labels? The Case of Taiwan. *J. Prod. Brand Manag.* **2007,** *16* (6), 368–376.

Mishra, S.; Malhotra, G.; Saxena, G. In-Store Marketing of Private Labels: Applying Cue Utilisation Theory. *Int. J. Retail Distrib. Manag.* **2020.**

Mishra, S.; Malhotra, G.; Saxena, G. In-Store Marketing of Private Labels: Applying Cue Utilisation Theory. *Int. J. Retail Distrib. Manag.* **2021,** *49* (1), 145–163.

Morwitz, V. G.; Steckel, J. H.; Gupta, A. When do Purchase Intentions Predict Sales? *Int. J. Forecast.* **2007,** *23* (3), 347–364.

Mostafa, R. H. A.; Elseidi, R. I. Factors Affecting Consumers' Willingness to Buy Private Label Brands (PLBs) Applied Study on Hypermarkets. *Span. J. Mark. ESIC* **2018,** *22* (3), 341–361.

Muruganantham, G.; Priyadharshini, K. Antecedents and Consequences of Private Brand Purchase: A Systematic Review and a Conceptual Framework. *Int. J. Retail Distrib. Manag.* **2017,** *45* (6), 660–682.

Naumovska, L. Marketing Communication Strategies for Generation Y – Millennials. *Bus. Manag. Strat.* **2017,** *8* (1), 123.

Nurafifah Jaafar, S. *Consumers' Perception, Attitudes and Purchase Intention Towards Private Label Food Products in Malaysia*, 2012.

Olson, J. C.; Jacoby, J. Cue Utilization in the Quality Perception Process. *ACR Special Volumes* **1972,** *SV-02.*

Oosthuizen, M. D. The Relationship between Perceived Price and Consumers' Purchase Intentions of Private Label Wine Brands. *Afr. J. Hosp. Tour. Leis.* **2015,** *4* (2).

Park, C. I.; Namkung, Y. The Effects of Instagram Marketing Activities on Customer-Based Brand Equity in the Coffee Industry. *Sustainability (Switzerland)* **2022,** *14* (3).

Puiu, S. *Generation Z -- A New Type Of Consumers.: Ebscohost*, 2016.

Rahman, F.; Soesilo, P. K. M. The Effect of Information Exposure of Contract Manufacturing Practice on Consumers' Perceived Risk, Perceived Quality, and Intention to Purchase Private Label Brand. *J. Retail. Consum. Serv.* **2018,** *42*, 37–46.

Retail Industry in India-Indian Retail Sector, Market Size. (n.d.). Retrieved March 22, 2023, from

Riboldazzi, S.; Capriello, A.; Martin, D. Private-Label Consumer Studies: A Review and Future Research Agenda. *Int. J. Consum. Stud.* **2021,** 844–866.

Richardson, P. S.; Dick, A. S.; Jain, A. K. Extrinsic and Intrinsic Cue Effects on Perceptions of Store Brand Quality. *J. Mark.* **1994,** *58* (4), 28.

Richardson, P.; Jain, A. K.; Dick, A.; Richardson, P.; Jain, A. K.; Dick, A. The Influence of Store Aesthetics on Evaluation of Private Label Brands Richardson. *J. Prod. Brand Manag.* **1996,** *5* (1), 19–28.

Samdani, T. *Impact of Tesco's Private Label Brands on Buying Behavior of Millennials in Terms of Brand Preference in Irish Market Title of Thesis: Impact of Tesco's Private Label Brands on Buying Behavior of Millennials in Terms of Brand Preference in Irish Market*, 2020.

Sethuraman, R.; Cole, C. Factors Influencing the Price Premiums that Consumers Pay for National Brands Over Store Brands. *J. Prod. Brand Manag.* **1999,** *8* (4), 340–351.

Shahid, S.; Paul, J.; Gilal, F. G.; Ansari, S. The Role of Sensory Marketing and Brand Experience in Building Emotional Attachment and Brand Loyalty in Luxury Retail Stores. *Psychol. Mark.* **2022,** *39* (7), 1398–1412.

Shannon, R.; Mandhachitara, R. Private-Label Grocery Shopping Attitude and Behavior: A Cross-Cultural Study. *J. Brand Manag.* **2005,** *12* (6), 461–474.

Song, S. S. *An Abstract of the Dissertation Of Sarah Sungsook Song for the degree of Doctor of Philosophy in Design and Human Environment presented on May 3, 2013. Title: Building Brand Equity for Unfamiliar Asian Brands' Entry into Global Markets*, 2013.

Thanasuta, K. Thai Consumers' Purchase Decisions and Private Label Brands. *Int. J. Emerg. Mark.* **2015,** *10* (1), 102–121.

Thangavel, P.; Pathak, P.; Chandra, B. Millennials and Generation Z: A Generational Cohort Analysis of Indian Consumers. *Benchmarking* **2021,** *28* (7), 2157–2177.

Thomson, M.; MacInnis, D. J.; Park, C. W. The Ties that Bind: Measuring the Strength of Consumers' Emotional Attachments to Brands. *J. Consum. Psychol.* **2005,** *15* (1), 77–91.

Varki, S.; Colgate, M. The Role of Price Perceptions in an Integrated Model of Behavioral Intentions. *J. Serv. Res.* **2001,** *3* (3), 232–240.

Veloutsou, C.; Gioulistanis, E.; Moutinho, L. Own Labels Choice Criteria and Perceived Characteristics in Greece and Scotland: Factors Influencing the Willingness to Buy. *J. Prod. Brand Manag.* **2004,** *13* (4), 228–241.

CHAPTER 17

Intention and Behavior Gap in Green Purchase: A Study on Consumers of Jharkhand and West Bengal

RUCHI GAUTAM[1], AKANKSHA KUMARI[2], and MUSKAN AGGARWAL[2]

[1]*Jharkhand Raksha Shakti University, Ranchi, India*

[2]*Xavier Institute of Social Service, Ranchi, India*

ABSTRACT

Green consumption is the only viable alternative to the traditional way of consumption. It focuses on an ecological consumption model that seeks to minimize the negative impacts of individual behaviors on the ecological environment while meeting human needs. Even Sustainable Development Goal (SDG) 12 strongly emphasizes responsible consumption. A green customer uses fewer natural resources because they purchase environmental friendly goods such as ecological, organic, or energy-saving goods. When it comes to making purchases for daily requirements, green consumer behavior starts by prioritizing the environment before any personal needs and desires. Green consumer behavior has significantly increased during the past few years. It all started with a determination to shift in favor of becoming more ecologically friendly at the individual, corporate, and institutional levels. Nevertheless, despite many consumers knowing of environmental friendly items, they do not intentionally choose to buy them. Typically, consumers buy what they want without concern about how it may affect the environment. This attitude-intention gap has puzzled manufacturers and policymakers alike. The gap also hampers the development of the green market. Primary research was conducted for this study. A survey was conducted in two major

Agile Business Transformations: Priorities, Lessons, and Practices. Satyajit Chakrabarti, Subrata Chattopadhyay, Udit Chawla, Sundeep Singh Sondhi, & Arunava Dalal (Eds.)

cities—Jharkhand and West Bengal. A sample size of 114 was collected for this survey. A questionnaire was used for this survey which was disseminated online and offline. These surveys were systematically analyzed. Various Scopus and Google Scholar journals and e-contents were also studied. The researchers try to understand the green purchase patterns of Gen-Z behavioral gap and intention of buying in these two states. The paper also attempts to understand the drivers of green purchase behavior among Gen-Z and how it can contribute more toward SDG 12 targets.

17.1 INTRODUCTION

When compared to competing items that fulfil the same purpose, green purchasing (GP) is defined as choosing a product that has a lesser or reduced negative effect or higher positive effect on human health and the environment. The purchase of raw materials, production, fabrication, manufacture, packing, distribution, reuse, operation, maintenance, and disposal of the product are all considered when GP is incorporated into the procurement process. This phrase covers the procurement of products that are recyclable, recycled, reusable, or that conserve energy or natural resources. Environmentally preferable purchasing, or EPP, is another name for it.

With varying degrees of aggressivity, environmentally preferable products can focus on various environmental attributes and pursue sustainable features. Environmentally preferable products can concentrate on various environmental aspects and pursue sustainable features with varying degrees of vigor. They typically have some combination of the following qualities, such as recycled materials,—recycled or re-manufactured materials or parts, such as 100% recycled paper—minimize waste by using recyclable or reusable packaging; conserve water, energy, or other naturally occurring resources derived from sustainable sources; avoid pollution; contain fewer hazardous compounds; preserve open space; and promote environmentally friendly behaviors, among other things.

The market has started to show signs of being more ecologically sensitive. Although environmentally conscious customers first appeared in the late 1960s (Kinnear and Taylor, 1973), the debate over eco-friendliness and sustainable consumerism has grown over time. According to Greendex (2020), an index created by National Geographic and Globe Scan tracks how consumer behavior changes in response to environmental concerns. A thorough rating system is then created using the information that has been obtained. India received a Greendex score of 61.4, placing it top in the 2020 survey. The nation was praised for its housing, transportation, and culinary options. Consumers are more aware than ever of the impact that the things they use have on the environment. Most critically, Gen-Z is gradually becoming into an ecologically conscious generation (Dragoleo et al., 2023).

Gen-Z is expanding rapidly on a global scale. By 2025, Gen-Z's will account for one-fourth of the population in the Asia-Pacific area. The study by Gómez-Román et al. (2020) demonstrates that although Gen-Z is environmentally sensitive, there are times when they lack drive, which stops them from putting the spirit required for the desire to purchase an environmentally friendly product into practice. Accordingly, research indicates that any behavior involving the purchase of an ecological good will be altered for the good of society (Gierszewska and Seretny, 2019), and Gen-Z representatives' use of ecological products will increase (Jaciow and Wolny, 2021). People who fit the typology of generation, more so than other generations and in connection to the location of origin, people who are typologically included in Gen-Z cohorts manifest and materialize intents to buy ecological goods.

This research investigates the cognitive–affective behavior of adolescent consumers' conduct due to these factors concentrating on Gen-Z consumers, who are regarded as the generation that is currently most environmentally concerned (Nguyen et al., 2019). This study looks at customer views of environmental attitudes and their intentions to make sustainable purchases. It examines how young customers feel about ergonomics, eco-friendliness, and their environmental attitudes, and how those feelings may affect their purchasing decisions. The theory of planned behavior (TPB) was taken into consideration to thoroughly analyze the behavioral gap among Gen-Z consumers from Jharkhand and West Bengal.

17.2 LITERATURE REVIEW

GP is simply the practice of making purchases of sustainable and ecologically beneficial goods. Recycled bags, eco-friendly clothing, energy-efficient bulbs, and other examples of green products could be given. Buying environmentally friendly products is one approach to stop humans from destroying the environment. Nowadays, a lot of businesses use green product marketing techniques without paying much attention to the cost-benefit analysis from the perspective of the consumer (Meyer, 2001). Consequently, there is an increasing need for a strategic framework in the arena of green products' market. Lately, the concept of green brand positioning (GBP) has also emerged for the brands to look out for, because it allows a brand to have a more emotional relation with its consumers.

Gen-Z is the name given to the generation born between 1997 and 2012. This generation has seen a rapid advancement in technology and the digital sharing of information. It is the generation's desire for individualism and the expression of their genuine thoughts via social media and other internet resources (Sun and Xing, 2022). Gen-Z can outpace all other generations in terms of green goods consumption because they are a young cohort exposed to a variety of innovative products and technology. For this reason, our study includes both the working and nonworking segments of the Gen-Z generation.

According to the idea of planned behavior, beliefs about the behavior serve as the basis for attitudes, subjective standards, and perceived behavioral control (Ajzen, 1991). There is room for improvement even though many studies have focused on behavioral ideas and attitudes about behavior. Along with using the TPB components, contextual considerations like media, family, and friends were also made because people's decisions are also influenced by their environment and related players. Studying the elements that influence Gen-Z's purchasing decisions is essential given the constantly changing relationship between this generation and the media. Family dynamics are considered. Family influence is considered because parental influence plays a huge role in deciding the purchasing decisions of the young generation by instilling in them a sense of creativity, innovation, and concern for the environment (Caruana and Vassallo, 2003). A positive relationship has also been seen between friends' influence and purchasing behavior.

Furthermore, numerous studies highlighted the role of sustainability in the CapSEM Model—capacity building in sustainability and environmental management—thereby focusing on the importance of supply chain management and production techniques of companies to achieve sustainable development goals, namely, SDG 12 (responsible consumption and production) and SDG 9 (industry, innovation, and infrastructure).

Consumers' level of environmental awareness and willingness to help solve problems is what matters (Dunlap and Jones, 2002; Kim and Choi, 2005; Wei et al., 2018). There are many ways that a pro-environment mindset might show itself, from views to behaviors, such as recycling and using green products (Choi and Johnson, 2019). Although the implications of consumers' environmental concerns have been researched, the outcomes of these behaviors are still unclear. According to Kim and Choi's 2005 survey of college students, there is a clear and significant link between environmental concerns and green consumer behavior. Furthermore, Maichum et al. (2016) found a link between young Thai consumers' purchases of eco-friendly goods and their environmental worries. In addition, Dagher et al. (2014) discovered that pro-environmental behavior, similar to the theory by Irawan and Darmayanti (2012), who focused on Indonesian students, stabilized the positive association between environmental concerns and intention to buy green items.

Two key theoretical constructs that can aid in understanding the intention and actual purchase gap are the theory of reasoned action (TRA) (Fishbein and Ajzen, 1975) and the TPB. TPB was preceded by the TRA. The Rational Idea of Action is improved by the TPB model, which is an extension of the TRA (Ajzen and Madden, 1986) developed by Ajzen (1985). TPB was rated as the top model for predicting intentions and, consequently, predicting behavioral intentions (Yadav and Pathak, 2016). Social psychologists frequently employ this model (Fielding et al., 2008). An intentional action plan with a specified behavior and a decision to act constitutes the purpose (Patch et al., 2005).

17.3 METHODOLOGY OF STUDY

This section will explore the research methods used to answer the research question. Primary research is employed here. A set of structured questions was circulated among Gen-Z consumers for our research. The quantitative data is analyzed and the hypothesis of theory of unplanned reason will be deduced. A subjective question has also been asked to check upon the motive for green purchase.

17.3.1 OBJECTIVE OF THE STUDY

For the study, the researchers have taken the following two vivid objectives:

i) To understand the gap and intentions of green purchase among Gen-Z
ii) To study the drivers of green purchase behavior among Gen-Z

17.3.2 RESEARCH METHODOLOGY

The Research methodology would elaborate and provide a direction this research.

A. *Research design*: Th research design would be exploratory based on the extent of study.
B. *Universe:* The universe for this study is two Indian states West Bengal and Jharkhand. The Gen-Z (i.e., people born between 1997 and 2012 according to Dimock, 2019) are the target population of

our universe. These two states were selected based on researchers' convenience for primary data collection.

C. *Sampling technique:* The sampling technique used here is convenience sampling. The data collection has been done on the reach of the internet and researchers' network.

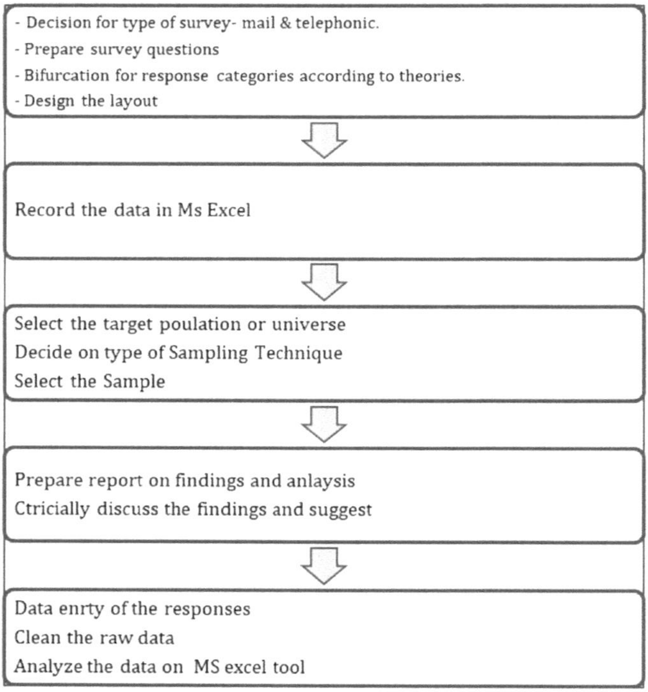

FIGURE 17.1 Research design flow chart.

TABLE 17.1 Sample Size Distribution in Two States.

Study area	No. of respondents
Jharkhand	68
West Bengal	46
Total	114

D. *Sample size:* The researchers have taken a sample of 114 for the study from the two states, namely, West Bengal and Jharkhand among major cities.

E. *Sources of data/tools for data collection:* The primary and secondary sources have been considered for the study.
   - Primary data: The questionnaire was developed to find the intentions and behavior gap of the green purchase among Gen-Z. The data is collected in Likert Scale. The questionnaire was circulated through google form among university students and some recent pass-outs.
   - Secondary data: A detailed literature review from Scopus journals, development journals, magazines, e-newspapers, etc., were taken into consideration for generating hypothesis and to understand the behavioral pattern.

17.3.3 LIMITATIONS

The findings of this study must be seen considering some limitations. They are:

1. The insufficient sample size used for statistical measurements, as it was an independent study with many financial constraints.
2. The lack of previous research studies done around GP in India, thereby narrowing the scope of research and providing less information on the related topic.

17.3.4 DATA ANALYSIS AND INTERPRETATION

Data analysis was done in MS Excel 365 and IBM SPSS 26 statistics to test the samples.

The interpretation is purely led to find out the significant difference between standard parameters and observed values.

Three Hypothesis tests have been generated by researchers to check significance difference pertaining to buying intentions and attitude by Gen-Z.

- Hypothesis Test 1:
  $H_{11:}$ The family does not influence the green purchase intention of Gen-Z.
  H_{12}: The family influences the green purchase intention of Gen-Z.
- Hypothesis Test 2:
  $H_{21:}$ The concern for the environment does not influences the purchase intention of Gen-Z.

H_{22}: The concern for the environment influences the purchase intention of Gen-Z.

- Hypothesis Test 3:

$H_{31:}$ For Gen-Z, green purchase decisions are not governed by individual choices.

H_{32}: For Gen-Z, green purchase decisions are not governed by individual choices.

17.4 FINDINGS AND ANALYSIS

In this section, the researchers discuss the primary data analysis. The survey was conducted among the Gen-Z of the two states Jharkhand and West Bengal. The researchers analyzed the data in Microsoft Excel using different statistical tools such as Correlation, Regression, Descriptive stats, etc. The data was analyzed considering the distinct factors of behavior and behavioral theories. The findings and analysis were divided into three parts: demographic profile, contextual factors (family/friends/media), and attitudes toward green purchase.

17.4.1 DESIGN AND CONSTRUCT OF QUESTIONNAIRE

In this research, the researchers utilized Ajzen's (2006) "Constructing a Theory of Planned Behavior Questionnaire" within the framework of TPB to address our research problem. The researchers employed direct measures in our questionnaire to answer our research question and opted for Ajzen's questionnaire design due to its high level of internal consistency. Additional items were added to make the questionnaire more relevant to our study. The research used the Likert Scale to create the questionnaire, which allows respondents to indicate the degree to which they agree or disagree with a series of belief statements about a given subject. The questionnaire to address research questions is presented in Table 17.2 for excel analysis, along with a level of significance extracted through the correlation tool.

17.4.1.1 DEMOGRAPHIC FACTORS

Gen-Z educational qualifications, income status, and eating habits influence green purchase behavior.

TABLE 17.2 Distribution of Questionnaire Constructs for Study.

Construct development		Questions	α
Demographic constructs	Age	Your age	
	Educational qualification	Your educational qualification	
	Income status	Your annual income (in Lakhs P.A)	
	Food preference	Your food preference (Veg/Non- Veg/Vegan/Eggetarian/Don't want to disclose)	
Contextual factors	Media	I like to watch environmental related documentaries.	$\alpha = 0.51$
		I pay attention to advertisements related to environmental issues.	
		I buy green products by seeing social media influencers' recommendations.	
	Family	My family members and I discuss environmental issues.	$\alpha = 0.34$
		My family members suggest me to buy green products.	
	Friends	I discuss environmental related topics/issues with my friends.	$\alpha = 0.35$
		My family members and I discuss about environmental issues.	
Theory of planned behavior	Attitude toward green purchase	Green products are good for my health.	$\alpha 1 = 0.52$
		I like to buy green products.	$\alpha 2 = 0.45$
		I will be buying green products in the future.	
	Perceived behavioral control (PBC)	Do you think prior knowledge is required to purchase green products?	$\alpha = 0.15$
		My purchase decisions are influenced because of my knowledge of environmental issues.	
		I see recycle tags before buying green products.	
		I follow the rules of waste segregation before disposing garbage.	
		I take my own bag for grocery shopping.	

TABLE 17.2 *(Continued)*

Construct development	Questions	α
Subjective norms	My family members and I discuss environmental issues.	$\alpha = 0.35$
	My family members suggest me to buy green products.	
	I discuss environmental related topics/issues with my friends.	
	My purchase decisions are influenced because of my knowledge of environmental issues.	
	What motivates you to buy green products?	

17.4.1.2 CONTEXTUAL FACTORS

Media influence: Three questions have been developed to measure how respondents come across media messages/ documentaries that led to their buying behavior for green purchases. On checking the Significance, the value of $\alpha = 0.51$

Family influence: Two questions have been developed to determine how respondents perceive family influence on environmental issues and whether family asks to make green purchases. On checking the Significance, the value of $\alpha = 0.34$.

Friends influence: Two questions have been developed to determine how respondents perceive friends' influence on environmental issues and whether friends ask to make green purchases. On checking the Significance, the value of $\alpha = 0.35$.

17.4.1.3 THEORY OF PLANNED BEHAVIOR (TPB)

Attitude toward green purchase: The questions have been designed to determine respondents' attitudes influence purchase intentions. On checking the significance, I will buy green products showing $\alpha = 0.52$. Similarly, "I will be buying green products in the future" shows significance, $\alpha = 0.45$.

Subjective norm: The questions have been designed to determine whether others influence respondents' beliefs. On checking the significance, $\alpha = 0.31$.

Perceived behavioral control: The five questions have been designed to check the important conscience factors for a person. On checking the significance, say I see I recycle tags before buying green products, researchers got $\alpha = 0.15$.

17.4.2 DEMOGRAPHIC PROFILE

The demographic variables used were age, educational qualification, income status, and eating preference. Age constraints: out of 114 respondents, 73.68% of Gen-Z respondents belong to the 21–25 years category. They are born between 1997 and 2002. At the same time, 26.32% of respondents are born after 2003.

- Educational constraints: Out of 114 respondents, 41.23% are graduates, 34.21% are postgraduates and 24.56% are intermediate. This can be seen as the sample is knowledgeable enough to understand green purchases and their significance in life.

TABLE 17.3 Descriptive Distribution of Demographic Constraints.

Demographic constraints	Frequency	%
Age (in years)		
21–25	84	73.68%
Below 20	30	26.32%
Education		
Graduate	47	41.23%
Post-graduate	39	34.21%
Intermediate	28	24.56%
Income status (in lakhs P.A)		
10,00,000 and above	10	8.77%
5,00,000–10,00,000	14	12.28%
2,00,000–5,00,000	13	11.40%
Below 2,00,000	10	8.77%
Nil	67	58.77%
Food preference		
Non-vegetarian	66	57.89%
Vegetarian	39	34.21%
Vegan	3	2.63%
Eggetarian	3	2.63%
Don't want to disclose	3	2.63%

- Income status: The annual income of the respondents is considered in lakhs. It is noticed that 58.77%, a huge portion of respondents do not earn as they are students and dependent on their family income for any purchases. This helps to boost family as an influence (contextual factor) or moderates the behavior of Gen-Z. Only 8.77% of the respondents earn more than 10 lakhs, 12.28% earn between 5 and 10 lakhs, 11.40% earn between 2 and 5 lakhs, and 8.77% earn below 2 lakhs.
- Food preference constraints: A massive portion of 57.89% of the respondents are nonvegetarian while 34.21% are vegetarian. The researchers also surveyed vegans and eggetarians. It is reported that only 2.63% of respondents have their eating preferences as vegan and Eggetarian.

17.4.3 ANALYSIS FOR GEN-Z

The descriptive statistics shown in Table 17.4 help determine some significant problems with Gen-Z consumers' perceptions of green purchases. The average to be seen for the importance of using green products for health is often regarded as being at the greatest level (mean value = 4.43, refer to Table 17.4: Descriptive Statistics) on a 5-point Likert scale. The second-highest priority, which differs from the previous element, is the intention to take own shopping bag (mean value = 4.36) influence to reduce waste. Third, purchasing green products in the future (mean value = 4.25) is thought to be influenced favorably by education. In contrast to these characteristics, family and concern for environmental thoughts significantly impact the purchasing intentions of Gen-Z consumers. From Table 17.4, family suggestions to Gen-Z give a mean value of 3.62 on a Likert scale of 5. Also, environmental concern among Gen-Z gives a 3.56 mean value. Additionally, parents' contributions to children's GP behavior have been accorded the second-lowest priority (mean value: 3.39 and 3.44). TV shows are thought to have a marginally larger (Mean Value = 3.64) potential to influence young customers' intentions to purchase eco-friendly goods.

TABLE 17.4 Descriptive Statistics for Constructs on Likert Scale.

Constructs	N	Mean	Std. Deviation
Watch environmental-related documentaries	114	2.82	1.113
Pay attention to advertisements related to environmental issues	114	3.21	1.181
Family members and I discuss about environmental issues	114	2.89	1.111
Family members suggest me to buy green products	114	3.62	1.272
Discuss environmental-related topics/issues with my friends	114	3.24	1.139
Good for my health	114	4.43	.651
Will buy green products	114	3.87	1.052
Influenced because of knowledge of environmental issues	114	3.56	.903
seeing social media influencers' recommendations	114	2.75	1.094
Buy green products in the future	114	4.25	.750
Own bag for grocery shopping	114	4.36	1.074
Follow the rules of waste segregation before disposing of garbage	114	3.45	1.183
Valid N (listwise)	114		

17.4.4 KMO AND BARTLETT'S TEST

TABLE 17.5 KMO and Bartlett's Test Statistics for Sample Study.

Kaiser-Meyer-Olkin measure of sampling adequacy		**.810**
Bartlett's test of sphericity	Approx. chi-square	325.577
	df	55
	Sig.	.000

The KMO assesses sample adequacy for each variable in the model and the entire model. It checks whether your data are suitable for factor reduction. KMO has a value between 0 and 1. The general rule for interpreting statistics is that data is better acceptable for factor analysis when KMO is higher in value. The value of KMO is shown in Table 17.5 above as 0.810, which is greater than the threshold limit of 0.7. As a result, the data are sufficient for the study's ongoing analysis. The chi-square value is 325.57 with 55 degrees of freedom (df) at significance level .000 according to Bartlett's test of sphericity.

17.4.5 FACTOR ANALYSIS

This section identifies the relationship between various variables of a factor.

TABLE 17.6 Exploratory Factor Analysis Table.

Communalities: EFA		
	Initial	**Extraction**
I like to watch environmental0related documentaries	1.000	.675
I pay attention to advertisements related to environmental issues	1.000	.598
My family members and I discuss about environmental issues	1.000	.448
My family members suggest me to buy green products	1.000	.563
I discuss environmental related topics/issues with my friends	1.000	.568
Green products are good for my health	1.000	.654
I like to buy green products	1.000	.621
My purchase decisions are influenced because of my knowledge of environmental issues	1.000	.444
I buy green products by seeing social media influencers' recommendations	1.000	.580
I will be buying green products in the future	1.000	.543
I take my own bag for grocery shopping	1.000	.588
Extraction method: Principal component analysis.		

The factor loadings for each item are shown in Table 17.6. According to the factor loading discussion, values should be greater than 0.4, hence all values shown above for each item are higher than 0.4. Items with factor loading lower than 0.4 were excluded, and the remaining items were considered for additional analysis. Only one of the variables has been excluded, that is, following rules of waste segregation under TPB (i.e., PBC), which had a factor loading of less than 0.4, was removed from the study before the analysis.

17.4.6 RELIABILITY AND VALIDITY TEST

TABLE 17.7 Reliability Statistics.

Reliability statistics					
	Cronbach's alpha	**Cronbach's alpha based on standardized items**	**Scale statistics mean**	**Scale statistics std. dev.**	**No. of items**
Contextual factors	.736	.739	15.83	4.037	5
Theory of planned behavior	.676	.706	23.92	3.535	6

Here, the researchers show how each component of the factor relates to the others. The Cronbach alpha coefficient, which measures the dependability of the variables, indicates excellent internal consistency of the variable by a high value. To measure the reliability values Cronbach's alpha statistic is used; values better than 0.6 are thought to be adequate for measuring each construct. The standardized items show all values greater than 0.6.

17.5 HYPOTHESIS TESTING

The hypothesis testing serves the justification of the second objective, that is, to study the drivers of the purchase behavior of Gen-Z.

The paired samples correlations presented in Table 17.8 suggest a relationship between the variables being tested. To formally test whether these correlations are statistically significant, the researchers conducted a hypothesis test.

Null hypothesis: There is no significant correlation between the two variables in each pair.

TABLE 17.8 t-Test Paired Samples Correlation Table for Three Pairs.

Paired samples correlations				
		No	Correlation	Sig.
Pair 1	My family members suggest me to buy green products and I like to buy green products	114	.512	.000
Pair 2	I pay attention to advertisements related to environmental issues and I buy green products by seeing social media influencers' recommendations	114	.148	.116
Pair 3	Green products are good for my health and I like to buy green products	114	.522	.000

Alternative hypothesis: There is a significant correlation between the two variables in each pair.

To test this hypothesis, the researchers used a two-tailed t-test with a significance level of alpha = 0.05. If the test's p-value is less than alpha, the null hypothesis is rejected, concluding a significant correlation between the two variables. If the p-value is greater than alpha, researchers fail to reject the null hypothesis and conclude that there is not enough evidence to suggest a significant correlation.

Hypothesis 1:

For Pair 1, the correlation coefficient is 0.512 with a p-value of 0.000. Therefore, we can reject the null hypothesis and conclude that there is a significant slightly positive correlation between family members suggesting green products and the individual's willingness to buy green products.

Hypothesis 2:

For Pair 2, the correlation coefficient is 0.148 with a p-value of 0.116. Therefore, we fail to reject the null hypothesis and conclude that there is not enough evidence to suggest a significant correlation between paying attention to advertisements related to environmental issues and buying green products by seeing social media influencers' recommendations.

Hypothesis 3:

For Pair 3, the correlation coefficient is 0.522 with a p-value of 0.000. Therefore, we can reject the null hypothesis and conclude that there is a significant positive correlation between the belief that green products are good for one's health and the individual's willingness to buy green products.

TABLE 17.9 t-Test Paired Samples Table.

	Paired samples test							
	Paired differences					t	df	Sig. (2-tailed)
	Mean	Std. deviation	Std. error mean	95% confidence interval of the difference				
				Lower	Upper			
Pair 1 Family influence—attitude	−.246	1.164	.109	−.462	−.030	−2.253	113	.026
Pair 2 Environment concern—attitude	.474	1.477	.138	.200	.748	3.425	113	.001
Pair 3 Awareness—attitude	.561	.903	.085	.394	.729	6.641	113	.000

Keynote:

I like to buy green products & I buy green products by seeing social media influencers' recommendations—Attitude.

My family members suggest me to buy green products—Family Influence (Contextual Factor).

I pay attention to advertisements related to environmental issues—Environment Concern (PCB)

Green products are good for my health—Awareness (PCB).

17.6 CONCLUSION AND SUGGESTION

17.6.1 CONCLUSION

The study examined the key factors that influence consumers' decisions to purchase environmentally friendly or "green" products, including their knowledge of eco-friendly products, attitudes toward green brands, and willingness to pay. The research findings indicate that all these factors directly and positively impact consumers' intentions to purchase green products. Specifically, the study emphasizes the behavioral gap in the two states. The test of significance (α) showed that Gen-Z is aware of the green facts, but intentions are not that strong to buy them. The reliability and validity tests showed the constructs are good, and if handled strategically, green purchase intentions would rise. Therefore, social marketing campaigns should be the focus to enable the SDG12 indicators as this will also fulfill green purchase consumption and awareness. The theoretical implications such as contextual factors (i.e., media, family, and friends) showed a weak correlation when r was tested. In the end, researchers would like to suggest some measures that could boost green purchases among Gen-Z as well as other buyers.

17.6.2 SUGGESTIONS

1. Various influencer campaigns might be performed to include Gen-Z in the market for green products due to Gen-Z's low awareness of green products.
2. According to the study, Gen-Z's purchasing intentions may improve with increased wealth, encouraging them to purchase more environmentally friendly goods.
3. The pricing of eco-friendly products should also be reorganized to convince Gen-Z to buy them.
4. The government should also take note of this issue by establishing GP policies and persuading all parties to cooperate.

Therefore, companies should prioritize understanding consumers' attitudes and focus on making their environmentally friendly products more attractive to them.

KEYWORDS

- **green purchase**
- **sustainability**
- **SDG12**
- **intent**
- **consumption**

REFERENCES

Ajzen, I. The Theory of Planned Behavior. *Organ. Behav. Hum. Dec. Proc.* **1991,** *50* (2), 179–211.

Ajzen, I.; Madden, T. J. Prediction of Goal-Directed Behavior: Attitudes, Intentions, and Perceived Behavioral Control. *J. Exp. Soc. Psychol.* **1986,** *22* (5), 453–474. https://doi.org/10.1016/0022-1031(86)90045-4

Caruana, A.; Vassallo, R. Children's Perception of their Influence over Purchases: The Role of Parental Communication Patterns. *J. Consum. Mark.* **2003,** *20* (1), 55–66.

Chan, R. Y. Determinants of Chinese Consumers' Green Purchase Behavior. *Psychol. Mark.* **2001,** *18* (4), 389–413.

Choi, D.; Johnson, K. K. Influences of Environmental and Hedonic Motivations on Intention to Purchase Green Products: An Extension of the Theory of Planned Behavior. *Sustain. Prod. Consum.* **2019,** *18.*

Dagher, G.; Itani, O. Factors Influencing Green Purchasing Behavior: Empirical Evidence from the Lebanese Consumers. *J. Consum. Behav.* **2014,** *13.* 10.1002/cb.1482.

Dimock, M. Defining Generations: Where Millennials End and Generation Z Begins. *Pew Res. Center* **2019,** *17* (1), 1–7.

Dragolea, L. L.; Butnaru, G. I.; Kot, S.; Zamfir, C. G.; Nuţă, A. C.; Nuţă, F. M.; Cristea, D. S.; Ştefănică, M. Determining Factors in Shaping the Sustainable Behavior of the Generation Z Consumer. *Front. Environ. Sci.* **2023,** *11*, 1096183. DOI: 10.3389/fenvs.2023.1096183

Escap, U. SDG 12: Responsible Consumption and Production: Ensure Sustainable Consumption and Production Patterns. [Online] 2018. https://repository.unescap.org/bitstream/handle/20.500.12870/872/SDG%2012%20Goal%20Profile.pdf?sequence=1&isAllowed=y

Fauzan, N.; Azhar, F. N. The Influence of Environmental Concern and Environmental Attitude on Purchase Intention Towards Green Products: A Case Study of Students College in Universitas Muhammadiyah Yogyakarta. *SSRN Electron. J.* **2020.** http://dx.doi.org/10.2139/ssrn.3525917

Fielding, K. S.; McDonald, R.; Louis, W. R. Theory of Planned Behavior, Identity and Intentions to Engage in Environmental Activism. *J. Environ. Psychol.* **2008,** *28* (4), 318–326. https://doi.org/10.1016/j.jenvp.2008.03.003

Fishbein, M.; Ajzen, I. In *Belief, Attitude, Intention and Behavior: An Introduction to Theory and Research*, 1975.

Gierszewska, G.; Seretny, M. Sustainable Behavior–The Need of Change in Consumer and Business Attitudes and Behavior. *Found. Manag.* **2019,** *11*, 197–208. 10.2478/fman-2019-0017.

Godin, G.; Kok, G. The Theory of Planned Behavior: A Review of its Applications to Health-Related Behaviors. *Am. J. Health Promot.* **1996,** *11* (2), 87–98.

Gómez Román, R.; Wang, L. F.; Lee, B.; Halpin, K.; de Wit, E.; Broder, C. C.; Rahman, M.; Kristiansen, P.; Saville, M. Nipah@20: Lessons Learned from Another Virus with Pandemic Potential. *mSphere* **2020,** *5* (4), e00602–20. https://doi.org/10.1128/mSphere.00602-20

Jaciow, M.; Wolny, R. New Technologies in the Ecological Behavior of Generation Z. *Procedia Comput. Sci.* **2021,** *192*, 4780–4789, ISSN 1877-0509. https://doi.org/10.1016/j.procs.2021.09.256

Kinnear, T. C.; Taylor, J. R.; Ahmed, S. A. Ecologically Concerned Consumers: Who are They?: Ecologically Concerned Consumers CAN be Identified. *J. Mark.* **1974,** *38 (2)*, 20–24. https://doi.org/10.1177/002224297403800205

Maichum, K.; Parichatnon, S.; Peng, K. C. Application of the Extended Theory of Planned Behavior Model to Investigate Purchase Intention of Green Products among Thai Consumers. *Sustainability* **2016,** *8* (10), 1077. MDPI AG. http://dx.doi.org/10.3390/su8101077

Meyer, A. What's in it for the Customers? Succesfully Marketing Green Clothes. *Bus. Strat. Environ.* **2001,** *10 (5)*, 317–330. 10.1002/bse.302

Patch, C. S.; Tapsell, L. C.; Williams, P. G. Attitudes and Intentions Toward Purchasing Novel Foods Enriched with Omega-3 Fatty Acids. *J. Nutr. Educ. Behav.* **2005,** *37* (5), 235–241. https://doi.org/10.1016/s1499-4046(06)60277-7

Sun, Y.; Xing, J. The Impact of Social Media Information Sharing on the Green Purchase Intention among Generation Z. *Sustainability* **2022,** *14* (11), 6879.

Wang, Y. M.; Zaman, H. M. F.; Alvi, A. K. Linkage of Green Brand Positioning and Green Customer Value with Green Purchase Intention: The Mediating and Moderating Role of Attitude Toward Green Brand and Green Trust. *Sage Open* **2022,** *12* (2), 21582440221102441.

Yadav, R.; Pathak, G. S. Young Consumers' Intention Towards Buying Green Products in a Developing Nation: Extending the Theory of Planned Behavior. *J. Clean. Prod.* **2016,** *135*, 732–739. https://doi.org/10.1016/j.jclepro.2016.06.120

CHAPTER 18

Sustainable Development Goal Indicators: Opportunities and Challenges in Monitoring and Assessment of Sustainable Development Goals and Their Targets and Indicators

ANIRBAN DATTA[1] and SUSHMITA CHOUDHURY[2]

[1] *West Bengal State Centre, The Institution of Engineers (India), MIE, C Eng, PE, Kolkata, West Bengal, India*

[2] *Pinnacle Infotech, Durgapur, West Bengal, India*

ABSTRACT

The 2030 Agenda for Sustainable Development, which consists of a set of 17 sustainable development goals (SDG) with 169 specific targets, was adopted by 193 member countries of the United Nations General Assembly on September 25, 2015. A set of global indicators are used to track and evaluate progress over and against both the overall goals and the individual targets. United Nations Statistical Commission (UNSC) established the Inter-Agency and Expert Group on SDG indicators (IAEG-SDGs) at its 46th session in 2015. The IAEG-SDGs initiated the development of the global indicator framework in conjunction with the SDGs and targets. In the start, totalling 300, the proposed indicators have undergone an inclusive, open, and transparent consultation process in which countries, regional and international agencies, civil society, academia, and the private sector had been involved to comment and indicate their views and opinions. This process had spawned adjustments, deletions, and replacements in the initial

Agile Business Transformations: Priorities, Lessons, and Practices. Satyajit Chakrabarti, Subrata Chattopadhyay, Udit Chawla, Sundeep Singh Sondhi, & Arunava Dalal (Eds.)

indicator list, providing the basis for a final proposal of 230 SDG indicators proposed at the 47th session of the UNSC. These were finally accepted at the 48th session of the UNSC held in March 2017. The indicator framework has been proposed to be updated annually by appending new indicators as they emerge. The IAEG-SDGs proposed 36 substantial improvements to the framework as part of the 2020 Comprehensive Review in accordance with the group's objective. These suggestions were approved by the 51st Statistical Commission of the UN in March 2020. Next adaption of comprehensive modification is scheduled in 56th session to be held in 2025, wherein the global indicator framework will be complemented by indicators intended for and relevant at the regional and national levels, to be developed by member countries. The abundance of indicators is regarded as valuable in a management context and for the development of (statistical) ability, but it also increases the effort necessary to assess the overall effectiveness of attaining sustainable development. The fact that there are so many targets and indicators could potentially skew clear policy guidance toward reaching an SDG is a major problem in this regard regarding the monitoring process of SDGs, along with their associated targets and indicators. Additionally, there should be targets and/or indicators that are country- and region-specific because the developmental challeges vary among nations and even within a single nation. The goals outlined in the 2030 agenda are dwelling in extremely difficult circumstances as the globe deals with escalating and interconnected global crises and conflicts, including the COVID-19 pandemic and war/conflict conditions. This chapter focuses on the potential and problems in monitoring and evaluating the SDGs, their targets, and their indicators in both a broad and detailed way.

18.1 INTRODUCTION

Sustainable Development Goals (SDGs) and their 2030 Agenda established a comprehensive approach to sustainable development, addressing many facets of sustainability and allocating national-level accountability for prioritization, monitoring, and reporting. Opportunities to evaluate and monitor sustainable development are provided within the SDG framework by organized initiatives to collect and harmonize indicator data internationally. The SDG framework, which consists of 17 goals, 169 related targets, and 248 indicators (the global indicator framework includes 242 unique indicators, and there are 6 indicators which are under the umbrella of two or three different targets), establishes a roadmap for sustainable development that all UN member nations must accomplish by the year 2030. The implementation of the 2030 Agenda would require not only a great deal of effort and involvement from a wide range of stakeholders at various socio-economic-political spatial levels ranging from local to global, but also adequate assessment methodologies to support evidence-based decision-making, so that the pledge that "*NO ONE WILL BE LEFT BEHIND*" is accomplished. While there is a general agreement that the focus of SDG monitoring would be at the national levels, backed up by ground-level monitoring at regional and local levels, with supplemental monitoring at global levels, it goes without saying that data produced within the SDG framework must also be sufficiently disaggregated to address specific challenges for different stakeholders. To adequately address such issues with an often inherent spatial component, a need for the localization of the SDG framework has emerged. Considering the scope, complexity, interdependence, and time frame of the 2030 Agenda for Sustainable Development, there is immense concern in the development of subsets of indicators to enable more timely and targeted monitoring of sustainable development, which should be limited in number; simple, intuitive, inclusive, policy-relevant; consensus-based, in line with international standards, relevant to all countries and all people; and to track progress for all relevant groups.

18.2 FORMATION

18.2.1 SUSTAINABLE DEVELOPMENT GOALS (SDGS)

17 SDGs are pledged to stimulate action in the key areas, known as 5 Ps:

- People.
- Planet.
- Prosperity.
- Peace.
- Partnerships.

These aggregate economic, social, and ecological dimensions of sustainable development of the globe. Although not binding legally or legislatively, all UN member nations are expected to acknowledge those and to move forward for their achievement. However, the UN also recognizes each country's specific challenges and struggles to achieve sustainable development, and the specific challenges and obstacles being faced or to be faced the countries which are most vulnerable (UN-GA, 2015), as summarized by the UN:

"The Sustainable Development Goals and targets are integrated and indivisible, global in nature and universally applicable, taking into account different national realities, capacities and levels of development and respecting national policies and priorities. Targets are defined as aspirational and global, with each Government setting its own national targets guided by the global level of ambition but taking into account national circumstances. Each Government will also decide how these aspirational and global targets should be incorporated into national planning processes, policies and strategies (UN-GA 2015)."

FIGURE 18.1 Sustainable development goals (SDGs).

Source: United Nations. https://social.desa.un.org/issues/disability/sustainable-development-goals-sdgs-and-disability

18.2.2 SDG WEDDING CAKE

SDG Wedding Cake shows the interconnection and significance of economic, social, and ecological systems to accomplish global goals. In 2016, the Stockholm Resilience Centre launched the so-called SDG Wedding Cake. It is a visual representation of the UN SDGs in the form of a multilayered cake, with each layer representing a different group. The lowest layer of the biosphere system contains environmental sustainability goals, comprising life on land and in water, clean water and sanitation, and most importantly, actions toward climate change. The middle layer of the social system includes the social goals of sustainable development, including the absence of poverty, zero hunger, good health and well-being, quality education, peace and justice, gender equality, clean energy and sustainable cities and communities. The upper layer of the economic system includes the goals of sustainable economic development, including decent work and economic growth, reduction of inequality, responsible consumption and production, industry, innovation and infrastructure. The SDG Wedding Cake is an innovative way to visualize the SDGs. It is a convenient mechanism to promote participation of people and increase awareness of the prerequisite to work toward the 17 SDGs, emphasizing their mutual relationships. In addition, nesting shows the importance of individual systems in achieving sustainability goals. Social and environmental systems are critical and fundamental to the economic system and its functioning.

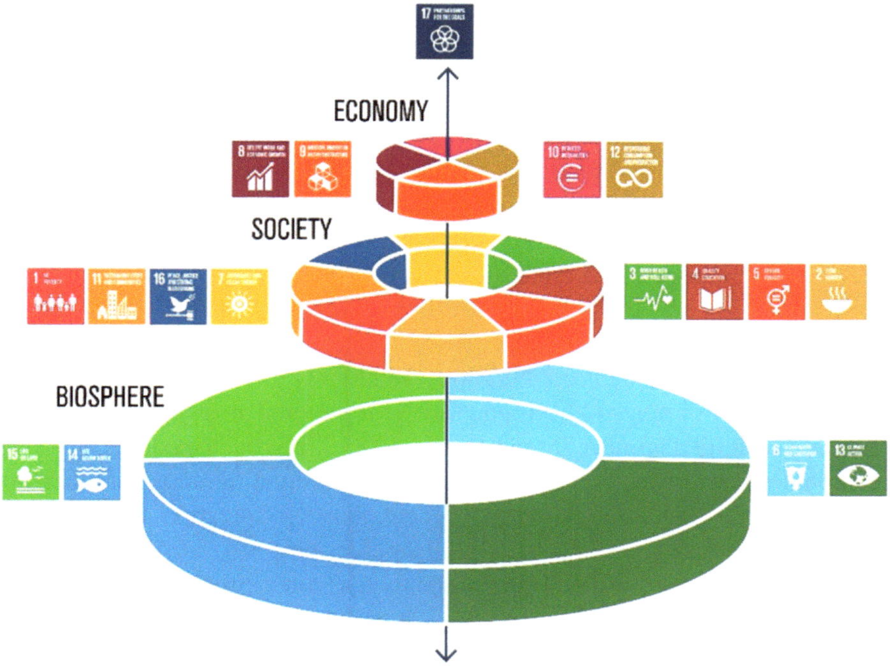

FIGURE 18.2 SDG wedding cake.

Source: Reprinted from Azote for Stockholm Resilience Centre, Stockholm University (2016). https://creativecommons.org/licenses/by-nd/3.0/

18.2.3 SDG INDICATORS

To expedite the pathway for the global SDG indicator framework, all indicators are categorized by the IAEG-SDGs into three tiers, the basis of which is their level of development methodology and the availability of data associated with them at the global level, as indicated in Table 18.1.

TABLE 18.1 Tier Classification for Global SDG Indicators.

Tier	Definition
Tier I	Indicator is conceptually clear, has an internationally established methodology and standards are available, and data are regularly produced by countries for at least 50% of countries and of the population in every region where the indicator is relevant.
Tier II	Indicator is conceptually clear, has an internationally established methodology and standards are available, but data are not regularly produced by countries.
Tier III	No internationally established methodology or standards are yet available for the indicator, but methodology/standards are being (or will be) developed or tested.

Source: https://unstats.un.org/sdgs/iaeg-sdgs/tier-classification/.

Note: As per the statistics available upto 54th session of the UNSC in March 2023, the updated tier classification contains 157 nos. Tier I indicators, 85 nos. Tier II indicators and 6 indicators are grouped under multiple tiers (different components of the indicator are grouped into different tiers), and so far there are no Tier III indicators in the global indicator framework.

As mentioned earlier, the above classification of tier for the SDG indicators is based on development methodology and availability of data at the global level, and may or may not be aligned with the national or regional level. Since the responsibilities for accomplishing the SDGs lie at the local level, regional/national governments and subnational contexts must be taken into account in an extremely focussed manner. This refers to "localization of the SDGs," involving a multi-level and multi-stakeholder approach, with integration of national, regional, and local governments and authorities as well as stakeholders/target population/beneficiaries. It is a mechanism to empower local stakeholders and leverage their respective advantages through mustering their specific economic, social, technological, cultural, and creative resources. It is intended for making sustainable development more receptive and pertinent to local needs and objectives.

18.2.4 ROADMAP

Global Taskforce of Local and Regional Governments, formed in 2013 to collaborate the joint activities of the major international networks of local governments, propagated SDG and Habitat III processes and presented the opinions of local leaders/representatives of stakeholders to the international deliberations on financing for development, disaster risk mitigation and climate change, and had drawn up the roadmap for localizing the SDGs, jointly with UNDP and UN Habitat, to provide back-up to the regions and cities to adhere to the 2030 Agenda. This roadmap contains five parts:

1. AWARENESS-RAISING: Identification of SDGs at the subnational level.
2. ADVOCACY: Inclusion of subnational perspective in formulation of national SDG strategy.
3. IMPLEMENTATION: The SDGs go local!
4. MONITORING: Data capturing, analyzing, evaluating, and collating "lessons learnt" from the process.
5. WAY FORWARD: WHERE DO WE REACH FROM HERE?

Following key factors, which are essential in this process, emerged out from this roadmap:

- Role of regional and local governments/authorities are crucial for stimulating inclusive sustainable development within their zones/jurisdictions and, therefore, they are the stakeholders/partners in the process of implementation of SDGs.
- Competency of local governments/authorities can enable the inclusion of widely diverse local stakeholders, to bring broad-based commitment, accountability, and complete ownership.
- A cohesive multilevel and multistakeholder strategy is essential to promote implementation plans at the local level.
- It requires a strong national commitment to provide suitable institutional, financial, and legal support.

In this roadmap, the following five recommendations have been made:

i. Development of a set of localized and specific indicators is required.
ii. Use of information gathered by the regional and local governments in monitoring and reporting at the national level is to be ensured.
iii. Participation of regional and local and regional governments and authorities and other stakeholders in the mechanism and process of review of national plans is to be brought in.

iv. SDG indicators are to be used as a starting point in assessing and monitoring regional and local strategies.
v. Regional and local accomplishments are to be recognized and included as part of the national/regional progress reports of achievement of SDGs.

To integrate local priorities with national priorities and other international development frameworks, targets and methods for achieving them must be defined locally. By advocating for formulating solutions through the establishment of genuine partnerships, localizing is not just seen as a technical or predefined process but rather as a mechanism which is sensitive to local opportunities, priorities, and ideas and moves beyond simply adapting or aligning global goals to the local level. This results in more inclusive, needs-driven, local-level responses to global challenges and objectives. In the long run, localizing entails empowering local authorities, communities, and stakeholders to act as change agents to aid in the accomplishment of global objectives.

18.3 CHALLENGES, OPPORTUNITIES, AND PROPAGATION

18.3.1 CHALLENGES

There are multiple challenges in segregating, propagating, implementing, and monitoring SDGs and their indicators at local levels. One of the key challenges is to set a balance between the need for keeping fluency in what is being monitored and reported on and the need for innovation to mitigate the challenges of new elements fetched by the SDGs and their indicators. Monitoring progress largely requires depending on existing data and monitoring mechanisms, for tracking SDG progress over a clearly-defined or not-so-clearly-defined period of time, until the introduction of new metrics and monitoring mechanisms required to measure achievement of new goals or to fill significant gaps in the collection and processing of data.

For local governments, there are three (3) primary challenges in this regard:

18.3.1.1 AVAILABILITY OF DATA

Availability of data is very much location-specific, that is, it varies significantly from region to region, country to country, province to province, or even city to city. Even for locations with abundance of data, the challenge lies in collection, segregate and analysis of those.

18.3.1.2 KNOWLEDGE AND COMPETENCE OF PERSONNEL

These include shortage in number and skillset of personnel who are involved in collection and analysis of the data.

18.3.1.3 "DATA SILOS"

There are obstacles when one agency restricts the data within them and does not share with other agencies involved, thus not building up inter-governmental harmony and coordination.

Practically all SDG proposals as of now acknowledged the need to include a judicious analysis of social, environmental, and economic dimensions of sustainable development. While monitoring systems and indicators for many issues may be re-validated/re-adopted, there may be new goals where establishing pertinent and technically comprehensive indicators may pose a substantial challenge. Data gaps emerge from gaps in monitoring systems and competency, capacity, and efficiency of workforce handling the systems, mittigating measures shall call for investment in human capital development, so that the role of monitoring and reporting necessities can be addressed in all segments of the policy cycle, from goal setting to planning, implementing, evaluating and learning, so that the potential of the system can be aligned with SDG-related decision making. Monitoring mechanisms and indicators are to be taken into account at the inception phase to establish the key baselines for the definition of goals and setting of targets.

18.3.2 OPPORTUNITIES

Apart from the challenges, there are several opportunities that are advantageous in monitoring and reporting the progress toward achievement of SDGs, due to significant progresses by United Nations Statistical Commission and United Nations Statistics Division (UNSTAT) and Organisation for Economic Co-operation and Development (OECD), in the conceptual and technical framework of measurement. If there is adequate support and political backing at the local level, significant improvement in synchronization of monitoring and reporting can be achieved. Although a common metric for political backup of monitoring, measurement, and reporting is yet to be developed (as this aspect is grossly dependent on country, region, and location), increased awareness, alignment and understanding of their roles in refining the approach toward policy making is being observed among the leadership in many countries. Although indicators that cannot be used readily pose a big challenge, there are also many instances where measured content is being managed effectively and efficiently. With pros and cons, "evidence-based policy," that is, the policy that uses monitoring information as evidence, is being accepted, with the formulation of location-specific indicators systems and web/cloud-based, real-time reporting. This necessitates to formulate a global measurement reform agenda in a way by not merely adding a set of metrics, also improving the effectiveness of governance. The growing variety and number of projects aimed at tracking and reporting on components of the SDGs and associated indicators are important, because, despite having diverse starting points, they all aim to improve the substantiation for SDG implementation as a whole. It is also notable to observe the diversity of participants, including intergovernmental organizations, an association of professionals, scientific and technology forums, and organizations with a major interest in the economy, in addition to representatives of national statistical offices. With the involvement of numerous groups and forums, it is important to ensure that the SDGs become a true game changer in the propagation of sustainable development. Interactions between these groups and forums also result in general or sector-specific reviews and analyses of potential targets and indicators, which are specific to a country, a region or a location.

18.3.3 PROPAGATION

While the statistical community is primarily responsible for monitoring networks and reporting data on a regular basis, in order to ensure that targets and indicators accurately reflect the impact of development on the state of the Earth's resource base, the science, and technology community would need to be deeply involved. They should concentrate on connecting SDG targets and indicators to planetary boundaries and reflecting new scientific knowledge about the Earth as a dynamically changing system, moving toward the "Beyond GDP" agenda. This philosophy has the potential to create a unique opportunity for different nations to join hands and formulate a common agenda for aligning with the shared task of monitoring, selecting proper indicators and reporting, and redefining the comprehensive structure of progress measurement collaboratively and inclusively. Governments would play the most crucial role in this process, not only because they are the ones legislative authority to propel the SDGs and associated targets and indicators, but also due to the advantage of possessing a substantial portion of the institutional infrastructure of data collection and monitoring, as well as having the constitutional authority to combine different cross-sections of society, from industry to academia to science and technology community to citizens, in order to proceed in a collaborative approach. This propagation must be achieved in parallel paths on multiple levels. It is inevitable for regions, countries and communities to develop their own goals and corresponding monitoring and reporting systems, keeping the following in mind:

- While there would be synchronization of SDGs on critical global issues, national-level diversities would be needed to be addressed via sub-goals and targets. Wherever feasible, indicators linked with common goals should be grouped together, for macro-level aggregation and comparisons.
- Governments ought to engage national statistical offices and geospatial data communities at an initial stage to identify specific SDG indicators and review their alignment in the national perspective.
- Governments are to recognize, and where possible, develop other monitoring and reporting mechanisms and capacities at subnational level (communities, associations, sectors, etc.).
- Governments are to advocate for broader societal engagement toward goal setting, which is essentially a science-policy process, not only to establish specific and realistic targets, but also to attach wider societal ownership of the goals, targets, their associated indicators and, finally, their implementation.
- Governments must understand that the goal of tracking and reporting progress based on indicators is to enhance the effectiveness and accountability of implementation, and they should, whenever possible, establish direct links between strategies, plans, programs and budgets and SDG reports and indicators.

18.4 GLOBAL STANDING IN ACHIEVEMENT OF SDGS

18.4.1 FALLOUT

The Sustainable Development Goals Report 2022 of United Nations showcase the negative impacts and disruptions due to COVID-19 and conflicts/war situations toward reaching the SDGs. The Pandemic itself has so far cost 15 million lives, either directly or indirectly. Global health systems have almost come to a collapse with disruptions in many essential health infrastructures and services, leading to major threats to combat other life-threatening diseases such as tuberculosis and malaria, due to a huge drop in the immunization process, for the first time in the decade. The pandemic also practically annihilated progress on poverty eradication achieved in around previous 4 years and dragged nearly 93 million additional population into extreme poverty, in 2020 only. Prolonged closures of educational institutions put nearly 24 million learners, from different levels (pre-primary to university), at risk of permanent termination of learning. About 147 million children were barred from more than 50% of their in-person learning in major portions of 2020 and 2021, significantly upsetting their learning as well as psychological well-being. Women have suffered excessively from the socio-economic domino effect of the pandemic, hit with loss of income, increased loads of care work grossly unpaid, and escalating domestic violence.

The ill effects of the pandemic are now eclipsed by the rapidly increasing threat of climate change. Billions of people around the globe are already being affected by increased heat-waves, droughts, wildfires, and floods which are leading to potentially irreversible damage to the Earth's ecosystems. To evade the most awful effects of climate change, as pledged in the Paris Agreement, global greenhouse gas emissions would have required to reach to peak before 2025 and then decline by 43% by 2030, reducing to net zero by 2050. On the contrary, under the present scenario and different nation's current voluntary climate action goals, greenhouse gas emissions would rise by almost 14% by 2030.

Apart from the aforementioned, civilization is enduring the highest number of conflicts since the creation of the United Nations in 1946, with nearly 25% of the global population now living in conflict-affected countries. As of May 2022, an all-time high number of around 100 million people have been by force uprooted from their homes, with 6.5 million evacuating from Ukraine alone, mostly women and children.

The current recovery process across the globe is neither consistent nor reliable, with concerns related to the threat of newer COVID-19 variants and/or other virus outbreaks, rising inflation, major disruptions of supply-chain, mounting pressures on labor market, and unmanageable debt in developing and third world countries. It has been observed that the distribution of COVID-19 vaccine has been in gross disparity across the world, resulting in a blunt double-standard recovery from COVID-19, planting an intensifying feeling of injustice and persistent inequalities around the world.

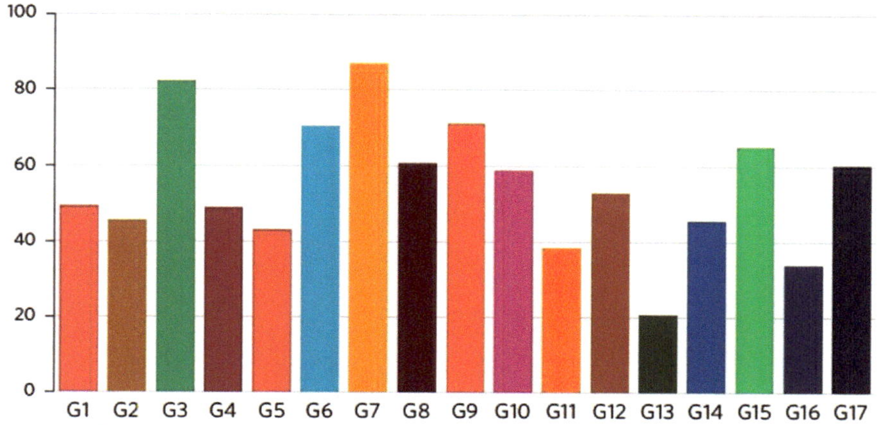

FIGURE 18.3 Countries or areas with data available since 2015, by goal (%).

It is challenging to completely comprehend the pace of development toward the progression and achievement of the 2030 Agenda, disparities among areas, and "who is being left behind" due to significant data gaps that persist in terms of geographic coverage, timeliness, and amount of disaggregation. Less than 50% of the countries or regions have globally comparable/analogous data from 2015 or later for 8 of the 17 SDGs. Around 20% of nations have substantial data for Goal 13 (climate action), although Goals 3 (health) and 7 (energy) have the highest percentage of data availability (more than 80% of the countries have a minimum of one data point since 2015) (Figure 18.3).

The substantial danger COVID-19 posed to already resistant national statistics systems served as a reminder of the necessity for robust and resilient statistical and ICT frameworks. Due to widespread lockdown measures, 96% of countries stopped collecting face-to-face data completely or in part in May 2020. Face-to-face data-gathering issues persisted in 57% of nations as of May 2021. Before the pandemic, countries that depended solely on face-to-face or in-person mode of data collection suffered greatly, whereas those who were capable of remote data collection or had tried it out benefited greatly. Figure 18.4 depicts this scenario.

It is essential to gather information on population groups that are vulnerable, such as immigrants and people with disabilities, in order to comprehend their difficulties and locate the "left behind" cross-section. Traditional surveys that solely look at residential premises overlook people staying in institutions, including hospitals, other residential care facilities, homeless shelters, and prisons, all of which have been severely impacted by the pandemic. Additionally, the greatest barrier to linking some cross-sections throughout the epidemic had been the digital divide in mobile phone ownership and Internet access. 39% of the countries polled had trouble gathering adequate data on migrants, 27% confronted hitches gathering information on the elderly, and 27% struggled to gather information on those with various impairments (Figure 18.5).

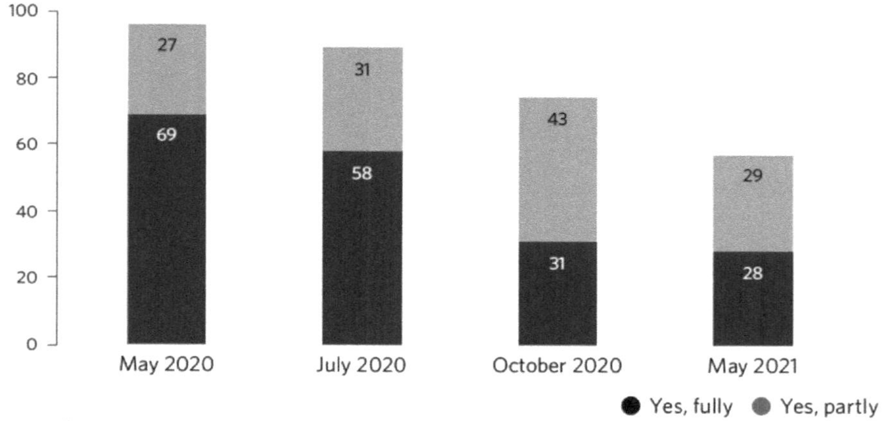

FIGURE 18.4 Countries that stopped face-to-face data collection, May 2020–May 2021 (%).
Source: The Sustainable Development Goals report 2022 of United Nations.

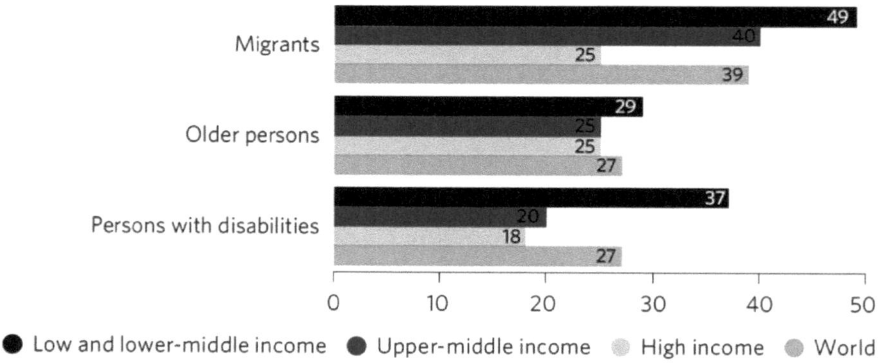

FIGURE 18.5 Countries facing difficulty in collecting data on specific population groups, by income group, May 2021 (%).
Source: The Sustainable Development Goals Report 2022 of United Nations.

Status up to June 2022 is summarized in TABLE 18.2.

TABLE 18.2 Summary of Status for 2030 Agenda up to June 2022.

Goals		Status
Goals 1	No poverty	• Derailed progress due to COVID-19 and Ukraine crisis.
		• Rise in percentage share in number of workers living in the severest levels of poverty in 2020 (first time in two decades).
		• Cash benefits to unemployed: Over 50% in high-income countries via-avis to nearly 1% in low-income countries.
		• Rise in disaster-related deaths over 6 times in 2020, largely attributable to the after-effect of a pandemic.
Goals 2	Zero hunger	• Undermined food security globally, attributable to COVID-19, conflicts, growing inequalities and climate change.
		• Low labor productivity associated with small-scale food producers.
		• Very slow progress on overcoming child malnutrition due to the pandemic and growing food insecurity.
		• Sharp rise in a number of affected countries due to high food prices in 2020.
Goals 3	Good health and well-being	• Direct and indirect death of nearly 15 million people in two years of the pandemic.
		• Significant rise in sense of insecurity, anxiety, and depression among young groups in particular, and in all demographic cross-sections as a whole.
		• Some progress toward improvement in maternal and child health, but with prominent disparities across different countries, regions, and locations.
		• Inconsistent progress and results toward universal health coverage.
		• Widespread disorders with respect to progress in the fight against HIV, tuberculosis, and malaria.
		• Disruptions in essential vaccinations of children due to the pandemic.
		• Large number of deaths of health and care workers, in most regions, due to COVID-19.
Goals 4	Quality education	• Prolonged school closures and discontinuation from school.
		• Shadow on learning outcomes.
		• Entrenched inequities in education during the pandemic.
		• Overlooked psychosocial support for students after the reopening of schools.

TABLE 18.2 *(Continued)*

Goals		Status
Goals 5	Gender equality	• Although growing awareness of violence against older women, data remaining limited. • Persistent human rights violations on the front of juvenile marriage and mutilation of female genital. • Sluggish progress in women's admittance to political and economic leadership positions. • Lack of legal right in many countries toward autonomy to women over their own bodies. • Large shortfall in protection of rights of women's to land and property. • Accelerated growth required to allocate public financing with diversity and gender equality objectives.
Goals 6	Clean water and sanitation	• Need of four times increase in the pace of progress to meet targets for potable water, sanitation, and hygiene (WASH) by 2030. • Loss of wetlands at an alarming rate; protection and restoration required on a massive scale. • Lack of active monitoring for early remediation of water pollution in the poorest countries. • Increasing stress on water resources in Western Asia and Northern Africa at an alarming rate. • Lack in cooperation agreements on shared water resources by most of the countries; a potential source of conflict.
Goals 7	Affordable and clean energy	• Slow progress in electrification. • Need of intensified efforts in lesser developed nations to access clean fuels and efficient technologies for cooking. • Need of major thrust in spread of renewable energy systems, with substantial finance mobilization to meet global energy and climate objectives. • Target for global energy conservation remains within reach, however it needs significant investment in balanced manner. • Sluggish international public financing toward renewable energy (even since before pandemic), in spite of the mounting perseverance of climate change.

TABLE 18.2 *(Continued)*

Goals		Status
Goals 8	Decent work and economic growth	• Hindrance in robust economic recovery due to various shocks, including the war in Ukraine. • Volatile swings in labor productivity, mostly affecting small businesses and economically backward nations, due to pandemic. • Shaky labor market recovery. • Lack of informal employment option for many workers evacuated due to pandemic. • Rising poverty and disruptions due to pandemic forcing millions of children into child labor. • Massive disruptions in youth training, education, and employment, with women facing the biggest challenges.
Goals 9	Industry, innovation and infrastructure	• Manufacturing in many developed countries rebounded, leaving least developed countries behind, and jobs lost during the pandemic not getting regained. • Struggle by passenger airline industry to recoup catastrophic losses. • Lack of credit or other support has for many small-scale industries. • Hi-tech industries being established as much more resilient in crisis situations than their low-tech counterparts. • Most of the world now covered by a mobile-broadband network, but gaps in economically weaker countries.
Goals 10	Reduced inequalities	• Record numbers of refugees added worldwide due to war in Ukraine. • Large numbers of migrants either got killed or lost their lives due to hunger and illness on migratory routes in 2021–2022 alone. • Relative poverty increased in many countries due to COVID-19. • Hike in income inequality, leading two decades of balanced progress to vulnerability, due to the pandemic. • Increasing widespread discrimination against women and persons with disabilities. • Eroding workers' share of national income, aggravates income inequality.

TABLE 18.2 *(Continued)*

Goals		Status
Goals 11	Sustainable cities and communities	• Need of increased emphasis on urban slums, that is, home for nearly 1 billion people. • Although ambient air quality now being monitored in large number of cities, but still below the desirable coverage worldwide. • Only about 50% of world's population living in cities having proper access to public transportation. • Municipal solid waste disposal/treatment/conversion, a historically longstanding challenge, continues to pile up, as urban population continue to increase. • Insufficient access to public open spaces in crowded urban areas. • More local and civic bodies and authorities adopting disaster risk mitigation and reduction strategies, but still there is a need for broader and comprehensive disaster and climate risk mitigation policy and approach.
Goals 12	Responsible consumption and production	• Increasing dependency on natural resources pulling the Earth on unsustainable consequence. • Loss or waste of too much food in every country every day. • Lack of safe management of world's vast electronic waste. • Positive growth of renewable energy in developing countries, but not substantially in economically backward nations. • Alarmingly high fossil fuel subsidies, despite a temporary drop in 2020. • National education systems to include and focus on mainstream sustainable development and significance of global citizenship.
Goals 13	Climate action	• Mounting emissions of greenhouse gas globally, leading to unprecedented ambient temperatures and more extreme weather conditions in near future. • Emissions due to combination of fossil fuel bounced back to a record high in 2021, wiping out the positive effect pandemic-related reductions. • Climate financing remained just a fraction of the recommendation of UN for averting the worst scenarios.

TABLE 18.2 *(Continued)*

Goals		Status
Goals 14	Life below water	• Hindrance in the capacity of oceans and seas to absorb effects of climate change due to increasing acidification. • Loss of marine life due to rise in deposition of plastic, lack of nutrient, and other wastes. • Large areas of the ocean and sea are now under protection, however, there is still requirement for more pragmatic and intensive. • Global fish stocks still in danger. • Pressure on fish stocks is pulling down the role which sustainable fisheries play in economic growth in some regions. • Fast-tracked action required to support the livelihoods of small-scale fishers, many of whose sustenance collapsed during pandemic.
Goals 15	Life on land	• Continuos shrink in world's forest area, mainly due to expansion in agricultural, industrial, and real-estate sectors. • Gain of momentum in efforts across the globe to stimulate access and leverage of genetic resources. • Rise in risk of species extinction; highest in Asia and small island developing countries. • Inportance of conservation of biodiversity being reflected in national planning policies in many countries; still, with very sluggish progress. • Nearly 50% of areas identified as crucial for global biodiversity conservation now under protection, however 4 regions still having gaps in progress.
Goals 16	Peace, justice, and strong institutions	• Brunt of violent conflicts being borne by civilians, with record numbers forcibly displaced. • Need of strengthening the tracing through better global cooperation to curb illegal small arms trade. • Perception of about 1/3rd of the world's population—mostly women—of feeling unsafe in their localities after sunset. • Decreasing rates of homicide reflect strong gender differences. • Need of streamlined and transparent business processes to curb corruption prevailed worldwide.

TABLE 18.2 *(Continued)*

Goals		Status
Goals 17	Partnerships for the goals	• Although rise in official development assistance was observed, largely due to COVID-19-related relief work, but still lagging behind the target. • Significance of data, information, and statistics for a comprehensive decision-making process gained momentum, but funding for this is still under stagnation. • Additional debt burdens on economically weaker countries due to pandemic. • Surge in internet usage propelled due to pandemic, however with sharp contrast in economically backward countries and/or many of third world countries who are still lagging. • Foreign direct investment (FDI) bounced back sturdily in 2021 across the globe, but only modest growth in flows to the poorest countries. • Fund flows to economically weaker nations has been strong, reinforced by strong infrastructural development, economic activities, and employment generation.

Source: The Sustainable Development Goals Report 2022 of United Nations.

18.4.2 SILVER LINING

18.4.2.1 COVID-19 SET THE CLEAR THE MANDATE FOR THE NEED OF STRONG STATISTICAL FOUNDATION FOR DIFFERENT COUNTRIES

Countries that relied solely on face-to-face data collection before the pandemic suffered the most, while those with hands-on experience with remote data collection remained significantly ahead over the others.

18.4.2.2 PATHWAY FOR THE FUTURE OF INNOVATION HAS BEEN SET BY THE PANDEMIC

The pandemic has brought up an unprecedented challenge in different countries, zones, and locations, for national or local statistical systems. It also provided a gateway to test innovative methods of collecting data, to explore sources of new data, and to upgrade Information and Communication Technologies (ICT) infrastructures to meet the data requirements of policy design. During this process, the importance of comprehensive information was made clear. In the future, the lessons learned during the pandemic can be used for the future of public statistical updates.

18.4.2.3 NATIONAL STATISTICS OFFICES (NSO) REQUIRE TO REINFORCE COORDINATION WITHIN NATIONAL LEVEL DATA ECOSYSTEMS

During the COVID-19 wave peaks, tie-ups were established between government bodies and public sectors, academic institutions, local authorities, private companies, and citizen forums to collect the data required for policy formulation. These collaborations have brought up new ideas, concepts, and resources. It also enhanced the comprehensiveness, timeliness, and usability of the resulting data. In many countries, national statistical offices played a stronger coordinating role.

18.4.2.4 EFFECTIVE COMMUNICATION STRATEGIES HELPED TO COMBAT MISINFORMATION AND DISINFORMATION

Due to the pandemic, pressure on NSOs around the world has been enormous. These bureaus were expected not only to set the gold standard for the quality of data in their respective countries but also to lead in correcting the mass distortion in the forms of misinformation and disinformation that have been spreading about the impact of a pandemic. To do so, NSOs are required to share insights on new and traditional approaches to outreaching various data users.

18.5 CONCLUSION

In spite of a balance sheet showing the negative scores higher, the underlying silver lining indicates toward formulation of region/country/location-specific segregation and/or aggregation of SDG targets and indicators. Otherwise, it would be practically impossible the bridge the gap between pledged and achieved with respect to the 2030 Agenda.

KEYWORDS

- **SDG**
- **target**
- **indicator**
- **policy**
- **development**

REFERENCES

Global Evaluation Agenda 2016–2020, Developed by a Global, Multi-Stakeholder Consultative Process; Developed by a Global, Multi-Stakeholder Consultative Process, Jan 15, 2016; pp 9–15.

Measuring, Monitoring and Evaluating the SDGs, Iclei Briefing Sheet-Urban Issues, No. 06, November 2015, pp 2–3.

Monitoring and Reporting on Sustainable Development Goals: Cross-Scale Linkages László Pintér, Ph.D. Crisis Communications, SDplanNET Briefing Note April 2014, pp 1–3.

National Evaluation Capacity Development: Practical tips on how to strengthen National Evaluation Systems; A Report for the United Nations Evaluation Group (UNEG) Task Force on National Evaluation Capacity Development; pp 6–16.

Recommendation of the Council on Good Statistical Practice, OECD Legal Instruments, OECD; pp 6–7.

Report on the Implementation of the OECD Recommendation on Good Statistical Practice; OECD, 2020; pp 6–46.

Resolution Adopted by the General Assembly on Sept 25, 2015.

Roadmap For Localizing The Sdgs: Implementation And Monitoring At Subnational Level, pp 2–4.

Sustainable Development Goal 16: Focus On Public Institutions - World Public Sector Report 2019, Prepared by Department of Economic and Social Affairs, United Nations, 2019; pp 9–31.

Sustainable Development Outlook. Achieving SDGs in the Wake of COVID-19: Scenarios for Policymakers, Prepared by Department of Economic and Social Affairs, United Nations, 2020; pp 13–33.

The 5Ps of the Sustainable Development Goals, [Online].

https://www.coursera.org/lecture/sustainable-development-ban-ki-moon/summary-JvkbC

The Sustainable Development Goals Report 2022, United Nations, 2022.

United Nations Sustainable Development Cooperation Framework 2019, United Nations Sustainable Development Group, 2019; pp 6–15.

Voluntary National Reviews Synthesis Report, prepared by Department of Economic and Social Affairs, United Nations, 2019; pp 14–24.

CHAPTER 19

Neuromarketing Practices in Marketing Campaigns: A Case of Forecasting Consumer Behavior

KOUSIK MANDAL and SUDIN BAG

Department of Business Administration, Vidyasagar University, Midnapore, India

ABSTRACT

Various research methodologies have been used over the last decade to explain and forecast the performance of marketing campaigns. However, most traditional approaches have been shown to be ineffective. Understanding and modeling cognitive reactions to commercials are difficult because emotions influence how consumers interpret messages. This has been a methodological difficulty. Neuromarketing is an important step forward in understanding how the subconscious mind impacts customer decision making. Despite initial debate, the area has quickly earned legitimacy and respect among advertising and marketing experts. Marketers expertly entice people to buy their products, fueling significant research in a variety of fields of brain research. Neuroscientists are always developing new approaches and digging further into the topic of neuroscience. Products are strategically positioned to attract customers by creatively influencing consumer behavior. Traditional approaches for assessing and forecasting the efficacy of advertising campaigns have often fallen short, relying on consumers' willingness and capacity to verbalize their sentiments when exposed to adverts. Modern techniques that directly access the human mind without requiring demanding cognitive or conscious engagement are introduced by neuromarketing. In this

Agile Business Transformations: Priorities, Lessons, and Practices. Satyajit Chakrabarti, Subrata Chattopadhyay, Udit Chawla, Sundeep Singh Sondhi, & Arunava Dalal (Eds.)

study, the promising potential of the developing discipline of neuromarketing is explored, with the suggestion that it can greatly improve the efficacy of commercial and cause-related advertising messages globally.

19.1 INTRODUCTION

Marketing's fundamental purpose is to elicit an emotional reaction through different communication channels, such as commercials. Researchers have spent many years attempting to comprehend and assess the success of marketing strategies. Emotions influence how people comprehend information, making it difficult to understand and analyze cognitive reactions to advertisements. As a result of the difficulties in measuring consumer emotions, marketing research has worked to establish new models of value and individual rationality. To obtain a competitive advantage, managers constantly investigate aspects connected to attitudes and customer behavior. Previously, marketing and advertising researchers depended on focus groups to gain information on goods and brand communication. However, as the market advances, new technologies are required to get a scientific grasp of the thoughts of customers. Researchers have been developing numerous neurophysiological tools to analyze consumer behavior and the influence of advertising in recent years. Their objective is to shed light on many areas of marketing (Yadava et al., 2017).

Typically, a consumer's purchase decision begins with recognizing the need for a product or service and progresses to deciding whether to buy. The customer decision-making process, on the contrary, is not always clear. Understanding how customers make decisions is critical in marketing but it cannot be fully reached through traditional tactics such as surveys, personal interviews, or observations. This is because numerous unconscious mental processes have a significant impact on the decisions of customers.

Recent advances in neuroscience have demonstrated that emotions are the underlying foundation for people's ideas, behaviors, and actions (Tornati, 2012). As a result, there is increased interest in a method centered on the brain and the relationship between consumer behavior and brain activity (Hsu, 2016; Potter and Bolls, 2012). This growing subject is known as neuromarketing, which is the intriguing convergence of two distinct disciplines, namely, neuroscience and marketing. The term "neuromarketing" emerged organically around 2002 without any specific individual being credited for its inception. During that time, pioneering U.S. companies such as Brighthouse and SalesBrain spearheaded the provision of neuromarketing research and consulting services. They advocated leveraging insights and technology derived from cognitive neuroscience to enhance marketing strategies. In essence, neuromarketing can be likened to the relationship between neuropsychology and psychology. Just as neuropsychology delves into understanding the connection between the brain and human cognitive and psychological functions, neuromarketing emphasizes the significance of interpreting consumer behavior from a neurological perspective.

Manufacturers and managers throughout the world confront considerable challenges in forecasting customer attraction to new items, defining appropriate prices, and analyzing the efficiency of marketing messages (Gazdzik, 2017). Qualitative research, such as focus group interviews or blind taste tests, is based on self-reports, and the responses of participants give significant insights into product acceptability, taste preferences, or commercial response. This model, however, implies that customers are always truthful, which is not necessarily the case, since consumers may occasionally lie or reply with worries and prejudices. This assumption may jeopardize the trustworthiness of studies in this sector (Tekin et al., 2017). Furthermore, during focus group interviews, people' perspectives may be affected by dominating personalities, resulting in possibly incorrect study conclusions. Individual answers may not be completely independent of one another as a result (Gazdzik, 2017).

Neuromarketing research and application have gained prominence as a result. Neuromarketing studies employ neuroscience and psychology tools to investigate the neurological and psychological factors underlying people's decisions and behavior. So, a study on this mechanism is better for understanding the efficacy of marketing stimuli on consumers, and there is a potential of acquiring objective data utilizing present technology and breakthroughs in neuroscience.

Neuromarketing is a breakthrough in overcoming the constraints of traditional approaches for testing and forecasting the impact of advertising spending. Traditional tactics frequently rely on the availability and capacity of customers to communicate their thoughts about advertising, which can be inaccurate. Neuromarketing, on the contrary, offers a novel technology that directly accesses customers' thoughts without requiring considerable cognitive input (Morin, 2011). Neuromarketing, by using neurotechnology and cutting-edge neuroimaging techniques, enables an unparalleled examination of neural activity, including its frequency, location, and timing (Bakardjieva and Kimmel, 2017). Neuromarketing explores how changes in product design, packaging, and in-store displays affect customers by using neurology. It also goes into the reasons why customers choose some items and brands over others. Furthermore, neuromarketing evaluates the amount to which advertising content and execution impact consumers (Bakardjieva and Kimmel, 2017).

The major goal of this research is to investigate the impact of neuromarketing on consumer behavior and how it might help improve the efficacy of commercial advertising messages. This examination attempts to provide light on the function of neuromarketing in changing consumers' decision-making processes through a thorough analysis of current literature and research data. Unlike prior studies that just compiled material, this study goes beyond by investigating real-world neuromarketing applications from several worldwide case studies. The research investigates how positive and negative emotions influence consumer choices by analyzing experimental studies and real-life instances. Furthermore, the study assesses the influence of organizations' advertising messages on customer behavior in both positive and negative aspects. This study's findings have implications for marketing managers since they provide significant insights into the efficiency of neuromarketing methods in influencing customer behavior. Furthermore, it advances understanding of how neuromarketing may be used to optimize advertising efficacy and customer reactions, which contributes to the theoretical element of market research.

19.2 LITERATURE REVIEW

Firms that are marketing a product confront the issue of developing effective advertising campaigns in a highly competitive market. It is critical to address concerns such as reaction time, product diversity, and competitive strategies (Nyoni and Bonga, 2017b). Surprisingly, a large percentage of customers' decision-making process—roughly 95%—occurs subconsciously. Neuroscience can assist shed light on this process by uncovering the causes behind customers' purchasing behaviors (Nyoni and Bonga, 2017a; Ramsoy, 2014). Purchasing decisions are significantly more complicated and interrelated than the classic concept of plain, rational choices offered by Muth's rational-choice model (Muth, 1961). A recent study reveals that even seemingly reasonable cognitive judgments are highly impacted by emotions, eventually influencing the results (Hazeldine, 2014). Understanding the complexities of decision making is difficult since the brain operates as a "black box," concealing emotions and consumer preferences. Neuroeconomics, on the contrary, provides a valuable "window" into the underlying neurological processes of the individual being investigated (Green and Holbert, 2012).

Neuromarketing is still a subject that needs further research and knowledge. Several studies have previously been carried out to collect data on the number of matches and differences in heat points across various demographics on certain quadrants of a website. Štrach and Slivkin (2017) investigated cross-cultural disparities in business-to-business website evaluations, whereas Boz et al. (2017) investigated a tourism website. These studies demonstrated the significance of neuromarketing in these specific fields. Contrary to common assumption, corporations are increasingly using neuromarketing to improve promotional efforts for clients via traditional marketing channels (Glaenzer, 2016). Rather than altering customer behavior, the emphasis is on developing more effective and targeted advertising techniques.

To obtain significant information and insights, neuromarketing utilizes a variety of traditional methodologies such as surveys, focus groups, experiments, and ethnography (Cascio et al., 2015). Its primary goal is to improve the precision of predicting consumer preferences and behavior when combined with conventional methods (Boksem and Smidts, 2015; Smidts et al., 2014). To assess precise brain activity in reaction to advertising messages, researchers use modern technologies such as functional magnetic resonance imaging (fMRI) and electroencephalography (EEG). Companies acquire insights into the causes behind consumers' decisions and the underlying brain processes that govern their behaviors by analyzing this data (Ghorpade, 2017). According to Nick Lee, Honorary Professor of Marketing and Organizational Research at Aston University, CEOs are enthusiastic about adopting brain scans. Neuromarketing businesses are projected to extract ever more comprehensive data on the elements affecting people's wants to acquire or avoid certain items as brain imaging and neuroscience develop. However, whether Neuromarketing can effectively trigger a "buy button" in the human brain needs to be shown (Nyoni and Bonga, 2017b).

The limited implementation of neuromarketing approaches is one notable gap in the area (Feenstra and Pallarés-Domnguez, 2017). Although some skeptics and detractors refer to neuromarketing as "brainwashing" (Ghorpade, 2017), these approaches may give useful insights into how businesses manage ethical problems (Feenstra and Pallarés-Domnguez, 2017). Given the current capabilities and execution of neuromarketing research, claims regarding risks to consumer autonomy, privacy, and control lack considerable ethical consequences (Stanton et al., 2017). Neuromarketing could benefit society and consumers, which is often disregarded in ethical debates regarding the subject (Stanton et al., 2017). Nonetheless, many businesses decide to limit or avoid utilizing this sophisticated monitoring tool. While it is relatively straightforward for firms to observe what consumers buy, understanding the underlying reasons for such transactions is more difficult (Ghorpade, 2017). Neuromarketing could bridge this critical gap by providing practical and managerial implications that can enhance decision making and customer engagement.

19.3 COMPREHENDING THE CONSUMER'S MIND

Marketing research methodologies have long attempted to comprehend and forecast the performance of advertising efforts. Traditional tactics, however, have mostly failed in this endeavor. Emotions influence how consumers receive information, making it difficult to understand and predict their cognitive responses to advertising, offering a methodological challenge. Researchers have generally relied on consumers' self-reported sentiments about individual advertising to gauge consumer reactions to marketing messages. These reports are frequently compiled using confidential methods such as face-to-face interviews, questionnaires, or group settings such as focus groups. Unfortunately, these approaches have significant drawbacks. First, they believe that individuals can adequately express their own cognitive processes, ignoring the considerable role of subconscious aspects in decision making. Much of cognition happens outside of conscious consciousness, according to our developing knowledge of it. Second, a variety of conditions might cause study participants to exaggerate their emotional reporting. Incentives, time restrictions, and peer pressure might all influence their replies, resulting in less trustworthy results. Given these limitations, there is a growing need to investigate new and more subtle approaches capable of delving into the complex interplay between emotions, cognition, and advertising efficacy. Only via such techniques can we acquire a better understanding of how advertising affects consumers' perceptions and behaviors.

Among these difficulties, the development of neuroimaging methods has provided potential methodological options. Even though our minds have a tremendous impact on our behaviors, many areas of our brain remain unknown and undiscovered. Research done at the California Institute of Technology's Psychology and Social Sciences Division by John O'Doherty gives insight into how advertising impacts certain centers in our brain linked with pleasure, satisfaction, and anxiety. These regions, which are situated in the midbrain and diencephalon, are also implicated in drug addiction and some mental illnesses. The brain responds to advertising by associating stimuli with items. Advertisements work by giving a sensation and linking it with a product, therefore appealing to our brain's pleasure and reward centers. This association process is the foundation of advertising's efficacy.

Magnetic resonance imaging (MRI) enabled neurologists to observe the activity of the diencephalon and mid-brain in volunteers and evaluate their reactions to juice. Neurologists created visual stimulations related to the subjects' preferences, revealing the mid-brain's more intense activity when stimulated with their favorite flavor. The diencephalon reacted with up and down fluctuations, revealing subjects' preferences and individual choices. The limbic system, a part of the diencephalon, is involved in emotions, mood, and self-awareness, determining individual behavior. The limbic lobo, hippocampus, thalamic nuclei, limbic bark, and amygdala can influence human behavior and mood.

The amygdala is connected to the cerebral cortex, which regulates relations with the outside world. The amygdala's instinctive function, ear emotion, could provide advantages in decision making, as automatic responses caused by fear could be stronger than our rational ability to voluntarily inhibit them. The amygdala is also the center of anxiety, and understanding customer anxiety through coherent advertisements and fMRI analysis can lead to new horizons in understanding purchasing dynamics and the role of neurological marketing processes.

Tears, a uniquely human emotional signal, are activated by the amygdala, a region of the brain responsible for storing emotional memories. Surprisingly, our emotions are handled by a different system within the brain that is separate from rational mental processes. According to research done by Drazen Prelec and George Loewenstein, boosting product costs while increasing consumption causes psychological anguish similar to physical pain. This brain process sheds light on loss avoidance ideas as well. One effective marketing approach supported by neuroscientific data is the creation of product bundles in which the prices of separate goods contribute to a discounted overall. This method streamlines the selling process and has been shown to be successful in neuromarketing studies. Selling individual items might be difficult, but using packages allows for a more efficient and effective marketing strategy.

19.4 THE MAIN METHODS FOR THE ANALYSIS OF BRAIN ACTIVITY

In this research, we will investigate how distinct stimuli impact specific brain areas, with a particular emphasis on the midbrain and diencephalon, particularly the amygdala, in relation to consumer behavioral reactions. We will use three standard methods to analyze brain activity in response to stimuli: EEG, positron emission tomography (PET), and MRI, or fMRI. The spatial resolution capabilities of these brain imaging modalities, especially PET and fMRI, differ. We will also utilize eye tracking to detect eye movements and find the most fascinating places in the stimulus image. Biometric measures will also be coupled with EEG to supplement our study.

These findings are often used to better understand two crucial aspects: the level of attention induced by the stimuli and the level of emotional involvement it elicits. In general, researchers want to know if customers respond positively to stimuli and how well the stimuli are remembered (Chater and Loewenstein, 2016). Based on this information, useful supplemental information may be acquired, such as: (1) analyzing the desire to purchase a product; (2) measuring the distinctiveness of the suggested product in comparison to rivals; and (3) rating the stimulus's efficiency in delivering its message. All of these hypotheses have been thoroughly investigated in empirical investigations.

Eye-opening research on the influence of various commercial videos was undertaken on a sample of 30 university students, 15 men and 15 women. Surprisingly, the EEG data revealed no significant brain activity within the first 10 s of the films. However, as the images moved to emphasize values, notably family unity, favorable brain responses in the individuals were detected. Notably, scenes aimed mainly at guys produced negative responses from females, but scenes with supernatural themes or foggy colors failed to pique female attention (Tekin et al., 2017). This study reveals unique behaviors displayed by men and women during EEG testing. In comparison to males, women are more impacted by hedonistic settings (Lucia-Palacios et al., 2017). Similarly, in shopping-related research, females were shown to be more vulnerable to environmental cues (Lucia-Palacios et al., 2017; Wirtz et al., 2000).

Furthermore, using both EEG and fMRI methods, Suomala et al. (2012) showed the importance of neuromarketing as a significant tool for studying the brain's activity during client involvement. Their research included a virtual trip scenario replicating an advice sales procedure, as well as brain scans. A total of 16 participants were shown video clips and images of sales interactions at Nokia flagship stores. The individuals might immerse themselves in the experiences, engaging with the persons and events represented in the movies, during this process. Surprisingly, they felt safe during the consultative sales process. These findings show the potential of virtual labs as environments akin to genuine sales environments, allowing customers to actively engage in the purchasing process and respond to events depicted on the screen. In this scenario, the use of neuromarketing is crucial, providing consumer insights that cannot be extrapolated from other sources.

Although it can only record the most superficial brain waves, EEG stands out as a more accessible, cost-effective, and non-invasive examination (Costa Rozan Fortunato and de Moura Engracia Giraldi, 2014). Henry Walter used fMRI to measure the brain activity of 12 young men while showing them with 66 black-and-white photos of sports cars, sedans, and utility vehicles in a well-known Daimler Chrysler experiment. The study found that watching sports vehicles caused a unique activation of the nucleus accumbens, which was triggered by dopamine release. This research suggests that men's demand for perceived sports automobiles is connected to the effect of advertising, implying that these vehicles are very desired. Lindstrom (2008) presents research in his book "*Buyology*" that reveals how labels emphasizing the beneficial benefits of cigarettes act as visual stimuli for smokers, urging them to consume more. Rather than reducing their urge to smoke, these labels serve as advertising signals that increase desire inside the nucleus accumbens, the part of the brain linked with pleasure anticipation.

Barbasso et al. (2015) did an enthralling study to learn how packaging, independent of cost, may add value to a product. The study included 24 people ranging in age from 24 to 40 and with varied levels of education. Two brain imaging technologies, fMRI and magnetoencephalography (MEG), were used to analyze the participants' reactions, utilizing magnetic fields created by the brain's electrical activity (Żurawicki, 2010). The researchers were able to determine the cortical regions active in response to consumer behavior and experiences using these cutting-edge methodologies (Gazzaniga, 2004). The study's findings indicated that packaging, or the suitability of packaging within its intended setting, plays a critical influence in molding customers' perceptions of the value of a product.

Consumers' focused attention, visual gaze fixation patterns, pupil dilation, and focus and micro-focus behavior have all been measured using eye-tracking research. However, eye tracking alone does not offer information on the emotions linked with specific areas of focus (Costa Rozan Fortunato and de Moura Engracia Giraldi, 2014). However, research utilizing PET shares a degree of validity with fMRI since both techniques provide useful neuroimaging data. Nonetheless, PET uses radioactive positrons, which can be invasive and difficult in neuromarketing applications since they must travel through people to obtain data (Lin et al., 2010). As a result of its invasiveness, PET is a less desirable alternative for neuromarketing investigations.

19.5 RESEARCH METHODOLOGY

Through the literature research, this study examined "neuroscience, the consumer's brain and thinking style, neuromarketing applications, and neuromarketing research techniques." The research part of the study examined the new generation of neuromarketing applications of technological developments developing with the digital economy. Using neuromarketing techniques in marketing research was attempted to reveal "not only what the consumer says, but what their feelings are in their subconscious mind." To explain this situation, the result of the prior neuromarketing research was assessed as case studies.

The study used the "descriptive case study analysis" method, and the sample of the study that is business selected for the research was examined by selecting them using the "judgmental sampling" method. The reason why well-known global brands such as Unilever and Coca-Cola or Pepsi were chosen is that they are both popular in advertising and research and provide more information about the global consumer. In the study, which was prepared as case studies, the study and evaluation of consumer behavior in the neuromarketing studies that were previously carried out were conducted.

19.6 ASSESSMENTS

In the case study examined for this purpose, the positive and negative facets of consumer behavior were assessed on the effects of advertising and packaging studies made by companies. This study includes case studies based on neuromarketing research; using neuromarketing measurement techniques, we attempted to increase the positive impact created on the target consumers during packaging studies and advertising campaigns. When consumers' negative effects and emotional strain were observed in advertising campaigns, necessary basic regulations were made, and the marketing campaign's success rate increased for the brand. The brand's advertising campaign aims to create a positive impression about the brand among the consumers, and if there are negative facets for the brand, these have been amended. Thus, it has been observed that the brand's sales, profits, and turnover have been positively impacted. Also, it creates a positive brand image on consumer behavior. From these echoes, it is notable that applications of neuromarketing techniques may be useful for achieving a more suitable assessment of the efficiency of communication, and brands have been increased success rates in influencing consumer behavior.

19.7 CASE STUDIES

19.7.1 COCA-COLA OR PEPSI: A CONSUMER'S PERSPECTIVE

According to research, up to 95% of consumer goods and service transactions are possibly impulsive purchases (Koc and Boz, 2014a, 2014b). This chapter examines customer behavior in relation to a specific product (a well-known beverage) and a service. This product was the subject of one very interesting neuromarketing research undertaken by McClure et al. (2004). Researchers monitored brain activity as individuals drank either Coca-Cola or Pepsi during the trial. The study made use of fMRI technology and included two conditions: a blind-tasting test and a brand-cued delivery. Surprisingly, brain activity in the blind tasting test was remarkably comparable between Coca-Cola and Pepsi. Significant variations in brain activity were seen in the brand-cued condition, notably in the ventromedial prefrontal cortex.

The crucial finding was that when brand information was not present, no significant variations in brain activity were detected. When brands were recognized, however, brand familiarity and product preference had a major effect on the brain response. Coca-Cola was chosen as the favorite beverage by the subjects, resulting in increased activity in the ventromedial prefrontal cortex. The participants made no explicit decisions in this study, and the drink was administered to them in small amounts while they were within the fMRI. The manipulation depended on whether the brand was revealed beforehand, and the conclusions were based on the fMRI-measured activation areas.

In their study, Koenigs and Tranel (2008) discuss the "Pepsi paradox," which emphasizes an unusual phenomenon. During blind taste testing, people either prefer Pepsi over Coca-Cola or have no consistent preference. Despite this, Coca-Cola routinely outsells Pepsi. When brand information is given, Coca-Cola becomes the favored option. In the absence of brand knowledge, no consistent preferences are detected.

Cola preference was counterbalanced in the study done by McClure et al. (2004) to achieve impartial results. Koenigs and Tranel (2008) corroborate these findings by looking at people who have had prefrontal cortex injury. Surprisingly, even when these individuals are supplied with brand information, their choices remain unchanged. This finding is consistent with the effects seen in normal people during blind taste tests and under their own blind taste test circumstances.

19.8 A NEUROMARKETING INVESTIGATION OF THE ADVERTISEMENT "SHARING HAPPINESS WITH ALGIDA DURING RAMADAN"

Algida, a Unilever subsidiary, is an ice cream firm that distinguishes its product line, which is accessible globally, by integrating native flavors distinct to each location. Their marketing efforts are centered on cultural characteristics, effectively implementing the "think global, act local" concept in the worldwide market.

In Turkey, a unique advertisement film has been created for the month of Ramadan. The commercial opens with a youngster buying a pita from a grocery shop while the sound of a cannon firing announces the evening meal. As the youngster exits the store, he stumbles upon an Algida freezer that miraculously glides across the neighborhood and stops in a garden where the entire family is breaking their fast. "While it might not be easy for an Algida freezer to reach you this Ramadan," the film adds, "we hope you'll visit the nearest Algida freezer after iftar this summer and share your joy with Algida during this Ramadan." However, despite conducting an AdNeuro™ test by ThinkNeuro for the advertisement, the results have been less than satisfactory, with all scores falling below the desired and expected levels.

With a rating of 67.47, the advertisement's attention score stayed below the general average of all advertisements assessed thus far, while the Emotional Impact obtained a rating of 66.63. Both the attention and emotional impact curves initially exhibited an increasing trend, indicating that viewers were interested and inclined to keep watching the commercial.

The commercial opens with a cannon blasting sound, which first elevates tension levels, but is quickly followed by fast-paced music that triggers emotions. When the Algida freezer is added, both the emotional strain and attention curves begin to grow. However, when the freezer approaches people, the emotional effect curve begins to diminish. The "Hey!" callout at the conclusion, accompanied by an external voice, elicits a negative emotional response in consumers, with an emotional strain score of 44.68, much higher than the norm. As a result, the created emotional bond eventually deteriorates.

The scene where people are seen enjoying the ice cream helps recapture viewers' interest. Notably, when the brand name is highlighted, the audience focuses their attention on the Unilever logo in the upper right corner and the Algida logo in the center.

ThinkNeuro partner Eda Ocak characterized the observed drop in subconscious perceptions as follows: "The downward motion of the freezer triggered emotional strain and anxiety in consumers." Because of the emotional link built between the freezer's emblem and the brand, viewers associated worry with the brand itself. Recent neuromarketing research has found two essential variables as influential on consumers: the "celebrity effect" and the "negative impact of unpleasant emotions on the brand' included in commercial films to improve the plot. These elements are quite important in advertising films. Brands must carefully pick the correct people to represent their goods and avoid inadvertently triggering unfavorable internal reactions and emotions in customers, all while attempting to conjure a positive and realistic picture inside the advertisement's story.

The neuromarketing experiment carried out as part of the research underlined the need of paying attention to these aspects, notably in the formation of story patterns that trigger pleasant emotions, inside the Unilever commercial video for the Algida brand. The study findings demonstrated that, although initially properly and efficiently capturing consumer sentiments and ideas, the commercial eventually lost its attraction as simplicity was degraded. As a result, while Algida intended for this particular Ramadan commercial to convey delight to customers, it accidentally elicited dread, resulting in a progressive alienation of the consumer from the message."

19.9 DISCUSSION

Through a series of case studies, this study investigates the influence of advertising and packaging methods on customer behavior, focusing on both good and negative elements. Using neuromarketing research, this study sought to increase the positive impact on the target audience by incorporating neuromarketing measuring tools into packaging and advertising efforts. When the emotional strain and negative consequences of advertising campaigns were recognized, suitable modifications were made to improve the brand's campaign performance. The emphasis was on creating advertising campaigns that left a pleasant impression, and any bad parts were addressed and corrected as soon as possible. As a result, the brand had a significant beneficial impact on customer behavior, resulting in improved sales, profits, and total turnover. The brand's potential to favorably influence customer behavior improved significantly as well.

Using efficient neuromarketing approaches not only allows companies to obtain insights into their customers' cognitive processes but also helps them comprehend their emotions. Brands that understand both the emotional and rational sides of their customers are better positioned to meet sales goals and develop everlasting client loyalty. Neuromarketing, from a theoretical standpoint, provides a potential to go beyond standard marketing techniques by offering unbiased scientific data for analyzing customer behavior. Marketers may now use neuromarketing to measure consumers' unconscious and emotional responses to advertising campaigns, messaging, and brand pictures, among other things. When the brain's dynamic state switches from neutral to active, the essential point of consumer decision making emerges. By analyzing customers' beliefs and behaviors toward the brand, marketers may develop strong brand relationships with their audiences and strengthen their market position by employing neuromarketing.

19.10 IMPLICATIONS

Neuromarketing, from a theoretical aspect, provides a unique chance to transcend the subjectivity commonly associated with traditional marketing methods such as focus groups by delivering objective scientific facts. This allows for a more precise examination of client behavior. On the managerial front, neuromarketing enables the objective assessment of the influence of various advertising campaigns, commercials, brand images, and other factors. Among the numerous neuromarketing strategies, fMRI is the preferred method by both scientists and businesses. EEG is also often used to measure the influence of items in television advertising. PET, on the contrary, is less popular since it is very intrusive, and MEG is not adequate for assessing the deepest subcortical and cerebral regions and needs expensive equipment. Eye tracking is another approach that is less commonly employed since it does not offer information on the emotional associations associated with the areas of focus.

Neuromarketing and related technologies have emerged as a modern and fast-developing subject, provoking heated arguments over ethical concerns and the precision of its applications. Concerns have been raised concerning the possible hazards and abuse of these approaches. This research offers a complete "state of the art" assessment of how neuromarketing affects customer behavior. Future studies can back up these results with empirical evaluations of clients from diverse industries and geographical regions. Neuromarketing is a unique method of marketing comprehension. It could help marketing professionals promote and sell items more successfully when applied appropriately and with a strong emphasis on ethical ideals. It can be a useful technique for determining the appropriate target audience for certain items (Glaenzer, 2016). Finally, acquiring a thorough grasp of the cognitive operations of the brain may provide solutions to a variety of marketing-related concerns (Costa et al., 2014).

KEYWORDS

- **neuromarketing**
- **neuroscience**
- **consumer behavior**
- **advertising**
- **purchase decision**

REFERENCES

Bakardjieva, E.; Kimmel, A. J. Neuromarketing Research Practices: Attitudes, Ethics, and Behavioral Intentions. *Ethics Behav.* **2017,** *27* (3), 179–200.

Barbasso, L.; Cortez, J.; Butter, W. Studio Reazioni Corticali e Subcorticali a Diverse Tipologie di Packaging Attraverso fMRI. Unpublished Study, 2015.

Berns, G. S.; Moore, S. E. A Neural Predictor of Cultural Popularity. *J. Consum. Psychol.* **2012,** *22* (1), 154–160.

Bigne, J. E.; Andreu, L. Emotions in Segmentation: An Empirical Study. *Ann. Tour. Res.* **2004,** *31* (3), 682–696.

Boksem, M. A. S.; Smidts, A. Brain Responses to Movie Trailers Predict Individual Preferences for Movies and their Population-wide Commercial Success. *J. Mark. Res.* **2015,** *52,* 482.

Boz, H.; Arslan, A.; Koc, E. Neuromarketing Aspect of Tourısm Pricing Psychology. *Tour. Manag. Perspect.* **2017,** *23,* 119–128.

Bryman, A.; Bell, E. *Business Research Methods,* 3rd ed.; Oxford University Press: Oxford, 2011.

Cascio, C. N.; O'Donnell, M. B.; Bayer, J.; Tinney, F. J., Jr.; Falk, E. B. Neural Correlates of Susceptibility to Group Opinions in Online Word-of- mouth Recommendations. *J. Mark. Res.* **2015,** *52* (4), 559–575.

Chater, N.; Loewenstein, G. The under-appreciated drive for sense-making. *J. Org. Behav. Org.* **2016,** *126* (b), 137–154.

Costa Rozan Fortunato, V.; de Moura Engracia Giraldi, J. A Review of Studies on Neuromarketing: Practical Results, Techniques, Contributions and Limitations. *J. Manag. Res.* **2014,** *6* (2), 201–220.

Feenstra, R. A.; Pallarés-Domínguez, D. Ethical Debates on Political Neuromarketing: The Technological Advance and its Potential Impact on the Formation of Public Opinion. *Veritas* **2017,** *36,* 9–28.

Gazdzik, T. Neuromarketing: Seller New World Order. *Вісник Львівського університету-Серія економічна* **2017,** *37,* 264–266.

Gazzaniga, M. S. *The Cognitive Neurosciences*. Cambridge,MIT Press: MA/London, 2004.

Ghorpade, R. Neuromarketing: New Science of Consumer Behavior. *AADYA-Natl. J. Manag. Technol. (NJMT)* **2017,** *7,* 199–206.

Glaenzer, E. Are the Brain and the Mind One?: Neuromarketing and How Consumers Makedecisions. 2016. http://digitalcommons.colby.edu/cgi/viewcontent.cgi?article=1831a ndcontext=honorstheses. (accessed Jan 3, 2018).

Google Trends. *Google Trends.* 2018. https://trends.google.it/trends/. (accessed Jan 3, 2018).

Green, S.; Holbert, N. Gifts of Neuroimaging: Science and Speculation in the Age of Neuromarketing. *Mark. Res.* **2012** *24* (1), 10–14.

Hazeldine, S. *Neuro-sell: How Neuroscience can Power Your Sales Success*. Kogan Page Limited: Croydon, 2014.

Hilderbrand, M. L. *Neuromarketing: An Essential Tool in the Future of Advertising and Brand Development*. Master thesis, University of Texas, 2016.

Hsu, M. *Neuromarketing: Inside the Mind of the Consumer.* 2016. http://faculty. haas.berkeley. edu/mhsu/papers/Neuromarketing.pdf. (accessed July 27, 2016).

Koc, E. The Role of Family Members in the Family Holiday Purchase Decision-Making Process. *Int. J. Hosp. Tour. Admin.* **2004,** *5* (2), 85–102.

Koc, E.; Boz, H. Triangulation in Tourism Research: A Bibliometric Study of Top Three Tourism Journals. *Tour. Manag. Perspect.* **2014a,** *12,* 9–14.

Koc, E.; Boz, H. Psychoneurobiochemistry of Tourism Marketing. *Tour. Manag.* **2014b,** *44,* 140–148.

Koenigs, M.; Tranel, D. Prefrontal Cortex Damage Abolishes Brand-cued Changes in Cola Preference. *Soc. Cogn. Affect. Neurosci.* **2008,** *3* (1), 1–6.

Lin, C. H.; Tuan, H. P.; Chiu, Y. C. Medial Frontal Activity in Brand-loyal Consumers: A Behavior and Near-infrared ray Study. *J. Neurosci. Psychol. Econ.* **2010,** *3* (2), 59–73.

Lindstrom, M. *Buyology: Truth and Lies About Why We Buy and the New Science of Desire*. Crown Publishing Group: Danvers, 2008.

Lucia-Palacios, L.; Pérez-Lòpez, R.; Polo-Redondo, Y. Atmospheric Excitement, Customers' Moods and Gender: A Study of Young Shoppers. *J. Strat. Mark.* **2017,** 1–16.

McClure, S. M.; Li, J.; Tomlin, D.; Cypert, K. S.; Montague, L. M.; Montague, P. R. Neural Correlates of Behavioral Preference for Culturally Familiar Drinks. *Neuron* **2004,** *44,* 379–387.

Morin, C. Neuromarketing: The new Science of Consumer Behavior. *Society* **2011,** *48* (2), 131–135.

Muth, J. F. Rational Expectations and the Theory of Price Movements. *N. Class. Macroecon.* **1961,** *1,* 3–23.

Nyoni, T.; Bonga, W. G. Neuromarketing: The Journey to Better Consumer Understanding. *J. Econ. Financ.* **2017a,** *2,* 1–10.

Nyoni, T.; Bonga, W. G. Neuromarketing: No Brain, no Gain! *J. Econ. Financ.* **2017b,** *2,* 17–29.

Plassmann, H.; O'Doherty, J.; Shiv, B.; Rangel, A. Marketing Actions can Modulate Neural Representations of Experienced Pleasantness. *PNAS of the USA* **2008,** *105* (3), 1050–1054.

Plassmann, H.; Venkatraman, V.; Huettel, S. A.; Yoon, C. Consumer Neuroscience: Applications, Challenges, and Possible Solutions. *J. Mark. Res.* **2015,** *52,* 427.

Potter, R. F.; Bolls, P. D. *Psychophysiological Measurement and Meaning: Cognitive and Emotional Processing of Media*. Routledge: New York, 2012.

Prelec, D.; Loewenstein, G. The Red and the Black: Mental Accounting of Savings and Debt. *Mark. Sci.* **1998,** *17* (1), 4–28.

Qui, F.; Wu, M. An Experimental Research on the Influence of Cognitive Styles and Negative Emotions on Tourism Decision-making. *Psychol. Sci.* **2005,** *28* (5), 1112–1114.

Ramsoy, T. Z. *Introduction to Neuromarketing and Consumers Science*. Kindle Editions, Kindle Locations, Neurons: Holbæk, 2014.

Smidts, A.; Hsu, M.; Sanfey, A. G.; Boksem, M. A. S.; Ebstein, R. B.; Huettel, S. A.; et al. Advancing Consumer Neuroscience. *Mark. Lett.* **2014,** *25,* 257–267.

Stanton, S. J.; Sinnott-Armstrong, W.; Huettel, S. A. Neuromarketing: Ethical Implications of Its use and Potential Misuse. *J. Bus. Ethics* **2017,** *144* (4), 799–811.

Štrach, P.; Slivkin, N. In *Adaptation Needed: Eye-Tracking Study of Cross-cultural Differences in Perception of B2B Websites*. International Business and Economy Conferences, XVI International Business and Economy Conference, Chile 2017, 2017. https://papers.ssrn.com/sol3/papers. cfm?abstract_id=2920998

Suomala, J.; Palokangas, L.; Leminen, S.; Westerlund, M.; Heinonen, J.; Numminen, J. Neuromarketing: Understanding Customers' Subconscious Responses to Marketing. *Technol. Innov. Manag. Rev.* **2012,** *2* (12), 12–21.

Swarbrooke, J.; Horner, S. *Consumer Behavior in Tourism*.Routledge: Stockport/ Cheshire, 2007.

Tekin, M.; Köylüoğlu, A. S.; Koyuncuoğlu, L. Ö. Research on Consumers' Brain Activations by Means of Electroencephalography Method. *Eur. J. Multidiscip. Stud.* **2017,** *5* (1), 313–322.

Tornati, I. *Il Ruolo Delle Emozioni nei Processi Decisionali del Consumatore: Dalle Neuroscienze al Neuromarketing*. Master Thesis in Marketing and Communication, University Ca' Foscari of Venice, Venice, 2012.

Wirtz, J.; Mattila, A. S.; Tan, R. L. P. The Moderating role of Target-arousal on the Impact of Effect on Satisfaction: An Examination in the Context of Service Experiences. *J. Retail.* **2000,** *76,* 347–365.

Witt, S. T.; Moutinho, L. *Tourism Marketing and Management Handbook*.Prentice Hall Europe: Hertfordshire, 1995.

Yadava, M.; Kumar, P.; Saini, R.; Roy, P. P.; Dogra, D. P. Analysis of EEG Signals and its Application to Neuromarketing. *Multimed. Tools Appl.* **2017,** *76* (18), 19087–19111.

Yoon, C.; Gonzalez, R.; Bechara, A.; Berns, G. S.; Dagher, A. A.; Dube, L.; et al. Decision Neuroscience and Consumer Decision Making. *Mark. Lett.* **2012,** *23,* 473–485.

Żurawicki, L. *Neuromarketing: Exploring the Brain of the Consumer*. Springer, 2010. http://info.4imprint.com/wp-content/uploads/1P-07-0710-July-Blue-Paper Neuromarketing.pdf. (accessed July 27, 2016).

CHAPTER 20

Patient Incivility Experiences in Healthcare Systems: An Exploratory Study

MITALI SENGUPTA[1], ARIJIT ROY[2], SAPTAPARNA GHOSH[1], SATYAJIT CHAKRABARTI[1], and INDRANEEL MUKHOPADHYAY[3]

[1]*Institute of Engineering & Management, School of University of Engineering and Management, Kolkata, India*

[2]*Chikitsa Medicare Pvt. Ltd, Kolkata, West Bengal, India*

[3]*Amity Institute of Information Technology, Amity University, Kolkata, India*

ABSTRACT

Patient incivility experiences are detrimental for long-term relationships among healthcare providers and service recipients. Aspects of incivility are often reported by healthcare personnel (e.g., nurses), but patient incivility remains an area of in-depth research for better patient satisfaction. The Indian healthcare system has also faced aspects of incivility experienced by patients and/or their families.

The researchers undertook a qualitative study (N = 24) with patients and their families who visited public and private healthcare facilities to seek treatment. The leading question underlying this study was "Have you ever felt any form of incivility mated out to you by healthcare practitioners (doctors, nurses, house staff, administrative and billing team, or any other healthcare personnel)? If yes, describe the event."

Based on the responses from study participants, interpretative phenomenological analysis (IPA) was utilized and four main themes were identified. The

---

Agile Business Transformations: Priorities, Lessons, and Practices. Satyajit Chakrabarti, Subrata Chattopadhyay, Udit Chawla, Sundeep Singh Sondhi, & Arunava Dalal (Eds.)

themes were (a) insensitive and rude behavior, (b) social status and identity, (c) mismatched expectation, and ignorance (d) poor communication.

It is important that healthcare personnel be aware of experiences of patients that might seem perceptually discriminative in nature. For a better patient experience and engagement, such situations must be avoided for a congenial healthcare atmosphere.

20.1 INTRODUCTION

One of the most common forms of interpersonal ill-treatment experienced by people across organizations worldwide is incivility of any form. Researchers have revealed that the trends of incivility are on the rise with the passing of time (Schilpzand et al., 2016; Porath and Pearson, 2013). Incivility refers to deviant behavioral attributes at workplaces that are generally of significantly low intensity and have been found to have little-known harmful outcomes (Andersson and Pearson, 1999). According to Cortina et al. (2001) dimensions of incivility are quite diverse and range from factors of perpetration, the context of workplace relationships, psychological well-being, work-related targets, and healthcare implications (Adams and Webster, 2013).

Incivility and its attributes are therefore, pervasive in nature and a number of studies have reported aspects of incivility in workplaces (Guidroz et al., 2010; Spence Laschinger et al., 2009). Most of the incidences of incivility have been reported by nurses or hospital employees (D'ambra and Andrews, 2014). Interestingly, little research has been done on different attributes of incivility, faced by patients or their families. A few researchers highlighted deviant behaviors experienced by patients that include abuse of some kind (Daly et al., 2011; Maya et al., 2018). Ha et al. (2010), have identified interpersonal problems to be one of the major focuses of patient–physician communication. It is important to note that while these studies identify interpersonal problems, however, not all of these issues lead to disrespect or problems that have behavioral aspects. Most importantly, the construct "incivility" is largely multidimensional in nature and has been perpetrated beyond the horizon of physicians or nurses but also includes other healthcare personnel that fall outside the purview of the communication process. Therefore, the range of uncivil behavioral attributes faced by patients might not be fully covered during the process.

The Indian healthcare system comprises of both public- and private-funded healthcare facilities (Selvaraj et al., 2022). The corresponding waiting time, infrastructure, mode of operations, and customer service of these facilities are quite different from one another. The private-funded hospitals mostly rely on out-of-pocket expenditures and therefore financial solvency of patients and their families is an integral factor in deciding the choice of the facility in a number of scenarios.

This study has attempted to investigate a comprehensive series of experiences that patients and their families face in a hospital. The researchers have identified the instances that have been captured regarding workplace incivility that has been experienced by patients and families during their interactions in hospitals/ healthcare setups. However, workplace incivility targeting any specific group has not been explored. Additionally, aspects of incivility faced by nursing personnel could be very different from the experiences faced by patients and their families.

20.2 METHODOLOGY

These data are part of a larger qualitative study that has documented attributes of patient experience during visits to healthcare facilities. Study respondents (N = 35) were recruited from eastern parts of India and verbal informed consent was taken from them. The major pertinent questions asked to the study participants included, "Have you ever felt any form of incivility mated out to you by healthcare practitioners (doctors, nurses, house staff, administrative and billing team, or any other healthcare personnel)? If yes, describe the event." The same question was also translated in Hindi and Bangla, for the respondents to answer it. The vernacular answers were translated to English without altering the meaning, using the back translation method (Tyupa, 2011; Sengupta et al., 2019). The participants had to fill up their experience in detail in the corresponding form provided to them. Out of 35 respondents, 11 (31%) indicated that they had never experienced any form of incivility in hospital settings. The rest of the participants had experienced some form of incivility at least once in hospital settings.

The detailed sociodemographics are given in Table 20.1. Interpretative phenomenological analysis (IPA) was used for identification and interpretation of the data (Smith and Osborn, 2008; Griffin and May, 2012). The detailed reports shared by participants were read closely numerous times by the authors, MS and AR, and these annotations were then developed in preliminary themes based on experiences of incivility. These themes were a result of participant's experience and therefore the final themes were carefully integrated with the experiences of participants. Revaluation and revisiting of definitions of incivility was constantly done independently by the two researchers and the final themes were devised after mutual agreement among all four authors. Details of themes and quotes demonstrating the exact statements and their closed relationship with patient incivility have been described in details in the result section.

TABLE 20.1 Socioeconomic Details of the Respondents.

Description		Healthcare recipients		Total
		Patients	Next of kin	
Sample Size		11	13	24
Gender	Male	5	7	12
	Female	6	6	12
Education	High school	5	3	8
	Graduation	4	6	10
	Postgraduation	2	3	5
	Above Postgraduation	0	1	1
Monthly income (in INR; 1 USD = 75 INR approximately)	Below 20,000	3	2	5
	20,000–50,000	7	8	15
	Above 50,000	1	3	4

20.3 RESULTS

The total study participants were found to be $N = 24$. The participation ratio of males and females was found to be equal, that is, 50 males and 50% females. The participants belonged to both urban and rural settings. These participants had the experience of visiting public and private healthcare facilities. The inclusion criteria included patients and families that have at least faced one instance of hospital incivility during their visit to any healthcare facility.

Four main themes were identified from the written anecdotes shared by participants (Figure 20.1). These are described in the following.

20.3.1 INSENSITIVE AND RUDE BEHAVIOR

The participants reflected on the rude behavior they faced during their interactions with hospital authorities. This is one of the most common forms of incivility experienced by almost all the participants. Many of the participants (approximately 29%) also documented "rude" behavior from one or more healthcare personnel.

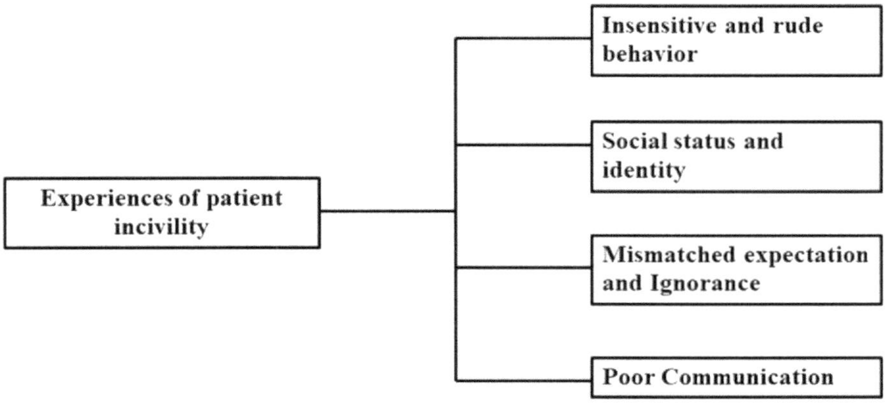

FIGURE 20.1 The different themes underlying patient incivility as experienced by study respondents.

A few excerpts shared by the respondents

> *"The OPD receptionist stopped responding when I asked twice about the arrival update of the doctor. My son (aged 6 years) was coughing badly and I was anxious to see the doctor. Felt as if I had come for free treatment."* (A 39-year-old mother describing her experience in a private healthcare facility.)
>
> *"I requested the doctor to check on my father as I felt something was not right. He was rude and reminded that he understands symptoms more than me. Gave some medicines and I got my father back. After two days, he landed in the ICU of another hospital with acute chest infection."* (A 27-year-old daughter of a 61-year-old male patient.)

20.3.2 SOCIAL STATUS AND IDENTITY

The socioeconomic status of individuals has a direct impact on the quality of healthcare service they experience. A few of them identified their social identity (e.g., their profession or socioeconomic status) to be contributory to the outcome they received.

As outlined by the patients,

> *"I was mostly asked to wait while the other patients were taken inside for check up. Whenever, I finally went, there were no dialogues but decisions given out regarding what I needed to do. I mainly never got chance even to ask questions. Sometimes, I was given free medicines."* (A 48-year-old male diabetic patient.)

"I stay very far from the government hospital. It takes me about 2 hours to reach the place. I have noticed that no one wants to talk to me or answer my queries. They are very busy. I wish I had money to go to those big hospitals." (A 57-year-old female patient.)

"I met with an accident and was wheeled in to one of the big corporate hospitals (names it). When the emergency doctor realized, I might not afford the same, she gave two pain killers and wrote my discharge advice. I was not even given the wheel chair as I waited for my family to pick me from the hospital." (A 41-year-old female patient.)

20.3.3 MISMATCHED EXPECTATION AND IGNORANCE

Healthcare institutions are places where the service providers and service recipients mutually interact with one another. The perceptions, experiences, and circumstances often create room for mismatched expectations and feelings of ignorance.

The same has been cited as follows:

"I was due for my surgery and even when I told the doctor that I could still feel sensations in my leg, the team didn't take me seriously and instead ignored my moans... I could feel the razor going through my leg and screamed in pain. That is when they realized I wasn't lying. Still, nobody consoled or accepted their mistake." (A 25-year-old male sportsperson.)

"I took my mother to the emergency department. The nurse informed that all the beds were full. I need to keep her in the floor or take her to some other facility. I did not have enough money or knew where to go. I had to no choice but to keep her in the floor, just with a bed-sheet underneath as I held the saline bottle, since there was no stand... Never thought in my life that I will have to go through this." (A 19-year-old boy of a 46-year-old patient.)

20.3.4 POOR COMMUNICATION

Communication is integral to all healthcare interactions. However, communication attributes can create issues and dissatisfaction in situations of inadequacy, inefficiency and ineffectiveness. Many respondents including patients and families identified communication laxities to be overwhelming and have severe negative outbursts. One of the most commonly encountered instances of poor communication reflected a discussion of a condition or disease without any compassion. Moreover, the absence of enough or adequate information from the healthcare providers made it difficult for the recipients to undertake an informed decision or give consent.

As described by the respondents is as follows:

> *"I still remember when I had just given birth and came back to my ward after a couple of hours. I was eagerly waiting for my child to be given next to me, however, when I asked the nursing attendant, she couldn't tell when the child would be handed over. Only after 8-9 hours, I was taken to the nursery and was allowed to feed her. I was emotionally vulnerable and as I wanted to stay there for some more time, another attendant came and wheeled me out of the nursery without even telling me anything."* (A 31-year-old patient.)
>
> *"I took my father, a farmer, to the doctor since he had fainted twice in three days. I wanted to understand why this was happening to him. The on-duty doctor did not even look at me, nor did he touch my father. He simply wrote some medicines and asked me to give it to him. Even the instructions were not clearly told."* (A 22-year-old son.)

20.4 DISCUSSION

This study has been instrumental in capturing the incivility faced in health-care settings from the perspective of patients. As the study respondents are experts in terms of their experiences they have gathered, four major themes have been identified. We have found that the reflections of incivility seem to be present in almost many of the patient experiences that have been identified from different sources. For instance, when an individual reaches the reception desk and interacts after entering the hospital, whether public or private, they might experience some degree of changes in behavioral dynamics due to their appearance, social perception, and prior knowledge (Vargas and Mahalingam, 2020). Similarly, questions or clarifications asked to the emergency department personnel might not always be dealt with as per patient/ family expectations. Therefore, the themes identified above have successfully captured the dynamic interactions and interpersonal experiences of patients and families which could be different from any forms of incivility that is faced by other hospital employees. This is one of the first studies that have underscored the importance of only focusing on incivilities faced by patients and families in the Indian healthcare system.

Numerous forms of uncivil behaviors were reported by the study respondents. These included ignorance, social perception and underlying discrimination, rude behavior, insensitivity to the need and situation and communication inadequacy. Many researchers have identified that incivility among individuals, although pervasive, definitely undermines the process of controlling individuals and eventually it also undermines the quality of healthcare and associated services (Wallston et al., 1978).

Interestingly, there were also a few observations that emerged during these interactions with participants. For instance, while incivility mostly referred to minor forms of mistreatment, the fact that overlooking certain observations by patients or families or not considering some symptoms seriously, resulted in serious implications and is a clear stance of discrimination. Many people also documented aspects of trauma associated with the inability to secure timely treatment and therefore, the actual health implications of patient incivility need to be explored in greater detail considering multidimensional attributes.

Further, follow-up studies are required to narrow down to specific attributes of patient incivility and its direct and indirect implications on health consequences. More research on the availability of exact medical history and other factors in the underlying context shall go a long way to make informed choices and identify patient incivility and its consequences.

20.5 CONCLUSION AND RECOMMENDATION

Healthcare incivility and associated behavioral experiences of patients during their visits to hospitals and healthcare facilities of different statures reflect the dynamic instances of interactions, experiences, and perceptual differences faced by patients and families. Preliminarily, it is clear that patient incivility definitely has a negative impact on health outcomes and long-term healthcare provider–recipient relationships.

Furthermore, in-depth research on patient incivility and corresponding training and awareness programs for healthcare personnel can help in patient engagement and also keep the patient–provider conflicts at bay.

KEYWORDS

- **patient incivility**
- **interpersonal relationship**
- **satisfaction healthcare**
- **India**

REFERENCES

Adams, G. A.; Webster, J. R. Emotional Regulation as a Mediator Between Interpersonal Mistreatment and Distress. *Eur. J. Work Org. Psychol.* **2013,** *22* (6), 697–710.

Andersson, L. M.; Pearson, C. M. Tit for Tat? The Spiraling Effect of Incivility in the Workplace. *Acad. Manag. Rev.* **1999,** *24* (3), 452–471.

Cortina, L. M.; Magley, V. J.; Williams, J. H.; Langhout, R. D. Incivility in the Workplace: Incidence and Impact. *J. Occup. Health Psychol.* **2001,** *6* (1), 64.

Daly, J. M.; Merchant, M. L.; Jogerst, G. J. Elder Abuse Research: A Systematic Review. *J. Elder Abuse Negl.* **2011,** *23* (4), 348–365.

Griffin, A.; May, V. Narrative Analysis and Interpretative Phenomenological Analysis. *Research. Soc. Cult.* **2012,** *3,* 441–458.

Guidroz, A. M.; Burnfield-Geimer, J. L.; Clark, O.; Schwetschenau, H. M.; Jex, S. M. The Nursing Incivility Scale: Development and Validation of An Occupation-Specific Measure. *J. Nurs. Meas.* **2010,** *18* (3), 176–200.

Ha, J. F.; Longnecker, N. Doctor-patient Communication: A Review. *Ochsner J.* **2010,** *10* (1), 38–43.

Maya, E. T.; Adu-Bonsaffoh, K.; Dako-Gyeke, P.; Badzi, C.; Vogel, J. P.; Bohren, M. A.; Adanu, R. Women's Perspectives of Mistreatment During Childbirth at Health Facilities in GHANA: FINDINGS from a Qualitative Study. *Reprod. Health Matters* **2018,** *26* (53), 70–87.

Porath, C.; Pearson, C. The Price of Incivility. *Harv. Bus. Rev.* **2013,** *91* (1–2), 114–121.

Schilpzand, P.; De Pater, I. E.; Erez, A. Workplace Incivility: A Review of the Literature and Agenda for Future Research. *J. Org. Behav.* **2016,** *37,* S57-S88.

Selvaraj, S.; Karan, K. A.; Srivastava, S.; Bhan, N.; Mukhopadhyay, I.; World Health Organization. India: Health System Review. *Health Syst. Transit.* **2022,** *11* (1).

Sengupta, M.; Chakrabarti, S.; Mukhopadhyay, I. Waiting Time: The Expectations and Preferences of Patients in a Paediatric OPD. *J. Health Manag.* **2019,** *21* (3), 427–442.

Smith, J. A.; Osborn, M. Interpretative Phenomenological Analysis. *Qualitative Psychology: A Practical Guide to Research Methods,* 2nd edn.; Sage: London, 2008; pp 51–80

Spence Laschinger, H. K.; Leiter, M.; Day, A.; Gilin, D. Workplace Empowerment, Incivility, and Burnout: Impact on staff Nurse Recruitment and Retention Outcomes. *J. Nurs. Manag.* **2009,** *17* (3), 302–311.

Tyupa, S. A Theoretical Framework for Back-translation as a Quality Assessment Tool. *New Voices Transl. Stud.* **2011,** *7* (1), 35–46.

Vargas, E. A.; Mahalingam, R. Experiences of Patient Incivility: A Qualitative Study. *J. Patient Exp.* **2020,** *7* (4), 615–620.

Wallston, K. A.; Strudler Wallston, B.; DeVellis, R. Development of the Multidimensional Health Locus of Control (MHLC) Scales. *Health Educ. Monogr.* **1978,** *6* (1), 160–170.

CHAPTER 21

Brand Hatred and Its Effect on Business Performance: A Conceptual Understanding

ASHUTOSH RAI[1], UDIT CHAWLA[2], and SUBRATA CHATTOPADHYAY[2]

[1]*University of Engineering and Management, Kolkata, India*

[2]*Institute of Engineering & Management, School of University of Engineering and Management, Kolkata, India*

ABSTRACT

Marketing managers need to show their contribution to the performance of the brand. There are very few research studies that link marketing to the firm's ability of performance. This conceptual paper serves as a foundation for advancing knowledge and uncovers areas of further research. The concepts here give a high-quality, in-depth understanding of the subject. This paper highlights the development of concepts on brand hatred and its effect on business performance. This paper shows the important link between brand hatred and business performance. This study will motivate and give a valuable framework for advancing research in brand hatred. This paper summarizes and categorizes the existing knowledge. Brand hatred and business performance are described conceptually and logically. Future studies can be done empirically to show the relationship between brand hatred and business performance. This paper tries to put a right balance between the conceptual depth and relevant theoretical maturity of brand hatred.

Agile Business Transformations: Priorities, Lessons, and Practices. Satyajit Chakrabarti, Subrata Chattopadhyay, Udit Chawla, Sundeep Singh Sondhi, & Arunava Dalal (Eds.)

21.1 INTRODUCTION

Brand hatred has been researched recently by many scholars. Literate review of brand hatred has been done by many scholars recently (Yadav and Chakrabarti, 2022; Aziz et al., 2022; Rai et al., 2023). This paper tries to methodologically understand the brand hatred phenomenon (Zarantonello et al., 2016, 2018) and its effect on business performance. The first part of the paper focuses on the conceptualization of brand hatred (Hegner et al., 2017; Fetscherin, 2019). The second part of the paper focuses on various concepts that are widely used by researchers in their business performance studies. Concepts are the systematic ordering of ideas in any field of research. Concepts are concerned with understanding, explanation, and prediction of the phenomenon. Concepts are the application of the methodological approach. The general purpose of the concept is to understand reality. The possible functions of concept can be characterized as being descriptive, analytical, or explanatory in nature, predictive to some extent, and prescriptive in nature. A concept is a unit of knowledge that includes research and deep understanding. This paper shows how facts are organized for the present and future works of research. A scientific theory must match facts. Concepts can be tested by experiment or systematic observation. A conceptual framework usually focuses on selected aspects of the phenomenon under consideration. Brand hatred has the potential to affect business performance. It is very necessary to study the business performance in various aspects and how it affects business.

21.2 LITERATURE REVIEW

Most of the professional and scholarly literature on consumer behavior has neglected consumer hatred toward a brand. Brand bad experiences spread very rapidly in the market and consumer domain. Brand love is more studied, researched, and popular than brand hate. The existing literature can be categorized into three different categories psychoanalysis, social psychology (intergroup/hate crime), and basic emotion research (Johnson et al., 2011; Alba and Lutz, 2013; Romani et al., 2012; Bryson et al., 2013; Farhat and Chaney, 2021). Brand hate has various angles and dimensions. Hate has various psychological and emotional complexities. Consumers may hate a brand because of the brand's symbolic meaning. Alternatively, consumers may feel dislike toward a brand if its parent company disrespects basic human right. Consumers may feel irritated and annoyed due to brand slogans. This theory emphasizes vengeance against slight to one's identity. Negative emotions toward a brand have influence on consumer goodwill and brand finance. As antibrand websites are becoming very common, consumers can easily raise online complaints. Brand hate can be caused due to negative attitudes related to past worst experiences with the product (Kucuk, 2016, 2018a, 2018b, 2021). Most of these research works have been done in non-Indian contest which have got a poor resemblance with the Indian cultural system. Moreover, most of the research papers out of the available limited ones tried to conceptualize brand hatred from a very fragmented point of view. There is a dearth of research that has dealt with a consolidated model which implies brand hatred among consumers.

21.3 RESEARCH METHODOLOGY

The present paper is placed as a theoretical paper. Theoretical studies do not present data, but rather an integration of the concepts. We have integrated concepts and logic from various brand hatred research works and their effect on business performance. The objective of it was to identify the various theories and understand their logical contribution toward the conceptualization of brand hatred and business performance. We have shown how theories have been incorporated from human psychology, marketing practices, and consumer choices.

21.4 BUSINESS PERFORMANCE

As managers have been challenged to prove the significance they bring to their operations, the requirement to correlate marketing with business performance has become increasingly critical. Recent developments in the commercial–finance interface have also started to offer greater evidence of the effects of particular marketing initiatives and other usiness-related assets on businesses' economic performance and financial results.

Atkinson (1998) defines business performance measurement as how an organization achieves its primary and secondary objectives. This concept of business performance measurement is based on strategic performance. The primary objective is defined by the owner and the secondary objective is defined by the stakeholders (Atkinson et al., 1997). This performance management system focuses on senior management planning, outputs, and how stakeholders are negotiated for scope and objectives.

According to the study by Bititci et al. (1997), business performance measurement is very important and critical information system which is used for effective functional performance measurements (Bourne et al., 2003). The business performance management system is used for measurements of planning and business. It is a set of procedures that can have different dimensions (Forza 2000). Business performance measurement is the processing and performance delivery of products, processes, and business units Gates (1999) defined performance measurement as how a company achieves its financial, strategic, and operational targets. Kaplan (1996) defined how business is achieved as organizational financial, customer, internal, and growth in performance.

According to Kerssens et al. (2003), performance is measured internally and externally by evaluating targets of stakeholders and inside managers Maisel (2001). Business performance measurement is how an organization plan, control, and evaluate sales, performance, and operations Neely (1998). Performance management enables us to quantify past and future performance. Rogers (1990) defined business performance measurement as a link between the individual and organizational goals and targets. We have marketing performance measurements also that measure how marketing activities like advertisement, sales, and promotion can be done.

There is a lack of consensus on the business performance definition. Every definition gives a different perspective. Researchers need to work more on business performance. Marketing performance measurement is very crucial and give an important framework for brand management and other marketing future and present direction.

TABLE 21.1 Business Performance Management (BPM) System.

Features of BPM	Role of BPM	Process of BPM
Performance measurements	Strategy implementation	Data evaluation
Marketing impact	Control	Target validity
Financial implications	Internal communication	Rewards
Strategic validity	External communication	Strategy objectives
Rewards	Measurements	Review
	Planning	Performance evaluation
	Relationship maintenance	Measurement design
	Feedback	
	Rewards	

Source: Prepared by Author (2023)

21.5 DOES BRAND HATRED EFFECTS BUSINESS PERFORMANCE?

This is very important question and it needs to be explored and answered. First, we need to understand hate and then we need to understand how it impacts business and past incidents regarding it. We need to place a framework to define a set of procedures to show marketing performance and its link to the brand performance. Hate has a bad influence on customers and can harm organization performance, this is theoretically and conceptually linked but it is not proven empirically. Atwal et al. (2021) studied how the Italian luxury fashion house Dolce and Gabbana brand is affected by hatred in China. Various stages of brand hatred are studied and it should be managed proactively (Atwal et al., 2021).

Brands must be seamlessly included in the strategic planning of the organization. Brand equity has awareness, quality, association and loyalty has four important factors (Aaker, 1996). Brand trust (Gail et al., 2017) and brand orientation (Yu et al., 2018) affect brand performance. Brand performance leads to business performance and is about brand awareness in the market. Customers drive the financial performance of the brand. Brand success is whenever a customer thinks of product category then he must think of the brand. Brand hatred has a significant effect on brand performance and brand performance affects the financial business performance of the organization (Baumgarth, 2010; Gromark et al. 2011). There is a positive significant association between brand performance onto financial performance (Wong and Merrilees, 2008; Brïdson and Evans, 2004). Business performance can be measured through market share (O'Cass and Ngo, 2011), growth in sales, and profitability (Hajipour et al., 2010).

21.6 MANAGERIAL IMPLICATION AND FUTURE DIRECTION

Recently, managers and academicians have been focusing and working more on business performance as it is very vital for the brand's success. A manager's action on the brand has to be justified and result in positive business performance as brand performance success is very critical and has long-term effect on the brand. Recently work on brand business performance has seen more publications based on different frameworks and different variables. However, still there is a need for a more comprehensive framework of brand hatred and its effect on business performance. Future research can be done on various brands and other countries. It is very essential to decide what needs to be measured in business performance and how the procedure and process will be followed for the performance measurements.

21.7 CONCLUSION

Both branding researchers and managers must gain a thorough understanding of how marketing is related to business performance. The field needs a broad framework that will enable the data from several research to be progressively incorporated over time, as few studies can never cover the spectrum of factors and correlations crucial in tying marketing with company performance.

KEYWORDS

- **brand hatred**
- **business performance**
- **conceptual domain**

REFERENCES

Alba, J. W.; Lutz, R. J. Broadening (and Narrowing) the Scope of Brand Relationships. *J. Consum. Psychol.* **2013,** *23* (2), 265–268.

Aaker, D. A. Measuring Brand Equity across Products and Markets. *Calif. Manag. Rev.* **1996,** 102–120.

Atkinson, A. A. Strategic Performance Measurement and Incentive Compensation. *Eur. Manag. J.* 1998, *16* (5), 552–561.

Atwal, G.; Bryson, D.; Kaiser, M. The Chopsticks Debacle: How Brand Hate Flattened Dolce & Gabbana in China. J. Bus. Strat. **2021,** *43* (1), 37–43. doi: ttps://doi.org/10.1108/JBS-07-2020-0160

Atkinson, A.A.; Waterhouse, J. H.; Wells, R. B. A Stakeholder Approach to Strategic Performance Measurement. *Sloan Manag. Rev.* **1997,** *38* (3) 25–37.

Aziz, R.; Rahman, Z. Brand Hate: A Literature Review and Future Research Agenda. *Eur. J. Mark.* **2022,** *56* (7), 2014–2051.

Baumgarth, C. Living the Brand‖: Brand Orientation in the Business-to-Business Sector. *Eur. J. Mark.* **2010,** 653–671.

Bititci, U. S.; Carrie, A. S.; Mcdevitt, L. Integrated Performance Measurement Systems: A Development Guide. *Int. J. Oper. Prod. Manag.* **1997,** *17* (5–6), 522–534.

Bourne, M. C. S.; Neely, A. D.; Mills, J. F.; Platts, K. W. Implementing Performance Measurement Systems: A Literature Review. *Int. J. Bus. Perform. Manag.* **2003,** *5* (1), 1–24.

Bryson, D.; Atwal, G.; Hult′en, P. Towards the Conceptualisation of the Antecedents of Extreme Negative Affect Towards Luxury Brands. *Qual. Mark. Res. Int. J.* **2013,** *16* (4), 393–405.

Bridson, K.; Evans, J. The Secret to a Fashion Advantage is Brand Orientation. *Int. J. Retail Distrib. Manag.* **2004,** 403–411.

Hegner, S. M.; Fetscherin, M.; van Delzen, M.; Determinants and Outcomes of Brand Hate. *J. Prod. Brand Manag.* **2017,** *26* (1), 13–25.

Farhat, Z.; Chaney, D. Introducing Destination Brand Hate: An Exploratory Study. *Curr. Issues Tourism.* **2021,** *24* (17), 2472–2488.

Fetscherin, M. The Five Types of Brand Hate: How They Affect Consumer Behavior. *J. Bus. Res.* **2019,** *101*, 116–127.

Forza, C.; Salvador, F. Assessing Some Distinctive Dimensions of Performance Feedback Information in High Performing Plants. *Int. J. Oper. Produc. Manag.* **2000,** *20* (3), 359–385.

Gates, S. *Aligning Strategic Performance Measures and Results*; The Conference Board: New York; 1999.

Gail, M. D.; Siphiwe, D. Does Brand Orientation Lead to Brand Loyalty Among Senior and Top Management in a South African Business-Tobusiness Organisation? *S. Afr. J. Bus. Manag.* **2018,** *49* (1), 1–28.

Gromark, J.; Melin, F. The Underlying Dimensions of Brand Orientation and Its Impact on Financial Performance. *J. Brand Manag.* **2011,** 394–410.

Hajipour, B.; Bagheri, M.; Ghanavati, M. The Impact of Socio-Cultural Innovation and Brand Management on Financial Performance and Brand Performance of the Companies Listed in Tehran Stock Exchange. *Int. Res. J. Int. Stud.* **2010,** *15,* 55–68.

Johnson, A. R.; Matear, M.; Thomson, M. A Coal in the Heart: Self-Relevance as a Post-Exit Predictor of Consumer Anti-Brand Actions. *J. Consum. Res.* **2011,** *38* (1), 108–125.

Kaplan, R. S.; Norton, D. P. Linking the Balanced Scorecard to Strategy (Reprinted From the Balanced Scorecard). *Calif. Manag. Rev.* **1996,** *39* (1), 53–79.

Kucuk, S. U. Legality of Brand Hate. In *Brand Hate. Palgrave Macmillan*; Cham, 2016. https://doi.org/10.1007/978-3-319-41519-2_6

Kucuk, S. U. Macro-level Antecedents of Consumer Brand Hate. *J. Consum. Mark.* **2018a,** *35* (5), 555–564.

Kucuk, S. U. *Brand Hate: Navigating Consumer Negativity in the Digital World*, 2nd ed.; Springer, 2018b.

Kucuk, S. U. Developing a Theory of Brand Hate: Where are We Now? *Strat. Change.* **2021,** *30* (1), 29–33.

Kerssens-Van Drongelen, I. C.; Fisscher, O. A. M. Ethical Dilemmas in Performance Measurement. *J. Bus. Ethics.* **2003,** *45* (1–2), 51–63.

Maisel, L. S. *Performance Measurement Practices Survey Results*; AICPA: US, 2001.

Neely, A. D. *Measuring Business Performance: Why, What and How*; the Economist and Profile Books Ltd.: London, UK, 1998.

O'Cass, A.; Ngo, L. V. Market Orientation Versus Innovative Culture: Two Routes to Superior Brand Performance. Eur. J. Mark. **2007,** *41* (7/8), 868–887.109.

Rai, A.; Chawla, U.; Chattopadhyay, S. Brand Hatred: a Literature Review and Research Agenda. *Int. J. Prof. Bus. Rev.* **2023,** *8* (3), 9.

Rogers, S. *Performance Management in Local Government*; Longman: London, UK, 1990.

Romani, S.; Grappi, S.; Dalli. D. Emotions that Drive Consumers Away from Brand: Measuring Negative Emotions towards Brands and their Behavioural Effects. *Int. J. Res.in Mark.* **2012,** *29,* 55–67.

Wong, H. Y.; Merrilees, B. The Performance Benefits of Being Brand-Orientated. *J. Prod. Brand Manag.* **2008,** 372–383.

Yadav, A.; Chakrabarti, S. Brand Hate: A Systematic Literature Review and Future Research Agenda. *Int. J. Consum. Stud.* **2022,** *46* (5), 1992–2019.

Yu, C.; Wang, X.; Dennis, B. Enhancing Firm Performance: The Role of Brand Orientation in Business-Tobusiness Marketing. *Indus. Mark. Manag.* **2018,** 1–9.

Zarantonello, L.; Romani, S.; Grappi, S.; Fetscherin, M. Trajectories of Brand hate. *J. Brand Manag.* **2018,** *25* (6), 549–560.

Zarantonello, L.; Romani, S.; Grappi, S.; Bagozzi, R. P. Brand Hate. J. Prod. Brand Manag. **2016,** *25* (1), 11–25.

CHAPTER 22

Factors Influencing the Adoption of Digital Transactions

SOUMIK GANGOPADHYAY, SUCHANA ROY, ARYAN DEB, PRIYANKA DEY, SAPTAPARNI DHOL, and SATYADIP BISWAS

Institute of Engineering & Management, School of University of Engineering and Management, Kolkata, India

ABSTRACT

In daily life, digital transactions are becoming increasingly important. The present paper has attentively focused on the respondents' perceptions of the acceptability of digital transactions. A structured series of questions were used to elicit the opinions of 200 respondents in the above-18 age group. The outcome of the dimension reduction study indicates that, out of the various studies that make up digital transactions, the perceived utility and threat of using cybercash are those that have the greatest influence on the general public. While people are taking advantage of every opportunity, convenience, and utility in general, they are also wary of some of its consequences, such as cybercrime and cyberattacks. By the detailed study of all the influencing factors and the knowledge gathered from the public, it is fair to say that majority of the people are looking forward to a bright digital economy for this country.

Agile Business Transformations: Priorities, Lessons, and Practices. Satyajit Chakrabarti, Subrata Chattopadhyay, Udit Chawla, Sundeep Singh Sondhi, & Arunava Dalal (Eds.)

22.1 INTRODUCTION

Everything in today's world is online, but is really everything online? In India, the use of mobile phones and the Internet has significantly increased during the past decade.

A significant factor in a nation's ability to flourish economically and socially is its payment system. The bulk of essential services provided to inhabitants require payment, which is at the heart of all economic activity in a city, including wages, consumer spending, business purchases, and tax collection. As a result, more and more cities are realizing the benefits of smart payment technology and the crucial role it plays in realizing the nation's vision for smart cities. With the introduction of "Digital India," the government of India desires to create a cashless society in India. Digital payment methods include BHIM-UPI, IMPS, NACH, RTGS, NETC, AePS, credit cards, debit cards, RTGS, NEFT, PPI, Internet banking, mobile banking, and mobile wallets. To encourage cashless transactions, a number of digital payment methods are available, including UPI, Micro ATMs, Internet Banking, and Banking Cards. It has momentum in providing service at home to customers and thus earned commercial value. Several of the 20 communities selected for this vision are already far on their way to benefiting from their payment's digital activities, while others have recently deployed projects toward accomplishing the same.

TABLE 22.1 Modes of Digital Transaction Methods in India.

Digital payment mode	Year of introduction	Source
RTGS	2004	Reserve Bank of India (RBI)
NEFT	November 2005	RBI
IMPS	22 November 2010	National Payments Corporation of India (NPCI)
UPI	11 April 2016	NPCI

Source: Secondary data.

Digital India is a step forward toward a "faceless, paperless, and cashless" economy. When merchants wish to increase their digital payment alternatives in response to rising consumer demand, the rate of digital payment in India increased to 53% in 2022 from 38% in 2021. The monthly UPI transaction value reached ₹3 lakhs crores in September 2020, 4 years after its launch in 2016. And it has nearly doubled to ₹7 lakhs crores in a year. Digital

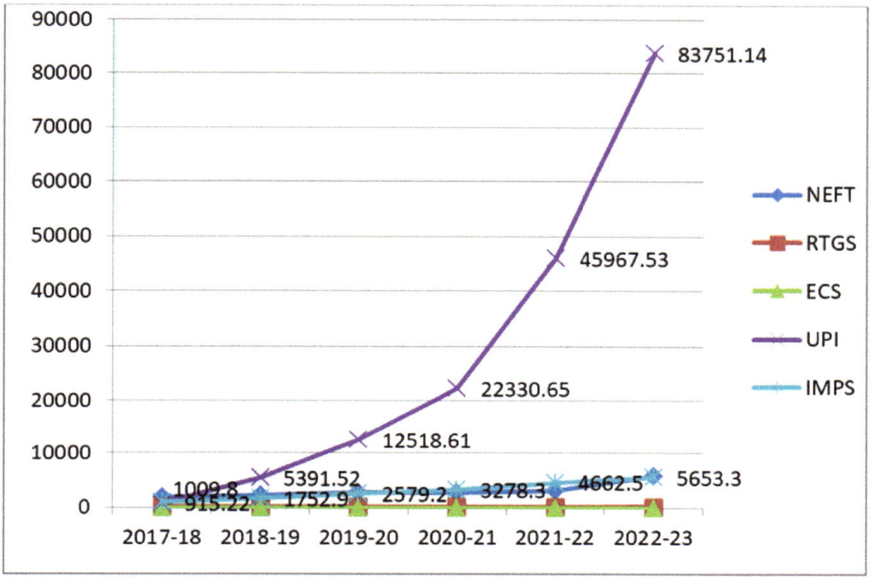

FIGURE 22.1 Total number of digital transactions in India.
Source: Reserve Bank of India (RBI)

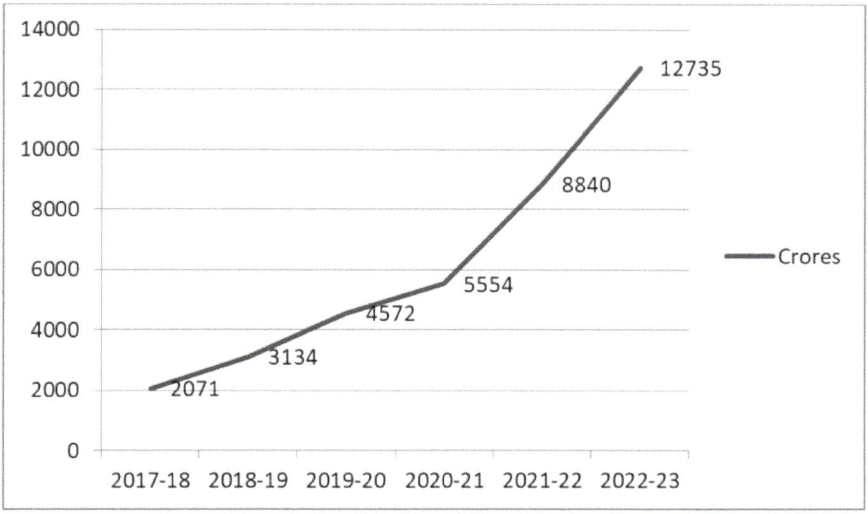

FIGURE 22.2 Trends of digital transactions in India.
Source: Reserve Bank of India (RBI)

transactions have sparked various payment trends that are expected to have an impact on both consumers and enterprises. They are essential to the concept of the "smart city," and local governments and their constituents are beginning to recognize the value they provide. According to estimates, UPI is used by customers to make about 47% of all payments in FY22, with only 6% using mobile wallets. Customers use UPI for over 47% of all payments in FY22, compared to mobile wallets for only 6% of payments.

While the nation started the process of converting to a cashless economy, it is inevitable that companies of all sizes digitize their operations and accept payments via an assortment of methods, including cards, mobile wallets, UPI, etc. The Point of Sale is one of a company's most crucial components.

The research's overarching goals were to: (a) comprehend the preference for digital transactions; (b) apprehend the elements affecting the change; and (c) pinpoint the causes of the change in payment.

22.1.1 PERCEIVED VALUE OF DIGITAL TRANSACTION

Consumer adoption of new technology, such as digital currencies, is significantly influenced by perceived value. "Idiosyncratic analysis" that derive from a good or service in comparison to its price is known as perceived value. The perceived value of the e-rupee can be quantified in terms of its practicality, security, accessibility, and cost-efficiency.

22.1.2 PERCEIVED OBJECTIVE OF DIGITAL TRANSACTION

The variables affecting Indian customers' acceptance of digital payments have been the subject of several research. According to research, Indian consumers' acceptance of digital payments was largely impacted by their perceptions of their utility, usability, and security. Additionally, the adoption of digital payments among Indian customers is greatly influenced by trust, convenience, and perceived risk. Digital exchanges have always been seen as cashless. With the addition of contactless payment, it enables rapid payments (Joshi, 2017), a complete and accurate history of transactions, and a greater degree of security (Dimitrova et al., 2022). Digital payment techniques have improved accessibility by lowering late payments and processing costs (Somasundaram and Litt, 2020) compared to conventional cashless alternatives. The use of any digital payment system has been seen to vary with age

(Chawla and Joshi, 2019). The rapid and simple setup of digital payment systems makes it possible to reduce carbon footprint (Tenhunen and Penttinen, 2010). Other perks such as rewards (Garg and Kaur, 2019) and low risk of theft (Sujith and Julie, 2017) have turned out to be very convenient for the public creating a strong background and financial stability. Digital payment methods as a whole have been very efficient (Pal et al., 2018). Even though there are so many great qualities of digital payment methods, the adverse effect of overspending (Hussain, 2022) and issues related to the availability of the Internet (Hussain, 2022) still prevail over time which further can have payments blocked during crucial transactions (Hussain, 2022). People are also worried about being vulnerable to cases of cyberattack.

22.1.3 PERCEIVED SUBJECTIVE VALUE OF DIGITAL TRANSACTION

Recently introduced digital currency has been perceived as more secure and suitable for transacting privately. It has become more popular among national policymakers due to its centralized mode of control, controlled supply, control over beneficiaries, irreversible transaction flawless cross-border transaction, ease of offline mode of transaction, and anonymity of transaction (Darbha and Arora, 2020), reduced illicit transaction (Soderberg et al., 2022), zero charge of interest (Priyadarshini and Kar, 2021), easy recoverability (Miedema et al., 2020) and least chance of cyberattack (Tian et al., 2023). Further, e-transaction has also been preferred due to the option of direct transfer of money (Bossu et al., 2020), reduced transactional cost, and instant settlements (Ahmat and Bashir, 2017). The rise in e-commerce (Didenko and Buckley, 2018) has been fueled by the ease of shift in large volume (Bordo and Levin, 2017), public trust (Hussain, 2022), the least cost of implementing (Morales-Resendiz et al., 2021). However, most concerns over the recently introduced options were network effects and less public education. Overall, this makes it easier to avoid forgeries, have simple tracking, and readily exchange like currency. Additionally, this may promote creativity and competition in the realm of payment systems.

The available research shows that many characteristics of mass perception, such as perceived benefit, perceived ease of use, perceived usefulness, perceived control, perceived danger, and perceived behavioral regulation, all have a role in how people perceive the value of e-transactions. However, exploring the characteristics or elements driving people's intentions to choose e-transactions is the potential study direction.

22.2 METHODS

This research is the summation of secondary and primary data. Secondary data has been collected from different websites, newspaper articles, and journals. As evidenced by the previous researchers, cashless transaction (Var 1), hassle free (Var 2), convenience (Var 3), accessibility (Var 4), rewards (Var 5), transaction record (Var 6), secured transaction (Var 7), processing cost (Var 8), contactless payment (Var 9), risk of threat (Var 10), efficient (Var 11), carbon-foot print (Var 12), quick (Var 13), duration of the transaction (Var 14), cyberattack (Var 15), Internet and server facility (Var 16), Overall spending (Var 17), Urban choice (Var 18), Easy sharing of information (Var 19), Positive attitude toward cashless transaction (Var 20) have been considered as variables influencing the perceived value of the digital transaction.

Primary data has been collected in the form of questionnaires from both the earning as well as the dependent classes of people. It contains close-ended questions that have collected the reflection of the respondents on a 5-point Likert scale anchored as "strongly agree," "agree," "undecided," "disagree" and "strongly disagree," which are coded as 5, 4, 3, 2, and 1. 30 observed variables as explored by the previous researchers have been identified as variables that can influence the choice of digital or e-transactions. The survey questionnaire has been developed based on a literature review and expert input. The questionnaire includes questions on the perceived value of digital transactions, digital literacy, business size, frequency of using e-payment methods, and other demographic information.50 respondents have been chosen equally from four parts of Kolkata, India as sample respondents. So, a total of 223 responses have been received from which 200 have been considered for final selection.

Primary data collected by such a technique has been coded and standardized. The primary data has been analyzed by using Excel and other statistical software.

22.3 ANALYSIS AND RESULTS

The primary data analysis explored that 46% of the respondents are female and 54% account for male in which 37% aged between 18 and 25 years, 23% are belonged to the 25–32 years age group, 20% are between 32 and 39 years age group, 10% are aged between 39 and 45 years and last but not the least, and 10% are above 46 years of age. It has also come to light that amongst our respondents 25% of the groups are undergraduates, 33% are graduates,

26% are postgraduates and 16% have acquired higher degrees after their postgraduation studies. The data has revealed that among the respondents 4, 13, 15, 21, and 47% fall into the monthly household income of less than ₹25,000, ₹25,001–50,000, ₹50,001–75,000, ₹75,001–100,000, and above ₹00,000, respectively. In the studied group 44% work in the service sector, 7% have businesses, 9% are professionals, 5% are homemakers and the rest 35% are dependent on others.

The study has also observed that in today's time, cashless transactions are preferred to cash or other forms of payments by majority of the respondents. Majority of the respondents have agreed that digital payment methods are hassle free, involves less time to transact and are more efficient than other offline methods. Respondents have also agreed that the setups of digital payment methods/digital wallets are quicker and easier. This study has supported the prior research that, digital wallets/digital payment methods are more convenient along with being more accessible than other offline methods. Results also indicated the subjective inclination toward receiving rewards like cash back and coupons. Respondents have also confirmed that transaction history provided by digital wallets/digital payment methods help to keep a track of day-to-day transactions, unlike cash transactions. The transaction history provided by digital wallets/digital payment methods helps to keep a track of daily transactions. Most of the respondents have also agreed that digital transacting provides more security than other traditional non-digital methods and digital payment methods help saving more processing cost as compared to others. The contactless payment options that digital payment platforms provide make a huge difference for its users. Subjective respondents also confirmed that there is a lower risk of theft during a digital transaction than that of cash.

It is interesting to observe, that irrespective of age majority agreed that digital payment methods have potential to minimize the carbon footprint. The maximum number of respondents oscillate from agreeing and remaining undecided about whether digital payment methods are more prone to cyberattacks or not. Further, a dominating number of the respondents have agreed to the statement that online payments face Internet and other server problems. The analysis adds value to the existing research when the result explores that respondents perceive that digital transaction enhances overall spending as a by-product of the current trend of using digital payment techniques. Interestingly, respondents agree that cash transactions are preferred to digital payment by urban users.

Further, respondents have confirmed that information about various forms of digital payments is explicitly shared with the users. Therefore, the analysis signals that amount of positive attitudes toward a completely cashless economy is increasing.

To reveal the factors influencing the adoption of digital payments, Factor analysis has been done. The dataset has 200 plus responses which is 5 times more than the variables studied. The Cronbach's alpha value, that is, the scale reliability coefficient is 0.7788. Kaiser–Meyer–Olkin (KMO) measure of sampling adequacy is a statistic) value of the said analysis is 0.621. All the values are conforming to the thumb rule. Hence, we may proceed with factor analysis. The factor analysis has revealed the following 4 factors with eigenvalues greater than 1, i.e., 3.68, 1.20, 1.03 and 0.95 respectively for factor 1, factor 2, factor 3, and factor 4. Only, the first two factors have variables with loading greater than 0.5.

Factor I – Var 1, Var 3, Var 4, Var 7, Var 8, Var 9, Var 10

Var 1: Cashless transactions are preferred to cash or other forms.
Var 3: Digital wallets/digital payment methods are more convenient.
Var 4: Digital payment methods are more accessible than offline methods.
Var 7: Transacting digitally is more secure than the other traditional non-digital methods.
Var 8: More processing costs are saved when opting for digital payment methods.
Var 9: The contactless payment options that digital payment platforms provide make a huge difference for its users.
Var 10: There is lower risk of theft when transacting digitally than that of cash.

Factor II – (Var 10), Var 15

Var 10: There is lower risk of theft when transacting digitally than that of cash.
Var 15: Digital payment methods are more prone to cyberattacks.

Factor I explores the variables, that is, cashless transactions, convenience, accessibility, security, less processing cost, contactless payments, and lower risk of theft. So, Factor I can be termed as "perceived utility" whereas, Factor II has revealed variables like lower risk of threat and cyberattack-like issues. So, Factor II can be termed as "perceived risk."

To justify the value of the perceived comparative importance of adopting digital transactions (Var 20) has to be assessed with respect to the comparative security of digital vs traditional mode of the transaction (Var 7), risk of theft in the transaction (Var 10), and risk of cyberattack in the digital transaction

(Var 15). Therefore, a two-way analysis of variance (ANOVA) has been done between Var 7, Var 10 and Var 20 and between Var 7, Var 15, and Var 20. In both cases, the probability value is less than 0.05 (0.00006 and 0.0000017). So, the null hypothesis has to be rejected in both cases. Therefore, the adoption interest of digital transactions has profound dependence on perceived security of transactions, perceived risk of theft, and perceived risk of cyberattack.

22.4 CONCLUSION

Digital payment methods are shaping the economy in ways more than one. From any tradesman to a regular consumer, everyone tends to make transactions digitally on a daily basis. People are leaning toward digital payment for its own convenience and advantages. They also have a very positive attitude toward the growth of a complete digital economy. Although people are blindsided by the glamour of the trending digital payment options, there are plenty of drawbacks which if not treated can lead to be very harmful. What is important is that the upsides are more than the downsides.

India is pacing toward a cashless economy. With increasing digital dependency, it is necessary to explore the problems usually and regularly faced by users. Utility-related, that is, convenience, and accessibility must be promoted as a homogeneous facility by the digital transaction service providers. Digital transaction service providers must transform their service immune to cyberattacks or security threats. They should highlight issues related to cyberattack and what actions they have taken to minimize it and promote this as unique selling proposition.

KEYWORDS

- **digital transactions**
- **cashless transactions**
- **convenience**
- **accessibility**
- **security**
- **less processing cost**
- **contactless payments**

REFERENCES

Ahmat, N.; Bashir, S. *Central Bank Digital Currency: A Monetary Policy Perspective*; Bank Negara Malaysia Cenral Bank of Malaysia Staff Insights, 2017; vol. 11, pp 1–7.

Bordo, M. D.; Levin, A. T. *Central Bank Digital Currency and the Future of Monetary Policy (No. w23711)*; National Bureau of Economic Research, 2017.

Bossu, W.; Itatani, M.; Margulis, C.; Rossi, A.; Weenink, H.; Yoshinaga, A. Legal Aspects of Central Bank Digital Currency: Central Bank and Monetary Law Considerations. *IMF Working Paper No. 20/254*; 2020.

Central Bank Digital Currency [Online]. Wikipedia. https://en.wikipedia.org/wiki/Central_bank_digital_currency (accessed Jun 30, 2023).

Chadha, S. Explained: How India is Outpacing the World in Digital Payments. *The Times of India*; Dec 30, 2021. https://timesofindia.indiatimes.com/business/india-business/explained-how-india-is-outpacing-the-world-in-digital-payments/articleshow/88580555.cms

Chavda, V. An Empirical Study on Factors Affecting Consumer Adoption of Mobile Payments in Rural Area. *Sankalpa* **2018,** *8* (1), 64–71.

Chawla, D.; Joshi, H. Consumer Attitude and Intention to Adopt Mobile Wallet in India–An Empirical Study. *Int. J. Bank Mark.* **2019,** *37* (7), 1590–1618.

Darbha, S.;.; Arora, R. *Privacy in CBDC Technology (No. 2020-9)*; Bank of Canada, 2020.

Didenko, A. N.; Buckley, R. P. The Evolution of Currency: Cash to Cryptos to Sovereign Digital Currencies. *Fordham Int. Law J.* **2018,** *42,* 1041.

Dimitrova, I.; Öhman, P.; Yazdanfar, D. Barriers to Bank Customers' Intention to Fully Adopt Digital Payment Methods. *Int. J. Qual. Serv. Sci.* **2022,** *14* (5), 16–36.

Garg, S.; Kaur, S. A Comparative Study: Digital Payment Modes vs. Cash on Delivery. *ZENITH Int. J. Multidiscip. Res.* **2019,** *9* (5), 40–45.

Hussain, H. Central Bank Digital Currencies: Reinforcing Public Trust. *Amsterdam LF.* **2022,** *14,* 21.

Immediate Payment Service [Online]. Wikipedia. https://en.wikipedia.org/wiki/Immediate_Payment_Service (accessed May 30, 2023)

Joshi, M. *Digital Payment System: A Feat Forward of India. Research Dimension*; 2017. ISSN: 2249–3867.

Kameswaran, V.; Hulikal Muralidhar, S. Cash, In *Digital Payments and Accessibility: A Case Study from Metropolitan India*, Proceedings of the ACM on Human-Computer Interaction, 3(CSCW), 2019; pp 1–23.

Karjaluoto, H.; Shaikh, A. A.; Leppäniemi, M.; Luomala, R. Examining Consumers' Usage Intention of Contactless Payment Systems. *Int. J. Bank Mark.* **2020,** *38* (2), 332–351.

Kumari, J. M. Central Bank Digital Currency (CBDC) Can It Replace Notes and Coins in India. *Shanlax Int. J. Manag.* **2021,** *8* (S1-Feb), 21–28.

Lee, Y.; Son, B.; Park, S.; Lee, J.; Jang, H. A Survey on Security and Privacy in Blockchain-based Central Bank Digital Currencies. *J. Internet Serv. Inf. Secur.* **2021,** *11* (3), 16–29.

Miedema, J.; Minwalla, C.; Warren, M.; Shah, D. *Designing a CBDC for Universal Access (No. 2020–10)*; Bank of Canada, 2020.

Morales-Resendiz, R.; Ponce, J.; Picardo, P.; Velasco, A.; Chen, B.; Sanz, L.; ... Hodge, A. Implementing a Retail CBDC: Lessons Learned and Key Insights. *Latin Am. J. Cent. Bank.* **2021,** *2* (1), 100022.

National Electronic Funds Transfer [Online]. Wikipedia. https://en.wikipedia.org/wiki/National_Electronic_Funds_Transfer (accessed Jan 2, 2023).

Nelson, B. Financial Stability and Monetary Policy Issues Associated with Digital Currencies. *J. Econ. Bus.* **2018,** *100,* 76–78.

Pal, J.; Chandra, P.; Kameswaran, V.; Parameshwar, A.; Joshi, S.; Johri, A. In *Digital Payment and Its Discontents: Street Shops and the Indian Government's Push for Cashless Transactions*, Proceedings of the 2018 CHI Conference on Human Factors in Computing Systems, 2018; pp 1–13.

Priyadarshini, D.; Kar, S. Central Bank Digital Currency (CBDC): Critical Issues and the Indian Perspective. *Institute of Economic Growth Working Paper*, 2021; p 444.

Real-time Gross Settlement [Online]. Wikipedia. https://en.wikipedia.org/wiki/Real-time_gross_settlement (accessed May 6, 2023).

Reserve Bank of India—Annual Report [Online]. n.d. ttps://m.rbi.org.in/Scripts/AnnualReportPublications.aspx?Id=1322

Schilling, L. Risks Involved with CBDCs: On Cash, Privacy, and Information Centralization. Privacy, and Information Centralization; Nov 1, 2019.

Soderberg, G.; Bechara, M.; Bossu, W.; Che, N. X.; Davidovic, S.; Kiff, J.; ... Yoshinaga, A. *Central Bank Digital Currency Behind the Scenes: Emerging Trends, Insights, and Policy Lessons*; International Monetary Fund: Washington, DC, 2022; p 07.

Somasundaram, M.;Litt, D. A Study on Perception of Consumers towards Digital Payment. *Mukt Shabd J.* **2020,** 9 (6), 2246–2255.

Sujith, T. S.; Julie, C. D. Opportunities and Challenges of E-payment System in India. *Int. J. Sci. Res. Manag.* **2017,** *5* (9), 6935–6943.

Tenhunen, M.; Penttinen, E. In *Assessing the Carbon Footprint of Paper vs. Electronic Invoicing*, ACIS 2010 Proceedings, 2010; p 95

Tian, S.; Zhao, B.; Olivares, R. O. Cybersecurity Risks and Central Banks' Sentiment on Central Bank Digital Currency: Evidence from Global Cyberattacks. *Finance Res. Lett.* **2023,** *53,* 103609.

Unified Payments Interface [Online]. Wikipedia. https://en.wikipedia.org/wiki/Unified_Payments_Interface https://www.npci.org.in/what-we-do/upi/product-statistics (accessed Jun 23, 2023).

CHAPTER 23

Does Customer Co-Creation Influence Customer Loyalty? A Special Reference to Online Video Games

RIKITHA SHETTY[1], JEANNE POULOSE[1], SANJIB BHATTACHARJEE[2], VINOD SHARMA[3], and MANOHAR KAPSE[3]

[1]*School of Business and Management, CHRIST (Deemed to be University), Delhi, India*

[2]*School of Management, Presidency University, Bengaluru, Karnataka, India*

[3]*Symbiosis Center for Management and Human Resource Development (SCMHRD), Symbiosis International (Deemed University), Pune, Maharashtra, India*

ABSTRACT

The research investigates the factors influencing consumer loyalty through co-creation in online video games in Delhi National Capital Region (Delhi-NCR). The study focuses on four independent variables, social motivation, personal motivation, utilitarian motivation, and hedonic motivation, to examine customer engagement through value co-creation, which is mediated through attitudinal and behavioral loyalty. The study collected 200 respondent data through an online survey administered to online video game players in the Delhi-NCR region and analyzed the data using the Statistical Package for the Social Sciences (SPSS) software. The study has several implications for online video game companies operating in the Delhi-NCR region to improve their co-creation strategies and enhance customer loyalty through value co-creation. The study backs to the body of knowledge on co-creation,

Agile Business Transformations: Priorities, Lessons, and Practices. Satyajit Chakrabarti, Subrata Chattopadhyay, Udit Chawla, Sundeep Singh Sondhi, & Arunava Dalal (Eds.)

customer engagement, and loyalty in the online video game industry. However, the stud has a limitation which include the sample size as the data has been collected only from Delhi NCR.

23.1 INTRODUCTION

The online video games industry has grown tremendously in recent years and has become a highly lucrative market. According to a report by Newzoo, the global games market was valued at $174.9 billion in 2020, and it is projected to reach $217.9 billion by 2023, growing at a Compound annual growth rate (CAGR) of 9.4%. The report also states that there were over 2.7 billion gamers worldwide in 2020, with mobile games accounting for 48% of the market. A study by Limelight Networks found that 48% of gamers play online games for more than 7 h a week, with 26% playing for more than 12 h a week. The study also found that 44% of gamers prefer to play with others online rather than alone. This highlights the social aspect of online gaming and the importance of engaging players in a community.

One of the reasons why the online video games industry is so lucrative is the increasing number of gamers worldwide. The rise of mobile gaming has increased access to games, and the pandemic has also increased the demand for online entertainment. Another reason for the industry's success is the emergence of new revenue streams such as in-game purchases, subscriptions, and advertising. In-game purchases, which allow gamers to buy virtual items or currency, accounted for 57% of the mobile games market in 2020. The importance of the online video games industry cannot be overstated. It has created thousands of jobs and significantly contributed to the global economy. The industry has also helped foster creativity and innovation, providing a platform for social interaction and community building.

In the world of online video games, competition is fierce as many companies compete for the attention and loyalty of gamers. To succeed in this environment, it is essential for companies to not only attract new customers but also maintain the loyalty of their current ones. Customer loyalty is vital to any business, and online video games are no exception. Loyal customers are likelier to repeat purchases and recommend the game to others. They are also less likely to switch to a competitor's game, even if it offers similar features. In the online video games industry, customer loyalty can result in long-term profitability and sustainability, an increase in the player base, and a positive reputation for the game.

In addition, the cost of acquiring new customers can be much higher than retaining existing ones. Therefore, companies need to focus on retaining customers through various strategies, such as providing excellent customer service, offering personalized experiences, and creating a sense of community around the game. There are numerous ways to build customer loyalty; one essential method is value co-creation.

Co-creation is a collective process in which customers and corporations create a product or service. In online video games, co-creation can involve allowing players to provide feedback, suggestions, and ideas for the game. This can be done through forums, surveys, or social media platforms. Co-creation has several benefits for companies, such as increased customer engagement, improved product quality, and reduced development costs. For customers, it provides a sense of ownership and involvement in the game, which can lead to increased loyalty. An example of successful co-creation in the online video game industry is Minecraft. The game has a large and active community of players who provide feedback and suggestions to the developers. Many of these suggestions have been implemented in the game, which has helped to create a loyal player base.

In conclusion, customer loyalty is essential for the success of any business, and the online video games industry is no exception. To ensure customer loyalty, companies must provide exceptional customer service, offer personalized experiences, create a sense of community, and consider co-creation as a method to involve players in the development process. By doing so, they can make a loyal player base, increase profitability, and sustain the long-term success of their game. Thus, this study tried to understand the position of co-creation in producing customer loyalty in online video games.

23.2 LITERATURE REVIEW

Before the commencement of this study, a detailed literature review was undertaken to understand the studies that have been done so far in the domain of customer loyalty and, specifically, co-creation. The details of the literature review have been summarized below.

The literature review must begin by examining current theories and phenomena. It is imperative to note that among the various theories, the uses and gratification theory (UGT) and the technology acceptance model (TAM) are prominent. This research paper utilizes the UGT as it is of utmost importance to focus on why individuals use specific media or technologies. This theory sheds light on why customers engage in co-creation activities and how these activities impact their loyalty towards a brand. On the contrary, TAM is more focused on adopting and using new technologies and may need to be more relevant to understanding the complex motivations behind co-creation in the online video games industry. Therefore, UGT is the underpinning theory for this research.

The variables in the UGT are social motivation, personal motivation, utilitarian motivation, hedonic motivation, customer engagement through value co-creation, attitudinal loyalty, and behavioral loyalty.

23.2.1 SOCIAL MOTIVATION

Consumers place a significant value on social connections, according to research on online communities (Claffey and Brady, 2017; Hilvert-Bruce et al., 2018; Nambisan and Baron, 2009). This is so that like-minded people with similar interests can be brought together, which can result in beneficial experiences (Dholakia et al., 2004). Customers must connect and speak with one another to meet their social demands, relying on social features offered by game distributors and designers (Chuang, 2020; Poretski et al., 2019). According to (Dholakia et al. 2004), loneliness relief and social support are two prominent reasons people use virtual platforms. Socialization is therefore essential for encouraging users to engage more actively in online media (De Vries and Carlson, 2014). Furthermore, co-creation necessitates a great deal of engagement and communication (Hoyer et al., 2010; Prahalad and Ramaswamy, 2004), which enables customers to forge social connections with other actors. According to Chuang (2020), social relationships among users, players, and developers influence engagement behavior within online video game platforms, enabling an unrestricted flow of ideas and widening networks.

23.2.2 PERSONAL MOTIVATION

Personal incentives are connected to gaining a sense of self-efficacy through strengthening one's reputation and pursuing status, claim (Nambisan and Baron 2009). By providing constructive criticism and recommendations, consumers hope to be thanked and recognized by the community for their efforts (Füller, 2010). This entails exchanging knowledge, answering inquiries, and resolving problems to help users increase their level of expertise (Dewalska-Opitek and Hofman-Kohlmeyer, 2021). Wasko and Faraj (2005) provided evidence in favor of this claim, showing that improving one's reputation in a virtual environment encourages people to offer wise counsel to their peers, resulting in emotions of satisfaction and fulfilment (Chuang, 2020; Kim and Kim, 2018). For instance, content producers on live streaming websites for video games such as Twitch. To acknowledge and thank viewers for their support, TV and YouTube gaming frequently reveal their names during live broadcasts (El Afi and Ouiddad, 2021). This may improve consumer engagement in co-creation activities and boost consumer pride (Dvorak, 2013). According to De Almeida et al. (2018), consumers' motivation to participate in co-creation in virtual communities is strongly influenced by their sense of personal accomplishment and self-efficacy.

23.2.3 UTILITARIAN AND HEDONIC MOTIVATION

According to Hoehle and Venkatesh (2015), hedonic motives are factors that are associated to entertainment. People are motivated to participate in fun and exciting activities. According to studies (Dholakia et al., 2004; Vander Schee et al., 2020), engaging in playful interactions with peers and taking on challenges can be a source of happiness and fun as well as a means of unwinding and escaping reality. Due to their gamified aspects, such as emotes and competitions, video game platforms are especially good at offering these motivations (Hilvert-Bruce et al., 2018; Merhabi et al., 2021). Consumer participation increases with the degree of gamification (Abou-Shouk and Soliman, 2021; O'Brien and Toms, 2008). Being altruistic and taking part in problem-solving can both be fun and thrilling (Füller, 2010; Hoyer et al., 2010). This dimension captures the delight of working with others online and exchanging opinions and experiences regarding goods and services (Dvorak, 2013).

Because of the nature of virtual communities in video games, players are encouraged to let off steam or take on difficult tasks. As a result, the notion of enjoyment directly affects online consumers' participation in value co-creation. Altruism and community involvement can both contribute to this happiness (Hollebeek et al., 2021).

23.2.4 CUSTOMER ENGAGEMENT THROUGH CO-CREATION

Loyalty is the preferred result of consumer interaction when compared to other notions, claim Bowden (2009), Brodie et al. (2011), and Van Doorn et al. (2010). This is accomplished through forging strong psychological bonds with customers and fostering interactive relationships that go beyond the just material requirement for purchases (Brodie et al., 2011; Vivek et al., 2012). Customers are drawn to gaming platforms because they provide them with the knowledge, interaction, social identity, and personal value they seek (Chuang, 2020), which can result in both rational and emotional responses that can increase their loyalty (Bowden, 2009; Brodie et al., 2011; Hollebeek et al., 2021). This entails exerting mental, emotional, and physical energy through the creation of content and communication activities (Algesheimer et al., 2005; Cheung et al., 2011). Through online gaming platforms, Poretski and Arazy (2017) contend that engaging in value co-creation practices can increase customer loyalty.

23.2.5 CUSTOMER LOYALTY

The perception of customer loyalty is multifaceted, and different perspectives exist in defining it. Loyalty can be defined as the willingness to repeatedly purchase a product or service and promote it through positive recommendations (Majumdar, 2005; Kandampully and Suhartanto, 2000). Two types of loyalty have been acknowledged in the literature: behavioral and attitudinal. Behavioral loyalty is demonstrated through repeated purchases, while attitudinal loyalty is customers' emotional attachment to a product, service, or retailer, even if they do not repurchase it (Baloglu, 2002; Kumar et al., and2006; Kursunluoglu, 2011).

Customers who are highly involved in delivering a service tend to spend more time seeking information. However, if the service meets their expectations, their frequency of purchase increases, and they are less likely to look for alternatives (Beatty et al., and1988; Yang et al., 2014). While some studies suggest that satisfaction plays a mediating role in describing loyalty (Lam et al., and2004), the direct influence of value co-creation on loyalty is also significant to consider. Value co-creation may act as a barrier to switching alongside satisfaction and directly influence customers' loyalty (Majumdar, 2005; Kandampully and Suhartanto, 2000).

23.3 RESEARCH DESIGN

This study aimed to identify the factors influencing customer engagement through co-creation in online video games. The scale items were identified through earlier studies on similar research topics. A quantitative approach was adopted. Delhi NCR residents who often play online video games were the study's participants.

23.3.1 OBJECTIVES

- To study the influence of individual motivation on customer engagement
- To study the influence of customer engagement on customer loyalty
- To study the influence of individual motivations on customer loyalty mediating through customer loyalty

23.3.2 HYPOTHESIS

H1: Social motivation influences customer engagement
H2: Personal motivation influences customer engagement
H3: Utilitarian motivation influences customer engagement
H4: Hedonic motivation influences customer engagement
H5: Customer engagement influences attitudinal loyalty
H6: Customer engagement influences behavioral loyalty
H7: Attitudinal loyalty influences behavioral loyalty
H8: Customer engagement mediates the relationship between social motivation and attitudinal loyalty
H9: Social motivation influences behavioral loyalty mediated through customer engagement and attitudinal loyalty
H10: Customer engagement mediates the relationship between social motivation and behavioral loyalty
H11: Customer engagement mediates the relationship between personal motivation and attitudinal loyalty
H12: Personal motivation influences behavioral loyalty mediated through customer engagement and attitudinal loyalty
H13: Customer engagement mediates the relationship between personal motivation and behavioral loyalty
H14: Customer engagement mediates the relationship between utilitarian motivation and attitudinal loyalty
H15: Utilitarian motivation influences behavioral loyalty mediated through customer engagement and attitudinal loyalty
H16: Customer engagement mediates the relationship between utilitarian motivation and behavioral loyalty

H17: Customer engagement mediates the relationship between hedonic motivation and attitudinal loyalty

H18: Hedonic motivation influences behavioral loyalty mediated through customer engagement and attitudinal loyalty

H19: Customer engagement mediates the relationship between hedonic motivation and behavioral loyalty

H20: Customer engagement mediates the relationship between attitudinal loyalty and behavioral loyalty

23.3.3 SAMPLE SIZE AND POPULATION

A total of 200 responses were collected around the –Delhi NCR region. To conduct the research, the sampling technique used is a snowball and judgmental technique.

23.3.4 PRIMARY METHOD

Primary data was collected to obtain quantitative data for conducting the research. The variables for the study were identified using exploratory research. Descriptive research was done for data analysis. Search engine marketing (SEM) was the tool used to check the appropriateness of the model.

23.3.5 RESEARCH INSTRUMENT

The study included 200 online video game participants, and a 5-point Likert scale was used for the survey. The questionnaire used a 5-point Likert scale to measure all questions. ranging from 1 (strongly disagree) to 5 (strongly agree). Multiple sections were created for the questionnaire. The first section focused on gathering sociodemographic information such as the respondent's gender, age, educational background, and family's annual income. The other sections were concentrated on the following "scale items:"

1) **Social Motivation** was measured using three items (adapted from Nambisan and Baron, 2009).
2) **Personal Motivation** was measured using four items (adapted from Nambisan and Baron, 2009)
3) **Utilitarian Motivation** was measured using three items (adapted from Hartman et al., 2006).

4) **Hedonic Motivation** was measured using four items (adapted from Hartman et al., 2006).
5) **Customer Engagement through Value Co-creation** was measured using five items (adapted from Yi, and Gong, T. 2013)
6) **Attitudinal Loyalty** was measured using three items (adapted from Kaur et al.. 2019)
7) **Behavioral loyalty** was measured using six items (adapted from Kaur et al., 2019)

There were 27 items altogether which covered all 5 scale items.

23.3.6 DATA COLLECTION

Data was collected from university students who play online video games using an online questionnaire created with Google Forms. The survey was shared through personal chats on WhatsApp and Instagram.

23.4 DATA ANALYSIS AND RESULTS

23.4.1 SOCIODEMOGRAPHIC PROFILE

The data presents the sociodemographic profile of active gamers in Delhi NCR. It shows that most gamers are male (67%) compared to female (33%). In terms of age, the highest percentage of gamers falls within the 20–24 age group (60.5%), followed by the 25–29 age group (16%). The education level of gamers is relatively high, with 42% being graduates and 33.5% being postgraduates. Regarding family income, the highest percentage falls within the 6–10 lakhs bracket (40.5%). The data also reveals that gamers above the age of 40 constitute 5.5% of the total active gaming population in Delhi NCR.

23.4.2 MODEL FITNESS

There are several indicators used to evaluate the fitness of a model. The Chi-square fit index (χ^2) is sensitive to sample size and measures how well the model fits the observed variables. The ratio of Chi-square to degree of freedom (χ^2/df) is a better indicator for large sample sizes. The goodness of fit (GFI) index is less sensitive to sample size and is considered a good fit if above 0.9. The adjusted goodness of fit (AGFI) modifies GFI, and values above 0.9 indicate a good fit. The nonnormed fit index (NNFI) is good if above 0.9, as is the comparative fit index (CFI). The root mean square error of approximation (RMSEA) is considered a better index for populations, with values less than 0.08 indicating a good fit. Finally, the standardized root mean squared residual (SRMR) is better for smaller sample sizes and nonnormal data.

TABLE 23.1 Model Fitness Indicators.

Fitness Indicators	Extracted Values	Threshold Limit
CMIN	18.157	
DF	7	
Sig	0.011	< 0.05
CMIN/DF	2.594	< 5.0
Standardized RMR	0.035	< 0.06
Goodness of Fit Indox (GFI)	0.975	> 0.9
Adjusted Goodness of Fit Index (AGFI)	0.900	> 0.9
Normed Fit Index (NFI)	0.972	> 0.9
Comparative Fit Index (CFI)	0.982	> 0.9
RMSEA	0.089	< 0.06

The study found that the ratio of Chi-square to degrees of freedom is below the acceptable limit of 2, with $df = 7$ and $\chi^2/df = 2.594$. Other indicators, including the GFI = 0.975) AGFI = 0.9, NNFI = 0.972, CFI = 0.982, RMSEA = 0.089, and SRMR = 0.035, all suggest a firm fit. These results align with previous research by Diamantopoulos and Siguaw (2000) and MacCallum et al. (1996), indicating that the model is well-suited for the data. In essence, the study confirms that the model fits well, as shown by various statistical indicators, and thus is a reliable tool for analyzing the data.

23.4.3 STRUCTURE EQUATION MODELING ANALYSIS

The given research analysis presents estimates of direct effects between variables. The first column indicates the estimate of the direct effect, while the second column shows its standard error (SE). The third column presents the critical ratio (CR), calculated by dividing the estimate by its SE. The fourth column shows the significance level (p) of the direct effect, and the fifth column indicates the label for the variables involved in the direct effect.

TABLE 23.2 Direct Effect.

	Estimate	S.E.	C.R.	P	Label
CE <— SM	.203	.069	2.813	.005	par_1
CE <— PM	.355	.066	5.244	***	par_2
CE <— UM	.128	.062	2.134	.033	par_3
CE <— HM	.187	.064	2.945	.003	par_4
AL <— CE	.573	.055	9.862	***	par_5
BL <— CE	.476	.066	7.140	***	par_6
BL <— AL	.229	.070	3.437	***	par_7

H1 Social motivation influences Customer Engagement

This research analysis's null hypothesis (H0) posits that social motivation does not affect customer engagement. The results from the study demonstrate a significant relationship between social motivation and customer engagement, with a p-value of 0.005. This suggests that social motivation positively influences customer engagement, leading to the "rejection of the null hypothesis."

H2 Personal motivation influences Customer Engagement

The research analysis had a null hypothesis (H0) stating that personal motivation does not impact customer engagement. However, the analysis results indicate a significant association between personal motivation and customer engagement, with a p-value of 0.000. This implies that personal motivation has a favorable effect on customer engagement, which leads to the "null hypothesis being rejected."

H3 Utilitarian motivation influences Customer Engagement

This research analysis hypothesized that there is no connection between utilitarian motivation and customer engagement, which is the null hypothesis (H0). However, the study results indicate a statistically significant correlation between utilitarian motivation and customer engagement, with a p-value of 0.033. Therefore, the "null hypothesis is rejected," implying that utilitarian motivation positively impacts customer engagement.

H4 Hedonic motivation influences Customer Engagement

In this research analysis, the null hypothesis (H0) suggests that hedonic motivation does not influence customer engagement. However, the analysis results show a significant correlation between hedonic motivation and customer engagement, with a *p*-value of .003. Hence, hedonic motivation favors customer engagement, leading to the "rejection of the null hypothesis."

H5 Customer Engagement influences Attitudinal Loyalty

The research analysis assumes a null hypothesis (H0) that states no relationship between customer engagement and attitudinal loyalty. However, the study results indicate a significant and positive relationship between customer engagement and attitudinal loyalty, as evidenced by a low p-value of .000. Therefore, "the null hypothesis is rejected."

H6 Customer Engagement influences Behavioral Loyalty

This research analysis's null hypothesis (H0) posits that customer engagement does not affect behavioral loyalty. The results from the study demonstrate a significant relationship between customer engagement and behavioral loyalty, with a p-value of .000. This suggests that customer engagement positively influences behavioral loyalty, leading to the "rejection of the null hypothesis."

H7 Attitudinal Loyalty influences Behavioral Loyalty

In this research analysis, the null hypothesis (H0) states that customer engagement has no impact on behavioral loyalty. However, the study findings indicate a significant correlation between customer engagement and behavioral loyalty, with a p-value of .000. This implies that customer engagement has a favorable effect on behavioral loyalty, "refuting the null hypothesis."

H8 Customer engagement mediates the relationship between social motivation and attitudinal loyalty

The null hypothesis (H0) posits that customer engagement does not mediate the relationship between social motivation and attitudinal loyalty was tested in this research analysis. The results indicate that social motivation significantly indirectly affects attitudinal loyalty through customer engagement, with a *p*-value of 0.002. Therefore, "the null hypothesis is rejected," and it can be concluded that customer engagement mediates the relationship between social motivation and attitudinal loyalty.

H9 Social motivation influences behavioral loyalty mediated through customer engagement and attitudinal loyalty

In this research analysis, the null hypothesis (H0) suggests that the relationship between social motivation and behavioral loyalty is not mediated by customer engagement and attitudinal loyalty. However, the results show a significant indirect effect of social motivation on behavioral loyalty through customer engagement and attitudinal loyalty, with a *p*-value of 0.001. Thus, the "null hypothesis is rejected," indicating that customer engagement and attitudinal loyalty mediate the relationship between social motivation and behavioral loyalty.

TABLE 23.3 Mediation Effect.

Indirect Path	Unstandardized Estimate	Lower	Upper	P-Value	Standardized Estimate
SM —> CE —> AL	0.104	0.049	0.172	0.002	0.117***
SM —> CE —> AL —> BL	0.025	0.012	0.049	0.001	0.117***
SM —> CE —> BL	0.091	0.039	0.161	0.002	0.097***
PM —> CE —> AL	0.186	0.108	0.275	0.001	0.203***
PM —> CE —> AL —> BL	0.045	0.021	0.089	0.001	0.203***
PM —> CE —> BL	0.163	0.093	0.246	0.001	0.169***
UM —> CE —> AL	0.071	0.011	0.131	0.058	0.074†
UM —> CE —> AL —> BL	0.017	0.005	0.040	0.029	0.074*
UM —> CE —> BL	0.063	0.012	0.119	0.052	0.061†
HM —> CE —> AL	0.101	0.033	0.185	0.016	0.107*
HM —> CE —> AL —> BL	0.025	0.008	0.054	0.010	0.107*
HM —> CE —> BL	0.089	0.033	0.164	0.013	0.089*
CE —> AL —> BL	0.130	0.068	0.208	0.001	0.131**

H10 Customer engagement mediates the relationship between social motivation and behavioral loyalty

In this research analysis, the null hypothesis (H0) suggested that there is no mediation effect of customer engagement between social motivation and behavioral loyalty. The results of the analysis revealed a significant indirect impact of social motivation on behavioral loyalty through customer engagement, with a *p*-value of 0.002. As a result, "the null hypothesis is rejected," and it can be inferred that customer engagement serves as a mediator in the relationship between social motivation and behavioral loyalty.

H11 Customer engagement mediates the relationship between personal motivation and attitudinal loyalty

This research analysis tested the null hypothesis (H0) that customer engagement does not mediate the relationship between personal motivation and attitudinal loyalty. The findings showed a significant indirect effect of personal motivation on attitudinal loyalty through customer engagement, with a *p*-value of 0.001. As a result, "the null hypothesis is rejected," and it can be concluded that customer engagement is a mediator between personal motivation and attitudinal loyalty.

H12 Personal motivation influences behavioral loyalty mediated through customer engagement and attitudinal loyalty

This research analysis tests the null hypothesis (H0) that customer engagement and attitudinal loyalty do not act as mediators between personal motivation and behavioral loyalty. However, the findings indicate a significant indirect influence of personal motivation on behavioral loyalty through customer engagement and attitudinal loyalty, with a *p*-value of 0.001. Hence, "the null hypothesis is rejected," meaning that customer engagement and attitudinal loyalty mediate the relationship between personal motivation and behavioral loyalty.

H13 Customer engagement mediates the relationship between personal motivation and behavioral loyalty

This research analysis aimed to test the null hypothesis (H0) that customer engagement does not influence the relationship between social motivation and behavioral loyalty. The results reveal a significant indirect effect of social motivation on behavioral loyalty through customer engagement, with a *p*-value of 0.001. As a result, "the null hypothesis is rejected," indicating that customer engagement mediates the relationship between social motivation and behavioral loyalty.

H14 Customer engagement mediates the relationship between utilitarian motivation and attitudinal loyalty

The null hypothesis (H0) posits that customer engagement does not mediate the relationship between utilitarian motivation and attitudinal loyalty, which was tested in this research analysis. The results indicate that utilitarian motivation significantly indirectly affects attitudinal loyalty through customer engagement, with a *p*-value of 0.058. Therefore, we "fail to reject the null hypothesis" hence we keep the null hypothesis. Customer engagement could not mediate the relationship between utilitarian motivation and attitudinal loyalty.

H15 Utilitarian motivation influences behavioral loyalty mediated through customer engagement and attitudinal loyalty

This research analysis aimed to test whether customer engagement and attitudinal loyalty mediate the relationship between utilitarian motivation and behavioral loyalty, as suggested by the null hypothesis (H0). However, the results indicate that there is indeed a significant indirect effect of utilitarian motivation on behavioral loyalty through customer engagement and attitudinal loyalty, with a *p*-value of 0.029. Therefore, the "null hypothesis is rejected," concluding that customer engagement and attitudinal loyalty mediate the relationship between utilitarian motivation and behavioral loyalty.

H16 Customer engagement mediates the relationship between utilitarian motivation and behavioral loyalty

The null hypothesis (H0) posits that customer engagement does not mediate the relationship between utilitarian motivation and behavioral loyalty was tested in this research analysis. The results indicate that utilitarian motivation significantly indirectly affects behavioral loyalty through customer engagement, with a *p*-value of 0.058. Therefore, we "fail to reject the null hypothesis" hence we keep the null hypothesis. Customer engagement was unable to mediate the relationship between utilitarian motivation and behavioral loyalty.

H17 Customer engagement mediates the relationship between hedonic motivation and attitudinal loyalty

The research analysis examined the null hypothesis (H0) that customer engagement does not mediate the relationship between hedonic motivation and attitudinal loyalty. However, the findings reveal that hedonic motivation has a significant indirect impact on attitudinal loyalty through customer engagement, with a *p*-value of 0.016. Hence, "the null hypothesis is rejected," and it can be inferred that customer engagement mediates the connection between hedonic motivation and attitudinal loyalty.

H18 Hedonic motivation influences behavioral loyalty mediated through customer engagement and attitudinal loyalty

The research analysis tested the null hypothesis (H0) that customer engagement does not mediate the relationship between hedonic motivation and behavioral loyalty. However, the results reveal a significant indirect effect of hedonic motivation on behavioral loyalty through customer engagement and attitudinal loyalty, with a p-value of 0.001. Consequently, "the null hypothesis is rejected," suggesting that customer engagement and attitudinal loyalty act as mediators between hedonic motivation and behavioral loyalty.

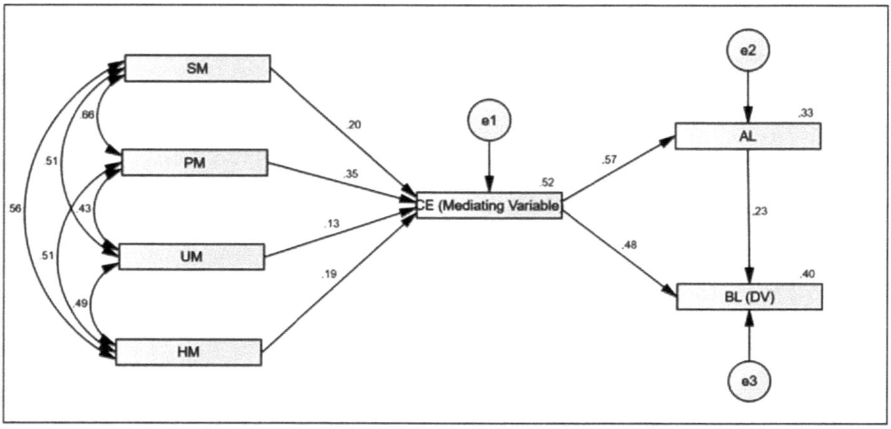

FIGURE 23.1 Structural model.

H19 Customer engagement mediates the relationship between hedonic motivation and behavioral loyalty

The research analysis aimed to test the null hypothesis (H0), which suggests that customer engagement does not influence the relationship between hedonic motivation and behavioral loyalty. However, the findings indicate a significant indirect effect of hedonic motivation on behavioral loyalty through customer engagement, with a p-value of 0.013. As a result, "the null hypothesis is rejected," indicating that customer engagement mediates the relationship between hedonic motivation and behavioral loyalty.

H20 Customer engagement mediates the relationship between attitudinal loyalty and behavioral loyalty

The research analysis tested the null hypothesis (H0), which suggests that customer engagement does not mediate the relationship between attitudinal and behavioral loyalty. However, the study's results demonstrate that customer engagement significantly indirectly affects behavioral loyalty through attitudinal loyalty, with a p-value of 0.001. As a result, "the null hypothesis is rejected," and it can be concluded that customer engagement mediates the relationship between attitudinal loyalty and behavioral loyalty.

23.5 DISCUSSIONS AND IMPLICATION

Based on our data analysis, it is evident that social motivation, personal motivation, utilitarian motivation, and hedonic motivation have a significant impact on customer engagement. Our research indicates that positive attitudes and behaviors towards a brand are more likely to occur when customers are engaged. Moreover, customer engagement acts as a mediator in the relationships between social motivation and both attitudinal and behavioral loyalty, personal motivation and both types of loyalty, and social motivation and behavioral loyalty. It is worth noting that customer engagement has the potential to mediate the relationship between utilitarian motivation and attitudinal loyalty as well.

The study's results suggest that customer engagement is critical in building attitudinal and behavioral loyalty. The study findings indicate that customers more engaged with the brand are likelier to be loyal. Companies may engage their customers to build loyalty and increase customer retention. The study's findings also suggest that social motivation, personal motivation, utilitarian motivation, and hedonic motivation are essential drivers of customer engagement. Customers motivated by social, personal, utilitarian, or hedonic factors are likelier to engage with the brand, leading to increased loyalty. Therefore, companies may identify what motivates their customers and design their marketing strategies to appeal to these motivations.

The study results also indicate that customer engagement serves as a mediator in the connection between social motivation and attitudinal loyalty, social motivation and behavioral loyalty, personal motivation and attitudinal loyalty, personal motivation and behavioral loyalty, and social motivation and behavioral loyalty. This suggests that customer engagement is crucial in converting motivation into loyalty. Companies may focus on enhancing customer engagement to strengthen the relationship between motivation and loyalty. The study's findings also revealed that customer engagement is essential for building attitudinal and behavioral loyalty, regardless of the type of motivation. The study results demonstrate that customer engagement is a critical mediator between motivation and loyalty. Therefore, companies may focus on improving customer engagement to build brand loyalty.

In conclusion, the study's findings suggest that customer engagement is critical in building attitudinal and behavioral loyalty. The study results demonstrate that social motivation, personal motivation, utilitarian motivation, and hedonic motivation positively impact customer engagement. Moreover, customer engagement serves as a mediator in the relationship between motivation and loyalty. Therefore, companies may prioritize customer engagement to build brand loyalty and retain customers.

23.5.1 IMPLICATIONS

The implications of the research analysis are essential in helping businesses and organizations understand the role of social motivation, personal motivation, and utilitarian motivation in influencing customer engagement, attitudinal loyalty, and behavioral loyalty. The rejection of the null hypothesis in each case implies that these motivations positively impact customer engagement, attitudinal loyalty, and behavioral loyalty. Therefore, businesses and organizations may motivate customers socially, personally, and utilitarianly to increase engagement and loyalty.

The research analysis also reveals the mediating role of customer engagement and attitudinal loyalty in the relationship between motivations and loyalty behaviors. This suggests that customer engagement and attitudinal loyalty are critical factors businesses and organizations must consider when developing strategies to foster customer loyalty. Organizations can influence and strengthen the relationship between motivations and behavioral loyalty by enhancing customer engagement and attitudinal loyalty. Furthermore, the study's results indicate that different motivational factors have varying levels of impact on customer engagement and loyalty. For instance, while social motivation significantly influences attitudinal loyalty, personal motivation significantly affects behavioral loyalty. Businesses and organizations may tailor their motivational strategies to match specific loyalty behaviors to achieve optimal results.

The findings also underscore the importance of customer engagement as a predictor of attitudinal and behavioral loyalty. Businesses and organizations may develop engagement strategies that connect customers and the brand emotionally. Such strategies include creating personalized experiences, providing excellent customer service, and leveraging social media to build relationships.

23.6 CONCLUSION AND LIMITATION

The research analysis shows that social motivation, personal motivation, utilitarian motivation, and hedonic motivation all have a positive impact on customer engagement. This is evidenced by the rejection of the null hypotheses that suggest otherwise. Furthermore, the results indicate that customer engagement is crucial in the relationship between these motivational factors and attitudinal loyalty and behavioral loyalty. This is supported by the significant indirect effects observed in the analysis.

These findings highlight the importance of understanding and leveraging motivational factors to increase customer engagement, ultimately leading to greater loyalty and retention. By focusing on these factors and implementing strategies to promote customer engagement, online video game businesses can improve their bottom line and strengthen customer relationships.

23.6.1 LIMITATIONS

This study on customer loyalty through co-creation in online video games in the Delhi NCR region has potential limitations. The sample size may be limited, and the respondents may not represent the entire population. Self-selection bias could also affect the results. Additionally, respondents may provide socially desirable answers, and the study's short timeframe may limit its ability to capture long-term effects. The study's limited scope could affect generalizability to other regions and types of video games. The lack of a control group could limit the ability to attribute observed effects to co-creation. Finally, subjective measures of customer loyalty and the need to consider external factors could determine the study's accuracy.

KEYWORDS

- **loyalty**
- **consumer engagement**
- **value co-creation**
- **motivations**
- **online video games**

REFERENCES

Abou-Shouk, M.; Soliman, M. The Impact of Gamification Adoption Intention on Brand Awareness and Loyalty in Tourism: The Mediating Effect of Customer Engagement. *J. Destinat. Mark. Manag.* **2021,** 20.

Algesheimer, R.; Dholakia, U. M.; Herrmann, A. The Social Influence of Brand Community: Evidence from European Car Clubs. *J. Mark.* **2005,** *69,* 19–34.

Baloglu, S. Dimensions of customer loyalty: Separating Friends from well Wishers. Cornell Hotel and Restaurant Administration Quarterly **2002,** *43* (1), 47–59.

Beatty, S. E.; Homer, P.; Kahle, L. R. The Involvement-commitment Model: Theory and Implications. *J. Bus. Res.* **1988,** *16* (2), 149–167.

Bowden, J. L.-H. The Process of Customer Engagement: A Conceptual Framework. *J. Mark. Theory Pract.* **2009,** *17,* 63–74.

Brodie, R. J.; Hollebeek, L. D.; Jurić, B.; Ilić, A. Customer Engagement: Conceptual Domain, Fundamental Propositions, and Implications for Research. *J. Serv. Res.* **2011,** *14,* 252–271.

Cheung, C. M. K.; Lee, M. K. O.; Jin, X.-L. In *Customer Engagement in an Online Social Platform: A Conceptual Model and Scale Development.* International Conference on Information Systems; 2011, ICIS 2011, 3105–3112, 2011.

Chuang, Y.-W. Promoting Consumer Engagement in Online Communities through Virtual Experience and Social Identity. *Sustainability* **2020,** *12,* 855.

Claffey, E.; Brady, M. Examining Consumers' Motivations to Engage in Firm-Hosted Virtual Communities. *Psychol. Mark.* **2017,** *34,* 356–375.

de Almeida, S. O.; Scaraboto, D.; dos Santos Fleck, J. P.; Dalmoro, M. Seriously Engaged Consumers: Navigating Between Work and Play in Online Brand Communities. *J. Interact. Mark.* **2018,** *44,* 29–42.

De Vries, N. J.; Carlson, J. Examining the Drivers and Brand Performance Implications of Customer Engagement with Brands in the Social Media Environment. *J. Brand Manag.* **2014,** *21,* 495–515.

Dewalska–Opitek, A.; Hofman–Kohlmeyer, M. Players as Prosumers–How Customer Engagement in Game Modding May Benefit Computer Game Market. *Central Eur. Bus. Rev.* **2021,** *10,* 77–97.

Dholakia, U. M.; Bagozzi, R. P.; Pearo, L. K. A Social Influence Model of Consumer Participation in Network- and Small-group-based Virtual Communities. *Int. J. Res. Mark.* **2004,** *21,* 241–263.

Dvorak, T. Co-Innovation: Customer Motives for Participation in Co-creation Processes via Social Media Platforms. *Undefined* **2013,** Retrieved from https://www. semanticscholar. org/paper/Co-Innovation%3A-customer-motives-for-participation Dvorak/0086c0ae88ff1ed99f4be912448abe7519e22095.

El Afi, F.; Ouiddad, S. The Rise of Video-Game Live Streaming: Motivations and Forms of Viewer Engagement. In *HCI International 2021 – Posters*; Stephanidis, C., Antona, M., Ntoa, S., Eds.; Springer International Publishing: Cham, 2021; pp 156–163.

Füller, J. Refining Virtual Co-Creation from a Consumer Perspective. *California Manag. Rev.* **2010,** *52,* 98–122.

Hilvert-Bruce, Z.; Neill, J. T.; Sjöblom, M.; Hamari, J. Social Motivations of Live- Streaming Viewer Engagement on Twitch. *Comput. Hum. Behav.* **2018,** *84,* 58–67.

Hoehle, H.; Venkatesh, V. Mobile Application Usability: Conceptualization and Instrument Development. *MIS Quart.* **2015,** *39,* 435–472.

Hollebeek, L. D.; Das, K.; Shukla, Y. Game on! How Gamified Loyalty Programs Boost Customer Engagement Value. *Int. J. Inform. Manag.* **2021,** *61,* 102308. https://doi.org/10.1016/j.ijinfomgt.2021.102308.

Hoyer, W. D.; Chandy, R.; Dorotic, M.; Krafft, M.; Singh, S. S. Consumer Cocreation in New Product Development. *J. Serv. Res.* **2010,** *13,* 283–296.

Lam, S. Y.; Shankar, V.; Erramilli, M. K.; Murthy, B. Customer Value, Satisfaction, Loyalty, and Switching Costs: An illustration from a Business-to-business Service Con-text. *J. Acad. Mark. Sci.* **2004,** *32* (3), 293–311.

Kandampully, J.; Suhartanto, D. Customer Loyalty in the Hotel Industry: The Role of Customer Satisfaction and Image. International *J. Contemporary Hosp. Manag.* **2000,** *12* (6), 346–351.

Kim, M.; Kim, J.The Effects of Perceived Online Justice on Relational Bonds and Engagement Intention: Evidence from An Online Game Community. *Comput. Hum. Behav.* **2018,** *84,* 410–419.

Kumar, V.; Shah, D.; Venkatesan, R. Managing Retailer Profitability-one customer at a Time! *J. Retail.* **2006,** *82* (4), 277–294.

Kursunluoglu, E. Customer Service Effects on Customer Satisfaction and Customer Loyalty: A field Research in Shopping Centers in İzmir city–Turkey. *Int. J. Bus. Soc. Sci.* **2011,** *2* (17), 52–59.

Majumdar, A. A Model for Customer Loyalty for Retail Stores Inside Shopping Malls—An Indian Perspective. *J. Serv. Res.* 2005, 47–64 (SpecialIssue).

Merhabi, M. A.; Petridis, P.; Khusainova, R. Gamification for Brand Value Co-Creation: A Systematic Literature Review. *Information* **2021,** *12,* 345.

Nambisan, S.; Baron, R. A. Virtual Customer Environments: Testing a Model of Voluntary Participation in Value Co-creation Activities. *J. Prod. Innov. Manag.* **2009,** *26,* 388–406.

O'Brien, H. L.; Toms, E. G. What is User Engagement? A Conceptual Framework for Defining user Engagement with Technology. *J. Am. Soc. Inform. Sci. Technol.* **2008,** *59,* 938–955.

Poretski, L.; Arazy, O. In *Placing Value on Community Co-creations: A Study of a Video Game "Modding" Community,* Proceedings of the 2017 ACM Conference on Computer Supported Cooperative Work and Social Computing, CSCW '17, Association for Computing Machinery: New York, NY, USA, 2017; pp 480–491.

Poretski, L.; Zalmanson, L.; Arazy, O. The Effects of Co-Creation and Word-of-Mouth on Content Consumption - Findings from the Video Game Industry. In *ICIS*, 2019.

Prahalad, C. K.; Ramaswamy, V. Co-creation Experiences: The Next Practice in Value Creation. *J. Interact. Mark.* **2004,** *18,* 5–14.

Van Doorn, J.; Lemon, K. N.; Mittal, V.; Nass, S.; Pick, D.; Pirner, P.; Verhoef, P. C. Customer Engagement Behavior: Theoretical Foundations and Research Directions. *J. Serv. Res.* **2010,** *13,* 253–266.

Vander Schee, B. A.; Peltier, J.; Dahl, A. J. Antecedent Consumer Factors, Consequential Branding Outcomes and Measures of Online Consumer Engagement: Current Research and Future Directions. *J. Res. Interact. Mark.* **2020,** *14,* 239–268.

Vargo, S. L.; Lusch, R. F. Institutions and Axioms: An Extension and Update of Service-dominant Logic. *J. Acad. Mark. Sci.* **2016,** *44,* 5–23.

Vivek, S. D.; Beatty, S. E.; Morgan, R. M. Customer Engagement: Exploring Customer Relationships Beyond Purchase. *J. Mark. Theory Pract.* **2012,** *20,* 122–146.

Wasko, M. M.; Faraj, S. Why Should I Share? Examining Social Capital and Knowledge Contribution in Electronic Networks of Practice. *MIS Quart.* **2005,** *29,* 35–57.

Index

H

I

K

M

N

T

U